Data Integrity By Design

Building Systems That Regulators Trust

Christopher L. Gent

AcceleraQA

Data Integrity by Design

Building Systems That Regulators Trust

For information about special discounts, bulk purchases or to contact the author email AcceleraQA sales at info@acceleraqa.com.

ISBN: 979-8-234-09397-4 (Print)

First Edition, 2026

Cover Design: Christopher Gent

Copy Editor: Christina Gent

Published in the United States of America

Printed in the United States of America

DEDICATION

TO MY WIFE, WHOSE BELIEF IN ME NEVER WAVERS.

"In all cases, we regard any lapse in data integrity as a risk to patient safety. Patients can't be assured of the safety and effectiveness of their medication when data has been altered."

— Scott Gottlieb, Former FDA Commissioner

"Accuracy of statement is one of the first elements of truth; inaccuracy is a near kin to falsehood."

— Tryon Edwards (19th-century theologian and author)

Contents

PART ONE: THE FOUNDATION

Understanding where we are and how we got here

CHAPTER ONE

The Cost of Getting It Wrong

On a Tuesday morning in March 2024, the head of data management at a mid-sized contract research organization in North Carolina received an email that would upend the next three years of his professional life. The subject line read: "FDA Warning Letter: Immediate Response Required." The letter was twenty-two pages long.

His organization had passed its last routine inspection with only minor observations. The warning letter did not cite poorly designed protocols or incompetent investigators. It cited data integrity: altered case report forms, audit trails in the electronic data capture system that had been disabled during key enrollment periods, and clinical research coordinators at multiple sites who had queried and re-entered data until implausible outliers disappeared from the dataset. None of this had been deliberate fraud, at least not at the organizational level. It had been accommodation, accumulated over years: sponsors pressing for clean data packages, coordinators under enrollment pressure, and a quality oversight function that reviewed metrics rather than records.

Within eighteen months, the CRO had spent $38 million on remediation and litigation. It had lost three major sponsor contracts, including a Phase III oncology program that was its largest active engagement. Its Chief Operating Officer had testified before a Senate subcommittee on clinical trial data reliability. The FDA had placed a clinical hold on two ongoing studies that had used the organization's data management platform. And it was operating under a consent decree that prohibited it from onboarding new sponsors until an independent data integrity auditor certified each of its eleven sites as compliant; a process the auditor estimated would take no fewer than four years.

The patients who had enrolled in those studies never learned that the data collected from their participation was under federal investigation. The sponsors who had relied on that data to support investigational new drug applications were required to notify FDA and assess whether any submitted analyses needed to be withdrawn or qualified. Two development programs were set back by more than two years.

This is not an unusual story. With variations in therapeutic area, site geography, and CRO size, it is a story that the FDA's Office of Scientific Investigations is writing with increasing frequency; the clinical research industry has been too slow to treat it as the systemic risk it is.

> *The FDA doesn't send warning letters as a formality. They are the agency's declaration that voluntary compliance has failed, and that escalation has begun.*

The Surge in Enforcement Activity

The surge in clinical data integrity enforcement is not an anomaly; it is the latest data point in a trajectory that has been building for more than a decade. The FDA's Office of Scientific Investigations conducted fewer than 200 bioresearch monitoring inspections annually in the late 2000s[1]. By the mid-2010s, inspection volume had grown substantially, driven by a pattern of source data manipulation, fabricated patient records, and audit trail circumvention uncovered at investigator sites across multiple international markets. By the early 2020s, data integrity had become the dominant finding category in OSI inspection outcomes, displacing protocol deviations, and informed consent failures that had historically defined GCP non-compliance.

Three converging forces have sustained and accelerated this trajectory. The first is the globalization of clinical trial conduct, which extended FDA's oversight reach into investigator sites and contract research organizations across Asia, Eastern Europe, and Latin America, regions where electronic data capture systems were adopted rapidly but site training, monitoring infrastructure, and data governance cultures did not keep pace. The second is the expansion of FDA's remote oversight toolkit: centralized monitoring programs, electronic records requests, risk-based site selection algorithms, and the remote inspection capabilities that were formalized during the pandemic and never fully retired. The third is a deliberate agency strategy to treat clinical data integrity as a first-order enforcement priority, reflected in FDA Commissioner statements, OSI program announcements, ICH E6(R3)'s explicit adoption of ALCOA+ as mandatory GCP expectations now being implemented by inspection programs globally, and the agency's consistent characterization of source data manipulation and audit trail circumvention as threats to the evidentiary foundation of the drug approval system itself.

The warning letter volume in any given reporting period is a lagging indicator. It reflects inspections conducted months earlier, investigations completed even earlier than that, and quality system failures that in many cases began years before anyone inside or outside the company recognized them as failures. The FDA is inspecting more, finding more, and acting on what it finds more consistently than at any point in the modern regulatory era.

How the Escalation Ladder Works

FDA enforcement operates as a graduated response. A standard inspection may produce no observations, or Form 483 observations: a list of objectionable conditions that require a company's response but carries no direct penalty. Warning letters come next, and their receipt changes a company's regulatory posture fundamentally.

A warning letter is a public document. It is posted on the FDA's website within days of issuance. For sponsors and CROs conducting clinical trials that support U.S. marketing applications, the consequences compound further. A warning letter from FDA's OSI can result in a clinical hold until the agency is satisfied that corrective actions are complete and sustainable. In the most serious cases, the FDA may refuse to file or refuse to approve an application that relies on flagged data; a consequence that can push a development program back by years and, in competitive therapeutic areas, permanently.

The Escalation Sequence

Stage	Action	Consequence
Form 483 Observations	Issued at close of inspection	FDA expects written response within 15 business days; no direct penalty
Warning Letter	Public enforcement action	Triggers sponsor audits across active engagements; potential clinical hold

Stage	Action	Consequence
Clinical Hold	Bar on new enrollment or continued use of flagged data	Study may be suspended pending corrective action
Refusal to File / Approve	FDA declines to accept or act on marketing application	Data integrity findings undermine evidentiary basis of submission[2]
Consent Decree	Court-ordered operating restrictions	Mandates independent data auditor and third-party oversight of all active trials
Disqualification Proceeding	FDA may disqualify investigator or CRO	Bars receipt of investigational products and future trial conduct under 21 CFR Part 312
Criminal Referral	DOJ prosecution	Personal liability for principal investigators, data managers, CRO executives, and sponsor quality personnel

What Warning Letters Actually Cost

The financial impact of an FDA warning letter is systematically underestimated upon receipt. Initial cost modeling typically captures direct remediation: hiring consultants, upgrading systems, and re-validating processes. It rarely captures the full picture. An analysis of enforcement actions across the clinical research sector over the past decade reveals a consistent pattern: total costs, measured across a three-to-five-year remediation horizon, run two to four times higher than initial estimates.

Direct Financial Penalties

Warning letters themselves carry no direct monetary penalty under the Federal Food, Drug, and Cosmetic Act. The costs begin the moment the letter is public.[3]

Illustrative Cost Ranges Derived from Enforcement Record Review		
Penalty Type	**Illustrative Range**	**Basis**
Remediation & Data Audit Consulting	$5M – $75M+	Derived from publicly reported CRO enforcement actions and consent decree remediation disclosures
Lost Sponsor Contracts	$15M – $400M+	Based on contract attrition patterns reported in SEC filings and industry analyst assessments
Clinical Hold Costs	$2M – $30M/month	Estimated from sponsor-reported program delay costs in annual reports and investor disclosures
Consent Decree Costs	$50M – $500M+	DOJ consent decree public filings and court records
Refusal to Approve / Program Abandonment	$100M – $2B+	Tufts CSDD estimates of full development program costs per approved compound (DiMasi et al., 2016)
Legal & Regulatory Affairs	$5M – $40M	Per major enforcement action; derived from litigation disclosures and industry benchmarking
eClinical Platform Liability	$10M – $150M+	Estimated from contract termination disclosures and revalidation cost benchmarks
Stock Price Impact (public sponsors)	8% – 35% decline	Academic and analyst studies of pharmaceutical enforcement event-driven equity reactions

Illustrative Cost Ranges Derived from Enforcement Record Review		
Penalty Type	**Illustrative Range**	**Basis**
Investigator / Site Disqualification	\$5M – \$50M+	Cost-of-re-execution estimates from clinical operations benchmarking literature

The ranges in this table are illustrative estimates derived from publicly reported enforcement outcomes and should be interpreted as order-of-magnitude guidance rather than precise benchmarks.

The Hidden Costs: Opportunity and Reputation

The costs that do not appear on remediation invoices are often the ones that define long-term competitive position. A CRO or sponsor operating under FDA scrutiny cannot onboard new studies or enroll new patients at flagged sites until compliance is restored. In therapeutic areas where trial timelines are existential, including oncology, rare disease, and gene therapy, a two-year remediation period is a strategic wound that competitors will not wait for you to recover from.

Talent is another casualty rarely captured in enforcement cost models. Skilled data integrity and compliance professionals who have built their careers on clean inspection records are reluctant to join organizations under enforcement action, and the organizations that most need experienced clinical quality leadership in the aftermath of a finding are precisely the ones least able to attract it at market rates.

Sponsor trust, once broken by a data integrity finding, recovers on a long lag. Pharmaceutical and biotechnology companies that have moved a program to an alternative CRO rarely return, even after FDA clearance is achieved. For eClinical technology vendors implicated in a finding, the damage extends further still: procurement cycles in the EDC and CTMS market run eighteen to thirty-six months, and a platform associated with an audit trail failure will be disqualified from consideration in evaluations that began before the warning letter was even issued.

> *Regulators remember. Customers remember. Investors remember. The warning letter is public forever; it does not expire from FDA's website when remediation is complete.*

Three Cases That Defined Modern Clinical Data Integrity Enforcement

CASE STUDY | Cetero Research (2010–2012)

Violation: Systematic data fabrication at Cetero's bioanalytical facilities, with the primary enforcement focus on the Houston, Texas laboratory. FDA found that study personnel had falsified analytical data across hundreds of bioequivalence and pharmacokinetic studies conducted between 2005 and 2010. Falsification included misreported extraction times, manipulation of equilibration samples, and analytical runs recorded as performed by technicians who were not present at the facility. [4]

Outcome: FDA's aggregate notification to sponsors covered approximately 1,900 studies across all Cetero facilities. Sponsors were required to assess whether affected studies could be relied upon for pending or approved applications. Dozens of generic drug approvals were delayed or required re-study. Cetero's clinical research operations were effectively destroyed.

The Cetero case is the defining clinical data integrity enforcement event of the modern era: not because the falsification was sophisticated, but because of its scale and its systemic invisibility. Cetero's facilities had passed sponsor audits. The downstream consequences fell primarily on sponsors who had relied on Cetero's data in good faith. The lesson that sponsor oversight obligations do not end at audit qualification, remains the most important takeaway for the clinical research industry.

CASE STUDY | Semler Research Center (2014–2016)

Violation: Data fabrication and source data falsification across multiple bioequivalence studies at the Bangalore facility. FDA found discrepancies between raw instrument data and reported results, substitution of subject samples, and audit trails that had been manipulated. Instrument audit trail capture was disabled for chromatographic systems during key study periods. [5]

Outcome: FDA issued an action rendering all Semler bioequivalence data unacceptable. Approximately 60 applications relying on Semler data were affected. Multiple generic drug approvals were delayed for two or more years. The facility never resumed regulatory operations.

The Semler case illustrates the geographic dimension of clinical data integrity risk. FDA's investigation revealed the specific failure modes now standard in clinical data integrity inspection protocols: chromatographic data files reprocessed until passing results were obtained; subject records that could not be reconciled with facility access logs; and an audit trail review program that existed in documentation but had never been operationally implemented.

CASE STUDY | GVK Biosciences (2014–2015)

Violation: Systematic manipulation of electrocardiogram data across hundreds of clinical studies at the Hyderabad facility. The French medicines agency found ECG tracings had been fabricated, substituted, or altered to remove findings that would have triggered safety reviews. Manipulations were detected in every one of the nine trials inspected, spanning at least five years. [6]

Outcome: EMA's CHMP recommended suspension of marketing authorizations for medicines lacking independent supporting data. The review covered approximately 700 medicines across EU member states. FDA issued parallel findings. An estimated 300+ generic applications in Europe required re-evaluation.

The GVK case is the most consequential clinical data integrity enforcement action in terms of its impact on approved medicines already on the market. The finding was not that development-stage data was unreliable; it was that safety data supporting medicines already dispensed to patients across Europe may have been falsified. Patients taking medicines whose authorizations were suspended faced abrupt treatment changes. The regulatory system's ability to protect patients depends entirely on the integrity of the data submitted to it.

Consent Decrees: When Warning Letters Are Not Enough

A consent decree is what happens when the FDA concludes that a company's voluntary compliance posture cannot be trusted. It is a court order, negotiated between the Department of Justice and the regulated entity, that imposes specific operational requirements and third-party oversight mechanisms. Non-compliance can result in contempt of court proceedings.

The structure of a consent decree matters enormously. Provisions typically include mandatory third-party expert certification before resuming operations at cited sites; prescribed timelines for Corrective Action and Preventive Action implementation with independent verification; financial assurance mechanisms; provisions requiring immediate notification of FDA for specified deviation categories; and personal liability clauses naming individual executives and quality leaders as parties to the decree. Modern consent decrees routinely name the CEO, President, and head of Quality as individual parties, creating personal legal accountability for ongoing compliance. A Quality director who signs a consent decree as a named party is, legally, personally responsible for its terms being met.

CONSENT DECREE FINANCIAL MECHANICS
Performance bond / financial assurance: $10M – $100M+ deposited or guaranteed at decree entry
Third-party Expert costs: $5M – $20M+ annually (fees plus internal management overhead)
Stipulated penalties for non-compliance: $15,000 – $30,000 per day per violation
Legal fees (ongoing): $3M – $10M+ annually during decree period
Internal compliance infrastructure: Typically requires 40–80+ dedicated FTEs at large facilities

The Reputational Cost: Quantifying the Unquantifiable

Clinical research organizations, eClinical technology vendors, and the sponsors that rely on them operate in markets where trust is, literally, part of the service. In clinical research, the product being sold is the integrity of the data, and a regulatory finding is a direct challenge to the credibility of that product.

Major pharmaceutical and biotechnology sponsors conduct regular regulatory risk screening of their CRO and eClinical vendor base. Receipt of a warning letter triggers automatic review that may result in immediate suspension of study activations; qualification of alternative providers; contract non-renewal at the next option period; or formal de-qualification requiring independent re-audit and FDA clearance confirmation before reinstatement. The aggregate impact of disqualification decisions made in the twelve to twenty-four months following a warning letter routinely rivals or exceeds the direct remediation cost.

The Human Cost

It is easy, in discussing consent decrees and stock price reactions, to lose sight of what FDA enforcement in clinical research ultimately concerns: the safety and rights of patients who volunteer to participate in trials on the understanding that the data collected from their participation will be handled with integrity. The cancer patient whose biomarker data was selectively reported. The rare disease patient whose quality-of-life assessments were reconstructed from memory days after they were due. The cardiac patient whose ECG findings were altered before they reached the safety review committee.

These are not hypotheticals. They are the documented fact patterns of the enforcement cases described in this chapter. The patients in those studies never knew. In most cases, they still do not.

> *Every enforcement statistic represents a quality system that failed to catch a problem before the FDA did. Some of those failures reached patients. Some did not. The margin between those two outcomes is often narrower than anyone inside the company understood at the time.*

What the Enforcement Trajectory Tells Us

The sustained rise in FDA clinical data integrity enforcement reflects several trends worth understanding as context for the chapters that follow.

FDA's post-pandemic oversight normalization is complete and accelerating. The agency has institutionalized remote assessment capabilities including electronic records requests, remote interactive evaluations, and centralized data monitoring that have expanded enforcement reach without proportionally expanding investigator headcount. The pandemic accelerated the development of the tools that make enforcement more efficient; it did not slow enforcement in any durable sense.

Data integrity remains the dominant citation category in clinical inspections not because sponsors and CROs are more dishonest than they were a decade ago, but because digitization has made integrity failures more visible and FDA investigators more sophisticated at identifying them. The tools available to OSI investigators, including audit trail analysis, EDC metadata examination, and cross-site data pattern analysis, can surface manipulation that would have been invisible under paper-based monitoring.

ICH E6(R3), adopted at Step 4 in January 2025 and now being implemented by inspection programs globally, has given the agency's clinical data integrity mandate international regulatory force.[7] The FDA and MHRA have formalized this convergent enforcement focus through joint GCP workshops, and the published output of the first joint workshop directly documents both agencies' common approach to audit trail review, data management practices, and the consequences of data integrity failures for marketing application acceptability.[8]

The guidance is not ambiguous. What remains ambiguous, for many organizations, is how to close the gap between the data governance policies on their quality system shelves and the day-to-day reality of how data is actually collected, transferred, queried, and reported across their trial portfolios. That gap is what this book is about.

CHAPTER ONE - KEY TAKEAWAYS
FDA clinical data integrity enforcement has risen consistently over more than a decade, with data integrity and GCP quality system failures now the leading citation categories in bioresearch monitoring inspections; no enforcement cycle in recent history has reversed the trend.
The total financial cost of a clinical data integrity enforcement action, measured across a three-to-five-year remediation horizon, typically runs two to four times higher than initial estimates, driven by sponsor contract attrition, program delay costs, and the compounding effect of reputational damage on future business development.
Consent decrees and disqualification proceedings impose court-ordered operating constraints, independent data auditor requirements, and personal liability for named executives, principal investigators, and clinical quality leaders.
Reputational damage compounds financial penalties through sponsor and partner disqualification, investor response, eClinical vendor procurement exclusion, and the long lag before clinical research credibility is restored.
The sustained enforcement trajectory reflects expanded FDA remote oversight capacity, increasingly sophisticated electronic data investigation tools, and the global adoption of ICH E6(R3)'s explicit data integrity requirements, a combination that makes detection of clinical data failures more likely in every successive inspection cycle.
The FDA and MHRA have formally documented their convergent clinical data integrity enforcement priorities through joint GCP workshop publications, confirming that data reliability concerns affect marketing application acceptability under both agencies' review frameworks simultaneously.
Organizations that receive clinical data integrity enforcement actions are not outliers; they are the predictable result of data management systems where documented policy diverged from operational reality, and where the divergence was neither detected nor corrected before investigators arrived.

CHAPTER TWO

Data Integrity by Design: The Core Philosophy

> *The difference between a compliant data governance program and a defensible one is not documentation. It is design.*

Recently a contract research organization based in the southeastern United States completed a comprehensive internal audit of its electronic data capture infrastructure. The audit found that every study-level EDC system was validated, that audit trails were enabled across all active trials, and that access controls met Part 11 technical requirements. The audit report was issued with no critical findings. The organization's clinical quality leadership reviewed it, approved it, and filed it.

Fourteen months later, the FDA's Office of Scientific Investigations concluded a for-cause inspection at two of the organization's investigator sites. The findings did not dispute that the EDC systems were technically validated. They documented something different: site coordinators who had been trained to use the audit trail function but had never been told why it mattered, query resolution workflows that systematically applied the same change reason text to hundreds of edits regardless of the actual basis for each change, and a data review program that flagged audit trail anomalies internally but had no documented escalation pathway that would have brought those anomalies to clinical quality leadership's attention. The technical controls were in place. The design that would have made those controls meaningful was not.

The inspection produced a Form 483 with seven observations. By the time the corrective action commitments were complete, the organization had spent more on remediation than it had originally spent building the data management infrastructure the inspection cited. The systems had not failed. The design had.

This chapter is about design. Specifically, it is about the recognition that data integrity in clinical research is not primarily a compliance achievement. It is a design outcome. Systems, processes, and cultures that are designed for integrity produce compliant data as a natural consequence of their operation. Systems, processes, and cultures that are designed for throughput and adapted to comply produce data integrity failures as a natural consequence of their operation, and compliance documentation that obscures those failures until inspection makes them visible.

> *Reactive compliance asks: are we covered? Proactive design asks: can this fail? These are fundamentally different questions, and they produce fundamentally different programs*

The Distinction That Changes Everything

The pharmaceutical industry has spent three decades developing an extensive vocabulary for clinical data integrity compliance. Validation documentation. Audit trail review. Source data verification. Risk-based monitoring. Data governance policies. Electronic signature controls. Each concept represents a real regulatory requirement, and organizations that implement them carefully are materially better positioned than those that do not.

But compliance is not the same as integrity, and the distinction is not semantic. Compliance is a property of documentation. Integrity is a property of systems. A clinical data management program can be fully documented and fundamentally compromised at the same time, and the warning letters that define the modern enforcement landscape are largely the record of organizations in exactly that condition: validated EDC systems with compliant audit trails that were generating unreliable data; source data verification programs that were completing 100% visit coverage and missing systematic reconstruction; risk-based monitoring dashboards that were flagging sites and producing action items that no one followed.

The regulatory framework governing clinical data integrity does not use the word 'design' with the specificity this chapter will. ICH E6(R3) requires data governance policies, validated systems, and audit trails. 21 CFR Part 312 requires adequate and accurate case histories and the ability to inspect them. PIC/S PI 041-1 describes what compliant records look like. What these frameworks do not, because they cannot, prescribe is how an organization builds the internal conditions under which ALCOA+-compliant data is generated consistently and reliably, across dozens of sites, hundreds of coordinators, and thousands of subjects, under the operational pressures of real clinical trial conduct.

That is a design question. And it is the question this book is ultimately about.

Why Integrity Failures Are Design Failures

The enforcement cases discussed in Chapter 1, Cetero, Semler, GVK, and the composite CRO scenario that opened this chapter, share a common structural feature that is rarely the focus of post-inspection analysis. The individuals involved in each case were not, in most instances, acting in deliberate defiance of regulatory requirements they understood. They were operating within systems that made the non-compliant path easier than the compliant one.

At Cetero, analysts reprocessed chromatographic data because the system they used allowed reprocessing without audit trail capture, because the supervisory review process did not check for reprocessed files, and because the production pressures they operated under made clean-on-first-analysis the implicit performance standard rather than accuracy-on-all-analyses. The design of the analytical laboratory's workflow made data manipulation structurally available, operationally convenient, and culturally normalized. No individual decision created the problem. The design did.

This pattern repeats with such regularity across documented clinical data integrity failures that it has become the most reliable diagnostic tool available. When an inspection finds systematic data manipulation at a clinical site or CRO, the question is not 'who decided to falsify data?' It is 'what design conditions made falsification easier than compliance?' In nearly every case examined across two decades of bioresearch monitoring enforcement, the answer is some combination of three factors: systems that permitted non-compliant actions without friction; processes that required non-compliant workarounds to meet legitimate operational objectives; and cultures that prioritized outcomes over documentation without explicitly endorsing falsification.

Design Failure Type	What It Looks Like in Practice	Regulatory Consequence
System design failure	EDC allows query resolution without change reason entry; audit trail does not capture the specific user who made each modification; access controls permit shared login credentials	Audit trail is present but uninformative; attribution is broken; the technical record cannot support the investigative questions an inspection will ask
Process design failure	Database lock timelines create pressure to close queries before they are adequately investigated; monitoring visit checklists focus on CRF-to-source agreement rather than audit trail review; deviation management workflow does not require root cause analysis	Systematic protocol deviations and data anomalies are closed without resolution; patterns that would indicate site-level fraud or systematic non-compliance are invisible in the process output
Culture design failure	Enrollment metrics are tracked and celebrated; data quality metrics are tracked and not discussed; coordinators understand that raising documentation concerns creates friction with sponsors; monitoring findings are managed as relationship issues rather than quality signals	Documentation pressure produces pre-completion, retrospective entry, and query response patterns that are individually explainable but collectively damning; inspectors recognize the cultural signature before they review a single record

Design Failure Type	What It Looks Like in Practice	Regulatory Consequence
Governance design failure	Data integrity policies exist at the corporate level but have not been operationalized in site-level SOPs; vendor qualification requirements do not include data integrity-specific assessment; organizational accountability for data integrity is diffuse	Corrective actions are reactive and site-specific rather than systemic; the same failure modes recur across studies and sites because the organizational conditions that produce them have not changed

The Design Mindset: From Compliance to Integrity

The shift from compliance-oriented to design-oriented data governance requires a fundamental change in the questions an organization asks about its clinical data management infrastructure. Compliance-oriented programs ask: do we have the required documentation in place? Design-oriented programs ask: under what conditions would this control fail, and have we designed against those conditions?

These are different questions, and they generate different programs. A compliance-oriented audit trail review program verifies that an audit trail review is occurring and that findings are being documented. A design-oriented audit trail review program asks whether the review methodology can reliably detect the specific manipulation patterns that appear in inspection findings, whether the reviewer has both the access and the analytical competency to recognize those patterns, and whether there is an escalation pathway that ensures anomalies identified in review reach someone with the authority and mandate to act on them. The compliance question produces a check in a box. The design question produces a surveillance program.

THE DESIGN QUESTIONS THAT CHANGE PROGRAMS

- For every data management control: under what operational conditions would this control fail, and have those conditions been designed against?

- For every ALCOA+ property: what specific system, process, or cultural condition is most likely to produce a failure of this property in this trial context?
- For every training program: does this training change behavior under pressure, or does it produce documented knowledge that does not survive the first enrollment deadline?
- For every monitoring program: is the methodology capable of detecting the specific manipulation patterns that appear in enforcement actions, or is it documenting visit completion?
- For every vendor relationship: have we verified the data integrity practices of this vendor, or have we accepted their contractual assurances as a substitute for verification?
- For every system deployment: has the system been designed so that compliant behavior is the easiest path, or does compliant behavior require additional effort that operational pressure will eventually eliminate?

The Seven Principles of Data Integrity by Design

The design philosophy described in this chapter is not a proprietary framework. It is the distillation of what distinguishes clinical data management programs that reliably produce ALCOA+-compliant data from programs that produce ALCOA+-compliant documentation. The seven principles below are not regulatory requirements. They are design requirements: the conditions that make regulatory compliance sustainable rather than episodic.

Principle One: Make Compliant Behavior the Path of Least Resistance

The single most powerful design principle in clinical data management is also the simplest: the compliant behavior should be easier than the non-compliant alternative. Every time a system, process, or workflow makes the compliant path harder than the workaround, it is accumulating a compliance debt that will eventually be collected.

In practice, this principle governs decisions that are rarely framed in data integrity terms: the configuration of EDC change reason dropdowns that include a specific, accurate option for every legitimate reason to modify a field, so that coordinators do not default to 'other' or 'transcription error' for changes that are neither; the design of query management workflows that provide coordinators with the information they need to resolve queries accurately, so that guessing or calling the sponsor data manager is not the path to closure; the timing of database lock milestones that allows adequate time for genuine query resolution rather than creating a window in which speed overrides accuracy. These are design decisions. They are made by clinical operations and data management teams, not by quality auditors. And they determine whether the data produced by the trial is reliably attributable, accurate, and contemporaneous, or whether it is those things in documentation and something else in practice.

Principle Two: Design Controls for the Failure Mode, Not the Standard Case

Regulatory controls in clinical data management are typically designed around what should happen. A well-functioning EDC system with a compliant audit trail, individual user credentials, and contemporaneous data entry will produce attributable, original records — this is not in dispute. The design question is what happens when the system is under pressure: when a coordinator is managing a monitoring visit and a database lock simultaneously; when a site is onboarding a new coordinator in the middle of enrollment; when a sponsor's data management team is under timeline pressure to close 300 outstanding queries before a scheduled lock.

Controls designed for the standard case fail under pressure. Controls designed for the failure mode hold. An access management control that works when IT has a full week to provision credentials fails when a coordinator needs access on the morning of a monitoring visit and the site administrator's workaround is to share the departing coordinator's login. A query management control that works when timelines are comfortable fails when a lock deadline creates a 48-hour window to resolve 150 queries. Designing for the failure mode means anticipating the pressure conditions under which each control is most likely to be circumvented and building friction into the circumvention path rather than the compliance path.

Principle Three: Build Verification Into the Design, Not the Audit

One of the most persistent structural failures in clinical data governance is the placement of data integrity verification at the audit stage, after data has been collected, transferred, and locked. Inspections find problems. Internal audits find problems. FDA's BIMO program finds problems. These mechanisms are essential, and they are not sufficient. By the time verification occurs at the audit stage, the design conditions that produced the failure have typically been in place for months or years. The failures they document are historical. The corrections they mandate address yesterday's problem. The underlying conditions that produced yesterday's problem are generating today's data, and today's data will be reviewed in tomorrow's inspection.

Verification built into the design means that data quality signals are surfaced continuously, not periodically. Centralized monitoring programs that review audit trail anomaly rates, missing data patterns, and query timing distributions across sites in real time are not merely efficient alternatives to on-site source data verification. They are the operational implementation of this design principle: quality signals detected as data is generated, rather than after it is locked, are actionable. Quality signals detected at inspection are the basis for a corrective action plan.

ICH E6(R3)'s requirement for risk-based quality management is the regulatory expression of this principle.[9] A trial design that prospectively identifies the data points and processes where integrity failures are most likely to occur, and builds monitoring mechanisms targeted at those specific risks, is implementing the principle. A trial design that retrospectively documents quality findings and generates corrective actions after they are detected at inspection is not.

Principle Four: Align Incentives with Integrity

The most technically sophisticated data integrity program will fail if the incentive structures governing the people who operate it point in a different direction. This is not an abstract behavioral claim. It is one of the most well-documented findings in the bioresearch monitoring enforcement record.

Clinical research coordinators who know they will be evaluated on enrollment numbers and visit completion rates, and who have no reason to believe that data quality metrics receive the same organizational attention, will systematically make trade-offs between speed and documentation under pressure. They will not necessarily falsify data. They will pre-complete forms. They will reconstruct entries from memory at the end of a long clinic day. They will resolve queries in whatever way closes them fastest. Each of these behaviors is individually explainable and collectively damning.

Sponsor medical monitors who know that raising data quality concerns may delay enrollment milestones, and who have no organizational support structure for doing so without personal cost, will manage monitoring findings as relationship problems rather than quality signals. Protocol deviations that should be formally documented will be resolved in phone calls. Site practices that deviate from the protocol will be coached rather than cited. The downstream consequences of this pattern are identical to those of deliberate falsification from an inspection standpoint, because the regulatory record shows the same gap between what should have happened and what did.

Aligning incentives with integrity means that the organizational metrics, performance evaluations, sponsor-CRO relationship dynamics, and escalation pathways that govern clinical trial conduct explicitly support data quality as an organizational value rather than treating it as a constraint on operational efficiency. This is harder than implementing a validated EDC system. It is also more consequential.

Principle Five: Design for the Inspector, Not for the Auditor

There is a meaningful difference between a data integrity program designed to pass an internal audit and one designed to withstand an FDA BIMO inspection. Internal auditors, however skilled, operate within the organizational context of the program they are reviewing. They have advance notice, defined scope, and a relationship with the quality function they are assessing. FDA investigators arrive without appointment, with the authority to examine any record, and with inspection methodologies specifically calibrated to identify the manipulation patterns and cultural signatures that distinguish data managed for documentation from data managed for accuracy.

Designing for the inspector means asking, for every record and every system, the question that the inspector will ask: what would an independent expert, with full access to all electronic records, instrument logs, training records, and personnel schedules, conclude about the integrity of this data? An organization that can answer that question confidently, for any record in its quality system, has built an integrity program. An organization that can answer it only for the records that were recently reviewed by the internal audit team has built a compliance program with integrity-shaped documentation.

Principle Six: Extend Design Obligations Through the Data Supply Chain

A clinical data management program is only as strong as its weakest link, and in a modern multi-site, multi-vendor clinical trial, the data supply chain includes a large number of links that are outside the sponsor's direct control. Central laboratories generating electronic source data. eCOA vendors hosting patient-reported outcome devices. IRT vendors managing randomization transaction logs. eTMF platforms archiving regulatory documents. Third-party imaging cores adjudicating radiological endpoints. Each of these vendors generates or manages clinical trial data that will ultimately support a regulatory submission. Each is subject to the same ALCOA+ requirements that apply to the sponsor's own systems. None can relieve the sponsor of its regulatory accountability for the data they handle.

The design implication is specific: sponsor data governance policies must extend to vendor qualification requirements that include explicit data integrity assessment, not merely GCP experience references and SOC 2 certifications. The qualification process must verify that vendor systems meet ALCOA+ requirements in practice, not merely in validation documentation. Ongoing oversight must include periodic access verification confirming that original records, not merely derived outputs, remain retrievable for the full retention period. And contractual data return provisions must ensure that device-level logs, transaction records, and original electronic files will be available to the sponsor independently of the vendor relationship, so that the sponsor's retention obligations are not hostage to a contract that may expire before the regulatory retention period does.

ICH E6(R3) makes this obligation explicit: sponsors cannot transfer their data governance responsibilities to CROs or vendors.[10] The February 2026 EMA/PIC/S joint consultation described in Chapter 4 proposes to formalize a clinical supply chain data integrity standard that will operationalize this requirement at a level of specificity no prior guidance has achieved. Sponsors who are waiting for that guidance to build supply chain data integrity requirements into their vendor oversight programs will be implementing it under regulatory pressure rather than by choice.

Principle Seven: Build for Change

Clinical trials are not static. Protocols are amended. Sites are added and closed. Vendor platforms are upgraded and retired. Personnel turnover. Data management systems are migrated. Regulatory expectations evolve. A data integrity program designed for the conditions that exist at the time of its implementation will be out of date before the trial it governs is complete.

Building for change means implementing data governance in a way that is robust to the operational changes that will inevitably occur. This includes documented change control processes that assess the data integrity implications of system upgrades, site staffing changes, and vendor transitions. It includes validated data migration procedures that ensure original records and metadata are preserved when platforms are replaced. It includes training designs that build ALCOA+ understanding rather than system-specific procedural knowledge, so that a coordinator who moves from one EDC platform to another understands what contemporaneous recording means in the new system rather than simply learning where the new entry fields are. And it includes a quality management cadence that periodically reassesses data integrity risk in light of how the trial has evolved, rather than treating the risk assessment completed at protocol finalization as a settled document.

Reactive Compliance vs. Proactive Design: The Critical Distinction

The difference between reactive compliance and proactive design is not a philosophical preference. It has a direct and quantifiable impact on the probability that a clinical program will generate an inspection finding, and on the magnitude of the consequences if it does.

Reactive compliance programs devote organizational resources to demonstrating that requirements have been met after the data exists. Validation documentation is produced after systems are deployed. Audit trail reviews are conducted as a retrospective quality check rather than as a prospective surveillance program. Corrective action plans respond to specific findings rather than to the conditions that produced them. Training is delivered when a gap is identified rather than when a new risk is introduced. Vendor qualification confirms historical GCP compliance rather than verifying current data integrity practices for the specific trial.

The consequences of this orientation are visible in the bioresearch monitoring enforcement record. Reactive compliance programs are well-documented. They can demonstrate, at any point in time, that the required documentation exists. What they cannot demonstrate is that the documentation accurately represents current practice, because the documentation was produced in response to requirements rather than the output of a functioning quality system. When an FDA investigator begins examining the relationship between what the documentation says should happen and what the electronic records show actually happened, that gap becomes the inspection narrative.

Proactive design programs build quality signals into operations from the beginning. Centralized monitoring programs designed to detect specific ALCOA+ failure modes generate continuous data on whether attributability, contemporaneity, and accuracy are being maintained across the site network. Training programs designed to produce ALCOA+ competency, not just ALCOA+ awareness, generate a workforce that understands why the controls exist. Vendor oversight programs designed to verify data integrity in practice generate evidence that the sponsor has fulfilled its oversight obligation. These programs generate more work at the design stage. They generate dramatically less work at the remediation stage.

Activity	Reactive Compliance Approach	Proactive Design Approach
EDC audit trail review	Periodic review confirms audit trail is enabled and entries are present; findings documented	Review methodology specifically targets attribution failures, timestamp anomalies, and query timing patterns; anomalies trigger site-level investigation; review frequency calibrated to site risk profile
Training program	Coordinators complete GCP training module at site initiation; completion documented	Training builds ALCOA+ competency mapped to specific role responsibilities; competency assessment confirms understanding under realistic scenarios; training updated when data integrity failure modes are identified in the site network
Vendor qualification	Vendor completes qualification questionnaire; GCP experience confirmed; contractual data integrity attestation obtained	Qualification includes data integrity-specific assessment of systems, practices, and prior inspection history; on-site or remote audit verifies actual practices; data return and retention provisions confirmed independently of contractual attestation

Activity	Reactive Compliance Approach	Proactive Design Approach
Protocol deviation management	Deviations documented and closed; root cause analysis completed per SOP; CAPA issued	Deviation patterns analyzed across sites for signals of systematic data management failures; sites with elevated deviation rates reviewed for audit trail anomalies; deviation root causes drive training and process design updates rather than site-specific remediation alone
Risk-based monitoring design	Sites selected for monitoring based on enrollment status and historical finding rates; visit coverage calibrated to protocol complexity	Monitoring strategy identifies specific ALCOA+ failure modes as critical risks; centralized review monitors real-time indicators of those failure modes; on-site verification targeted at anomalies identified in centralized review rather than at visit frequency targets

What Design-Level Accountability Looks Like

Translating the seven principles above into operational practice requires that data integrity accountability be assigned at the design level, not delegated to quality oversight after systems are in place. This means specific individuals, with specific authority and specific responsibilities, are accountable for each design decision that affects clinical data integrity.

In the sponsor organization, design-level accountability means that the clinical data management lead who selects and configures an EDC platform is accountable for the data integrity design decisions embedded in that configuration: whether change reason dropdowns are designed to support accurate attribution; whether audit trail review is built into the data management plan as a surveillance activity with defined frequency, scope, and escalation criteria; whether the EDC-to-clinical database transfer specifications preserve audit trail data or transmit only accepted values. These decisions are made during system setup and are rarely revisited unless a finding forces them to be. Making them consciously, with ALCOA+ requirements explicitly mapped to each configuration decision, is the operational expression of design-level accountability.

For CROs, design-level accountability means that the data management infrastructure deployed for a given sponsor cannot be treated as a configuration of commercial software that happens to satisfy technical requirements. It must be designed to support the specific ALCOA+ obligations of the specific trial, with documented rationale for each design decision and a quality review process that evaluates those decisions against the regulatory standard before the first subject is enrolled.

For investigator sites, design-level accountability means that site staff understand not merely what to do but why the requirements exist, so that the judgment required to apply them correctly under novel circumstances is present when no SOP covers the specific situation. A coordinator who understands that contemporaneous recording exists because memory is unreliable and outcome-biased will make better documentation decisions in unanticipated situations than a coordinator who knows the rule without understanding its basis.

COMPLIANT: What Good Looks Like	NON-COMPLIANT: What Inspectors Cite
Data management plan explicitly maps each ALCOA+ property to specific system configurations, process controls, and training requirements	Data management plan describes system features and procedural steps but does not map controls to ALCOA+ properties or identify failure modes
EDC configuration is reviewed against ALCOA+ requirements before first site activation; design decisions are documented with regulatory rationale	EDC is deployed as a commercially validated platform; sponsor validation is limited to technical IQ/OQ without review of data integrity design decisions embedded in configuration

COMPLIANT: What Good Looks Like	NON-COMPLIANT: What Inspectors Cite
Centralized monitoring program targets specific ALCOA+ failure modes identified in prospective risk assessment; anomaly thresholds are defined and documented	Centralized monitoring produces site scorecards and query metrics; no defined methodology for detecting ALCOA+ failure mode patterns
Vendor qualification includes data integrity-specific assessment with verification of actual practices, not solely documentation review	Vendor qualification relies on GCP experience attestation, SOC 2 reports, and contractual data integrity representations without independent verification
Deviation management program analyzes cross-site patterns to identify systemic data integrity signals rather than closing individual deviations in isolation	Protocol deviations are individually documented and closed; no cross-site pattern analysis; root cause analysis produces site-specific corrective actions without evaluation of systemic conditions

The Organizational Conditions That Enable Design

The seven design principles described above cannot be implemented in organizations where data integrity is owned by one department and operated by another. The most common structural failure in clinical data governance is exactly this configuration: quality owns the policy, data management owns the systems, clinical operations owns the sites, and no single organizational function is accountable for the design of the integrated program that connects them.

Under this configuration, quality produces policies that data management may not be aware of. Data management configures systems that quality has not reviewed. Clinical operations manages sites using practices that neither quality nor data management has approved. Monitoring finds problems that none of the three functions has the individual authority to resolve. The organizational design produces the compliance gap that the inspection will document.

Building organizational conditions that enable data integrity design requires, at minimum, three things. First, a single accountable owner for clinical data governance: not a shared committee responsibility, but a named individual with the authority to make design decisions across systems, processes, and training programs. Second, a governance structure that ensures data integrity design decisions are made prospectively, at the protocol and system design stage, rather than reactively in response to findings. Third, a leadership engagement model in which clinical program leadership reviews data integrity metrics with the same regularity and seriousness that it reviews enrollment metrics and database lock timelines.

This is what MHRA means when it requires that senior management create an environment in which data integrity is expected, supported, and verifiable.[11] The requirement is not satisfied by a management-approved data governance policy. It is satisfied when the organizational behaviors that policy describes are observable in practice: when monitoring concerns are escalated and acted upon; when database lock timelines accommodate quality resolution rather than overriding it; when clinical operations leadership treats a data integrity finding as a systemic signal rather than a site-specific incident.

E6(R3) as a Design Standard

ICH E6(R3), adopted at Step 4 in January 2025, is the most design-oriented regulatory document in the history of clinical GCP. Its requirements are not primarily technical, specific audit trail configurations, particular validation protocols, named documentation formats. They are organizational: quality management systems that identify critical data and processes prospectively; data governance policies covering the full data lifecycle; traceability requirements that link submitted data to original observations through every transformation. These are design requirements, and they are stated as such.

For sponsors implementing E6(R3) as a compliance exercise, producing the documentation that maps to each requirement, the guideline creates extensive documentation obligations. For sponsors implementing E6(R3) as a design standard, it provides the clearest regulatory articulation of what a well-designed clinical data governance program looks like: one in which critical risks are identified before they materialize, where organizational accountability is clear, where all systems are held to consistent data integrity standards regardless of their position in the data pipeline, and where the sponsor can demonstrate a verifiable chain from original source observation to regulatory submission.

The four foundational changes E6(R3) introduces, discussed in Chapter 2, are each, at their core, design requirements.[12] Making ALCOA+ explicitly mandatory means that every design decision in the clinical data management infrastructure must be evaluated against ALCOA+ properties. Requiring organizational data governance means that design accountability cannot be fragmented across departments. Extending obligations to all trial systems means that the design perimeter cannot stop at the EDC platform. Introducing a traceability requirement means that the design must support reconstruction of the data pathway from source to submission, not merely documentation of individual records. An organization implementing E6(R3) as a design standard is, in a precise regulatory sense, implementing what the guideline actually requires.

Where Design Fails: The Three Most Common Program Failures

Two decades of bioresearch monitoring inspection findings point to three structural program failures that appear, with remarkable consistency, across organizations of different sizes, therapeutic areas, and geographic markets. They are not exotic failures. They are the predictable consequences of implementing compliance documentation in the absence of integrity design.

The Validation-as-Compliance Fallacy

The most pervasive structural failure in clinical data management is the treatment of system validation as a data integrity control. A validated EDC system is a system that has been documented to function as intended. It is not a system that has been designed to produce ALCOA+-compliant data. These are different things, and the distinction is consequential.

Validation confirms that the system behaves according to its requirements specification. It does not confirm that the requirements specification was designed to produce attributable, contemporaneous, original data. A system validated to permit shared login credentials is a validated non-compliant system. A system validated to allow change reason fields to be left blank is a validated system that will produce attribution failures. A system validated to permit audit trail disabling is a validated system that will be manipulated.

Organizations that have treated validated EDC deployment as equivalent to ALCOA+-compliant data management have a specific remediation task: reviewing the design decisions embedded in their system configurations and identifying the specific ALCOA+ failure modes those configurations enable. This is not a re-validation exercise. It is a design review, and it requires the involvement of clinical quality professionals who understand both what ALCOA+ requires and how specific system configurations support or undermine it.[13]

The Documentation-Over-Function Inversion

The second structural failure is the subordination of function to documentation: designing data management programs that produce the required records rather than programs that manage data reliably. This failure is particularly insidious because it is indistinguishable from a compliant program in a documentation review. The policies are present. The procedures are current. The training records are complete. The monitoring reports describe visits conducted and observations documented.

What the documentation does not reveal is whether any of it reflects operational reality. A monitoring report describing 40 source data verification checks completed with zero discrepancies may accurately document a clean site. It may also accurately document a monitoring visit conducted by someone who understood the documentation requirement without understanding what source data verification is designed to detect. The records are the same. The quality of the quality function is different.

Distinguishing documentation from function requires the same approach FDA's inspectors use: examining whether the output of the quality system is consistent with the records the quality system produces. A site with a monitoring program that has never found a data discrepancy, across years of enrollment at a high-volume facility, is a site whose monitoring program deserves scrutiny. A CRO that has closed 300 queries without a single change reason other than 'transcription error' across multiple studies is a CRO whose query management culture deserves investigation. The documentation is compliant. The function is not.

The Escalation Gap

The third structural failure, and in many respects the most consequential, is the absence of an escalation pathway that connects data integrity signals to organizational accountability. In clinical data management programs of all sizes, quality signals are generated continuously: audit trail anomalies identified in review, query timing patterns that suggest retrospective data management, site coordinators whose entry habits differ from their colleagues in ways that warrant investigation, vendor systems that cannot produce requested records within the retention period. These signals are documented. They are closed. They are not, in most programs, connected to an organizational process that ensures they receive the attention of someone with the authority and mandate to act on the conditions that produced them.

The escalation gap is precisely what regulators look for when they ask whether an organization's quality system is functional. A quality system that generates findings and closes them at the site level is a documentation system. A quality system that generates findings, identifies patterns across findings, and connects those patterns to design decisions that require organizational attention is a quality system. The difference is not in the sophistication of the individual components. It is in whether the components are connected to each other and to organizational accountability in a way that makes the system capable of learning from its signals rather than merely recording them.[14]

Building the Design Mindset Into Practice

The chapters that follow this one are organized around specific domains of clinical data integrity design: the data lifecycle, computer system validation, audit trails, electronic records and signatures, and decentralized trial elements. Each chapter examines the design decisions that determine whether the systems and processes in that domain reliably produce ALCOA+-compliant data or reliably produce ALCOA+-compliant documentation.

Before entering those specific domains, two practical steps are worth identifying as the entry point for any organization seeking to shift from compliance to design orientation.

The first is a design audit: a structured review of each element of the clinical data management infrastructure that asks, for every system, process, and training program, whether the current design makes compliant behavior easier than the non-compliant alternative, whether the design has been evaluated against the specific ALCOA+ failure modes most likely in the trial context, and whether there is an escalation pathway connecting quality signals in this domain to organizational accountability. This is not a compliance gap assessment. It is a design review, and it requires different questions and different expertise.

The second is an incentive audit: a structured review of the organizational metrics, performance evaluations, sponsor-CRO relationship dynamics, and leadership engagement model to identify the specific conditions under which individuals in the organization face pressure to prioritize throughput over documentation quality. Not because every such pressure produces a data integrity failure, but because understanding where those pressures exist and whether the current design provides adequate counter-weight to them is the prerequisite for designing programs that hold under realistic operational conditions.

Neither of these audits requires external expertise, though experienced guidance helps. They require the intellectual honesty to ask the design questions that compliance audits are not designed to surface, and the organizational willingness to act on the answers.

> *The organizations that receive warning letters are not, in general, organizations that failed to implement the required controls. They are organizations where the gap between what the controls were designed to prevent and what they were actually capable of preventing, under real operational conditions, was larger than anyone inside the organization recognized until an inspector measured it.*

CHAPTER TWO - KEY TAKEAWAYS
The core distinction: Compliance is a property of documentation. Integrity is a property of systems. These are not the same thing, and the enforcement record confirms they can diverge dramatically.
Why failures are design failures: The documented clinical data integrity failures of the past two decades consistently reflect systems, processes, and cultures that made the non-compliant path easier than the compliant one, not deliberate fraud by individuals acting in isolation.
The seven principles: Make compliant behavior the path of least resistance; design controls for the failure mode rather than the standard case; build verification into operations rather than audits; align incentives with integrity; design for the inspector; extend design obligations through the data supply chain; and build for change.
Reactive vs. proactive: Reactive compliance demonstrates that requirements have been met. Proactive design builds conditions under which ALCOA+-compliant data is produced continuously and reliably, and where quality signals are generated, escalated, and acted upon before inspection surfaces them.
E6(R3) as design standard: ICH E6(R3)'s requirements for quality management, organizational data governance, and traceability are design requirements, not documentation requirements. Organizations implementing them as documentation exercises will have compliant records that do not reflect compliant operations.
Three structural failures: The validation-as-compliance fallacy, the documentation-over-function inversion, and the escalation gap account for the majority of bioresearch monitoring inspection findings and are the primary targets of design-oriented data governance programs.
Three structural failures: The validation-as-compliance fallacy, the documentation-over-function inversion, and the escalation gap account for the majority of bioresearch monitoring inspection findings and are the primary targets of design-oriented data governance programs.

CHAPTER TWO - KEY TAKEAWAYS
Where this leads: The specific design domains examined in the chapters that follow, including data lifecycle, computer system validation, audit trails, electronic records, and decentralized trial elements, are each governed by the same underlying question: under what conditions would this control fail, and have those conditions been designed against?

CHAPTER THREE

A Brief History of Clinical Data Integrity Regulation

> *Every major clinical data integrity regulation was written in response to something that went wrong. Understanding the history is understanding the failures the rules were designed to prevent.*

Regulation rarely arrives in a single, coherent document. It accumulates, in response to disasters, fraudulent studies, enforcement failures, and hard-won scientific consensus, across decades and jurisdictions. The regulatory framework that governs data integrity in clinical research today is the product of more than sixty years of exactly that kind of growth. Understanding where each rule came from, and why, is the fastest way to understand what it actually requires.

This chapter traces that history from FDA's first clinical research regulations in the 1960s through the most recent international harmonization guidance, including ICH E6(R3)'s landmark adoption of ALCOA+ as a binding Good Clinical Practice standard and the EMA's 2023 Guideline on Computerised Systems and Electronic Data in Clinical Trials, which formalized ALCOA++ in the EU framework. It is a roadmap, not an exhaustive commentary. The goal is for any clinical operations, data management, quality, or regulatory professional to finish this chapter with a clear mental model of which regulations apply to them, how they relate to each other, and what the underlying logic of clinical data integrity regulation actually is.

Before the Rules: The Era of Unregulated Human Experimentation

The Tuskegee and Willowbrook Legacy

The modern regulatory framework for clinical research data integrity cannot be understood without first understanding the ethical catastrophes that made it necessary. The Tuskegee Syphilis Study, in which the U.S. Public Health Service deliberately withheld treatment from African American men with syphilis and observed disease progression for forty years without informed consent, and the Willowbrook hepatitis experiments, in which intellectually disabled children were deliberately infected with hepatitis virus, were not outliers. They were extreme examples of a research culture in which the rights of human subjects, and the integrity of the data collected from them, were subordinate to scientific convenience. [15]

These studies produced data. That data was recorded, analyzed, and published. By the standards of their time, the records were complete. But the records documented procedures that were ethically indefensible, and the data they contained could not be separated from the conditions under which it was obtained. The first lesson of clinical data integrity history is that a technically accurate record can still be a profoundly corrupted one, if the conduct it documents violated the rights of the people from whom it was collected. [16]

Year	Event
1932	Tuskegee Syphilis Study begins. The U.S. Public Health Service enrolls 399 African American men with untreated syphilis in Macon County, Alabama, observing disease progression without informing them of their diagnosis or providing treatment.
1947	Nuremberg Code — Establishes ten principles for ethical human experimentation, including voluntary informed consent. The first international framework for protecting research subjects.
1955	Willowbrook hepatitis studies begin. Saul Krugman and Joan Giles deliberately infect intellectually disabled children at Willowbrook State School in Staten Island with hepatitis virus to study its natural history and test gamma globulin.

Year	Event
1964	Declaration of Helsinki — The World Medical Association adopts foundational ethical principles for medical research involving human subjects. Revised multiple times since; still the primary ethical framework for clinical research globally. [17]
1966	Henry Beecher publishes "Ethics and Clinical Research" in the *New England Journal of Medicine*, citing twenty-two examples of unethical research, including the Willowbrook studies, and catalyzing institutional scrutiny of research conduct.
1970	Willowbrook hepatitis studies end amid mounting public criticism.
1972	Tuskegee Syphilis Study exposed and halted. Jean Heller's Associated Press reporting reveals that subjects were never informed of their diagnosis and that treatment was withheld for forty years, including after penicillin became standard of care in the 1940s.
1974	National Research Act passed. Establishes Institutional Review Boards and the National Commission for the Protection of Human Subjects of Biomedical and Behavioral Research, directly in response to Tuskegee.
1979	Belmont Report issued. Articulates the three core ethical principles, respect for persons, beneficence, and justice, that underlie modern human subjects protection.

1962–1980: The Kefauver-Harris Foundation

1962: The Amendment That Created Modern Clinical Research Regulation

The modern regulatory framework for clinical data integrity in the United States traces directly to a single event: the thalidomide crisis, where the drug led to a sharp rise in phocomelia and other severe limb, organ, and craniofacial malformations in infants whose mothers had taken it during early pregnancy. The Kefauver-Harris Drug Amendments of 1962 transformed the clinical research landscape. For the first time, sponsors were required to demonstrate efficacy as well as safety through adequate and well-controlled clinical trials. The amendments gave FDA explicit authority over the conduct of clinical investigations, required investigators to obtain informed consent from research subjects, and created the investigational new drug application framework that governs clinical trials in the United States to this day.

Critically for data integrity, the 1962 amendments established the principle that clinical data submitted to FDA must be reliable, verifiable, and generated under conditions that can be inspected. The requirement was not stated in the language of ALCOA+, that framework was decades away, but the underlying demand was the same: data submitted to support a marketing application must accurately represent what actually happened to the patients from whom it was collected.

21 CFR Parts 312 and 314 — The Regulatory Architecture	
Issued by:	U.S. Food and Drug Administration (FDA). Year: 1963 (original); substantially revised 1987; amended periodically.
Scope:	All clinical investigations of drugs and biologics conducted in the United States or supporting U.S. marketing applications.
Key requirements:	Sponsor obligations: IND submission, protocol approval, safety reporting, investigator oversight. Investigator obligations: protocol compliance, informed consent, case history maintenance. Records: adequate and accurate case histories for all observations; retained per regulatory minimum periods. Inspection authority: FDA may inspect all records and facilities related to a clinical investigation. Disqualification: FDA may disqualify investigators found to have violated regulations or submitted false information.

1977–1996: The Birth of Good Clinical Practice

The Nonclinical Precedent: IBT, Searle, and the Regulatory Logic That GCP Inherited

Industrial Bio-Test Laboratories, Inc. was the largest contract toxicology laboratory operating in the United States in the early 1970s. Between 1971 and 1976, FDA investigators uncovered a systematic pattern of data fabrication and suppression. One animal facility, known internally as "the swamp," operated under conditions so poor that animal deaths went unrecorded, and pathological evaluations were never conducted.

Replacement animals were substituted into studies without documentation. The raw data, where it existed at all, bore no reliable relationship to the findings reported to the agency[18][19].

G.D. Searle & Company's failures had a different character but the same root. FDA investigators identified that the data in a revised study report had been rewritten to agree with the summary, rather than the summary being derived from the data. The sequence was inverted: conclusion first, data adjusted to match. That inversion is the failure mode the ALCOA principle of Original was subsequently designed to prevent. [20]

Congressional hearings chaired by Senator Edward Kennedy in 1975 and 1976 exposed the breadth of the problem to public scrutiny. The regulatory response was 21 CFR Part 58, the Good Laboratory Practices (GLP) regulations for nonclinical laboratory studies, promulgated in December 1978 and effective June 1979.[21] Each requirement in the GLPs was designed to address a specific documented failure mode: contemporaneous record-keeping to prevent backdating, raw data retention to prevent reconstruction, direct observation requirements to prevent fabrication, and a framework for independent audit that made changes visible rather than concealable. The parallel GCP rulemaking that followed applied the same regulatory logic to the clinical context.

GLP vs. GCP: The Distinction That Matters

The IBT and Searle cases are nonclinical research history. 21 CFR Part 58 governs nonclinical laboratory studies; Good Clinical Practice regulations govern clinical research involving human subjects. The connection between the two frameworks is causal, not regulatory: the congressional pressure and documented failure modes of the early GLP enforcement era directly shaped the GCP framework that followed. The GCP framework applied those same structural requirements to the human research context.

FDA published regulations for clinical investigators in 1977 and 1978, followed in 1981 by a consolidated set of GCP regulations that established the sponsor-monitor-investigator triad as the governing structure for clinical trial conduct. The 1981 regulations introduced the requirement for source data verification as a formal monitoring obligation. Source data verification is the first operational data integrity requirement in clinical research and the direct ancestor of the ALCOA principle of Original. [22]

Year	Development
1977–1981	21 CFR Parts 50, 56, 312 — Establishes sponsor-monitor-investigator framework. Introduces source data verification as a formal monitoring obligation. Creates the regulatory architecture ICH E6 would later harmonize internationally.

1996: ICH E6 — The First International GCP Standard

The International Council for Harmonisation was established in 1990 to develop harmonized technical requirements for pharmaceutical registration. The E6 guideline on Good Clinical Practice, published in 1996 and adopted by FDA, EMA predecessor bodies, and Japan's MHW, was one of the first outputs of this process.

The original ICH E6 guideline contains the first articulation of what would become the ALCOA framework, requiring that the data in clinical trial records be attributable, legible, contemporaneous, original, and accurate. The 1996 guideline was also the first international GCP document to address electronic records specifically, requiring that systems used for electronic data handling be validated, that audit trails be maintained, and that the investigator maintain control over trial data regardless of whether electronic systems were used. [23]

ICH E6 — Guideline for Good Clinical Practice (original)	
Issued by:	International Conference on Harmonisation. Year: 1996; implemented by FDA, EU, Japan simultaneously.
Scope:	All clinical trials of medicinal products intended for regulatory submission to ICH member authorities.
Key requirements:	Sponsor responsibilities: protocol development, CRO oversight, data management, safety reporting. Investigator responsibilities: protocol compliance, source data maintenance, CRF completion. Data and records: CRFs must accurately reflect source documents; source data must be attributable, legible, contemporaneous, original, and accurate. Electronic records: systems must be validated with audit trails maintained.

1997: 21 CFR Part 11 — Electronic Records Come to Clinical Research

21 CFR Part 11, published in March 1997, established the technical and procedural requirements under which electronic records could serve as the legal equivalent of paper records for FDA-regulated activities including clinical trials. For clinical research, this meant that an electronic case report form, an electronic informed consent, or an electronic investigator signature could satisfy regulatory requirements that had previously implied paper documentation, provided that Part 11's controls were in place. [24]

21 CFR Part 11 — Electronic Records; Electronic Signatures — Clinical Research Application	
Issued by:	U.S. Food and Drug Administration. Year: 1997 (effective); revised guidance 2003; clinical-specific Q&A guidance updated Revision 1.
Scope:	All electronic records and electronic signatures used in lieu of paper records required by FDA clinical research regulations (21 CFR Parts 50, 56, 312, 314).
Key requirements:	Audit trails: automatic, secure, computer-generated, date/time-stamped records of operator actions, applicable to EDC, CTMS, eTMF, and ePRO systems. System validation: documented evidence that clinical data systems function as intended. Access controls: unique login credentials; no shared accounts. Electronic signatures: unique to one individual, non-repudiable. Record retention: accurate, complete copies available for FDA review. Training: documented authority for all system users.

The 2003 Guidance and Its Clinical Research Consequences

FDA's 2003 guidance narrowing the scope of Part 11 had unintended consequences in clinical research. Some sponsors and CROs interpreted the guidance as reducing Part 11 audit trail requirements for clinical data systems, particularly for legacy EDC platforms that would require significant investment to upgrade. The result was a period in which some clinical data management systems in active use lacked compliant audit trails, a gap that became visible to FDA investigators as EDC adoption expanded, and inspection techniques matured. The 2003 guidance had not said audit trails were unnecessary. Its misapplication to clinical data systems created compliance gaps that took years to remediate. [25]

FDA's Clinical-Specific Part 11 Guidance: Questions and Answers

FDA subsequently published dedicated guidance on electronic systems, electronic records, and electronic signatures in clinical investigations (Electronic Systems Q&A, Revision 1), which is the authoritative clinical-context interpretation of Part 11 requirements.[26] Unlike the 2003 scope-and-application guidance, which was prepared primarily in a manufacturing and general regulatory context, the Electronic Systems Q&A guidance is written specifically for clinical investigations conducted under 21 CFR Parts 312 and 812. It addresses the application of Part 11 to EDC systems, electronic health records used as source data, digital health technologies used for remote data acquisition, and electronic signatures in the context of clinical trial operations.

The guidance clarifies that once data from an electronic health record or real-world data source enters the sponsor's EDC system, FDA assesses Part 11 compliance from that point forward. It confirms that for inspection purposes, source data recorded by digital health technologies is considered to be located in the durable electronic data repository, such as the EDC system or cloud platform, into which the data was transmitted via a pre-specified, validated process. These positions are directly relevant to decentralized trial conduct and are the operative FDA standard for any sponsor using patient-held devices, wearable sensors, or telemedicine platforms to generate clinical source data.

Year	Development
1997	21 CFR Part 11 effective — Establishes audit trail, access control, and electronic signature requirements for clinical data systems; makes electronic records legally equivalent to paper records when system requirements are met.
2003	Part 11 Scope and Application guidance — Narrows FDA enforcement interpretation; misapplied by some organizations to reduce audit trail requirements for clinical EDC systems.

Year	Development
Post-2003	FDA Electronic Systems Q&A for Clinical Investigations — Clinical-specific authoritative guidance interpreting Part 11 for EDC, EHR, and digital health technology contexts. Clarifies source data location for DHT-generated data.

2016: ICH E6(R2) — Risk-Based Monitoring and the EDC Transition

ICH E6(R2), finalized in 2016, was the most significant update to international GCP in twenty years. It introduced risk-based monitoring, the principle that monitoring intensity should be proportionate to the risks to subject safety and data integrity and explicitly acknowledged that centralized monitoring was a legitimate and often preferable approach to ensuring data quality. It updated the framework for electronic systems to reflect EDC as the norm rather than the exception.

E6(R2)'s most important data integrity contribution was its introduction of the quality management system concept into GCP. The guideline required that sponsors implement a systematic, prospective approach to identifying, evaluating, and managing risks to clinical trial quality, including data quality risks. This shifted data integrity from a retrospective compliance activity to a prospective quality management activity.

2013–2019: FDA's Clinical Data Integrity Guidance Portfolio

FDA published its guidance on risk-based monitoring in August 2013, predating ICH E6(R2) by three years and reflecting the agency's emerging view that traditional 100% on-site source data verification was an inefficient use of monitoring resources that did not reliably improve data quality. The guidance formally endorsed centralized monitoring and statistical data review as components of an effective monitoring strategy.[27]

FDA published its guidance on electronic source data in September 2013 (updated 2019), clarifying that where data is entered directly into an EDC system designed for that purpose, the electronic record is the source record. There is no requirement for a parallel paper record. But the electronic system must meet Part 11 requirements. This guidance effectively made Part 11 compliance a prerequisite for using EDC records as source data.[28]

Year	Development
2013	FDA Risk-Based Monitoring Guidance — Endorses centralized monitoring and statistical data review; establishes that monitoring must detect data integrity problems, not merely verify CRF-to-source agreement.
2013/2019	FDA Electronic Source Data Guidance — Direct electronic entry constitutes source data when system requirements are met; makes Part 11 compliance a prerequisite for treating EDC entries as primary source records.

The FDA-MHRA Joint GCP Workshop and Its Regulatory Significance

In October 2018, FDA and MHRA jointly convened the first formal cross-agency Good Clinical Practice workshop, bringing together officials from FDA's Center for Drug Evaluation and Research and MHRA's Inspection, Enforcement and Standards Division to establish a common published position on clinical data integrity. The published output of that workshop, authored by named FDA and MHRA officials, constitutes primary regulatory authority for the convergent positions of both agencies.[29]

The workshop documentation is significant for three reasons. First, it confirms that both agencies treat audit trail reliability, data blinding controls, and data management planning as direct determinants of marketing application acceptability, not merely as inspection findings. Second, it establishes that the regulatory consequences of data integrity failures are immediate and bilateral: a clinical dataset with documented data integrity concerns is simultaneously unacceptable to both FDA and MHRA, regardless of which authority conducts the inspection. Third, it signals the direction of international regulatory convergence: common inspection standards, shared training programs, and growing reliance arrangements between PIC/S member authorities mean that a finding by any major national competent authority increasingly carries weight with all others.

Year	Development
2018/2020	FDA-MHRA Joint GCP Workshop publication — Named FDA and MHRA officials document both agencies' common position on audit trail reliability, data management practices, and the impact of data integrity failures on marketing application acceptability. First formal joint regulatory authority publication on clinical data integrity.

The ALCOA Framework in Clinical Research: From Principle to Standard

The ALCOA framework, Attributable, Legible, Contemporaneous, Original, Accurate, was embedded in ICH E6 from its first publication in 1996. But its application in clinical research was inconsistent for two decades: understood by quality professionals, reflected in inspection findings, but not operationalized in most sponsor or CRO data management programs. This began to change as FDA's bioresearch monitoring inspection program intensified in the 2010s, and as the specific data integrity failure modes documented in enforcement actions against Cetero, Semler, and GVK made clear what ALCOA failures looked like in practice.

The extension of ALCOA to ALCOA+, adding Complete, Consistent, Enduring, and Available, was particularly significant in the clinical research context because the additional properties address failure modes specific to multi-site, longitudinal clinical trials.

ALCOA+ Principle	Specific Clinical Research Application
Attributable	Each CRF entry, query resolution, and data management action traceable to a specific authorized individual; not a shared site login or generic data manager account.
Legible	Source documents readable throughout the trial and retention period; eCRF data displayable in human-readable format including metadata.

ALCOA+ Principle	Specific Clinical Research Application
Contemporaneous	Clinical observations recorded at the time of the visit or procedure; EDC entry timestamps consistent with scheduled visit windows.
Original	Electronic source data retained in native format including audit trail; paper source documents not transcribed without retaining the original.
Accurate	CRF data truthfully represents the clinical event, including adverse events, protocol deviations, and missing assessments.
Complete	All data points required by the protocol are present; all queries resolved; no selective exclusion of site data from analysis datasets.
Consistent	Timestamps, visit sequences, and assessments are internally coherent; randomization dates consistent across source and CRF.
Enduring	Records maintained in readable format throughout the required retention period; archive systems validated; data migration documented.
Available	All trial records retrievable within the inspection window; eTMF accessible to regulators on request.

2023: ICH E6(R3) — The Defining Clinical Data Integrity Standard

ICH E6(R3), adopted at Step 4 by the ICH Assembly in January 2025 following the Step 2 public consultation in May 2023, represents the most fundamental restructuring of the international GCP framework since the original 1996 guideline. It is not an incremental revision. It is a reconceptualization of how clinical trial quality, including data integrity, should be designed, managed, and demonstrated throughout a trial lifecycle.[30]

ICH E6(R3) — Guideline for Good Clinical Practice — Third Revision	
Issued by:	International Council for Harmonisation (ICH) — adopted by FDA, EMA, PMDA, and 50+ additional authorities. Adoption: 6 January 2025; typographical correction: 24 October 2025.
Scope:	All clinical trials of medicinal products intended for submission to ICH member regulatory authorities.
Key requirements:	ALCOA+ explicitly adopted as the standard for all clinical trial data, paper and electronic. Data governance: sponsors must have documented policies covering the full data lifecycle. Quality by design: systematic identification of critical data and processes; prospective risk management. Electronic systems: validation, audit trails, and access controls required for all trial-related computerized systems. CRO oversight: sponsor cannot transfer regulatory responsibility; must verify CRO data integrity practices. Traceability: sponsor must be able to verify that submitted data accurately reflects original observations through all transfers and transformations.

E6(R3) changes clinical data integrity practice in four fundamental ways. First, it makes ALCOA+ explicitly mandatory. Second, it requires data governance at the organizational level, not merely system-by-system compliance. Third, it extends data integrity obligations to all trial systems, not just EDC, including CTMS, IRT, ePRO, and safety data management systems. Fourth, it introduces a traceability requirement that goes beyond the record level, requiring that sponsors be able to verify that data as submitted accurately reflects original observations at the investigative site through every data transfer, edit, query, and aggregation step.

2023: The EMA Guideline on Computerised Systems and Electronic Data

The European Medicines Agency's Guideline on Computerised Systems and Electronic Data in Clinical Trials (EMA/INS/GCP/112288/2023), adopted by the GCP Inspectors Working Group in March 2023 and effective September 2023, represents the most significant update to EU clinical computerized systems requirements since the 2010 Reflection Paper it formally replaced. This document is a primary EU regulatory authority for clinical data integrity and should be read alongside ICH E6(R3) as the operative EU standard for any sponsor or CRO conducting trials in EU member states.[31]

The guideline's most important contribution to the ALCOA framework is its explicit adoption of ALCOA++ as the EU clinical data integrity standard. Section 4.5 lists ten principles: the original five ALCOA properties, the four ALCOA+ extensions, and Traceable as the tenth discrete principle. This is a binding EMA guidance document, not an industry proposal or an aspirational framework. For sponsors conducting EU-regulated trials, Traceable is now a formally adopted regulatory requirement in the EU clinical context, not merely an emerging development. The specific language of Section 4.5 defines traceability as the ability to reconstruct the history of data actions throughout the data life cycle, explicitly extending beyond the record to the full data lineage from original capture to submitted value.

The guideline covers computerized systems across the full scope of clinical trial data capture, including EDC, eCOA, IRT, eTMF, electronic informed consent, and AI-assisted data management tools. Its treatment of AI use in clinical trials, including for participant recruitment, data clarification, and query processes, notes that requirements for AI beyond the generally applicable expectations to all systems will be addressed in a future annex, positioning the guideline as a living document with anticipated expansion.

Year	Development
2023	EMA Guideline on Computerised Systems and Electronic Data in Clinical Trials (EMA/INS/GCP/112288/2023) — Replaces the 2010 EMA Reflection Paper; formally adopts ALCOA++ including Traceable as the tenth principle as the EU clinical data integrity standard; covers EDC, eCOA, IRT, eTMF, eConsent, and AI tools.

2023: The EMA Data Quality Framework

The EMA Data Quality Framework for EU medicines regulation (EMA/326985/2023), adopted by the Committee for Medicinal Products for Human Use in October 2023, represents a strategic EMA initiative extending data quality governance beyond clinical trial records to encompass all data used in EU regulatory decision-making, including real-world data and evidence generated from electronic health records and secondary data sources.[32]

The framework is relevant to this history for two reasons. First, it establishes that the EMA's expectations for data quality are converging across traditional clinical trial data and the emerging real-world data sources that increasingly support regulatory decisions, including benefit-risk assessments, label updates, and post-authorization commitments. Second, it signals the direction of the EU regulatory landscape: data-driven regulatory decision-making, automated data quality assessment, and the integration of real-world evidence into the regulatory framework are EMA strategic priorities that will progressively shape the data integrity obligations of sponsors and data holders operating in the EU.

Year	Development
2023	EMA Data Quality Framework (EMA/326985/2023) — CHMP-adopted framework establishing EMA data quality governance for all regulatory decision-making, including real-world data; signals convergence of clinical trial data integrity standards with emerging real-world evidence requirements.

The Supporting Framework: Regulations That Complete the Picture

21 CFR Part 11 in the E6(R3) Era

21 CFR Part 11 remains in force and remains the primary U.S. technical standard for electronic records in clinical research. E6(R3) does not supersede Part 11; it adds to it. A clinical EDC system that meets Part 11's technical requirements but is deployed in an organization without an E6(R3)-compliant data governance framework satisfies the technical regulation but not the governance standard. Both are required. The FDA Electronic Systems Q&A guidance for clinical investigations provides the authoritative clinical-specific interpretation of how Part 11 requirements apply to EDC, digital health technologies, and real-world data sources used in FDA-regulated trials.

Updated computerized system validation guidance specific to clinical applications remains in development. Until that guidance is finalized, the combination of Part 11's technical requirements, the Electronic Systems Q&A guidance, and E6(R3)'s governance requirements is the operative standard for sponsors using cloud-hosted EDC, SaaS-based eTMF, and modern data management environments.

EU Clinical Trials Regulation (EU CTR 536/2014)

The EU Clinical Trials Regulation, fully applicable since January 2023, overhauled the EU clinical trial authorization framework and introduced new data integrity expectations for trials conducted in EU member states. EU CTR requires that clinical trial data be managed in compliance with EU GCP requirements, that electronic systems meet validation and audit trail standards, and that trial master file content be maintained in a way that allows reconstruction of the trial's conduct. The EMA Guideline on Computerised Systems now provides the primary operational guidance for EU CTR compliance with respect to electronic records and systems.[33]

MHRA's Clinical GCP Guidance Post-Brexit

The UK's MHRA maintains its own GCP framework following Brexit. UK GCP remains substantially aligned with ICH E6(R3). MHRA's inspection approach places the greatest weight on organizational culture and management accountability. MHRA inspectors assessing a sponsor operation will evaluate not only whether systems have audit trails, but whether the organization has a quality culture in which data integrity is genuinely expected and verifiable. For sponsors conducting trials in both EU member states and the UK, benchmarking against the more demanding of the two frameworks, which in most cases means MHRA's expectations, is the most efficient compliance strategy.

The Regulatory Roadmap: Which Rules Apply to Your Situation

If you are...	Primary clinical data integrity frameworks that apply
A sponsor conducting trials for FDA submissions	21 CFR Parts 50, 56, 312, 314; 21 CFR Part 11 and the Electronic Systems Q&A for clinical investigations; ICH E6(R3) as adopted by FDA; FDA 2013 risk-based monitoring guidance; FDA electronic source data guidance.
A sponsor conducting trials for EMA submissions	EU CTR 536/2014; ICH E6(R3) as adopted by EMA; EMA Guideline on Computerised Systems and Electronic Data (EMA/INS/GCP/112288/2023); national

If you are...	Primary clinical data integrity frameworks that apply
	competent authority GCP guidance for relevant member states.
A sponsor conducting trials for PMDA (Japan) submissions	ICH E6(R3) as adopted by PMDA; Japanese GCP Ordinance; PMDA computerized system guidance; Japan-specific requirements for informed consent and IRB approval.
A CRO performing clinical trial services	All frameworks applicable to the sponsors you serve; regulatory responsibility cannot be reduced because you are a service provider rather than a sponsor.
An eClinical technology vendor (EDC, CTMS, eTMF, RTSM)	21 CFR Part 11 and Electronic Systems Q&A for systems used in FDA-regulated trials; EMA Guideline on Computerised Systems for EU-regulated trials; ICH E6(R3) system requirements; customer-specific validation obligations under service agreements.
A clinical investigator site	21 CFR Parts 50, 56, 312 for site obligations; ICH E6(R3) investigator responsibilities; 21 CFR Part 11 if using electronic source records; institutional IRB/IEC requirements.
A sponsor conducting decentralized or hybrid trials	All frameworks above, with specific attention to E6(R3)'s provisions for remote data collection, ePRO, wearable device data, and FDA's Electronic Systems Q&A for inspection location of DHT-generated source data.

What the History Teaches

Tracing the arc from the Kefauver-Harris amendments through the GLP enforcement era and on to ICH E6(R3) and the EMA's 2023 Computerised Systems Guideline reveals the same pattern that characterizes every significant development in data integrity regulation: each rule was a response to a demonstrated failure. The 1962 amendments responded to inadequate clinical evidence. The GLP framework responded to fabricated nonclinical studies. The 1977-1981 GCP regulations responded to investigators who had not performed the procedures they documented. The 1996 ICH E6 guideline responded to the inconsistency of national GCP standards. The 2003 Part 11 guidance responded to disproportionate compliance burden. The 2013 risk-based monitoring guidance responded to monitoring programs that were expensive but did not reliably detect data integrity problems. ICH E6(R3) responded to a decade of documented clinical data integrity failures that demonstrated the existing framework was not preventing the failures it was designed to prevent. The 2023 EMA Guideline on Computerised Systems responded to the emergence of EDC, eCOA, IRT, and AI tools that had fundamentally changed how clinical trial data is generated and managed without a corresponding update to the regulatory expectations governing those systems.

The next regulatory development, whatever form it takes, will respond to failures that are occurring right now in organizations that believe their clinical data governance programs are adequate. The chapters that follow are designed to help organizations get ahead of the next regulatory response, rather than be the reason for it.

CHAPTER THREE - KEY TAKEAWAYS
1960s–1970s: The IBT and Searle enforcement actions demonstrated that fabricated nonclinical studies could reach FDA marketing applications without detection. The congressional response produced the first GLP regulations and established the regulatory logic that GCP would inherit: records must be contemporaneous, original, and traceable to their source.
1962: The Kefauver-Harris Drug Amendments created the foundational requirement for adequate and well-controlled clinical trials and established FDA's authority over clinical investigation conduct. The origin of clinical data integrity as a regulatory obligation.
1977–1981: FDA's first GCP regulations established the sponsor-monitor-investigator triad and introduced source data verification as a formal monitoring obligation, the operational ancestor of the ALCOA principle of Original.
1996: ICH E6 created the first internationally harmonized GCP standard and named the five ALCOA properties as the requirements for reliable clinical data records.
1997 onward: 21 CFR Part 11 established the technical framework for electronic records in FDA-regulated clinical research. The clinical-specific Electronic Systems Q&A guidance (Revision 1) is the authoritative interpretation of Part 11 for EDC, digital health technologies, and real-world data sources in clinical investigations.
2013–2019: FDA's risk-based monitoring guidance and electronic source data guidance established that monitoring programs must detect data integrity problems, and that direct electronic entry constitutes source data when system requirements are met. The 2018 FDA-MHRA joint GCP workshop produced primary regulatory documentation confirming both agencies' convergent positions on audit trail reliability and marketing application acceptability.
2016: ICH E6(R2) introduced risk-based monitoring and the quality management system approach to clinical trial conduct, shifting data integrity from a retrospective compliance activity to a prospective quality management responsibility.
2023 (March): The EMA Guideline on Computerised Systems and Electronic Data in Clinical Trials (EMA/INS/GCP/112288/2023) formally replaced the 2010 Reflection Paper, adopted ALCOA++ including Traceable as the tenth principle, and established the operative EU standard for EDC, eCOA, IRT, eTMF, eConsent, and AI tools used in clinical trials.

2023 (October): The EMA Data Quality Framework was adopted by CHMP, signaling convergence of clinical trial data integrity standards with real-world data quality governance across EU regulatory decision-making.
January 2025: ICH E6(R3) was adopted at Step 4, making ALCOA+ explicitly mandatory, requiring organizational-level data governance, extending data integrity obligations to all trial systems, and introducing a traceability requirement connecting submitted data to original source observations through every transformation step.
Core convergence: All major frameworks require the same foundations: ALCOA+-compliant data, validated systems with audit trails, organizational data governance policies, and management accountability. Regulatory responsibility cannot be transferred to a CRO or eClinical vendor.

CHAPTER FOUR

The Global Regulatory Landscape

> *A sponsor that conducts clinical trials across three continents does not operate under a single data integrity standard. Understanding which framework governs each activity, and where they converge, is the prerequisite for a compliance program that actually holds.*

A clinical operations team preparing for a combined FDA/EMA submission believed their data governance program was solid. Their EDC system was validated. Audit trails were enabled. The trial master file was maintained on a compliant eTMF platform. What the team had not confirmed was that their central laboratory retained raw electronic assay files in a format that their eTMF vendor's archive system could not render after a platform upgrade three years prior. When FDA inspectors requested the original electronic laboratory data during a pre-approval inspection, the sponsor could produce a derived PDF report for each subject's samples. The underlying files, the ones that constituted source data under FDA's 2013 electronic source data guidance and ICH E6(R3) retention and access requirements in section 4.2.7, were inaccessible. The inspection generated a complete response letter. The marketing application was delayed by eighteen months.

The scenario above is a composite, but every element of it is drawn from documented inspection findings. It illustrates the central challenge this chapter addresses: clinical trial data integrity is not governed by one framework. It is governed by several simultaneously, each originating from a different regulatory authority, each applying to a different aspect of the trial, and each capable of generating an independent compliance failure that has consequences in every market the sponsor is trying to reach.

This chapter maps the global regulatory terrain for clinical data integrity. For each of the six primary regulatory authorities, FDA, EMA, MHRA, WHO, PIC/S, and PMDA, we examine what they require of clinical trial sponsors and CROs, how they enforce those requirements, and what distinguishes their approach from the others. We then examine four emerging regulatory jurisdictions that are increasingly relevant for global clinical development programs. The chapter closes with an analysis of where international convergence is genuinely occurring and where meaningful divergence remains, anchored by the February 2026 EMA/PIC/S joint consultation that will define the next decade of global clinical data integrity standards.

> *Regulatory authorities regulate the same clinical trial data from different vantage points. Understanding what each authority is watching for, and why, is the foundation of a compliance strategy that works globally, not just domestically.*

The Landscape at a Glance

Before examining each authority in depth, the following matrix provides a practical reference showing how the six major frameworks address ten key clinical data integrity topics.

Topic	FDA	EMA	MHRA	PIC/S	WHO	PMDA
ALCOA+ Framework	Enforcement	Explicit	Explicit	Explicit	Explicit	Adopted
Audit Trail	Required	Required	Required	Required	Required	Required
Data Governance Policy	Guidance	Required	Required	Required	Required	Guidance
Risk-Based Monitoring	Guidance	Explicit	Explicit	Explicit	Explicit	Explicit
E-Source / EDC as Source	Guidance	Required	Guidance	Guidance	Guidance	Guidance

Topic	FDA	EMA	MHRA	PIC/S	WHO	PMDA
CRO Data Responsibility	Enforcement	Required	Required	Required	Required	Required
Decentralized Trials	Guidance	Guidance	Guidance	Emerging	Guidance	Guidance
AI / Digital Endpoints	Emerging	Guidance	Guidance	Emerging	Guidance	Active
Criminal Liability (DI)	Active	Active	Active	N/A	N/A	Active
Import/ Access Restrictions	Active	Parallel	Parallel	N/A	N/A	N/A

The status terms in the table above are not interchangeable, and the differences between them carry the analytical weight of the comparison.

- **Required** has been codified as a binding regulatory obligation, the body in question has written it into enforceable regulation or inspection program requirements, and a finding against it carries independent legal force.
- **Explicit** has been named and defined in published guidance, the body has committed to specific terminology and scope, but that commitment has not been codified into binding regulation.
- **Guidance** indicates advisory treatment only, inspectors may reference the concept, but it does not by itself constitute the legal basis for a finding.

These three terms describe progressively weaker degrees of formal commitment, and conflating them flattens a distinction this chapter depends on.

The remaining terms describe different kinds of regulatory posture rather than degrees of the same posture.

- **Enforcement** indicates that a body has not codified a concept by name but operationalizes it through inspection findings, warning letters, or consent decrees, this is the pattern the FDA follows for data integrity expectations generally.

- **Active** indicates a live legal mechanism, criminal referral or import restriction, currently in operation rather than merely available in statute.
- **Adopted** indicates incorporation through harmonization rather than independent origination, the pattern that describes most of PMDA's column.
- **Emerging** indicates that a body's position has not yet settled.
- **Parallel** indicates that a comparable mechanism exists but runs through a different legal pathway than the one FDA uses for the same purpose.
- **N/A** indicates the absence of the relevant authority altogether, typically because the body in question is a harmonization or standard-setting organization rather than a national regulator with prosecutorial or border control power.

With that vocabulary established, three patterns in the table merit discussion.

The first is the audit trail row, the only row in which all six bodies converge on Required. No other topic in clinical research data governance commands that degree of universal, binding consensus. If there is a single point of agreement across the global regulatory landscape on what constitutes minimum acceptable practice for electronic data, it is this one.

The second is the contrast between the FDA's column and every other column on the ALCOA+ Framework and CRO Data Responsibility rows. FDA is marked Enforcement on both, while EMA, MHRA, PIC/S, and WHO are marked Explicit or Required. This is not a gap in FDA's regulatory seriousness, the agency's enforcement record on data integrity is at least as aggressive as its counterparts. It is a difference in regulatory method. FDA has built its data integrity expectations primarily through the accumulated body of 483 observations, warning letters, and application integrity actions rather than through a single named regulation that defines ALCOA+ or CRO data responsibility as terms of art. EMA and the PIC/S-aligned bodies, by contrast, have published guidance documents that explicitly define these frameworks before any enforcement action occurs. A sponsor accustomed to FDA's case-by-case enforcement posture and unfamiliar with the EU's codified guidance can be caught off guard when an EMA inspector cites a specific, named data governance requirement that has no precise FDA analog. The substance of the expectation converges, the mechanism by which that expectation becomes binding does not.

The third is PMDA's position on AI and digital endpoints, the one row where Japan's regulator is marked Active while every other column reads Guidance or Emerging. PMDA's pattern elsewhere in the table is consistent with Japan's broader approach to ICH harmonization, adopting internationally agreed text rather than legislating independently.

The AI and digital endpoints row breaks that pattern, and the break is not incidental. It reflects Japan's Sakigake and related regulatory science fast-track initiatives, which have positioned PMDA ahead of its harmonization partners on emerging technology specifically, even as it continues to follow the consensus on more established topics. Decentralized trials and AI-derived endpoints remain, across the rest of the table, the two areas of genuine pre-consensus among all six bodies, which is itself a finding: forty years after Belmont and thirty after E6(R1), the regulatory apparatus built to govern data integrity is still catching up to the methodologies generating the data.

The N/A cells on criminal liability and import or access restrictions for PIC/S and WHO should not be read as findings about those bodies' seriousness on data integrity. They are findings about jurisdiction. PIC/S and WHO are standard-setting and harmonization organizations, not national regulators, and neither possesses the prosecutorial authority or border control mechanisms that make criminal referral or import restriction possible. The absence in those cells is structural, not substantive.

FDA: The World's Most Consequential Clinical Regulator

FDA — United States	
Primary instruments:	21 CFR Parts 50, 56, 312, 314; 21 CFR Part 11; Electronic Systems Q&A for Clinical Investigations; ICH E6(R3) as adopted; 2013 Risk-Based Monitoring Guidance; 2013/2019 Electronic Source Data Guidance; 2018 Data Integrity Q&A

FDA's jurisdiction over clinical data integrity is, by market size and enforcement consequence, the most influential in the world. Any sponsor conducting clinical investigations to support a marketing authorization application to FDA, regardless of where those trials are conducted, is subject to FDA's clinical data integrity framework. FDA enforces clinical data integrity through its Bioresearch Monitoring (BIMO) program, which conducts inspections of clinical investigator sites, sponsors, CROs, and IRBs. The enforcement outcomes of a BIMO inspection range from a Form 483 observation to a warning letter, a clinical hold, investigator disqualification, or, in cases involving knowing falsification of clinical data, criminal referral to the Department of Justice.

FDA's Distinctive Features in Clinical Enforcement

FDA has communicated many of its clinical data integrity expectations primarily through enforcement action, warning letters, BIMO inspection reports, and clinical hold letters, rather than through prescriptive prospective guidance. The 2013 risk-based monitoring guidance and the 2013/2019 electronic source data guidance formalized positions FDA had been expressing through enforcement for years before those documents were published. Sponsors tracking only published FDA guidance will consistently be behind the agency's current enforcement expectations.

FDA's 2013 guidance on electronic source data resolved an ambiguity that had persisted since Part 11's adoption: when data is entered directly into an EDC system designed to capture it, the electronic record is the source data. The FDA's clinical-specific Electronic Systems Q&A guidance further clarifies that once real-world data or digital health technology data enters the sponsor's EDC system, FDA assesses Part 11 compliance from that point forward. For inspection purposes, electronic source data recorded by a digital health technology is considered to be located in the durable electronic data repository into which it was transmitted via a validated, pre-specified process.[34,35]

FDA can refer clinical data integrity violations involving knowing falsification to the Department of Justice for criminal prosecution. This authority has been exercised. Individual investigators, CRO employees, and sponsor quality staff have faced criminal charges arising from clinical data falsification. The joint FDA-MHRA GCP workshop publication documents both agencies' convergent positions on the impact of data integrity failures on marketing application acceptability, confirming that a data reliability finding by one agency has direct implications for the acceptability of data under the other's review framework.[36]

FDA's Current Priorities in Clinical Data Integrity

As of early 2026, FDA's most active clinical data integrity enforcement areas are: EDC audit trail completeness and the adequacy of sponsor oversight of audit trail review programs; source data traceability through data transfers and external data providers including central laboratories and eCOA vendors; CRO oversight documentation demonstrating that sponsors have verified their CROs' data integrity practices rather than relying on contractual assurances; and the application of Part 11 and E6(R3) requirements to decentralized trial elements including wearable device data, electronic patient-reported outcomes, and telemedicine encounters.

EMA: The European Framework and Post-Brexit Complexity

EMA — European Union, 27 member states	
Primary instruments:	EU CTR 536/2014; ICH E6(R3) as adopted; EMA Guideline on Computerised Systems and Electronic Data in Clinical Trials (EMA/INS/GCP/112288/2023); EU GMP Guide Annex 11 (2011/2024 draft); EMA Data Quality Framework (EMA/326985/2023); GCP Inspectors Working Group guidance

The European regulatory framework for clinical data integrity operates through a structure that differs fundamentally from FDA's. EMA is not itself a GCP inspection authority for most purposes: GCP inspections of clinical trials supporting EU-authorized products are conducted by national competent authorities. EMA coordinates these activities, maintains the EU GCP inspection database, and can request inspections of critical studies. The inspection mandate sits primarily with national competent authorities.

The ICH E6(R3) guideline, adopted at Step 4 in January 2025, is the primary clinical data integrity standard within the EU framework. It has been adopted by EMA and by national competent authorities across EU member states as the binding GCP standard, replacing E6(R2). For clinical data integrity, E6(R3)'s explicit adoption of ALCOA+ as the mandatory standard for all clinical trial data means that an EU GCP inspection finding that data fails any ALCOA+ property is a direct E6(R3) non-compliance.[37]

The EMA 2023 Guideline on Computerised Systems: The New Operative EU Standard

The EMA Guideline on Computerised Systems and Electronic Data in Clinical Trials (EMA/INS/GCP/112288/2023) is now the primary EU-specific document for compliance with electronic record and system requirements in clinical trials. It formally replaced the 2010 EMA Reflection Paper on electronic source data, with the final version adopted by the GCP Inspectors Working Group on 7 March 2023 and coming into effect in September 2023.[38]

For clinical data integrity, three aspects of the EMA 2023 Guideline are of direct compliance significance. First, it formally adopts ALCOA++ (as opposed to ALCOA+) as the EU clinical standard in Section 4.5, including Traceable as the tenth discrete property. As discussed in Chapter 3, this elevates Traceable from an emerging expectation to a binding regulatory requirement for EU-regulated trials. Second, it provides the most comprehensive current EU guidance on validation, audit trail requirements, user management, security, and electronic signatures for EDC, eCOA, IRT, eTMF, electronic informed consent, and AI-assisted data management tools. Third, it addresses AI in clinical trials explicitly in its scope and notes that requirements for AI tools beyond the generally applicable expectations will be addressed in a future annex, signaling continuing regulatory development in this area.

Sponsors conducting EU-regulated trials should verify that their EDC, eCOA, IRT, and eTMF validation packages, audit trail review programs, and data governance policies address the specific requirements of the EMA 2023 Guideline, not merely the earlier Reflection Paper it replaced.

The EMA Data Quality Framework: The Strategic Direction

The EMA Data Quality Framework (EMA/326985/2023), adopted by the CHMP in October 2023, represents the EMA's strategic framework for data quality governance across all data types used in EU regulatory decision-making, including real-world data, electronic health records, and secondary data sources.[39]

For sponsors and CROs, the DQF's significance is forward-looking. It establishes that the EMA's expectations for data quality will progressively converge across traditional clinical trial records and the emerging real-world data sources that increasingly support regulatory decisions. Sponsors whose development programs rely on real-world evidence to support label extensions, post-authorization commitments, or benefit-risk assessments should anticipate that EMA's data quality expectations for those datasets will be structured around the DQF dimensions and will converge toward the ALCOA+-aligned standards that govern traditional clinical trial data.

The EU Clinical Trials Regulation: CTIS and Data Implications

The EU Clinical Trials Regulation (EU CTR 536/2014), fully applicable since January 2023, overhauled the EU clinical trial authorization framework. All clinical trials within the EU must be registered, authorized, and have their results reported through the Clinical Trials Information System (CTIS). CTIS creates new data integrity obligations: the data submitted to CTIS must be consistent with the trial master file and the clinical study report. Discrepancies between CTIS-registered information and trial conduct are an integrity finding, not merely a procedural one. The EMA 2023 Guideline provides the operative system requirements for the computerized systems used to generate and manage data submitted through CTIS.[40]

The Annex 11 Revision and Post-Brexit Complexity

The 2024 draft revision of Annex 11, published for consultation, represents the most significant update to EU computerized systems requirements in over a decade. While Annex 11 is formally a manufacturing GMP document, its principles apply to computerized systems used in GCP-regulated activities through the cross-reference structure of EU GMP and GCP guidance. The draft's provisions on cloud and SaaS systems, AI and machine learning, and organizational data governance are directly applicable to clinical sponsors using cloud-hosted EDC, eTMF, and CTMS platforms.

The United Kingdom's departure from the EU in 2021 created a regulatory bifurcation that sponsors running trials in both EU member states and the UK must navigate. UK GCP remains substantially aligned with ICH E6(R3), which MHRA adopted promptly following its Step 4 finalization in January 2025. But the two frameworks are diverging over time. For clinical data integrity, MHRA's framework is in several areas more demanding than the current EU GCP baseline. Sponsors running trials across both jurisdictions should benchmark against the more stringent of the two frameworks, which in most cases means MHRA's expectations.

MHRA: The Culture-First Regulator

MHRA — United Kingdom	
Primary instruments:	MHRA GMP Data Integrity Guidance (2018); UK GCP Guide (ICH E6(R3)-aligned); MHRA-FDA joint GCP workshop documentation; Expectation for Industry statements on decentralized trials and digital endpoints

MHRA occupies a distinctive position in global clinical data integrity regulation. It is simultaneously the authority that has published the most accessible and practically useful data integrity guidance and the authority whose inspection approach places the greatest weight on organizational culture and leadership behavior rather than technical controls alone. For clinical quality professionals, MHRA's published guidance is valuable reading regardless of whether their organization operates in the UK.

MHRA's most important contribution to the global clinical data integrity framework is its insistence that data integrity is a question of quality culture, and that quality culture is a leadership responsibility. The MHRA guidance states explicitly that senior management must create an environment in which data integrity is expected, supported, and verifiable.

It requires that organizations conduct honest self-assessments of their data integrity risk, including assessment of whether commercial timelines, sponsor-CRO relationship dynamics, or organizational incentive structures are creating conditions that make integrity failures structurally likely.[41][42]

The FDA-MHRA joint GCP workshop publication, which reflects both agencies' convergent positions on clinical data integrity enforcement, is particularly relevant to understanding MHRA's approach in the context of multi-jurisdiction submissions. The joint documentation confirms that MHRA's data integrity expectations are substantively aligned with FDA's in the areas of audit trail reliability, data management planning, and the impact of data integrity failures on marketing application acceptability. A sponsor that satisfies MHRA's inspection standard has addressed the core clinical data integrity requirements of both agencies simultaneously.[43]

MHRA's Self-Inspection Requirement for Clinical Programs

MHRA CLINICAL DATA INTEGRITY SELF-INSPECTION: MINIMUM ELEMENTS
Data governance policy: Does the sponsor have a documented, management-approved policy covering the clinical data lifecycle from first capture through archival?
System inventory: Is there a complete, current inventory of all computerized systems processing clinical data (EDC, eTMF, CTMS, IRT, eCOA) with risk classification and validation status?
Audit trail review: Is there evidence that EDC and eTMF audit trails are routinely reviewed, with findings documented and escalated?
CRO oversight: Is there documented verification that CROs meet the sponsor's data integrity standards, not merely contractual attestation?
Source data traceability: Can the sponsor demonstrate that submitted data accurately reflects original site observations through every transfer?
Query management: Are query patterns reviewed for signs of retrospective data correction under time pressure?
Training effectiveness: Can key personnel articulate ALCOA++ requirements in the context of their specific roles?
Culture indicators: Are monitoring concerns raised and acted upon? Is there evidence of pressure to report passing results?
Management engagement: Does clinical program leadership review data integrity metrics and respond to adverse findings?

PIC/S: The Global Harmonizer for Clinical Inspection Standards

PIC/S — 55 member authorities globally	
Primary instruments:	PI 041-1 (Data Integrity Guidance, 2021); PI 006 (GCP Guide); PIC/S training materials and aide-memoires for GCP inspection

PIC/S does not regulate sponsors or investigators directly. What it does, with substantial practical effect, is harmonize the inspection standards and practices of its 55 member authorities. When a national competent authority that is a PIC/S member conducts a GCP inspection, it does so using inspection procedures, training materials, and guidance documents that PIC/S has developed and that all member authorities have agreed to apply.

PIC/S Guidance Document PI 041-1 (2021) is the most operationally detailed data integrity guidance document available from any regulatory body. Its treatment of hybrid record systems, audit trail review programs, and data integrity investigation methodology is substantially more detailed than any FDA or MHRA clinical guidance document. Clinical quality organizations that have not read it are missing the most comprehensive operational articulation of ALCOA++ requirements available in any single document.[44]

The February 2026 EMA/PIC/S joint consultation on a revised data management and integrity concept paper is the most significant joint regulatory initiative in pharmaceutical data integrity since ICH E6(R3) was adopted. For clinical sponsors, the relevant provisions of the concept paper directly address digital clinical data environments, AI-assisted data management, and supply chain data integrity across CRO and vendor networks. The consultation period runs through mid-2026. Finalized guidance is anticipated in 2027.

WHO: Clinical Standards for Global Health Development

WHO — Global: focus on LMIC markets, prequalification, and international health procurement	
Primary instruments:	WHO TRS 996 Annex 5 (2016); WHO GCP Guidelines; WHO Prequalification Programme assessment framework

WHO's role in clinical data integrity is distinct from the national regulatory authorities in this chapter. WHO is not a regulatory authority with binding enforcement power over sponsors. What it does is establish normative clinical research standards through its Technical Report Series and operate the WHO Prequalification Programme, which evaluates medicines and vaccines intended for procurement by UN agencies and other international health procurement mechanisms for low- and middle-income countries.

For sponsors developing products for global health markets, WHO prequalification is not a secondary consideration. It is the gateway to the largest pooled pharmaceutical procurement system in the world. WHO prequalification requires clinical data that meets WHO's GCP standards, which are formalized around ALCOA++ and are substantively equivalent to the standards applied by PIC/S member national competent authorities. WHO inspection reports are made public, a transparency feature that distinguishes WHO assessments from national regulatory inspections, creating reputational consequences that extend well beyond the immediate prequalification decision.[45]

PMDA: Japan's Rigorous and Harmonized Framework

PMDA — Japan	
Primary instruments:	GCP Ministerial Ordinance (revised 2021); MHLW GCP Notifications; ICH E6(R3) as adopted; PMDA computerized system guidance; J-GCP requirements for Japan-specific trial elements

Japan's pharmaceutical regulatory framework is based on the ICH E6 guidelines and is substantially harmonized with EU GCP and FDA requirements. The 2021 partial revision of Japan's GCP ordinance explicitly adopted ALCOA++ as the standard for clinical data quality, required audit trails for computerized systems used in GCP contexts, and introduced data governance policy requirements at the organizational level for sponsors and CROs operating in Japan.[46]

PMDA inspections are recognized for their methodical, documentation-intensive approach. PMDA inspectors typically request extensive advance documentation, then conduct detailed document review before arriving on-site. Data integrity assessments focus heavily on EDC and eTMF system validation records, user access management documentation, and evidence of audit trail review as a routine quality activity. PMDA has been actively strengthening its data integrity inspection capacity since 2020, with inspector training in EDC audit trail analysis and electronic source data review techniques comparable to those used by FDA's Office of Scientific Investigations.

Emerging Regulatory Authorities: The New Enforcement Frontier

The six established authorities above represent the frameworks that have historically defined global clinical data integrity standards. But the global clinical development industry is rapidly expanding into markets governed by authorities that are themselves modernizing their GCP frameworks. Four emerging authorities deserve specific attention.

China: NMPA and the World's Largest Clinical Trial Market

China has become one of the world's most significant clinical trial jurisdictions by volume. NMPA's 2020 revised GCP regulations introduced requirements substantively aligned with ICH E6(R2) standards. NMPA Announcement No. 74 (2020) requires audit trails for GMP and GCP-relevant computerized systems, unique user identification, and original electronic record retention. Sponsors who have historically operated dual-standard trial management between domestic China trials and multi-regional programs are operating with a data integrity risk that mirrors the manufacturing dual-standard problem documented in FDA warning letters against Chinese facilities.[47]

India: CDSCO and the World's Largest Supplier of Generic Medicines

India is a major global clinical trial site jurisdiction. The New Drugs and Clinical Trials Rules 2019 introduced requirements for clinical data management and electronic records that represented a substantial advance on prior Indian GCP requirements, including audit trail requirements for computerized systems and unique user identification for EDC access. India has been pursuing PIC/S membership, with CDSCO engaged in pre-membership alignment activities; formal membership, if achieved, would significantly strengthen CDSCO's inspection equivalence recognition with other PIC/S member authorities.[48]

Brazil: ANVISA and Latin America's Regulatory Leader

ANVISA published dedicated clinical data integrity guidance in 2023 that explicitly adopts ALCOA++ as the evaluative framework. RDC 658/2022, addressing computerized systems in GCP environments, requires audit trails for all GCP-relevant computerized systems, unique user identification, system validation, and electronic records management consistent with ALCOA++ properties. Brazil is a PIC/S member, which means ANVISA GCP inspection certificates carry recognition among other PIC/S member authorities.[49]

South Korea: MFDS and the Advanced Economy Standard

South Korea's MFDS published dedicated data integrity guidance for clinical trials in 2020 that explicitly adopts ALCOA++ as the evaluative standard, requires audit trails for all GCP-relevant computerized systems, and introduces organizational data governance policy requirements. MFDS is a full PIC/S member whose inspections are conducted at equivalence with EU national competent authority inspections. MFDS published guidance on AI/ML in clinical applications in 2024, positioning Korea as an Asian jurisdiction where AI clinical data integrity requirements are developing concurrently with, and in some respects ahead of, Western regulatory guidance.[50]

Where Frameworks Converge and Where They Diverge

Points of Firm Convergence

Convergence Point	Status Across Frameworks
ALCOA++ as mandatory evaluative standard	ICH E6(R3) makes ALCOA+ (nine properties) explicitly mandatory for all clinical trial data. The EMA 2023 Guideline on Computerised Systems formally adopts ALCOA++ including Traceable as the EU clinical standard (Section 4.5). Adopted by FDA, EMA, MHRA, PIC/S, WHO, PMDA, and MFDS.

Convergence Point	Status Across Frameworks
Audit trails for EDC and eTMF systems	Universally required. Automatic generation, unique user attribution, secure storage, tamper-evident design, and routine review required across all major frameworks.
Management and sponsor accountability	Explicitly required by MHRA, PIC/S, WHO, and ICH E6(R3). Applied by FDA through enforcement. Sponsor cannot contract away data governance responsibility to a CRO.
Electronic source data retention	Universally required. FDA 2013 guidance and Electronic Systems Q&A, E6(R3) Section 4.9.3, and PIC/S PI 041-1 all require original electronic records (not derived PDFs) to be retained as primary source records.
CRO oversight as sponsor obligation	Universally established across all frameworks. Sponsors are responsible for data integrity at CRO sites regardless of contractual arrangements and must verify, not merely attest, CRO compliance.
System validation for clinical data systems	Required universally for all systems generating or managing regulatory-relevant clinical data. EDC, eTMF, IRT, eCOA, and central laboratory systems all carry explicit validation obligations.

Points of Remaining Divergence

Divergence Point	Nature of the Difference
Scope of electronic record requirements	FDA Part 11 applies only to electronic records used in lieu of paper for predicate rule compliance. E6(R3) and EU frameworks apply to all GCP-relevant computerized systems regardless of paper backup. Practical impact: broader scope under EU/ICH framework.

Divergence Point	Nature of the Difference
AI-assisted clinical data management tools	FDA: guidance in development, not finalized. EMA: addressed in 2023 Guideline scope and 2026 concept paper; future annex announced. MHRA: addressed in guidance. MFDS: guidance published 2024. Significant jurisdictional specifics to monitor until 2027 guidance finalized.
Traceable as named ALCOA++ property	EU (EMA 2023 Guideline): formally adopted as discrete tenth property in Section 4.5. ICH E6(R3): operationalized through Sections 4.9.3 and 5.5.8 without naming Traceable separately. Practical impact is equivalent; terminology differs.
Audit trail review documentation requirements	PIC/S PI 041-1 provides the most operationally detailed requirements. Other frameworks require review but are less prescriptive about frequency, scope, escalation criteria, and documentation of the review process itself.
Organizational data governance policy level	MHRA and PIC/S explicitly require an organizational-level data governance policy. FDA addresses this through enforcement expectation. E6(R3) requires it; EMA 2023 Guideline reinforces it. Convergence is occurring; FDA-specific prescriptive guidance remains in development.
Decentralized trial source data requirements	FDA's Electronic Systems Q&A guidance (Revision 1) is the most operationally specific on source data location for digital health technologies. E6(R3) addresses in principle. EMA 2023 Guideline covers eCOA and ePRO specifically. Operational specificity varies significantly across frameworks.
Supply chain clinical data integrity	Currently the most significant gap across all frameworks. E6(R3) requires traceability but does not specify supply chain verification methodology. The 2026 EMA/PIC/S concept paper proposes the first comprehensive clinical supply chain data integrity standard.

Which Framework Governs Your Situation: A Decision Guide

Situation	Primary Clinical Data Integrity Frameworks
You sponsor clinical trials for FDA submission	21 CFR Parts 50, 56, 312, 314 apply to all trial operations regardless of site location. 21 CFR Part 11 and the Electronic Systems Q&A for Clinical Investigations (Revision 1) apply to EDC, eTMF, IRT, and eCOA systems. ICH E6(R3) as adopted by FDA is the binding GCP standard; ALCOA+ is explicitly mandatory. FDA 2013 risk-based monitoring and electronic source data guidance apply. CRO oversight is an active enforcement priority.
You sponsor trials for EMA submission (EU/EEA)	EU CTR 536/2014 governs trial authorization; CTIS data consistency is a compliance requirement. ICH E6(R3) as adopted by EMA is the binding GCP standard. EMA Guideline on Computerised Systems (EMA/INS/GCP/112288/2023) is the operative standard for all clinical computerised systems; ALCOA++ including Traceable is explicitly required. National competent authority GCP inspection standards apply for the relevant member state(s).
You sponsor trials for PMDA (Japan) submission	ICH E6(R3) as adopted by PMDA applies; ALCOA++ explicitly mandatory since 2021 revision. J-GCP specific requirements apply to Japan-specific trial elements; advance preparation for PMDA documentation requests is essential. PMDA conducts overseas inspections; computerized system validation documentation packages must satisfy J-GCP standards.

Situation	Primary Clinical Data Integrity Frameworks
You are a CRO providing clinical services to multiple sponsors	Your data integrity obligations are determined by the markets your sponsors supply; you are subject to every framework they are. No framework allows sponsors to transfer their data integrity obligations to you. Expect sponsor-initiated data integrity audits as a routine part of qualification and ongoing oversight. Best practice: implement to MHRA + FDA + E6(R3) + PIC/S as the common high standard.
You conduct trials in China, India, Brazil, or South Korea	China (NMPA): 2020 GCP regulations and Announcement No. 74 are the domestic baseline; FDA/EMA/PMDA requirements apply additionally for multi-regional programs. India (CDSCO): New Drugs and Clinical Trials Rules 2019 apply; site-level EDC training and audit trail oversight are priority areas. Brazil (ANVISA): RDC 658/2022 and 2023 clinical DI guidance apply; Brazil is PIC/S member. South Korea (MFDS): Full PIC/S member; ALCOA++ explicitly required; AI/ML guidance (2024) applies to digital endpoint and eCOA tools.
You sponsor decentralized or hybrid clinical trials	All frameworks above apply, with specific attention to E6(R3) provisions for remote data collection and the FDA Electronic Systems Q&A guidance on source data location for DHT-generated data. Source data traceability through device logs to transmitted composite scores to EDC must be documented. Vendor qualification for eCOA and wearable device providers must include data integrity-specific assessment.

Where Global Clinical Data Integrity Harmonization Is Heading

The trajectory of global clinical data integrity regulation is toward convergence on a single universal standard. Not because regulatory authorities have agreed to unify their frameworks in a formal sense, but because the underlying principles are already unified through ICH E6(R3)'s universal ALCOA+ mandate, the inspection community is increasingly internationalized through PIC/S membership and cross-authority training programs, and the February 2026 EMA/PIC/S joint consultation represents a deliberate push toward a single globally adopted document.

The EMA/PIC/S Guidance: The Central Development

The guidance that emerges from the 2026 consultation, once adopted by PIC/S member authorities, will be simultaneously applicable in most of the world's significant clinical regulatory jurisdictions. If it incorporates the supply chain data integrity standard and the AI-assisted data management requirements outlined in the concept paper, it will represent the most significant expansion of clinical data integrity obligations since ICH E6 named the five original ALCOA properties in 1996. Sponsors and CROs that engage with the consultation process will be positioned to implement the final guidance rather than react to it.

The Emerging Markets: The Next Enforcement Wave

The trajectory in China, India, Brazil, South Korea, and the Gulf is toward more rigorous clinical data integrity enforcement. In each jurisdiction, regulatory modernization is driven by domestic industry development goals, international market access ambitions requiring alignment with PIC/S or equivalent frameworks, and in several cases specific enforcement incidents that have created political pressure for more rigorous oversight. The historical compliance discount for these jurisdictions is no longer a reliable assumption for any of them.

AI and Digital Endpoints: The Next Major Compliance Challenge

Every major regulatory authority is developing or refining its approach to AI and machine learning in clinical data management and digital endpoint assessment. The EMA 2023 Guideline on Computerized Systems has already addressed AI in the scope of general system requirements, with a dedicated future annex announced. The 2026 EMA/PIC/S concept paper addresses AI-assisted data management specifically. For sponsors using AI-assisted anomaly detection in centralized monitoring, algorithmic query generation, automated safety data review, or digital biomarker scoring, the window between now and the finalization of AI clinical data integrity requirements is the time to build traceability and validation into those systems proactively rather than retrofitting them under regulatory pressure.

> *Regulatory harmonization does not eliminate compliance complexity; it shifts it. Instead of managing fundamentally different requirements across jurisdictions, global sponsors increasingly manage a single high standard with jurisdictional variations in scope, process, and enforcement style. Building to that single high standard is both the most rigorous and the most efficient approach.*

CHAPTER FOUR - KEY TAKEAWAYS
FDA: Enforcement-first communication; predicate rule structure; BIMO inspection program for clinical sites, sponsors, and CROs; criminal referral capacity; Electronic Systems Q&A (Revision 1) is the authoritative clinical-specific interpretation of Part 11 for EDC, DHT, and real-world data contexts.
EMA: GCP inspections conducted by national competent authorities; ICH E6(R3) is the binding standard; EU CTR 536/2014 introduces CTIS data consistency obligations; EMA Guideline on Computerised Systems (EMA/INS/GCP/112288/2023) is the operative EU standard for clinical computerised systems and formally adopts ALCOA++ including Traceable.
EMA Data Quality Framework (EMA/326985/2023): CHMP-adopted strategic framework for data quality governance across all EU regulatory decision-making, including real-world data; signals progressive convergence of clinical trial and real-world evidence data quality requirements.
FDA-MHRA joint GCP workshop documentation: Primary regulatory authority confirming that both agencies' data integrity enforcement positions are convergent; audit trail failures and data management deficiencies affect marketing application acceptability under both agencies' frameworks simultaneously.
MHRA: Culture-first regulator; most accessible published guidance; explicit management accountability requirements; self-inspection mandate specific to data integrity; MHRA + FDA + E6(R3) + PIC/S is the recommended multi-jurisdictional compliance baseline.
PIC/S: 55-member global harmonizer; PI 041-1 (2021) is the most operationally detailed ALCOA++ guidance available; February 2026 EMA/PIC/S joint consultation is the most significant joint regulatory initiative in clinical data integrity in a decade.
WHO: Standard-setter and prequalification gateway for global health clinical data; ALCOA+-based assessment framework; public inspection reports create reputational consequences beyond the immediate prequalification decision.
PMDA: Japan's framework substantially harmonized with ICH E6(R3) since 2021 revision; documentation-intensive inspection approach; expanding overseas inspection program.

CHAPTER FOUR - KEY TAKEAWAYS
Emerging authorities: NMPA, CDSCO, ANVISA, MFDS, and SFDA are all actively modernizing their clinical GCP frameworks. The historical compliance discount for these jurisdictions is eroding. Implement to PIC/S standards in all jurisdictions.
February 2026 EMA/PIC/S consultation: Expected to produce a globally adopted standard by 2027-2028 addressing digital trial environments, AI-assisted data management, and CRO supply chain data integrity.
Convergence: ALCOA++ via E6(R3) and the EMA 2023 Guideline, audit trails, management accountability, electronic source data retention, and CRO oversight obligations are converging across all jurisdictions. The compliance discount for regulatory arbitrage is closing.
Practical strategy: Design clinical data governance to the most stringent requirement across applicable frameworks. For most global development programs, this means MHRA + FDA + E6(R3) + PIC/S as the baseline, with jurisdiction-specific requirements layered on top and anticipatory implementation of 2024/2026 draft guidance for AI/ML and digital trial elements.

CHAPTER FIVE

ALCOA+ Decoded: What Regulators Actually Mean

> *An inspector examining a clinical trial dataset is not looking for a record of everything that happened. They are looking for evidence that the data meets ALCOA+. Each principle is a lens. A gap under any one of them is a potential citation.*

During an FDA bioresearch monitoring inspection at a Phase III investigator site, the Office of Scientific Investigations investigator requested the electronic audit trail for the site's EDC system covering a six-month enrollment window. The site coordinator produced the export within the hour. The investigator reviewed it for forty minutes, asked three questions, and left. Three weeks later, the sponsor received a Form 483 with seven observations. None of them were about the clinical outcomes of the enrolled subjects. All of them were about the records.

The observations described a pattern that the audit trail had made visible: EDC field entries timestamped hours after the clinic's documented closing time, query resolutions clustered in two-day bursts in the week before each monitoring visit, change reasons applied uniformly across hundreds of edits regardless of the actual basis for each correction, and a primary endpoint eCOA system whose session-level device logs had not been retained because no one had identified them as source data. The data itself may have been accurate. The record structure made that determination impossible. That is a data integrity failure under ALCOA+, and it is the kind that FDA's inspection program is specifically designed to find.

ALCOA+ is widely known in name and widely misapplied in practice. Most clinical research professionals can recite the acronym. Fewer can articulate what each principle looks like when an investigator opens their system, what the specific failure modes are that generate 483 observations and warning letters, and what the practical difference is between a compliant record and a defensible one. This chapter provides that practitioner-level breakdown, anchored throughout in clinical trial terminology, clinical systems, and the specific enforcement record that defines what regulators actually mean when they invoke each principle.

> *ALCOA+ defines what a compliant record looks like. It does not guarantee that compliant records are being created. That gap is where enforcement happens.*

ALCOA+ at a Glance: The Ten-Principle Standard

The ALCOA framework began with five properties named in the original 1996 ICH E6 guideline: Attributable, Legible, Contemporaneous, Original, and Accurate. Four extensions, Complete, Consistent, Enduring, and Available, were added in subsequent guidance documents and formalized as ALCOA+ through PIC/S PI 041-1 (2021) and ICH E6(R3) (adopted January 2025). The tenth principle, Traceable, has been adopted as a discrete named property in the EU clinical regulatory framework through the EMA Guideline on Computerised Systems and Electronic Data in Clinical Trials (EMA/INS/GCP/112288/2023, Section 4.5), which defines data integrity as compliance with ALCOA+ principles including Traceable. ICH E6(R3) operationalizes the same concept through its traceability requirements in Sections 4.9.3 and 5.5.8, though it does not enumerate Traceable as a separately named ALCOA+ property in the same explicit manner.

For purposes of this book, ALCOA+ is used to describe the ten-property framework that represents the current state of regulatory expectation across the combined EU and ICH standards. Sponsors, CROs, and eClinical technology vendors operating in EU-regulated environments should treat all ten properties as explicitly required. Those operating under FDA and ICH E6(R3) frameworks should treat the first nine as explicitly required and Traceable as an operational requirement derived from E6(R3)'s data lineage and traceability provisions.

	Principle	Core Question	Clinical Research Implication
A	Attributable	Can you prove who made this entry, and when?	Shared EDC logins, undated source document entries, and bulk investigator countersignatures are universal citation triggers.
L	Legible	Can it be read now and in twenty-five years?	Overwritten source entries, undefined abbreviations, and EDC formats not validated for long-term readability fail legibility.
C	Contemporaneous	Was it recorded at the time the activity occurred?	Retrospective CRF entry, pre-completed visit forms, and post-database-lock AE documentation are prohibited without exception.
O	Original	Is this the first, unaltered capture of the data?	eCOA composite scores retained without session logs, and CRF printouts replacing EDC originals, are the most common failures.
A	Accurate	Does it truthfully represent what was observed?	Selective omission of adverse events, unreported eligibility deviations, and query-driven outcome correction are accuracy failures.

	Principle	Core Question	Clinical Research Implication
C	Complete	Is everything there, including unfavorable data?	Missing visit windows, unresolved queries, and excluded site data in analysis datasets are completeness failures.
C	Consistent	Is the record internally coherent?	A subject with a post-baseline assessment timestamped before randomization, or randomization dates inconsistent across source and CRF.
E	Enduring	Will the record survive its full retention period?	eCOA vendor contracts that expire before the 25-year TMF retention period, and non-validated data migration, create endurance risk.
A	Available	Can it be produced when an inspector asks for it?	eTMF records that exist but cannot be retrieved within the inspection window are functionally non-compliant.
T	Traceable	Can the full data provenance be reconstructed?	Adopted in EU clinical framework (EMA/INS/GCP/112288/2023, Section 4.5); operationalized in ICH E6(R3) Sections 4.9.3 and 5.5.8. The chain from raw sensor reading through algorithmic derivation to submitted endpoint value must be reconstructable.

A | ATTRIBUTABLE

Every data point must be traceable to a specific person, at a specific time, performing a specific action.

Attributability is the foundational data integrity principle in clinical research. Before any other property of a record can be evaluated, there must be an answer to the question: who created this entry, and when? A record that cannot be attributed to a specific individual is, from a regulatory standpoint, anonymous, and anonymous data cannot support the conclusions that sponsors, investigators, regulators, and ultimately patients depend upon clinical trial records to provide.

In electronic data capture systems, attributability is established through unique user identification and authentication, the combination of login credentials and, where risk warrants, additional authentication factors required under 21 CFR Part 11 and addressed in the FDA's Electronic Systems Q&A guidance for clinical investigations. The core requirement is that each user's actions in an EDC system, a clinical trial management system, an eTMF platform, or any other system that touches trial data must be linked to that individual and to no other.[51]

The Shared Credential Problem

Shared login credentials are the single most universally cited attributability failure in clinical site inspections. The reasons are operationally understandable: EDC systems with complex password policies and short timeout periods create friction for coordinators managing multiple subjects across a busy clinic day; sites with high staff turnover may not promptly provision individual accounts for new hires or deactivate accounts for departing staff; CROs deploying team-based data management workflows may default to shared accounts for convenience. None of these pressures constitute a regulatory defense.

When shared credentials are discovered, the inspector's question is not only "who entered this data?" It is "can anything this system produced be trusted?" When individual user accountability cannot be established, the integrity of the entire dataset is in question. There is no way to verify who made which entries, whether any entries were made by individuals without the authority to make them, or whether query resolutions reflect the clinical judgment of a qualified investigator or the convenience of an unnamed data entry operator.

L | LEGIBLE

Records must be readable when created and must remain readable throughout the full retention period, which in clinical trials may span twenty-five years.

Legibility connects data integrity to records management and long-term archival strategy in ways that clinical data managers often underestimate. A record that is perfectly readable at creation but stored in a proprietary format that becomes inaccessible when the originating software is decommissioned is not a legible record when the inspector requests it decades later. The legibility obligation extends from the point of creation to the end of the retention period.

In electronic systems, legibility failures typically arise from: proprietary file formats that cannot be rendered without the originating application; EDC archive formats that display data but strip metadata and audit trail information essential for interpretation; and eCOA device logs stored in binary formats that require vendor-specific tools to render in human-readable form. Sponsors who have not specifically verified that their eTMF and EDC archive formats will remain renderable throughout the applicable retention period, independent of the originating vendor's continued operation, have accepted a latent legibility risk.

C | CONTEMPORANEOUS

Clinical observations must be recorded at the time the activity occurs, not reconstructed from memory, informal notes, or supervisory recollection.

Contemporaneity connects data integrity to the specific historical precedent of the IBT enforcement era. The IBT pathology report was backdated by more than two years, from May 1976 to March 1974. The regulatory framework that was built in response to that documented failure, including the GCP requirement that clinical observations be recorded contemporaneously, was designed to make the IBT failure mode structurally visible rather than structurally concealable. Modern EDC systems, with their server-side timestamps, make backdating visible in the same way that the regulatory framework was designed to require: the edit record shows the actual entry time, regardless of what date the user intended to document.

Contemporaneity failures in clinical trials generate a distinctive audit trail signature: EDC entries clustered outside the clinic's documented operating hours; batches of query resolutions occurring in the forty-eight hours before a scheduled monitoring visit; and clinical assessment entries timestamped after the site coordinator's access logs show they were at a different location. Each of these patterns tells a story about records that were created after the events they document.

The Pre-Completed Form Problem

One of the most specific contemporaneity failures cited in FDA warning letters is the pre-completed form: a case report form or visit checklist in which entries are made before the corresponding activities are performed. A pre-completed form is a falsified record regardless of whether the entries turn out to be accurate. Consider a site coordinator who pre-enters inclusion and exclusion criteria responses on a screening CRF before the eligibility interview is conducted, confident the subject will qualify. If the subject discloses a contraindicated condition during the visit, the pre-completed form creates pressure not to correct the discrepancy, because doing so would reveal that the form was completed in advance. This is precisely the dynamic that turns a minor data integrity failure into an unreported eligibility violation.

What Inspectors Look For	Common Failure Mode	Red Flag Indicators
Source data entries made at or near the time of observation; EDC timestamps consistent with scheduled visit windows.	CRFs completed retrospectively at the end of the clinic day, or following receipt of a monitor query.	EDC entry clusters outside visit windows; clusters of entries in the 48 hours before monitoring visits.
Protocol deviation, AE, and SAE records created at time of occurrence; reported within required timeframes.	Deviation and safety reports prepared retrospectively after unblinding, data lock, or regulatory query.	Deviation forms dated after database lock; AE forms bearing timestamps after the subject discontinued.

What Inspectors Look For	Common Failure Mode	Red Flag Indicators
EDC system clock synchronized to validated, controlled time server; adjustments documented and justified.	System clock at investigative site manipulated to permit backdated or post-dated electronic entries.	System logs show unexplained time adjustments; site internal clock inconsistent with sponsor reference time server.
eCRF screens left blank until data are available; no pre-population of expected results.	Pre-completed eligibility criteria checkboxes; anticipated laboratory ranges entered before sample results received.	Audit trail entries for fields timestamped before the scheduled visit window; eligibility data entered before consent date.

O | ORIGINAL

The first-captured, unaltered version of the data is the record, not a copy, transcription, derived score, or printout.

The original data principle addresses what, precisely, constitutes the record. In electronic clinical trial systems, the raw output of a central laboratory analyzer, the unprocessed electronic file containing the assay result, the sample identifier, the instrument timestamp, and the calibration parameters, is the original record. A PDF report generated from that file is a representation of part of that record. A data listing transferred to the sponsor's EDC system is a derived document. If the PDF is retained but the underlying laboratory data file is deleted or inaccessible to the sponsor, the original record does not exist, even if the printout appears identical to what was originally generated.[52]

The Historical Precedent: When the Summary Preceded the Data

The Original principle exists to prevent a specific and documented failure mode: the construction of a record that presents a desired conclusion as though it were derived from underlying observations, when in fact the data was adjusted to fit the conclusion. G.D. Searle & Company's submission of a revised study report to FDA in 1974 illustrates the failure with precision. FDA investigators identified that the data in the revised submission had been rewritten to agree with the summary, rather than the summary being derived from the data. The sequence was inverted: conclusion first, data adjusted to match.

In clinical data management, the equivalent pattern is a query resolution that changes a reported value to match the expected value for a patient in that treatment arm without a source document supporting the change; or a source document amendment created after a monitoring finding to provide retrospective justification for a value that was never actually observed. In both cases, the resulting record is not original: it reflects a conclusion about what the data should show rather than an observation of what actually occurred.

The eCOA Session Log Problem

The most common original data failure in clinical trials involving electronic outcome assessment systems is retaining the exported composite score in the EDC while discarding the underlying eCOA or ePRO device logs from which those scores were derived. This practice persists because sponsors frequently believe that the composite score is the record. It is not.

FDA's position is unambiguous: where data is generated by a computerized system, the electronic record is the primary record, and any derived output is a representation of that record. Retaining the exported score while discarding the device-level session log is equivalent, in regulatory terms, to discarding the original record while retaining a copy. The FDA Electronic Systems Q&A guidance for clinical investigations confirms that for inspection purposes, electronic source data is considered to be located in the durable electronic data repository into which DHT-generated data was transmitted via a validated, pre-specified process. Where an eCOA vendor retains device logs on infrastructure the sponsor cannot independently access, audit, or archive, the sponsor has not met its retention obligation. [53]

A | ACCURATE
Records must truthfully represent what was observed, measured, or performed, including events that were unfavorable.

Accuracy is the principle that ALCOA was, in a fundamental sense, designed to protect. The four preceding principles are procedural requirements that make accuracy verifiable. Accuracy itself is the substantive requirement: the record must tell the truth about what happened, including adverse events that resolved before the data lock, protocol deviations that occurred during high-enrollment pressure periods, eligibility exceptions identified retrospectively, and assessments that produced unfavorable results. Selective reporting is an accuracy failure even when every individual value reported is numerically correct.

The accuracy failures most frequently documented in FDA warning letters cluster around four patterns: unreported adverse events; unreported protocol deviations; query-driven outcome correction where data values are modified in response to monitor queries in ways that shift results toward protocol-defined thresholds without documented clinical justification; and the failure to document protocol-required assessments that were attempted but not completed.

Compliant: What Good Looks Like	Non-Compliant: What Inspectors Cite
All adverse events documented in the CRF regardless of investigator causality assessment, with onset date, resolution date, and action taken.	Adverse events verbally described to site staff but not entered into CRF; events classified "unrelated" without medical officer review.
Protocol deviations documented and reported at time of identification; root cause and corrective action completed for each.	Eligibility violation identified during monitoring but not entered as a deviation; site resolves the query informally without creating a deviation record.
Query responses supported by documented clinical rationale; change reasons specific to the actual basis for each correction.	Primary endpoint values modified in response to monitor queries; change reason for all edits recorded as "transcription error" regardless of actual basis.
Missing or uncollectable assessments recorded with a reason code per protocol specification; not left blank.	Required assessment fields left blank in EDC with no reason code; analysis dataset treats blank as missing at random

Compliant: What Good Looks Like	Non-Compliant: What Inspectors Cite
	rather than as an uncollected required data point.

ALCOA+: The Four Extensions

The extension of ALCOA to ALCOA+, adding Complete, Consistent, Enduring, and Available, was particularly significant in the clinical research context because the additional properties address failure modes specific to multi-site, longitudinal clinical trials. ICH E6(R3) incorporates all nine named properties as the evaluative framework for clinical trial data quality.[54]

C | COMPLETE
All data necessary to reconstruct the clinical activity must be present, with no missing visits, no unresolved queries, and no absent records.

The Complete principle extends accuracy in a specific direction: it requires not just that reported data is truthful, but that the full context necessary to understand and verify that data is present. The most common completeness failures in clinical trial data management are: missing visit windows not documented with a reason; unresolved or improperly closed queries at database lock; protocol deviation logs that do not include all deviations identified during monitoring; safety narratives for serious adverse events that do not include all follow-up communications; and analysis datasets from which site data has been excluded without a documented rationale in the statistical analysis plan.

In electronic systems, completeness has a specific meaning related to audit trail continuity. An EDC audit trail with gaps, periods during which system activity occurred but no audit trail entries were generated, is a completeness failure. The gap may reflect a system restart that interrupted logging, or it may indicate deliberate manipulation: audit trail disabled during a period of non-compliant data entry. Either way, the record is incomplete, and an incomplete record cannot support the conclusions drawn from the data it contains.

C | CONSISTENT

Records must be internally coherent: sequences, timestamps, and values must tell a plausible story that is physically and logically possible.

Consistency addresses the internal logical coherence of a clinical record or dataset. Consistency failures in clinical trials are often immediately apparent to an experienced inspector because they violate common sense. A subject cannot have a post-baseline assessment timestamped before their randomization date. A coordinator cannot have performed a physical examination at two different sites simultaneously. A blood draw result cannot be received by the central laboratory before the sample was drawn at the investigative site. A consent form cannot be dated after the subject's first study procedure.

Timestamp inconsistencies are among the most reliably detected consistency failures because the modern trial data infrastructure generates abundant time-referenced data across multiple independent systems that can be cross-compared. FDA investigators compare EDC entry timestamps against clinic appointment system records and EMR entries for the same subject visit; confirm that source document entries preceded EDC entries for the same observation; and check that informed consent dates precede first study procedure dates.

E | ENDURING

Records must remain intact, readable, and accessible throughout their full required retention period, which in clinical trials may span twenty-five years.

Endurance addresses the dimension of time. A clinical trial record that meets every other ALCOA+ requirement at the time of creation but cannot be retrieved and read throughout its full required retention period is a deficient record. Under 21 CFR Part 312.62, records must be retained for at least two years following the later of marketing application approval or discontinuation of the investigation and notification of FDA. Under EU CTR 536/2014 Article 58, the trial master file must be retained for at least twenty-five years after trial completion. For pediatric studies, gene therapy trials, and products subject to post-approval follow-up obligations, the operative period may be longer still.

The most prevalent endurance risk in modern clinical trial data management is the expiration of eClinical vendor agreements before the applicable retention period expires. An eClinical system vendor contract typically covers the active trial period plus a defined archival period. If that archival period is shorter than the regulatory retention requirement, the sponsor faces a situation where records exist on infrastructure to which it no longer has contractual access. The time to ensure that eClinical vendor agreements include explicit provisions for data return, continued access for regulatory purposes, and archive format specifications that meet the readability requirements of the retention period is before signature.

A | AVAILABLE

Records must be promptly retrievable when a regulator, monitor, or auditor requests them, not eventually, not with preparation, now.

Availability is the final ALCOA+ property and the one that most directly determines whether an organization passes or fails the operational test of an inspection. A record that meets every other ALCOA+ criterion but cannot be produced within the inspection window is functionally non-compliant. Under 21 CFR Part 312.58 and 312.62, FDA investigators have the right to access, copy, and verify all records related to a clinical investigation. The corresponding obligation on the sponsor and investigator is that those records are available for inspection, not that they can be located with effort and produced by next week.

Availability failures frequently result from: records distributed across multiple storage locations without a definitive index; eTMF completeness backlogs that leave documents unfiled at study close; and records held by CRO or vendor systems to which the sponsor has not retained direct access rights. An eTMF that the sponsor cannot independently access without requesting a vendor-generated export is not available in the regulatory sense during an inspection, because the time required to obtain the export may exceed the inspection window.

Traceable: The Tenth Principle

The Traceable principle is no longer emerging in the EU clinical regulatory framework. The EMA Guideline on Computerised Systems and Electronic Data in Clinical Trials (EMA/INS/GCP/112288/2023), which is operative law for EU GCP-regulated activities, names Traceable as the tenth discrete ALCOA+ property in Section 4.5. The Section defines data integrity as compliance with ALCOA+ principles of being attributable, legible, contemporaneous, original, accurate, complete, consistent, enduring, available when needed and traceable. For sponsors conducting EU-regulated trials, Traceable is a formally adopted regulatory requirement, not an aspirational development.

ICH E6(R3) operationalizes the same concept without enumerating Traceable as a separately named property. Section 4.9.3 requires that the sponsor be able to verify that data as submitted to a regulatory authority accurately reflects original observations at the investigative site through every data transfer, edit, query, and aggregation step. Section 5.5.8 requires that sponsors ensure the integrity of data through the complete data pathway from original capture to submission. These provisions create a traceability obligation for ICH E6(R3)-regulated trials that is functionally equivalent to the EMA's named Traceable principle, even if the terminology differs.

For practical purposes, all clinical sponsors and CROs should treat traceability as a fully operative requirement. The two most critical application contexts are eCOA and wearable sensor data, where a patient-reported outcome or physiological measurement passes through multiple systems before appearing in the efficacy analysis; and AI-assisted data management, where algorithmic tools are applied to clinical data for anomaly detection, endpoint scoring, or missing data imputation. In both contexts, the chain of custody from original patient observation to submitted value must be documentable and auditable at any point during the retention period.[55]

System Type	What Constitutes Original Raw Data	Traceability Documentation Required
EDC / eCRF	Data as originally entered by the investigative site, including the first-entered value for every field, all subsequent changes with full audit trail, and the timestamp and identity of every action.	Data pathway from site source document through EDC entry to analysis dataset; query correspondence retained as part of the audit trail.
eCOA / ePRO Devices	The device-level interaction log capturing each patient session: when the assessment was opened, individual item responses and any mid-session modifications,	Connection between device session log and composite score exported to EDC; algorithm version used to derive the composite score.

System Type	What Constitutes Original Raw Data	Traceability Documentation Required
	device clock synchronization records.	
IRT / RTSM	The complete transaction log for every randomization, stratification, dispensing, and resupply event, including date, time, site ID, subject ID, treatment arm, kit number.	Blinded allocation summaries are derived; the original transaction log must be retained and traceable to the submitted randomization listing.
Central Laboratory	The instrument output file as generated by the analyzer, including the raw assay result, sample identifier, instrument timestamp, and calibration parameters.	Chain from instrument output through PDF report to EDC-mapped value; any reprocessing or recalibration documented in the audit trail.
EHR / EMR Data (DCT)	The original record is held by the healthcare provider. The sponsor's obligation is to document the pathway from EHR data point through every transformation step to its representation in the clinical database.	EHR extract specification, transformation rules, reconciliation log, and audit trail for each step from extract to EDC are source data for the derived value.

Applying ALCOA+ in Practice: The Inspector's Operational Framework

Understanding ALCOA+ academically and applying it under inspection pressure are different skills. The most effective way to develop the latter is to read your own records through an inspector's eyes: not asking "does this record exist?" but asking "what questions would an inspector ask about this record, and can I answer them?" The ten questions below represent, in condensed form, the evaluative framework that a trained FDA or MHRA bioresearch monitoring investigator applies when reviewing a clinical trial record. An organization that can answer yes to all ten, with documented evidence, for any record in its trial master file, has a data integrity program that is defensible under inspection.[56] [57]

ALCOA+ Principle	The Inspector's Operational Question
Attributable	Can I identify, with certainty, who created or approved this specific entry, when, and under what documented authority?
Legible	Can I read this record now, and is it stored in a format I will be able to read when the twenty-five-year TMF retention period expires?
Contemporaneous	Is there objective evidence, EDC timestamps, appointment system records, EMR entries, that this was recorded at the time of the activity, not afterward?
Original	Am I looking at the original record, or a representation of it? If a representation, where is the original and can I access it within this inspection?
Accurate	Does this record represent everything that happened, including adverse events, protocol deviations, and assessments with unfavorable results?
Complete	Is everything I need to independently verify this result present in the record or in a retrievable, referenced document with a documented audit trail?

ALCOA+ Principle	The Inspector's Operational Question
Consistent	Do the timestamps, sequences, assessment dates, and personnel attributions in this record form a story that is physically and logically possible?
Enduring	Will this record still be readable and retrievable when the retention period expires, without action from a vendor that may no longer exist?
Available	If I ask for this record right now, without advance notice and without preparation, how long will it take to produce it, and in what form?
Traceable	If this value was derived from other data, can I follow the complete chain of transformation from the original patient observation to this submitted result?

ALCOA+ is not a compliance checklist. It is a framework for building records that tell the truth. Organizations that internalize that purpose, rather than treating ALCOA+ as a documentation exercise, build quality cultures that make data integrity failures structurally unlikely.

CHAPTER FIVE - KEY TAKEAWAYS
Attributable: Every CRF entry, query resolution, and data management action must be traceable to a specific named individual at a specific time. Shared EDC credentials and bulk investigator countersignatures are universal citation triggers.
Legible: Source documents and electronic records must remain readable throughout their full retention period, up to twenty-five years under EU CTR for trial master files. Format obsolescence and non-validated data migration are the primary risks.
Contemporaneous: Clinical observations must be recorded at the time they occur, not reconstructed from memory or informal notes. EDC timestamp analysis is the primary detection method; pre-completed forms are a falsified record regardless of accuracy.
Original: The first-captured unaltered electronic record is the source, not the derived score, the PDF export, or the summary report. eCOA session logs, EDC audit trails, and IRT transaction logs are original records that must be retained independently of derived outputs. The Searle case established the paradigmatic failure: a summary rewritten to match a desired conclusion rather than derived from underlying data.
Accurate: The record must represent the full reality of what occurred, including adverse events, eligibility deviations, and unfavorable assessments. Selective omission is an accuracy failure even when every reported value is numerically correct.
Complete: All data required to reconstruct and verify the clinical activity must be present. Missing visit documentation, unresolved queries at database lock, and EDC audit trail gaps are completeness failures.
Consistent: Timestamps, assessment sequences, and personnel attributions must form a physically and logically plausible account. Consent dates after study procedures and assessments timestamped before randomization are immediate inspection red flags.
Enduring: Records must survive their full retention period in a readable format. eClinical vendor contract expiration before the twenty-five-year TMF retention period is the most prevalent endurance risk in modern clinical data management.
Available: Records must be promptly retrievable, not with preparation, not through a vendor export request. eTMF completeness backlogs and records held on infrastructure the sponsor cannot directly access are availability failures.
Traceable: Formally adopted as the tenth ALCOA+ property in the EU clinical regulatory framework (EMA/INS/GCP/112288/2023, Section 4.5) and

CHAPTER FIVE - KEY TAKEAWAYS

operationalized through ICH E6(R3) Sections 4.9.3 and 5.5.8. The full data provenance, from original patient observation through every algorithmic derivation and system transfer to the submitted value, must be reconstructable. For sponsors conducting EU-regulated trials, Traceable is a binding requirement, not an emerging standard.

PART TWO: DESIGNING FOR INTEGRITY

The core practitioner contribution — building systems that cannot fail

CHAPTER SIX

The Data Lifecycle: From Creation to Archive

> *Regulatory authority over clinical trial data does not end when a study closes. It persists for as long as the data exists, and the integrity obligations that govern data at creation govern it equally at every subsequent stage of its life*

The unblinding request arrived without warning on a Thursday morning, eighteen months after the study database had been locked. The NDA was already under review. The agency had questions about a subset of primary endpoint data from three investigator sites, and it wanted to trace the complete history of that data: from the original clinical observation to the source document, from the source document to the EDC entry, from the EDC entry through every query and resolution to the clean dataset submitted in the application. A straightforward request. The kind that a well-organized clinical data management program should be able to fulfill within days.

It took four weeks. The eCOA vendor whose device data covered sixty-two of the flagged subjects had archived the original session logs to a legacy storage format that required specialized retrieval software no longer supported by the vendor's current platform. The IRT system that had managed randomization for the three sites had been migrated to a new version, and the migration documentation was insufficient to confirm that the original transaction logs had survived intact. Two of the investigator sites had stored their source documents at a third-party archive facility, and one of the two archives had changed ownership during the intervening months; the retrieval process involved three separate approval chains that had not existed when the records were deposited. The data itself was clean. The integrity of the data, in the regulatory sense that matters, was very difficult to demonstrate.

The agency's review was delayed by six weeks. When it concluded, the sponsor received a complete response letter with two clinical information requests referencing the traceability gaps the retrieval exercise had exposed. No allegation of falsification. No enforcement action. But a clear signal that data whose provenance cannot be reconstructed on demand is data whose integrity is, for regulatory purposes, in question regardless of what the values show.

The scenario above is not exceptional. It is representative of a class of clinical data integrity failure that receives less regulatory attention than falsification and manipulation but generates a significant share of NDA deficiencies, inspection observations, and complete response letters: data that was accurate at the time of creation and unreliable at the time of regulatory scrutiny, not because anyone changed it, but because the systems and practices governing its lifecycle failed to maintain the conditions under which its integrity could be verified.

Data integrity is not a property of values. It is a property of the complete pathway, from the moment of observation to the moment of submission, and through every year of retention that follows.

> *A lifecycle control that is designed at study close rather than study start is not a control. It is a remediation plan for a gap that has already materialized.*

The Lifecycle as a Regulatory Construct

Clinical data does not exist as a static artifact. It is generated at a specific moment under specific conditions, processed through a sequence of systems and human actions, reviewed and validated through defined workflows, transferred across organizational and technical boundaries, and ultimately preserved or destroyed under retention obligations that can extend for decades. Each of these stages is a regulated activity. Each creates specific ALCOA+ obligations. And each is a point at which integrity can be maintained or lost.

ICH E6(R3), adopted in January 2025, is the first iteration of the international GCP standard to address the data lifecycle explicitly rather than through the aggregated obligations of sponsor, investigator, and monitor roles. Section 4 of E6(R3) introduces a data governance framework that requires sponsors to define, document, and oversee the complete lifecycle of clinical trial data from initial generation through archiving and eventual destruction. This is not a restatement of prior guidance. It is a structural requirement that the sponsor's quality management system account for data integrity at every stage of the lifecycle, not merely at database lock or submission.[58]

The European regulatory framework has articulated the lifecycle concept with equal force through multiple parallel instruments. The EMA's 2023 Guideline on Computerised Systems and Electronic Data in Clinical Trials (EMA/INS/GCP/112288/2023) formally codifies ALCOA++ as the operative standard for all EU-conducted clinical trials and extends the lifecycle obligation explicitly to include the retirement phase of every system used in trial data management: decisions about data retention, archiving, migration, and destruction are part of the computerized system lifecycle, not its aftermath. The EMA Data Quality Framework, adopted by the Committee for Medicinal Products for Human Use in October 2023, further extends the European approach by establishing five quality dimensions, extensiveness, coherence, timeliness, relevance, and reliability, that map across the data lifecycle in ways that complement but do not duplicate the ALCOA+ structure. Together, these instruments mean that a clinical trial conducted within the EU is subject to a lifecycle governance framework as demanding as, and in some respects more structurally detailed than, its U.S. counterpart.[59][60]

The practical implication for sponsors operating across both frameworks is significant. A sponsor whose data governance program addresses EDC configuration, source data verification, and audit trail review, but does not address what happens to eCOA device logs after the platform contract expires, has a lifecycle gap under ICH E6(R3) Section 3.16.1(e) and Section 4.2 (Data Life Cycle Elements, a data integrity gap under PIC/S PI 041-1, and a computerised system lifecycle gap under the EMA's 2023 GCP guideline. All three findings are available to a GCP inspector from any EU national competent authority or to an FDA BIMO investigator conducting a for-cause inspection. The overlap is not coincidental. It reflects a sustained, multi-year convergence in how regulatory authorities on both sides of the Atlantic understand the relationship between lifecycle design and data integrity.[61]

PRIMARY REGULATORY FRAMEWORK: DATA LIFECYCLE
ICH E6(R3), Section 4.2 -- Data Life Cycle Elements: Requires sponsors and investigators to maintain oversight of the complete data lifecycle including generation, processing, review, reporting, transfer, storage, and archiving.
EMA Guideline on Computerised Systems and Electronic Data in Clinical Trials (EMA/INS/GCP/112288/2023): Defines the computerised system lifecycle to include all phases through retirement; requires that data retention, archiving, migration, and destruction be managed as part of the system lifecycle. ALCOA++ is the explicit operative standard.
EU CTR 536/2014, Articles 37 and 58: Clinical trial data submitted to CTIS must be consistent with the trial master file and clinical study report; clinical trial master file retention is 25 years after the end of the clinical trial.
EMA Data Quality Framework (EMA/326985/2023): Establishes five data quality dimensions -- extensiveness, coherence, timeliness, relevance, and reliability -- applicable across the lifecycle for regulatory decision-making.
21 CFR Part 312.62 -- Investigator Recordkeeping: Case histories must include source data adequate to verify subject enrollment, study procedures, and clinical observations for the retention period.
FDA Guidance: Electronic Source Data in Clinical Investigations (2013/2019): Electronic records generated directly in clinical systems are source data when system requirements are met; the electronic record, not any derived output, is the record of reference.
PIC/S PI 041-1 (2021): Data lifecycle governance must address each stage from initial data capture through final disposition, with defined controls at each transition point.
MHRA GxP Data Integrity Guidance (2018): Data governance must be applied across the whole data lifecycle; data transfer and migration must be validated; traceability of processing activities must be maintained regardless of whether outputs are ultimately used in reporting.

Stage One: Data Generation

Data generation is the stage at which a clinical observation becomes a record. A subject completes a patient-reported outcome assessment on an eCOA device. A coordinator measures a vital sign and enters it into a source document. A central laboratory instrument produces an assay result. An IRT system logs a randomization transaction. In each case, something that existed as a physical event or measurement becomes a documented datum, and the ALCOA+ clock starts at that moment.

The integrity requirements at generation center on attributability, contemporaneity, and originality. The record must identify the person responsible for the observation. It must reflect the time at which the observation was made, not the time at which it was convenient to document it. And the first recorded version of the data, whatever form it takes, is the original, with all the retention and reconstruction obligations that designation carries. These principles are established by decades of regulatory guidance and have been reinforced in every major update to the international GCP framework.

The EMA's 2023 GCP Computerised Systems Guideline adds a dimension to the generation-stage analysis that the U.S. framework addresses less directly: the concept of source data location and the regulatory significance of where, in a chain of systems, data is first captured. The guideline distinguishes between direct capture, where data is entered directly into the system designed to collect it, and transcription, where data observed in one context is entered into a clinical system from an intermediate record. For direct capture, the system's audit trail is the primary integrity record. For transcription, the original source from which the transcription was made is the primary integrity record, and its retention is an obligation independent of the EDC record. The practical consequence is that investigators and sponsors who design trials around direct electronic capture must ensure that the system receiving direct entry is validated for that purpose; those who design trials with intermediate paper capture must ensure the intermediate records are retained as source documents rather than discarded after transcription.

Two generation-stage failure modes appear with sufficient regularity in inspection findings on both sides of the Atlantic to warrant specific design attention. The first is the hybrid record: a clinical observation initially captured on an informal medium, an index card, a sticky note, a personal smartphone photograph, that is later transcribed into the official source document or EDC. The transcription is what the monitoring program sees, the data management program processes, and the regulatory submission contains. The informal original is discarded. The result is a source document that presents as an original contemporaneous record but is in fact a transcription from a source that no longer exists. Where the transcription is accurate, this creates an attributability and originality problem. Where the transcription differs from the original observation, it creates an accuracy problem that is invisible to every subsequent review process because the evidence of the discrepancy has been destroyed.

The second generation-stage failure mode is the pre-completed record: a source document or eCRF completed before the corresponding clinical activity is performed. Site coordinators who pre-populate eligibility criteria checkboxes before a screening interview, investigators who pre-sign safety assessment forms before a clinic visit, and clinical operations staff who enter anticipated protocol-completion endpoints before confirmatory procedures are performed, all create pre-completed records whose compliance problem exists independently of whether the pre-completed values turned out to be true.

COMPLIANT: Data Generation Practices	NON-COMPLIANT: Generation Failures Inspectors Cite
Clinical observations entered directly into validated EDC or source document at time of occurrence; entry timestamp consistent with scheduled visit window	Coordinator documents clinical observations on personal notes or informal worksheets during visits, transcribes to eCRF at shift end or following day; original notes discarded
eCOA device session logs retained in native format by sponsor or under vendor contract with confirmed access rights; device clock synchronized to controlled time server	Sponsor retains eCOA composite scores in EDC but does not confirm whether vendor has archived original session logs; device contract expires before retention period
IRT randomization transaction logs retained in original system format; event timestamps independently verifiable against site visit records	Investigator pre-completes screening eligibility checkboxes for subjects not yet interviewed, based on expectation that subjects will qualify
Source document design pre-specifies the medium of original capture; changes to capture medium require protocol amendment or deviation documentation	Source documents show uniform entry timestamps clustering outside visit windows, inconsistent with clinical workload patterns at the site
For direct capture systems (EMA GCP Guideline, Section 6.1.3): system validated for direct entry; no parallel paper record required where system meets validation requirements; audit trail constitutes the integrity record	For transcription-based workflows: intermediate paper records destroyed after eCRF entry, leaving EDC record without verifiable source; EMA GCP Guideline Section 6.1.1 violated

Stage Two: Data Processing and Transfer

Processing encompasses every action performed on data between its initial generation and its arrival in the sponsor's analysis-ready dataset. In a modern multi-site clinical trial, this stage is extensive. Central laboratory results are transmitted electronically and mapped into the sponsor's EDC through defined transfer specifications. eCOA composite scores are derived from individual item responses and exported through vendor APIs. Imaging data is assessed by independent core laboratories and adjudicated results are transmitted to the data management system. IRT transaction data is reconciled against dispensing records and subject exposure calculations. Each transfer, mapping, derivation, and reconciliation step is a processing action that creates the potential for data to change between its origin and its destination.

The ALCOA+ requirement for the processing stage is traceability: the ability to reconstruct the complete pathway from the original observation to the value as it appears in the analysis dataset. PIC/S PI 041-1 defines this explicitly as a data governance obligation applicable to every transformation in the data pathway. The MHRA's GxP Data Integrity Guidance frames the same requirement in terms that are operationally precise: if data processing has been repeated with progressive modification of processing parameters, this must be visible in the audit record to ensure that processing parameters are not being manipulated to achieve a more desirable result. The European formulation is notably stronger than its U.S. counterpart in specifying that the traceability obligation exists regardless of whether the output of a given processing step is ultimately reported or used for regulatory purposes. Every processing step is auditable, whether or not its output survives to the final dataset.[62]

ICH E6(R3) Section 4.2 requires that sponsors document and validate all data transformations and that the audit trail for any transformed data include a reference to its source. The EMA's 2023 GCP guideline reinforces this at the system level: data transfer between systems must be validated, including the transfer of metadata, and the receiving system must confirm that the transferred data is complete and matches the source. This is not a new requirement, but it is stated with greater operational specificity in the 2023 guideline than in prior instruments, and EU GCP inspectors have increasingly cited deficiencies in transfer validation as standalone findings rather than treating them as subissues of broader systemic problems.

The processing stage creates three categories of integrity risk. The first is mapping error: a mismatch between a variable as defined in the source system and the same variable as it appears in the receiving system after transfer. The second is transformation without retention: a processing step that produces a derived value without retaining the original from which it was derived. The eCOA composite score problem is the clearest example, but the same issue arises wherever complex derivation algorithms convert raw data into analysis-ready variables without version-controlled documentation. The third risk is transfer without validation: data transferred between systems without a defined reconciliation procedure confirming that what was sent was received completely and correctly.

Data Source	Processing Step	Key Integrity Control
EDC direct entry	Query and resolution workflow; field-level validation rules	Audit trail captures every entry, change, query, and resolution with user attribution and timestamp; query text retained
Central laboratory	Electronic data transfer via HL7 or proprietary API; field mapping to EDC	Transfer reconciliation confirms record count and field-level accuracy; mapping specification under version control; discrepancies resolved before EDC acceptance
eCOA / ePRO device	Score derivation from item responses; composite export to EDC	Algorithm version documented and under change control; original session logs retained; derivation validated and reproducible from original data
IRT / RTSM	Randomization transaction log; treatment assignment derivation	Original transaction log retained independently of sponsor reporting layer; blinded summary reports are derived documents only

Data Source	Processing Step	Key Integrity Control
Medical imaging (core lab)	Independent adjudication; results transmitted to EDC	Adjudication charter defines the decision process; original images retained; adjudication results transmitted with reader attribution and timestamp
Wearable / remote monitoring device	Raw signal processing; derived parameter calculation; transmission to data platform	Signal processing algorithm version documented; raw signal data retained; transmission log confirms data arrival and device calibration records retained

The European Regulatory Dimension: A Distinct Framework

The European regulatory framework for data lifecycle governance is not simply a regional variant of the ICH E6(R3) standard. It is a layered structure with instruments at the EU level, national competent authority level, and joint EU-UK level that collectively impose obligations the ICH standard does not fully capture. Understanding where these obligations exceed, parallel, and occasionally conflict with the U.S. framework is a prerequisite for designing a global data governance program that is compliant everywhere the data is generated, processed, and reported.

The EMA GCP Computerised Systems Guideline (EMA/INS/GCP/112288/2023)

The EMA's 2023 Guideline on Computerised Systems and Electronic Data in Clinical Trials is the most operationally detailed EU instrument on clinical data lifecycle management. It entered into effect in September 2023, replacing the 2010 reflection paper on electronic source data, and addresses the full range of systems used in modern clinical trials: EDC, eCOA, IRT/RTSM, electronic trial master files, and AI-assisted data review tools. Its treatment of the data lifecycle is structured around the concept of the computerized system lifecycle, which the guideline defines to include four phases: concept, project, operational, and retirement. The retirement phase encompasses all decisions about data retention, archiving, migration, and destruction. The guideline's explicit inclusion of retirement as a regulated phase means that the question of what happens to a system's data when the system is decommissioned is a validation and qualification question, not merely a vendor management question.

For audit trails specifically, the guideline states that audit trails must be retained for the same period as the data they cover, that they must be available for inspection on the same timeline as the underlying records, and that audit trail review is a required activity at defined intervals throughout the operational life of the system. The practical implication for EU-conducted trials is that a sponsor who manages audit trail review only at database lock, without periodic review during the operational phase, is operating outside the guideline's requirements regardless of whether the locked-database audit trail is complete.

The guideline's treatment of cloud solutions (Section 6.7) addresses the lifecycle challenge of systems hosted outside the sponsor's infrastructure. For cloud-hosted EDC and eTMF platforms, the responsible party must ensure that data remains accessible throughout the required retention period, that the vendor's data retention practices are contractually specified and audited, and that a validated data migration or export procedure exists before system retirement. The guideline explicitly requires that the responsible party not rely solely on the vendor's assurances; an in-depth examination of the vendor's quality system and data retention practices, including audit access, is required. This standard is applied by EU GCP inspectors and has produced findings against sponsors who could not produce evidence of vendor qualification that covered lifecycle obligations rather than merely operational validation.

EU Clinical Trials Regulation 536/2014 and CTIS

The EU Clinical Trials Regulation, fully applicable since January 2023, created data integrity obligations that have no direct U.S. equivalent. All clinical trials within the EU must be registered, authorized, and their results reported through the Clinical Trials Information System (CTIS). The data submitted to CTIS must be consistent with the trial master file and with the data in the clinical study report. This is a lifecycle consistency requirement: the registration data established at study initiation must remain consistent with the conduct and reporting data generated through the remainder of the trial, and any discrepancy requires documented justification rather than silent correction.

Article 58 of the EU CTR establishes a 25-year retention period for clinical trial master file records after the end of the clinical trial. This retention obligation exceeds the ICH E6(R3) minimum of 15 years and significantly exceeds the U.S. minimum under 21 CFR Part 312.62. The 25-year period is measured from study completion, not from the last regulatory action, which means that for major products, the practical retention horizon for EU-regulated trial records extends well into the mid-twenty-first century for trials being conducted today. System-of-record and archive design decisions made during current trial operations must accommodate retention periods that no current EDC or eTMF platform has been in existence long enough to have met.

The EMA Data Quality Framework

The EMA's Data Quality Framework, adopted by the CHMP in October 2023, introduces a conceptual layer that sits above the ALCOA+ standard and extends the European approach to data quality beyond the GCP context. The Framework defines five data quality dimensions: reliability (covering accuracy, precision, and truthfulness), extensiveness (covering completeness and coverage), coherence (covering consistency and standardization), timeliness (covering currency and availability), and relevance (covering fitness for the specific regulatory purpose). Each dimension is characterized by sub-dimensions and associated metrics, creating an assessment architecture that EU regulators are increasingly applying to the evaluation of submitted clinical data.

The Framework is not an inspection tool in the traditional sense; it is a regulatory assessment framework for submissions. But its dimensions map directly onto lifecycle stages where data quality must be maintained. Reliability is primarily a generation and processing-stage property. Extensiveness is a review and reporting-stage property. Coherence spans processing and reporting. Timeliness addresses the archive-stage question of whether data is available when needed. For sponsors seeking to anticipate how EU regulators will assess the data quality of submitted clinical evidence, alignment with the Framework's dimensions is an increasingly important design consideration.

MHRA and Post-Brexit Complexity

The UK's Medicines and Healthcare products Regulatory Agency maintains a GxP data integrity framework that is both the most operationally detailed in the world and, since Brexit, independent of the EU framework it originally helped to shape. The MHRA's 2018 GxP Data Integrity Guidance defines the data lifecycle as comprising all phases from generation and recording through processing, use, retention, archiving, and destruction, and requires that data governance be applied across the whole lifecycle. The guidance addresses each phase individually with specific requirements, including the obligation to validate data transfer and migration procedures, to maintain traceability of processing activities regardless of whether their outputs are used in reporting, and to verify that data remains accessible in human-readable form throughout the retention period.[63]

The MHRA's lifecycle framework differs from the EMA's in one operationally significant respect: it applies equally to all GxP activities, including both GMP and GCP, whereas the EMA's GCP Computerised Systems Guideline is specific to clinical trials. This cross-GxP scope means that MHRA data integrity inspectors bring GMP-derived lifecycle expectations into GCP inspections, including expectations about document control, process understanding, and the treatment of electronic worksheets that are more demanding than what GCP-only sponsors typically encounter in FDA BIMO inspections. Sponsors conducting trials in the UK who are primarily familiar with FDA GCP expectations frequently underestimate MHRA lifecycle requirements at the processing and archiving stages.

Requirement	European Framework	U.S. Framework
ALCOA++ standard for all clinical data	ALCOA+ (ICH E6(R3)) plus Traceable (T) as explicit 11th property; "Traceable" encompasses full provenance reconstruction	ALCOA+ as stated in ICH E6(R3); Traceable not separately enumerated in U.S. guidance but expected in practice
Computerised system lifecycle	Retirement phase (data migration, archiving, destruction) explicitly regulated as part of system lifecycle (EMA GCP Guideline 2023)	Lifecycle obligations implicit in Part 11 and 21 CFR 312 but no explicit lifecycle phase framework
Data retention -- TMF	25 years after the end of the clinical trial (EU CTR Article 58)	2 years after NDA approval or IND discontinuation (21 CFR 312.62); ICH E6(R3) minimum of 15 years often operative for global programs

Requirement	European Framework	U.S. Framework
Audit trail review frequency	Required at defined intervals throughout operational system life (EMA GCP Guideline Section 6.2.2)	Required; frequency not explicitly mandated in U.S. guidance
Cloud/SaaS vendor qualification	In-depth examination of vendor quality system required; sponsor cannot rely on vendor documentation alone (EMA GCP Guideline Annex 2)	Vendor qualification expected; depth of examination less explicitly prescribed
Transfer/migration validation	Explicitly required for all data transfers between systems; metadata transfer included (EMA GCP Guideline Section 6.1.2)	Transfer validation expected; less prescriptive on metadata requirements
CTIS registration consistency	Data submitted to CTIS must be consistent with TMF and clinical study report throughout lifecycle; discrepancies require documented justification (EU CTR Articles 37, 58)	No direct equivalent; ClinicalTrials.gov registration requirements are less tightly integrated with data integrity framework
Processing traceability	Applies regardless of whether processing output is used in reporting (MHRA GxP Guidance Section 6.9)	Applies to regulated records; scope less explicitly defined for non-reported outputs

Stage Three: Data Review and Query Resolution

Data review is the stage at which clinical data management intersects most directly with the investigator site workflow, and it is the stage that generates the largest volume of regulatory citation evidence in the form of query records, audit trail entries, and data clarification form correspondence. Review encompasses monitoring activities conducted at the investigator site, centralized statistical monitoring conducted by the sponsor or CRO, medical data review conducted by clinical teams, and biostatistical review prior to analysis. Each of these activities creates a record, and every record created during review is subject to ALCOA+ requirements independent of the data it concerns.

The integrity failure mode specific to the review stage is the coached correction: a query resolution in which the data correction is not driven by a genuine identification of an error, but by a reviewer's knowledge of the expected outcome or desired result. This pattern is among the most consequential in clinical data integrity enforcement because it operates entirely within the established procedures. Queries are issued. Responses are received. Changes are documented with stated reasons. The audit trail shows the complete sequence. The problem is that the sequence, taken in aggregate, reveals a pattern: endpoint values that move toward clinical significance following monitor visits; change reasons that are formulaic rather than informative; correction rates that are elevated at sites contributing subjects to a protocol-defined responder population.

FDA's 2013 guidance on risk-based monitoring identified statistical anomalies in site-level data patterns as a primary target of centralized monitoring review precisely because these patterns are not detectable by individual query review. ICH E6(R3) Section 3.11.4.2 makes this explicit: the monitoring strategy must be designed to detect data quality problems, including patterns that would not be apparent from the review of individual records. The EMA and MHRA have stated equivalent positions in GCP inspection findings and guidance. EU GCP inspectors apply the same aggregate-pattern analysis during inspections, examining correction rates by site, by endpoint category, and by temporal relationship to monitoring visits. The FDA-MHRA joint paper on data integrity in global clinical trials[64], published in 2020 following a joint workshop held in 2018, explicitly documented the convergence of inspection approaches between the two agencies on this point: both use audit trail pattern analysis as a primary inspection tool, though the analytical methods and specific metrics applied differ.[65, 66]

Query management as a data integrity control requires three properties that are often present individually but less frequently in combination. First, the query must be independently documented: the text of the query, the identity of the issuer, the date of issuance, the response received, and the identity of the responder must all be retained in the audit trail. Second, the stated reason for any data correction must be substantive: a reason that says "transcription error" without identifying the source of the corrected value provides no verifiable basis for the correction and is effectively an undocumented change. Third, the resolution timeline must be plausible: a pattern of queries resolved within hours of issuance on data that would require original source document review to verify is a signal that the resolution process is not functioning as described.

THE QUERY PATTERN INSPECTION APPROACH

When FDA's Office of Scientific Investigations reviews EDC audit trails during a bioresearch monitoring inspection, individual query records are a starting point, not the target. Investigators examine query patterns: the rate of corrections that move values toward clinical significance thresholds; the proportion of changes accompanied by substantive versus formulaic change reasons; the temporal relationship between monitor visit dates and query issuance clusters; and the comparison of correction rates across sites. A single query with a formulaic change reason is a minor observation. A pattern of two hundred queries with the same formulaic change reason, seventy percent of which resulted in corrections that moved subjects from non-responder to responder classification, is a data integrity finding.

EU GCP inspectors apply an equivalent analysis. The FDA-MHRA joint paper on data integrity in global clinical trials documented the convergence: both agencies use audit trail pattern analysis as a primary inspection tool. EMA GCP inspectors additionally examine query patterns against the ALCOA++ framework, specifically testing whether corrections undermine the contemporaneous property of the original record. An inspection finding at a European site that a data change was made without contemporaneous justification carries the same regulatory weight as a comparable FDA finding; under EU CTR, it can affect the integrity of CTIS-registered trial data for the entire program.

Stage Four: Data Reporting and Submission

Reporting encompasses all processes that transform clean, analysis-ready clinical data into summaries, listings, and outputs that support regulatory decision-making: from operational reports used in clinical oversight, through interim analyses and data monitoring committee reviews, to the integrated clinical and statistical reports submitted in marketing applications. The integrity obligation at the reporting stage centers on accuracy and traceability: the outputs must truthfully represent the underlying data, and the pathway from analysis dataset to reported result must be reconstructable.

Statistical analysis plan adherence is the primary integrity control at the reporting stage. A Statistical Analysis Plan (SAP) that specifies a primary endpoint analysis, followed by a reported result that reflects a different analysis without documented amendment, is a data integrity finding regardless of the clinical significance of the discrepancy. This applies to endpoint definitions, population definitions, handling of missing data, pre-specified sensitivity analyses, and the distinction between confirmatory and exploratory analysis.[67]

The CTIS registration requirements under EU Clinical Trials Regulation 536/2014 have added a specific traceability obligation with no direct U.S. equivalent: the primary endpoint as registered in CTIS must be consistent with the primary endpoint as analyzed and reported. Any discrepancy requires documented justification. This is not merely an administrative requirement. A sponsor whose primary endpoint shifts between CTIS registration and the clinical study report, without documented amendment, has a data integrity problem that is publicly visible through the CTIS portal and available to any national competent authority conducting a GCP inspection of a study supporting an EU marketing authorization application. The public transparency of the CTIS architecture converts what might otherwise be an internal data governance deficiency into an externally observable and verifiable discrepancy.[68]

EU CTR also mandates public disclosure of clinical trial results for all EU-conducted trials regardless of whether the results are favorable. This transparency requirement has indirect data integrity implications: a sponsor whose submitted dataset does not accurately represent the trial's actual results faces a compliance problem that is visible to the public, not merely to regulators in a non-public inspection. The reporting-stage integrity obligations in the EU are, as a consequence, both more technically specified and more publicly consequential than their U.S. equivalents.

Reporting-Stage Integrity Requirement	Design Control
SAP primary endpoint analysis must match submitted results	Final SAP locked before database lock; any post-lock amendments require documented justification with

Reporting-Stage Integrity Requirement	Design Control
	independent review; version control confirms amendment history
CTIS-registered endpoints must be consistent with analyzed endpoints (EU CTR)	Registration fields reviewed against final SAP before database lock; discrepancies resolved by amendment or documented justification before submission; CTIS record updated through authorized amendment process
Results disclosure obligations met (EU CTR)	Summary of trial results submitted to CTIS within 12 months of trial end; dataset consistent with clinical study report; no selective omission of unfavorable results
Cross-document value consistency (narrative, listings, summaries)	Systematic pre-submission consistency review with documented results; discrepancies resolved from source dataset, not by editing documents independently
Exploratory analyses clearly distinguished from confirmatory	Statistical report explicitly labels analysis type for every result; post-hoc analyses identified as such; ISS/ISE clearly identifies which analyses were pre-specified
Interim analysis results managed under firewall procedures	Interim analysis data and results accessible only to authorized personnel; unblinding procedures documented; monitoring committee recommendations and sponsor responses retained

Stage Five: Data Storage, Retrieval, and the Archive

Storage and archiving are often treated as administrative functions that begin when clinical operations end. This is a design error with significant regulatory consequences. The integrity properties that govern data at creation govern it equally at every subsequent stage of its retained life. An accurate, contemporaneous, original record that becomes inaccessible, illegible, or unverifiable during its retention period is a non-compliant record. The conditions of storage are not incidental to data integrity. They are part of it.

The retention period for clinical trial records is longer than the operational period of most clinical data management systems. Under 21 CFR Part 312.62, investigators must retain records for two years after the later of NDA approval or discontinuation of the IND. In the EU, Article 58 of EU CTR 536/2014 establishes a 25-year retention period for trial master file records after the end of the clinical trial. ICH E6(R3) Section 4.2.7 sets a 15-year minimum post-study completion. In practice, the retention requirement for most global development programs is determined by the most demanding jurisdiction, which in almost every case is the EU's 25-year TMF standard. Against this retention horizon, the operational lifecycle of any given EDC vendor, eTMF platform, eCOA system, or laboratory information system is short.[69]

The EMA's 2023 GCP Computerised Systems Guideline explicitly addresses the archive challenge for cloud-hosted systems: the responsible party must ensure that data remains accessible throughout the required retention period without depending on the vendor's continued commercial operation. This requires, at minimum, a validated export or migration procedure confirmed before the system enters its retirement phase, a data format capable of surviving the retention period without becoming unreadable, and contractual provisions that survive vendor insolvency or acquisition. The EMA and EU national competent authorities have cited archive-stage deficiencies with increasing frequency in GCP inspection findings as the 25-year retention clock runs forward on early post-EU CTR trials. The finding is straightforward: where a sponsor cannot demonstrate that archived data is accessible and readable on demand, the endurance and availability properties of ALCOA++ are compromised, and the inspection finding follows directly.

Vendor contract management is an underappreciated archive-stage integrity control. When an eCOA vendor contract expires, the sponsor's access to the original device-level session logs may expire with it unless the contract explicitly provides for post-contract data return. When an EDC platform is decommissioned, the audit trail data that constitutes the forensic record of the trial's data management history may be retained in a format that requires the decommissioned platform to read. These are not theoretical risks. They are recurring findings in for-cause inspections triggered by post-approval questions about specific studies. Sponsors who discover at the point of inquiry that their vendor relationships did not adequately protect their archive obligations are in a position that no amount of subsequent remediation fully resolves: the data retention obligation is the sponsor's, and the explanation that a vendor contract failed to preserve the records is an organizational failure, not a mitigating circumstance.

RETENTION PERIODS: KEY REGULATORY REQUIREMENTS
21 CFR 312.62(c): Investigator must retain records for two years after the later of NDA/BLA approval or IND discontinuation. Standard clinical trial record retention in the U.S.
21 CFR 312.57(c): Sponsor must retain records for two years after marketing application approval or IND discontinuation.
ICH E6(R3) Section 4.2.7: Essential documents must be retained for a minimum of 15 years after study completion. Individual jurisdiction requirements may be longer.
EU CTR 536/2014, Article 58: Clinical trial master file must be retained for 25 years after the end of the clinical trial.
ICH E6(R3) Section 4.2.7: Electronic records must be readable throughout the required retention period; format and system changes require validated migration.
PIC/S PI 041-1 Section 10: Archival procedures must include access verification, format durability assessment, and documentation of any record migration.
EMA GCP Computerised Systems Guideline (EMA/INS/GCP/112288/2023): System retirement must include validated data migration or export; sponsor cannot rely on vendor continued operation for long-term data accessibility.
MHRA GxP Data Integrity Guidance (2018) Section 6.17: Data retention must be in a format that allows full reconstruction of activities; backup is not a substitute for archive; access verification required throughout retention period.

Stage Six: Data Destruction

Data destruction is the stage that clinical data governance programs most consistently fail to plan for, and the omission matters more than it appears. The retention period is a floor, not a ceiling, and many organizations extend retention indefinitely for reasons ranging from genuine uncertainty about regulatory requirements to institutional reluctance to commit resources to a formal destruction program. Indefinite retention is not a neutral choice. It creates ongoing exposure from data that is no longer subject to active quality oversight, held in systems that may no longer receive security updates, and accessible to personnel whose roles have changed since the data was created.

ICH E6(R3) Section 4.2.8 requires that the destruction of essential documents be documented and approved. This means a defined destruction authorization process: confirmation that the retention period has been met, that no regulatory or legal hold is in place, that applicable jurisdiction-specific requirements have been reviewed, and that the destruction method is appropriate for the record type. For electronic records, appropriate destruction means methods that render the data unrecoverable. For paper records, it means physical destruction that renders the records unreadable. The documentation of destruction is itself a record subject to retention requirements.[70]

Destruction authorization becomes complex in multi-sponsor, multi-jurisdiction trials. A trial conducted simultaneously in the U.S., EU, and Japan with a co-development partner is subject to the retention requirements of all three jurisdictions plus any contractual obligations between the sponsors. The applicable retention period is the longest among applicable requirements. Under EU CTR's 25-year standard, a global program with EU sites will in almost every case determine the retention horizon for the entire trial. Organizations that manage destruction on an ad hoc basis, without a defined program that tracks retention periods across studies and jurisdictions, regularly discover that records they believed could be destroyed cannot be, and records that should have been destroyed long ago remain in active systems without the oversight that would be appropriate if the decision to retain them were intentional.

Data Flow Mapping: The Lifecycle as a Design Tool

The lifecycle framework described in the preceding sections is most valuable not as a compliance checklist but as a design tool. A data flow map that traces every data element in a clinical trial from its point of generation through every processing step, review activity, transfer, and archive destination does two things that no other quality tool does as efficiently: it identifies the complete population of records subject to ALCOA+ obligations, and it surfaces the transition points at which integrity controls are required but may not yet be designed.

An effective data flow map for a modern clinical trial is a complex document. It includes not only the EDC data pathway but the parallel pathways for central laboratory data, eCOA and ePRO data, IRT transaction data, imaging data, safety data, and any external data sources integrated into the trial. It identifies, for each data element, the system of generation, the transformation or derivation steps applied, the systems through which the data passes in transit, the system of record at database lock, and the archive destination at study close. And it identifies, at each transition point, the control that ensures ALCOA+ properties are maintained across the transition.

For trials conducted in the EU, the data flow map has an additional obligation dimension: it must account for CTIS data flows and the consistency requirement between trial registration data and conduct data. The CTIS architecture means that protocol amendments, endpoint changes, and population modifications are not merely internal document management actions. They are public regulatory events that change the registered basis against which the trial's results will be evaluated. A data flow map that does not trace the relationship between the clinical data management system and the CTIS registration is incomplete for EU purposes, regardless of how thoroughly it covers the EDC-to-submission pathway.

The practical process for building a data flow map begins at protocol finalization, not at study start. By the time a site is initiated, many of the design decisions that determine whether integrity controls can be implemented have already been made: vendor contracts signed, EDC configurations finalized, laboratory specifications locked. Data flow mapping at study start is a diagnostic exercise. Data flow mapping at protocol finalization is a design exercise, and it is the only timing that gives the clinical team the opportunity to identify and address lifecycle gaps before they become operational constraints.

Data Element	Point of Generation	Processing Steps	System of Record	Archive Destination	Key Control
Primary endpoint (eCOA)	Patient device, ePRO platform	Score derivation, composite export	Sponsor EDC (accepted value)	eTMF + vendor session log archive	Vendor contract data return clause; session log access verification
Vital signs (site)	Source document / EDC direct entry	SDV; query resolution	EDC	eTMF / site file archive	Contemporaneous entry policy; audit trail review

Data Element	Point of Generation	Processing Steps	System of Record	Archive Destination	Key Control
Central lab results	Instrument raw data, LIMS	HL7 transfer; EDC field mapping	EDC (mapped value)	Lab LIMS archive + EDC export	Transfer reconciliation; mapping specification version control
Randomization event	IRT/RTSM transaction log	Allocation derivation; site dispensing record	IRT transaction log	IRT archive (original); EDC (derived)	Original log retention; blinded summary as derived document only
Adverse event	Site source document	eCRF entry; medical coding; SAE narrative	EDC + safety database	eTMF; regulatory submission archive	Coding dictionary version retained; SAE timeline audit trail
Protocol deviation	Site deviation form	CRO review; deviation log	EDC / CTMS	eTMF	Deviation pattern analysis; root cause documentation

Data Element	Point of Generation	Processing Steps	System of Record	Archive Destination	Key Control
CTIS registration data (EU)	Protocol; IB; ICF	Authorized submission through CTIS portal	CTIS public registry	EU regulatory database (25-year retention)	Consistency review against SAP and CSR before and after submission; amendment documentation

Lifecycle Integrity and the ALCOA+ Framework

Every ALCOA+ property maps to specific lifecycle stages where it is primarily at risk. Understanding these mappings is a prerequisite for designing controls that are proportionate to risk rather than uniformly applied regardless of where in the lifecycle a given property is most vulnerable.

Attributability is primarily a generation-stage property. Records created with shared credentials, or attributed to a generic account rather than an identified individual, fail the attributability requirement at the point of creation, and no subsequent processing, review, or archiving step can restore attribution that was never captured. Contemporaneity is similarly a generation-stage property, though the review stage can create secondary contemporaneity problems where query resolutions or deviation reports are prepared retroactively. Originality is a property that spans generation and processing: the original record is created at generation, but its status as original can be compromised at the processing stage if transformations are performed without retaining the source.

Accuracy spans generation, processing, review, and reporting. A record can be accurate at generation and inaccurate at reporting if processing errors introduce mapping distortions, if review-stage corrections are driven by desired outcomes rather than identified errors, or if reporting-stage selections do not faithfully represent the underlying data. Completeness is a review and reporting-stage property as much as a generation-stage one: complete data at database lock requires that query resolution processes do not selectively close observations, that population definitions do not exclude inconvenient subjects, and that analysis populations are defined prospectively rather than constructed to optimize results.

Endurance and availability are archiving-stage properties with design implications that must be addressed at the generation and processing stages. Records that are generated in formats tied to proprietary platforms, or processed through transformation steps that do not retain source data, arrive at the archiving stage with endurance and availability vulnerabilities that archive procedures alone cannot remedy. The design implication is direct: format decisions made at the generation and processing stages must anticipate the endurance and availability requirements of the archiving stage.

The EMA GCP Computerised Systems Guideline explicitly lists "traceable" as the eleventh ALCOA++ property, distinct from the standard ten. Traceability, in the EMA's formulation, requires that the full provenance of a data value be reconstructable from initial capture through every algorithmic derivation and system transfer to the submitted value. This is a processing and archive-stage property whose risk is highest at transition points between systems and at the processing steps that produce derived values from original observations. Sponsors whose traceability controls address the EDC-to-submission pathway but not the device-to-EDC or laboratory-to-EDC pathways have an ALCOA++ deficiency under European standards regardless of how clean their submission datasets appear.

ALCOA+ Property	Primary Lifecycle Risk Stage and Control Point
Attributable	Generation: unique user credentials required before first data entry; shared accounts prohibited; delegation logs maintained for any role-based access
Legible	Generation and Archive: source document design standards; format requirements for electronic records maintained through migrations; legibility verification in archive access checks
Contemporaneous	Generation: entry timing policy with defined tolerance windows; audit trail review detects retrospective entry patterns; deviation procedure for late entries

ALCOA+ Property	Primary Lifecycle Risk Stage and Control Point
Original	Generation and Processing: first-captured record designated as original; transformation steps document source; derived values traceable to originals throughout retention period
Accurate	Generation, Review, Reporting: accuracy verification through SDV and central monitoring; query management controls prevent coached corrections; SAP adherence confirmed at reporting
Complete	Review and Reporting: query closure standards ensure all data fields resolved; population definitions pre-specified; missing data handling pre-defined in SAP
Consistent	Processing and Review: cross-system reconciliation confirms consistency of values across data sources; timeline verification confirms logical sequence of events
Enduring	Archive: format standards for long-term storage; validated migration procedures; access verification schedule; end-of-life procedures for all data systems
Available	Archive: retrieval procedure with defined timelines; disaster recovery tested; access rights maintained for authorized personnel throughout retention period
Traceable (ALCOA++)	Processing and Archive: complete audit trail from original capture to submitted value; derivation algorithms documented and version-controlled; data lineage preserved through migrations; provenance reconstruction required on demand (EMA GCP Guideline 2023, Section 4.5)

The Transition Point Problem

The most consistent finding across clinical data lifecycle analyses is that integrity failures concentrate at transition points: the moments when data moves from one system to another, one organization to another, one format to another, or one operational phase to another. The generation stage, the processing stage, and the archive stage each present defined technical requirements that experienced data management teams implement reliably. The gaps appear between stages, not within them.

The transition from site-level source documentation to EDC entry is a transition point. The transition from eCOA device to EDC via API export is a transition point. The transition from EDC to the analysis dataset is a transition point. The transition from operational system to archive is a transition point. And the transition from one vendor platform to another during a system migration is a transition point. Each of these transitions requires a defined handoff procedure: a control that confirms the data arrived at its destination with all required properties intact, and that the original source remains accessible if the transferred representation requires verification.

Designing transition controls requires identifying every transition in the data flow map and assigning a responsible party for each one. This sounds straightforward and in practice is consistently problematic, because clinical trial operations distribute responsibility for data integrity across organizations, contracts, and functional roles in ways that create accountability gaps at exactly the points where accountability is most needed.

ICH E6(R3) Section 3.6 addresses this directly: sponsors cannot transfer their regulatory accountability for clinical trial data to CROs or other vendors. The regulatory accountability for the completeness and accuracy of the data that enters a marketing application is the sponsor's accountability regardless of which party physically managed the systems through which the data passed. The EMA GCP Computerised Systems Guideline states this equivalent obligation in the EU context with equal clarity: all references to sponsors and investigators in the guideline also apply to their service providers, but the responsible party remains ultimately responsible for the validation of the computerised systems used in clinical trials and for the data those systems generate. Sponsors who discover during an inspection that they cannot demonstrate the integrity of a data transition because a vendor managed the relevant step without documented oversight have not transferred their accountability. They have failed it.[71]

CHAPTER 6 - KEY TAKEAWAYS
Data integrity is a lifecycle property: the ALCOA+ obligations that apply at the moment of data creation apply equally at every subsequent stage through which data passes until it is lawfully destroyed.
ICH E6(R3) Section 4.2 requires sponsors and investigators to design and oversee the complete data lifecycle, making lifecycle governance an explicit quality management system obligation rather than an implicit consequence of individual-stage controls.
The EMA GCP Computerised Systems Guideline (EMA/INS/GCP/112288/2023) defines the computerised system lifecycle to include the retirement phase; data migration, archiving, and destruction are regulated activities within the system lifecycle, not administrative tasks that follow it.
EU CTR 536/2014 establishes a 25-year retention period for trial master file records after the end of the clinical trial, the most demanding retention standard applicable to most global development programs, and requires CTIS registration data to remain consistent with trial conduct and reporting throughout the lifecycle.
The EMA Data Quality Framework's five dimensions -- reliability, extensiveness, coherence, timeliness, and relevance -- provide a lifecycle-spanning assessment structure that EU regulators apply to submitted clinical evidence and that sponsors should map to lifecycle stage controls.
Generation-stage controls must prevent hybrid records and pre-completed documentation; for EU trials, the distinction between direct capture and transcription determines which record constitutes the primary integrity source.
Processing-stage controls must ensure that every data transformation is documented, validated, and reversible; the MHRA GxP guidance requires traceability of all processing activities regardless of whether their outputs are used in reporting.
Query management requires aggregate pattern analysis, not merely individual record review; both FDA and EU GCP inspectors use audit trail pattern analysis as a primary inspection tool, as documented in the FDA-MHRA joint paper on data integrity in global clinical trials.
Reporting-stage integrity in the EU includes CTIS registration consistency and public results disclosure obligations under EU CTR that have no direct U.S. equivalent and that make reporting-stage deficiencies externally visible rather than solely subject to inspection.

CHAPTER 6 - KEY TAKEAWAYS
Endurance and availability requirements demand archive design at the generation and processing stages; format and vendor contract decisions made early in the trial determine whether archive obligations can be met under both U.S. and 25-year EU retention standards.
Regulatory accountability for data at transition points between systems, organizations, and formats cannot be transferred to vendors; sponsors must design oversight structures that confirm data integrity at every transition in the clinical data supply chain.
Data flow mapping at protocol finalization is a design tool; data flow mapping at study start is a diagnostic tool; for EU trials, the map must include CTIS data flows and the registration-to-conduct consistency requirement.

CHAPTER SEVEN

Computer System Validation in the Modern Era

> *A validated system that produces unreliable data is not a compliant system. Validation confirms that a computerized system functions per its intended use; it does not confirm that the organization has designed the right intentions, configured the right controls, or built the oversight program to detect when those controls fail.*

The sponsor had done everything the guidance documents said to do. The electronic data capture system deployed across its Phase III cardiovascular outcomes trial carried a validation package of considerable weight: installation qualification, functional testing, user acceptance testing, a traceability matrix mapping every system requirement to a test script, and a formal validation report signed by the system owner, the quality lead, and the clinical data manager. Audit trails were enabled. User access was controlled by role. The system vendor had provided its standard supplier qualification documentation, and the sponsor's quality team had audited the vendor confirming that the hosted environment met the technical specifications required under 21 CFR Part 11 and ICH E6(R3). Everything was in perfect order for a risk-based validation.

The FDA BIMO inspection, triggered eighteen months after database lock, began with those validation documents. The inspectors reviewed them methodically and found no significant gaps. Then they asked a different set of questions. They asked who reviewed the audit trail output and when. They asked what the escalation pathway was when audit trail review identified an anomaly. They asked whether the validation tests had ever been executed against the production environment or only against a test instance. They asked how the sponsor had verified that the configuration-controlled version of the system deployed at the beginning of the trial was the same version running at database lock.

None of the validation documents answered those questions. The validation package demonstrated that the system could perform as intended under test conditions. It said nothing about whether anyone had verified that it was performing as intended throughout two years of active enrollment, or whether the production environment had remained in its validated state across three software updates, two server migrations, and one vendor merger.

The Form 483 issued at inspection close contained six observations. Four concerned the gap between the validated state of the system and its operational management over the trial's lifecycle. The sponsor had built an excellent validation package and then treated it as a point-in-time filing artifact rather than a living framework. In the regulatory record, that distinction cost them significantly.

> *Validation is a well planned ongoing activity, not a voyage of discovery. The question regulators are asking is not whether the system was validated before first use. It is whether the sponsor managed that validated state through every update, migration, configuration change, and operational deviation that followed.*

The Regulatory Framework for Clinical System Validation

The obligation to validate computerized systems used in clinical research is not located in a single guidance document. It is distributed across 21 CFR Part 11, ICH E6(R3), the FDA guidance on electronic source data, and the general data integrity governance framework. The practical consequence is that sponsors sometimes approach validation as a Part 11 compliance exercise and miss the broader obligations imposed by the governance framework. Part 11 establishes the technical threshold; E6(R3) and the data integrity framework establish the organizational obligations that give those technical controls meaning.

21 CFR Part 11, Section 11.10 requires that systems used to create, modify, maintain, archive, retrieve, or transmit electronic records be validated to ensure accuracy, reliability, consistent intended performance, and the ability to discern invalid or altered records. The

phrase "consistent intended performance" is not a description of what the point-in-time validation package must demonstrate at the time of validation. It is a statement of what the sponsor must be able to demonstrate throughout the system's operational life. A system that performed consistently in testing but was never verified in production, or that was reconfigured without change control, or that drifted from its validated state through unmanaged software updates, fails this requirement.[72, 73]

REGULATORY SOURCE: Clinical System Validation Obligations
21 CFR Part 11, Sections 11.10(a) and 11.10(k): validation and audit trail requirements for electronic records systems in FDA-regulated clinical research.
ICH E6(R3), Section 4.3.4 (Validation): explicit requirement that sponsors are responsible for the validation status of all computerized systems used in clinical trials throughout the system lifecycle, using a risk-based approach that considers intended use, data criticality, and potential impact on participant safety and trial reliability.
EMA Guideline on Computerised Systems and Electronic Data in Clinical Trials (EMA/INS/GCP/112288/2023), Annex 2: comprehensive validation framework for EU-conducted clinical trials, including user requirements, traceability of requirements, periodic review, and change control obligations.
EU GMP Guide Annex 11 (2011; draft revision 2024): validation obligations for computerized systems used in EU-regulated activities; applies to clinical data management systems through the GMP/GCP cross-reference structure.
ICH E6(R3), Section 4.3.4: systems must be validated prior to use; subsequent changes require risk-based validation considering prior and new data; standard functionality, protocol-specific configurations, and system interfaces must all be validated; validation documentation must be maintained and retained.
FDA Guidance: Computerized Systems Used in Clinical Investigations (May 2007): recommends SOP-driven validation and functionality testing; requires validation of changes exceeding established operational limits or design specifications; and sets audit trail, access control, and source documentation retention requirements for systems generating electronic source data.

REGULATORY SOURCE: Clinical System Validation Obligations

PIC/S PI 041-1 (2021): supplier qualification includes assessment of quality management system, change control procedures, and data integrity controls -- not only product documentation.

ALCOA+ Properties Protected: Attributable, Accurate, Enduring -- validation ensures the system reliably attributes data to its originator, accurately captures what was entered, and preserves records in their original state.

The CSA Shift: From Prescriptive to Risk-Based

For most of the period following Part 11's 1997 implementation, computer system validation in regulated industries was heavily influenced by two differing approaches. The first was the FDA Guidance General Principles of Software Validation (1997) offering a pragmatic approach to computerized system validation, and a prescriptive approach derived from the GAMP (Good Automated Manufacturing Practice) guidelines. Both stated requirements to write requirements, write test scripts against each requirement, execute every test, document the results, and file the package. These approaches were expensive, slow, and disconnected from how modern software actually works.

FDA's shift toward Computer Software Assurance, described in the final guidance published in 2026, represents a fundamental reorientation. CSA does not ask how extensively you tested. It asks whether you tested the right things. The evaluative question is not coverage of requirements but management of risk. A clinical sponsor applying CSA principles to its eClinical system does not run a test script against every field on every CRF form. It identifies which system functions, if they failed, would create data integrity risk, and concentrates its testing there. A failure in the date-of-birth field on a demographic CRF is a data quality problem. A failure in the audit trail function, or the electronic signature workflow, or the data export interface used to generate analysis datasets, is a data integrity problem. CSA requires that sponsors know the difference and allocate testing effort accordingly.[74]

The EMA's approach to risk-based validation, codified in the 2023 GCP Computerised Systems Guideline (EMA/INS/GCP/112288/2023) Annex 2, reaches a substantially equivalent conclusion through a different doctrinal path. The EMA guideline does not use the CSA terminology, but Annex 2's framework, user requirements specified before testing, risk-based determination of the depth of validation activity, validation of trial-specific configurations in addition to platform validation, and periodic review throughout the operational life, describes the same risk-proportionate approach that CSA advocates. For global programs subject to both FDA and EU oversight, the convergence is practically significant: a single risk-based validation strategy calibrated to GxP-critical functions satisfies both frameworks more fully than a documentation-volume approach satisfies either.

For clinical research professionals, the practical translation of CSA is this: the validation strategy for an eClinical system should be built around the ALCOA+ properties the system is responsible for protecting. Attributability depends on access controls and audit trail function. Contemporaneity depends on system clock integrity and data entry workflow design. Originality depends on the system's ability to prevent unauthorized modification of locked records. Each of these functions carries higher validation risk than the system's ability to render a CRF page correctly in a supported browser. The testing effort should reflect that hierarchy.

Traditional Computer System Validation	Computer Software Assurance (CSA) Approach
Test script coverage of all CRF fields and workflows	Risk-based test coverage focused on data integrity-critical functions
Volume of documentation as proxy for compliance rigor	Fit-for-purpose testing with documented risk rationale
Vendor IQ/OQ/PQ packages accepted with minimal sponsor review	Sponsor-side testing of GxP-critical functions regardless of vendor qualification status
Validation report filed; compliance monitoring ad hoc	Validated state management: periodic review, change control, deviation documentation
Validation treated as IT function	Validation governed by data management and quality, with IT as operational support
EU equivalent: GCP IWG Q&A and 2010 reflection paper -- interpretation-dependent	EU equivalent: EMA GCP Computerised Systems Guideline 2023, Annex 2 -- risk-proportionate validation explicitly required; user requirements and traceability matrix mandatory

The European Regulatory Dimension: Annex 2 and the GCP Computerised Systems Guideline

The European regulatory framework for clinical system validation has historically operated through a patchwork of guidance: EU GMP Guide Annex 11, which covers manufacturing computerized systems and has been applied by analogy to clinical research; ICH E6(R2) and its predecessor's implicit validation requirements; and a series of GCP Inspectors Working Group questions and answers that addressed specific scenarios without providing a unified validation framework. The 2023 EMA Guideline on Computerised Systems and Electronic Data in Clinical Trials (EMA/INS/GCP/112288/2023) consolidates and supersedes that patchwork with an operationally detailed validation framework specific to clinical trials. Annex 2 of the guideline is the most comprehensive EU validation standard ever published for clinical computerized systems, and EU GCP inspectors have begun applying it in inspections since its entry into effect in September 2023.

Annex 2: The EU Validation Framework in Detail

Annex 2 of the EMA GCP Computerised Systems Guideline establishes a validation framework organized around eight elements: general principles, user requirements, trial-specific configuration and customization, traceability of requirements, validation and test plans, test execution and reporting, release for production, user helpdesk management, periodic review, and change control. The structure is more granular than the FDA's CSA framework and more explicit about what documentation is required at each stage.[75]

The general principles section (A2.1) states clearly that the responsible party remains ultimately responsible for the validation of all computerized systems used in clinical trials, regardless of whether those systems are developed on request, commercially available, or provided as a service. This formulation has direct implications for SaaS eClinical System Technology vendor systems: the vendor's qualification documentation may satisfy a portion of the validation obligation, but only if the responsible party has assessed the vendor's validation activities through an in-depth systematic examination, typically an audit, confirmed that the vendor's documentation covers the responsible party's specific intended use, and documented that examination in a report. Inspectors have access to that examination report. A sponsor that has accepted vendor documentation without audit, or whose audit report does not address the specific validation activities referenced in the vendor's documentation, has an Annex 2 gap regardless of the quality of the vendor's materials.

User requirements (A2.2) must be documented before validation testing begins and must address the specific functions the system will perform in the clinical trial, not merely the platform's general capabilities. For trial-specific configurations (A2.3), the guideline requires that customizations such as eCRF design, edit checks, and eCOA page configurations be validated as part of the system, not merely tested informally by the clinical team. The traceability requirement (A2.4) requires that every user requirement be traceable to a test case, and that every test case be traceable to a requirement -- a bidirectional traceability matrix that many sponsors operating under CSA thinking have moved away from. In the EU, that matrix remains expected.

The periodic review requirement (A2.9) is the element of Annex 2 most frequently absent from sponsor validation programs designed primarily for FDA compliance. The guideline requires that periodic reviews be conducted to assess whether the system can still be considered to be in a validated state, and specifies a non-exhaustive list of elements to evaluate: changes to hardware and infrastructure, operating system and platform changes, application changes, security procedure changes, backup and restore procedure changes, configuration changes, deviations, performance incidents, security incidents, open and newly identified risks, new regulation, user access reviews, and updates to service provider agreements. Each of these elements must be evaluated individually and in combination. This is a materially more structured periodic review than the majority of sponsors conduct for their eClinical systems, and it applies whether the system is hosted by the sponsor or by a service provider.

Change control under Annex 2 (A2.10) requires that change requests be documented and authorized, include details of the change, include a risk assessment covering data integrity, current functionalities, and regulatory compliance, identify impact on the validated state, and specify testing requirements. For trial-specific configurations, the change request must include details of any protocol amendment that prompted the change. The responsible party must ensure that changes to investigators' CRF and eCOA forms are clearly communicated, with documentation of when changes were implemented. This is not merely a change management best practice. For EU-conducted trials, it is an inspection expectation.

ANNEX 2 IN INSPECTION PRACTICE

EU GCP inspectors applying the 2023 EMA Computerised Systems Guideline have cited Annex 2 deficiencies in three primary categories since the guideline's September 2023 entry into effect. First, vendor qualification gaps: sponsors who accepted vendor validation documentation without demonstrating an in-depth examination of the vendor's quality system and specific validation activities. The guideline requires that if the examination is documented in an audit report, inspectors must be given access to that report. Second, periodic review gaps: sponsors whose validation programs conducted an initial validation but had no documented process for periodic review of the validated state during the system's operational life. Third, trial-specific configuration validation gaps: sponsors who validated the EDC platform but had not separately validated trial-specific configurations including eCRF design, edit checks, and data export specifications for the study in question.

Annex 11 and Its Clinical Application

EU GMP Guide Annex 11, last formally revised in 2011, remains the baseline GMP standard for computerized systems in EU-regulated activities. Its principles are applied to clinical data management systems by EU GCP inspectors through the cross-reference architecture of EU GMP and GCP guidance. The 2024 draft revision of Annex 11, published for consultation, would update the 2011 text to address cloud and SaaS-hosted systems, AI and machine learning, and organizational data governance in ways directly relevant to clinical sponsors.

Under the existing 2011 Annex 11, validation documentation must include change control records and deviation reports; an up-to-date inventory of all relevant systems with their GxP functionality must be maintained; user requirements specifications must be based on documented risk assessment and GxP impact; the regulated user must take reasonable steps to ensure that systems have been developed in accordance with an appropriate quality management system; and validation must include checks that data are not altered during migration between systems or formats. Each of these requirements applies to clinical EDC, eTMF, IRT, and eCOA systems when those systems are used in trials supporting EU marketing authorization applications.

The draft 2025 revision adds provisions that the 2011 text did not address: explicit requirements for cloud and SaaS system governance, including contractual provisions for data accessibility, audit trail retention, and migration support throughout the regulatory retention period; requirements for AI and machine learning system validation, including model change control and explainability; and strengthened vendor qualification requirements that parallel Annex 2's examination standard. For sponsors already compliant with Annex 2's current requirements, the 2025 draft represents an incremental rather than a structural change. For sponsors whose validation programs were designed around the 2011 text without reference to Annex 2 or the EMA GCP guideline, the draft's adoption will require material program updates.

Requirement	FDA (21 CFR Part 11 / CSA)	EU (EMA GCP Guideline 2023 Annex 2)	ICH E6(R3)
Validation approach	Risk-based (CSA 2026); fitness-for-purpose; reduce low-value documentation	Risk-proportionate; user requirements mandatory; traceability matrix required	Risk-based; both basic functionality and trial-specific configurations must be validated
Vendor qualification	Expected; depth not explicitly prescribed in regulation	In-depth systematic examination required; audit report must be available to inspectors	Responsible party ensures qualification documentation is maintained; cannot delegate accountability
Trial-specific configuration validation	Included in sponsor-side GxP-critical testing under CSA	Explicitly required as separate validation activity (Annex 2, A2.3)	Both basic system functionality and protocol-specific configurations must be validated (Section 4.5.5)
Periodic review	Validated state management expected; specific frequency not mandated	Required throughout system lifecycle; 12 specific element categories enumerated (A2.9)	Periodic review of cumulative helpdesk issues required; broader periodic review implied by lifecycle framework

Requirement	FDA (21 CFR Part 11 / CSA)	EU (EMA GCP Guideline 2023 Annex 2)	ICH E6(R3)
Change control	Required; impact assessment for validated state	Documented change request, risk assessment, validated state impact, testing requirements, protocol amendment linkage (A2.10)	Risk-based validation of changes; both previously collected and new data must be considered
Release for production	Production environment testing recommended	Formal release process required; all documentation updated and approved before production (A2.7)	Trial-specific systems implemented only after all approvals received
SaaS/cloud vendor reliance	Permitted; regulatory accountability not transferred	Permitted only after in-depth examination; vendor documentation must cover specific intended use	Responsible party ensures qualification and validation documentation maintained

The PIC/S and MHRA Positions

PIC/S PI 041-1 provides the most operationally detailed supplier qualification standard applicable to clinical computerized systems. The guideline requires that computerized system supplier qualification include assessment of the supplier's quality management system, change control procedures, software development lifecycle practices, and data integrity controls -- not merely review of the product's qualification documentation. The distinction is significant: a supplier whose product documentation appears to be in order but whose internal quality practices are inadequate does not satisfy PI 041-1's qualification standard regardless of what the documentation says. For sponsors qualifying eClinical

Technology vendors, this means that an audit of the vendor's internal processes, not merely a review of their validation packages, is what the standard requires.[76]

The MHRA's GxP Data Integrity Guidance applies the same lifecycle validation expectation to clinical data management systems that it applies to GMP manufacturing systems. Validation is a lifecycle activity requiring validated state management and change control throughout the system's operational life; commissioning a new system without considering its decommissioning is explicitly identified as a governance gap. The MHRA's cross-GxP scope means that clinical sponsors operating primarily under GCP frameworks may not have encountered these expectations in FDA BIMO inspections, where the validated state management framework is less prescriptively detailed. MHRA GCP inspections apply them consistently.[77]

Where Validation Ends and Oversight Begins

The most consequential misconception in clinical system compliance is the belief that a completed validation package constitutes ongoing evidence of system integrity. It does not. Validation establishes that the system met its specifications at a defined point in time. What happens between that point and database lock is governed by validated state management, and validated state management is not a validation activity. It is a quality oversight activity. As this chapter began, validation is a well defined activity, not a voyage of discovery.

Validated state management for a eClinical system requires, at minimum: a change control process that evaluates every software update, configuration change, or infrastructure modification for its impact on the validated state; periodic system reviews that confirm the production environment matches the validated configuration; documented procedures for handling vendor-initiated changes that occur outside the sponsor's change control window; and a deviation process for situations in which the system operates outside its validated parameters. The EMA's Annex 2 makes the periodic review component an explicit, enumerated obligation. FDA's CSA framework treats ongoing oversight as implicit in the lifecycle approach. Both lead to the same operational conclusion: the validation package is the baseline, and maintaining that baseline through the trial's full lifecycle requires continuous active management.

The vendor-initiated change problem is particularly acute for cloud-hosted and SaaS-deployed eClinical systems. A vendor that hosts an eClinical System platform on cloud infrastructure manages its own update and patching schedule, often without the ability to provide sponsors with advance notice of changes that fall below the vendor's significance threshold. Under 21 CFR Part 11, a sponsor is responsible for the validated state of the system it uses, regardless of who controls the infrastructure. Under the EMA's Annex 2, the responsible party must ensure that the vendor's process for validation prior to release for production is evaluated, and that changes are not implemented before the responsible party has validated the new functionality or reviewed and assessed the vendor's documentation. Neither framework permits the sponsor to pass this obligation to the vendor through contract.

COMPLIANT APPROACH	NON-COMPLIANT APPROACH
Sponsor maintains a system configuration log documenting the software version in production at all times. Vendor software updates above a defined risk threshold trigger a sponsor impact assessment before the update is applied to the production environment. Updates below that threshold are applied under a documented blanket change control authorization, with a post-implementation check confirming GxP-critical functions operate as validated. The validation summary report is updated to reflect each assessed change. Under EMA Annex 2, this process is documented and available to inspectors.	Sponsor receives notification of a vendor software update after it has been applied to the production environment. The notification describes the update as "bug fixes and performance improvements." No impact assessment is performed; no entry is made in the validation documentation. At EU GCP inspection, the sponsor cannot produce the examination report of the vendor's validation process required by Annex 2 A2.1, and cannot demonstrate that the production system matched the validated state during the update period.

Risk-Based Validation in Practice: A Framework for Clinical Systems

Risk-based validation is not permission to do less validation. It is a requirement to do validation more thoughtfully. The risk analysis that drives a CSA-compliant validation strategy must be documented, must be defensible, and must reflect an honest assessment of where the system could fail in ways that would compromise data integrity rather than merely inconvenience users. Under the EMA's framework, that risk analysis must be explicit: Annex 2 requires that both validation test plans and the determination of what constitutes trial-specific versus platform-level validation be grounded in documented risk assessments.

For eClinical systems, the risk analysis begins with function categorization. Every system function can be categorized by two dimensions: the consequence of failure (impact on data integrity, patient safety, or regulatory record quality) and the likelihood that standard software development and vendor qualification activities have already addressed that failure mode. Functions with high failure consequence require sponsor-side GxP-critical testing. Functions with low failure consequence, or functions whose failure modes are fully addressed by vendor testing, can be accepted based on vendor documentation with minimal or no sponsor-side testing. The ALCOA+ properties provide the most reliable test: a function is GxP-critical if its failure would compromise any ALCOA+ property for any clinical data record.

System Function	GxP Criticality	Validation Approach
Audit trail generation and retention	Critical	Full sponsor-side testing; verify completeness, immutability, and timestamp accuracy; EU Annex 2 requires traceability matrix entry
Electronic signature workflow and binding	Critical	Sponsor-side testing of signature binding, non-repudiability, and access control enforcement
Data export to analysis datasets (CDISC SDTM/ADaM)	Critical	Validation of data transformation accuracy; reconciliation testing between eClinical data and exported datasets
Access control enforcement (role-based, user-level)	Critical	Sponsor-side verification that role definitions enforce appropriate access; user access review included in Annex 2 periodic review

System Function	GxP Criticality	Validation Approach
Trial-specific configuration (eCRF design, edit checks)	Critical (EU)	EU: separately validated under Annex 2 A2.3; US: included in sponsor-side testing of GxP-critical functions
Query generation and resolution workflow	High	Functional testing of query lifecycle; confirm audit trail capture at each state change
CRF field rendering and data entry validation rules	Medium	Risk-based; test rules for primary endpoint and safety fields; accept vendor documentation for standard fields
User interface layout and navigation	Low	Accept vendor documentation; sponsor-side UAT sufficient
Backup and recovery function	High	Verify backup restores data in original unmodified form; EU Annex 2 periodic review includes backup procedures
System performance under load	Low (data integrity)	Accept vendor documentation; sponsor-side testing not required under CSA or Annex 2 risk-proportionate approach

The Vendor Qualification Problem

Most sponsors rely substantially on their eClinical System vendor's own quality system and validation documentation to satisfy a portion of their validation obligations. The logic is defensible: a vendor whose software has been validated and released through a mature software development lifecycle has already addressed failure modes that a sponsor-side test would only confirm. The CSA framework and Annex 2 both explicitly endorse this logic. They also both specify the condition under which vendor reliance is permissible: the sponsor must have assessed the vendor's validation activities and confirmed that the documentation covers the sponsor's specific intended use. That condition is where sponsors most consistently create compliance risk.

Vendor qualification under the EMA's Annex 2 is operationally specific in a way that FDA's framework is not. Annex 2 A2.1 requires that the responsible party be thoroughly familiar with the vendor's quality system and validation activities, which can usually be obtained through an in-depth systematic examination. This examination must be performed by qualified staff, must go sufficiently deep into actual activities, must review a suitable number of relevant key requirements and corresponding test cases, and must be documented in an examination report. If that examination is documented in an audit report, inspectors must be given access to the report. A sponsor whose vendor qualification consists of reviewing the vendor's standard qualification package without an in-depth examination of the underlying activities does not satisfy Annex 2's requirement, regardless of how comprehensive the vendor's documentation appears.

The shared responsibility model common to SaaS-deployed eClinical systems makes vendor qualification more complicated, not less necessary. In a typical SaaS deployment, the vendor operates the infrastructure, manages the application layer, and handles software updates. The sponsor may configure the system, or contract with eClinical system vendor, for its specific trial protocol, manages user access, and operates the clinical data management workflow. Both layers carry data integrity obligations. A validation strategy that addresses only the vendor's layer, or only the sponsor's layer, is incomplete under any regulatory framework.

VENDOR QUALIFICATION: REGULATORY EXPECTATIONS COMPARED
ICH E6(R3) Section 3.6.6: Sponsor cannot transfer regulatory responsibility through contracts. The ultimate responsibility for trial-related activities, including reliability of trial data, resides with the sponsor regardless of what has been delegated to a service provider. Vendor qualification must include verification, not merely contractual assurance.
21 CFR Part 11 Section 11.10(k): Persons using open systems must employ procedures designed to ensure authenticity, integrity, and confidentiality of electronic records -- regardless of vendor architecture.
FDA Guidance: Electronic Source Data in Clinical Investigations (September 2013, updated 2019): Source data must meet ALCOA requirements and satisfy regulatory recordkeeping obligations regardless of whether it is generated by sponsor-operated or

third-party systems. Sponsor and investigator responsibility for data quality is not diminished by use of vendor-operated electronic systems.
EMA GCP Computerised Systems Guideline (2023), Annex 2 A2.1: In-depth systematic examination of vendor quality system and validation activities required; examination report must be available to inspectors; vendor documentation accepted only if it covers the responsible party's specific intended use.
EU GMP Guide Annex 11 (2011), Section 4.5: Regulated user must take all reasonable steps to ensure the system has been developed in accordance with an appropriate quality management system; supplier assessed appropriately.
PIC/S PI 041-1 (2021): Supplier qualification includes assessment of supplier QMS, change control procedures, and data integrity controls -- not only product documentation.
MHRA Data Integrity Guidance (2018): Outsourcing data management does not diminish the regulated organization's data integrity responsibility. Third-party controls must be verified through audit and qualification.

Validation Lifecycle Management: From First Use to Decommission

A validation package that covers only the period from installation to first use addresses approximately ten percent of the system's compliance lifecycle. The remaining ninety percent is governed by what the industry has come to call the validated state: the ongoing confirmation that the system continues to perform as originally validated across every change, update, migration, and operational event that occurs between deployment and decommission.

The validated state has four principal threats in clinical research environments: uncontrolled software updates applied by the vendor, configuration drift resulting from operational changes made outside the formal change control process, data migration errors when records are transferred between platforms, and end-of-life risks when the system is decommissioned and clinical records must be preserved for the full regulatory retention period. The EMA's Annex 2 periodic review framework (A2.9) addresses all four by requiring periodic evaluation of changes to hardware, operating system, application, security procedures, backup and restore tools, configurations, deviations, performance incidents, security incidents, open risks, new regulation, user accesses, and service provider agreements. A sponsor implementing this framework consistently is also satisfying the validated state management expectations of FDA's CSA approach, because the substantive requirements converge even where the regulatory language differs.[78]

The decommission risk deserves particular attention because it is the point at which most sponsors discover that their validation strategy never addressed it. An eClinical system decommissioned at study closeout may hold audit trail data, query records, user access logs, and electronic signatures that constitute the forensic record of the trial's data management history. The EMA's Annex 2 requires that documentation relating to the validation of previous or discontinued system versions used in a clinical trial be retained; the GCP Computerised Systems Guideline Section 6.12 requires that database decommissioning be planned and managed with specific attention to record preservation, data migration, and audit trail accessibility. A validation strategy that does not address the retirement phase is an incomplete strategy under both U.S. and EU standards.

Automated Monitoring: The Next Tier of Validation Oversight

FDA's stated vision for the evolution of computerized system oversight in clinical research is one in which organizations implement automated monitoring tools that flag anomalies in real time: audit logs disabled unexpectedly, critical data fields modified outside query workflow, access control configurations changed without corresponding change control documentation. This vision describes what well-designed clinical data oversight programs do today, and it describes what inspectors are increasingly expecting to find when they review sponsor data management operations.[79]

Automated monitoring of system behavior is the logical extension of the validated state management framework. A validation package establishes what the system should do. Automated monitoring detects when it deviates. The two together constitute a closed-loop system: the initial testing establishes the baseline, and ongoing monitoring provides continuous evidence that the baseline is being maintained. Under the EMA's Annex 2 periodic review framework, automated monitoring outputs are directly relevant to the periodic review assessment: performance incidents, security incidents, and deviation patterns identified through monitoring are among the elements that must be evaluated in each periodic review. An organization with a functioning automated monitoring program therefore has the raw material for a substantially more efficient and defensible periodic review than one relying solely on manual checks.

The regulatory significance of automated monitoring extends beyond its operational utility. An organization that can demonstrate to an inspector that its eClinical system audit trail is reviewed systematically, that anomaly detection criteria are predefined, that flagged issues are investigated through a documented escalation pathway, and that the monitoring program itself is covered by a validated process is demonstrating something that a validation package alone cannot demonstrate: that the organization treats data integrity as an operational discipline rather than a compliance artifact.

Monitoring Signal	Data Integrity Risk Addressed	ALCOA+ Property
Audit trail continuity gaps (periods with no log entries during active data management)	Potential audit trail suppression or system interruption not captured in incident logs	Attributable, Contemporaneous
Query resolution patterns: same change reason applied to large numbers of edits in short windows	Systematic application of generic change reasons masking actual basis for data modification	Attributable, Accurate
Off-hours access patterns: significant data activity outside normal trial operating windows	Potential unauthorized access or data manipulation outside normal oversight environment	Attributable
Primary endpoint field modification after monitor visit completion	Retrospective data modification that may not have been subject to monitoring review	Contemporaneous, Accurate
Electronic signature events for records subsequently modified	Integrity of the signed record; modifications after signature require documentation and re-signature	Attributable, Original

Monitoring Signal	Data Integrity Risk Addressed	ALCOA+ Property
Configuration change events not preceded by change control documentation	Uncontrolled system changes that may have altered the validated state without assessment	Consistent, Enduring
Data export events outside the documented data management workflow	Unauthorized data extraction; risk of records modified outside the controlled eClinical environment	Original, Attributable
User account activity for accounts that should be inactive (departed staff, closed sites)	Potential unauthorized access via unrevoked credentials; access control failure	Attributable

Building the Monitoring Program: From Signal to Escalation

Automated monitoring produces value only when it is connected to a defined escalation pathway. A dashboard that flags anomalies that no one investigates is not a monitoring program. It is documentation that the organization knew about problems it chose not to address, which in regulatory terms is considerably worse than having no monitoring program at all. The escalation pathway is the structure that converts monitoring signals into defensible compliance evidence.

A functional escalation pathway for eClinical audit trail monitoring has four components: defined signal criteria that specify which patterns trigger review and at what threshold; a documented investigation process requiring clinical operations and data management functions to assess each signal; a resolution requirement specifying how each investigated signal is documented, remediated if warranted, and closed; and a periodic aggregate review that considers patterns across signals that individually fell below the investigation threshold but collectively warrant attention. The periodic aggregate review is the component most frequently missing. Individual audit trail anomalies are often explicable in isolation; viewed alongside complementary signals, they become a different kind of finding.

ICH E6(R3)'s quality management system framework explicitly supports this approach. Section 3.10.1.3 of E6(R3) requires that sponsors set pre-specified acceptable ranges, including quality tolerance limits at the trial level, where relevant to critical-to-quality factors, and evaluate deviations beyond those ranges throughout the trial's operational life. Audit trail anomaly rates, change reason specificity, and data modification patterns are legitimate quality metrics within that framework: each is mappable to a critical-to-quality factor in the data management process, and each is the kind of operational signal the QTL mechanism was designed to surface. A sponsor that has defined quality tolerance limits for its data management operations and monitors against them is doing precisely what E6(R3) requires. The EMA's Annex 2 periodic review aligns with this expectation: performance incidents and security incidents are among the twelve categories A2.9 requires periodic evaluation to address, making the cumulative output of the monitoring program a required component of the periodic review assessment.

Specific System Categories and Their Validation Implications

Clinical trials operate across a portfolio of interconnected computerized systems, each carrying its own validation obligations and characteristic failure modes. The validation strategy for a clinical program is not a single validation effort applied to a single system. It is a set of system-specific validation approaches coordinated by a unified data governance framework. The governance framework is what ensures that validated data from multiple systems can be integrated into a trustworthy clinical dataset.

Electronic Data Capture Systems

EDC systems are the primary locus of clinical data integrity obligation and the primary focus of BIMO and EU GCP inspection attention. The validation considerations specific to EDC systems include the audit trail architecture (field-level versus form-level; what is captured and what is not), the electronic signature binding (what data is signed and whether the signed state is preserved if underlying data is subsequently modified), the query lifecycle (whether query issuance, response, and resolution are audit-trailed with the same completeness as data entry), and the data export pathway (whether the data exported to analysis datasets is verifiable against the EDC source).

Under the EMA's framework, trial-specific EDC configurations require validation as a separate activity from platform qualification. An eCRF built on a validated EDC platform is not itself validated merely because the platform is qualified. The edit checks defined for the protocol's primary endpoint data fields, the electronic signature workflow for source document attestation, and the data export specification connecting the EDC to the analysis dataset are trial-specific configurations that require their own user requirements, test plans, and test execution under Annex 2 A2.3. For sponsors managing multi-regional trials, this obligation sits alongside FDA's parallel expectation under CSA that sponsor-side testing address the study-specific configuration rather than relying exclusively on the vendor's platform qualification.

Electronic Trial Master File Systems

eTMF systems carry validation obligations that differ from EDC in one critical respect: the eTMF is a document management system, not a data collection system, and its primary data integrity obligation is preservation rather than capture. The ALCOA+ properties most directly at risk are Enduring and Available. Validation of an eTMF system concentrates on document retention and retrieval: confirmation that documents cannot be modified after upload without creating an audit trail entry, that version control preserves prior versions, that the access control model prevents unauthorized deletion, and that the export and archive functions will produce a complete, searchable eTMF readable without the eTMF platform being operational.

The EU CTR 536/2014 twenty-five-year retention requirement for trial master file records creates an end-of-life validation obligation of unusual length. An eTMF selected today for a trial beginning now must be capable of preserving records in an accessible, vendor-independent format for a period that extends well beyond any current eTMF vendor's operational history. Validation of the eTMF's end-of-life functionality, including format durability, migration pathways, and audit trail accessibility independent of the vendor's continued operation, is as important as validation of its operational functionality, and it is the validation deliverable sponsors most consistently fail to plan at the time of system selection.

Interactive Response Technology and Randomization Systems

IRT systems occupy a category of particular sensitivity because their primary function, randomization and drug supply management, is connected directly to the clinical integrity of the trial. An IRT system that assigns subjects to treatment groups incorrectly, or that manages drug supply in a way that allows unblinding, creates an integrity problem that cannot be corrected after the fact. The validation of IRT systems requires specific attention to the randomization algorithm's implementation, the blinding maintenance architecture, and the audit trail for every assignment event.

Sponsor-side testing of the study-specific IRT configuration is a validation obligation that cannot be delegated to the vendor. The vendor's platform qualification package addresses platform-level failure modes. The sponsor's study-specific randomization scheme, stratification factors, and supply management logic are sponsor-configured parameters that the platform's generic validation package would not have tested. The EMA's Annex 2 A2.3 makes this obligation explicit for trial-specific configurations generally; for IRT systems, where configuration errors directly affect randomization integrity, the obligation is among the most consequential in the clinical validation portfolio.

External Data Systems and Integration Validation

Central laboratory data, eCOA and ePRO data, wearable device data, and electronic health record extracts represent a category of external electronic source data with distinct validation challenges. These systems are not operated by the sponsor, but the data they generate flows into the clinical database and ultimately into the submission dataset. The integrity of that data pathway, from external system capture through transfer, ingestion, and integration, is a validation obligation that the sponsor cannot outsource.

The EMA's GCP Computerised Systems Guideline Section 6.1.2 addresses data transfer explicitly: transfers between systems must be validated, including the transfer of metadata, and the receiving system must confirm that the transferred data is complete and matches the source. This is a more operationally specific transfer validation requirement than FDA's framework provides, and EU GCP inspectors have cited deficiencies in transfer validation as standalone findings. ICH E6(R3) Section 4.2.5 establishes the same foundational obligation: validated processes, or other appropriate processes such as reconciliation, must be in place to ensure that electronic data including relevant metadata retains its integrity when transferred between computerized systems, and the transfer process must be documented to ensure traceability. Section 2.12.2 requires that source data be verifiable regardless of where it originates, which means the sponsor must maintain access to originating system records, not merely transferred values in the EDC. For external data integrations, that verification requires a validated transfer pathway with documented reconciliation at each stage.

Practical Implementation: Building Validation Without Bureaucratic Waste

The tension between regulatory rigor and operational efficiency in computer system validation is real, and it is not resolved by choosing one over the other. Organizations that prioritize rigor without efficiency produce validation programs that consume resources disproportionate to their risk management value. Organizations that prioritize efficiency without rigor produce validation packages that satisfy the form of the requirement while leaving the failure modes that cause inspection findings unaddressed. The solution is a validation strategy calibrated to risk and designed to satisfy the applicable regulatory framework from the outset.

Define the validation approach before the validation plan. The validation plan is a document describing how the validation will be executed. The validation approach is a strategic decision about what will and will not be tested, and why. A solid validation approach for a clinical system must address how user requirements will be specified, how traceability will be maintained between requirements and test cases, and how trial-specific configurations will be validated separately from the vendor's platform. It must also document the risk categorization of system functions, which determines the depth of testing required for each component. Getting these decisions on paper before the validation plan is written prevents the common failure mode of a technically complete validation package that addressed the wrong things.

Validate the configuration, not just the platform. For commercially available eClinical systems, the vendor's platform qualification addresses platform-level failure modes. The sponsor's validation obligation is the study-specific configuration: eCRF design decisions, validation rules applied to specific fields, user role definitions, electronic signature workflows, data export specifications. These are where study-specific errors occur, and they are what both FDA and EU GCP inspectors examine. A sponsor who presents a vendor's qualification package in response to an inspection question about its own configuration has not answered the question.

Execute testing in the production environment, or document precisely why you did not. Testing conducted exclusively in a development instance and then deployed to production without equivalent verification leaves open whether the production environment matched the test environment. The cost of a production smoke test confirming that critical functions perform as validated is low. The cost of an inspection finding that the tested environment and the operational environment were never formally reconciled is not.

Treat change control as a validation activity. Every change to a validated clinical system is, in principle, a partial revalidation. Organizations that manage change control as an administrative approval process rather than a technical assessment frequently discover that accumulated changes have altered the validated state in ways not captured in documentation. Each change control record should contain a risk assessment covering data integrity impact, current functionality impact, and regulatory compliance impact. That standard is more demanding than what most sponsors apply in practice, and the gap between what change control records say and what was actually done is a recurring finding in both FDA BIMO and EU GCP inspections.

Build the retirement plan into the validation strategy. The question of what happens to the records in a clinical system when it is retired is not a question for the future. It is a design decision that affects system selection, configuration, and validation from the start. An organization that has never asked how its eClinical sytem audit trail data will be archived in a vendor-independent format is an organization that will face that question under time pressure, typically at database lock or system migration, when the leverage to extract favorable contractual terms from the vendor is gone. The retirement plan is not a convenience. Under any framework requiring multi-year post-trial record retention, it is a compliance obligation with a defined duration that begins at system decommission.

CHAPTER SEVEN - KEY TAKEAWAYS
Validation establishes that a computerized system met its specifications at a defined point in time; validated state management is the separate, ongoing obligation to confirm that it continues to do so across every change, update, and operational event that follows.
The EMA GCP Computerised Systems Guideline (EMA/INS/GCP/112288/2023) Annex 2 establishes the most operationally detailed validation framework for clinical computerized systems published to date, requiring user requirements documentation, bidirectional traceability matrices, trial-specific configuration validation, structured periodic review of twelve enumerated elements, and formal change control with risk assessment. For sponsors conducting trials in EU member states or seeking EMA review of their submissions, Annex 2 is the operative standard against which GCP inspectors will assess the validation program.
A risk-based validation strategy calibrated to GxP-critical functions satisfies Annex 2 more fully than a documentation-volume approach. Annex 2 explicitly endorses risk-proportionate validation: the depth of testing required is determined by the criticality of the function to participant safety and data reliability, not by the volume of documentation produced. Sponsors who treat validation as a paperwork exercise rather than a risk management activity tend to produce packages that are voluminous but incomplete where completeness matters, and that do not survive structured EU GCP inspection.
Vendor qualification under the EMA GCP Guideline requires an in-depth systematic examination of the vendor's quality system and specific validation activities. The examination must be performed by qualified staff, must go sufficiently deep into actual activities, must review a suitable number of relevant key requirements and corresponding test cases, and must be documented in an examination report that inspectors can access. Accepting vendor documentation without conducting that examination is a deficiency under the EMA GCP Guideline regardless of the documentation's apparent quality. For sponsors qualifying eClinical technology vendors, this means that a desk review of the vendor's standard qualification package does not satisfy the requirement; an audit of the vendor's actual processes does.
In SaaS and cloud-hosted deployments, shared infrastructure responsibility does not reduce sponsor regulatory accountability under the EMA GCP Guideline. The guideline explicitly requires that new vendor functionalities not be used in a clinical trial context until the sponsor has either validated those functionalities or assessed the vendor's own validation documentation covering them. That obligation applies to vendor-initiated updates, which in a SaaS environment the sponsor does not control

CHAPTER SEVEN - KEY TAKEAWAYS
and may not be notified of in advance. A sponsor whose vendor qualification and change control program does not address automatic vendor updates has a structural gap that EU GCP inspectors have cited as a standalone finding.
Trial-specific configurations, including eCRF design, edit checks, and data export specifications, must be validated as a separate activity from platform qualification. The EMA GCP Guideline requires this explicitly: platform-level vendor qualification and trial-specific configuration validation are distinct obligations, and satisfying one does not satisfy the other. FDA's risk-based approach under its Computer Software Assurance framework reaches the same practical conclusion, treating GxP-critical trial-specific functions as requiring their own testing regardless of the vendor's qualification status.
Computer Software Assurance and EU risk-proportionate validation both direct testing effort toward GxP-critical functions defined by their potential to compromise ALCOA+ properties; the ALCOA+ framework is the practical tool for making this determination.
Automated monitoring of audit trail behavior, user access patterns, and configuration integrity converts the validated state from a static document into a dynamic assurance; under Annex 2, monitoring outputs feed directly into the required periodic review assessment.
External data integrations, including central laboratory, eCOA, and wearable device data, carry sponsor-side validation obligations for the transformation and transfer pathway; the EMA GCP guideline Section 6.1.2 requires transfer validation including metadata, which exceeds what FDA's framework explicitly prescribes.
The decommission plan is a validation deliverable, not an afterthought; under EU CTR's twenty-five-year retention standard, the retirement planning obligation is among the most consequential validation decisions a sponsor makes at the time of system selection.
An organization whose monitoring program detects anomalies it does not investigate has documented knowledge of potential integrity issues it chose not to address; in regulatory terms, that is a more serious compliance problem than having no monitoring program.
The February 2026 EMA/PIC/S joint consultation on clinical data integrity harmonization is expected to produce additional convergence on validation requirements for digital trial environments, AI-assisted data management systems, and multi-party data supply chains.

CHAPTER EIGHT

Audit Trails: The Heartbeat of a Compliant System

> *An audit trail that has been disabled, filtered, or never reviewed is not a control, it is a liability. Every regulatory framework governing clinical trial data requires audit trails that are always on, tamper-evident, and subject to periodic human review.*

The query that started everything was unremarkable. A sponsor data management team reviewing edit history for a mid-stage oncology trial noticed that a site's primary endpoint entries showed an unusual pattern: the initial values, recorded close to the visit dates, had been revised in clusters, with multiple fields updated within the same narrow time window weeks after the corresponding clinic visits. Each revision carried a change reason. The change reasons were identical across all fields in each cluster: "Data entry error." No further specification. The time stamps showed the revisions had been entered late in the evening, after normal site hours. Three of the revisions crossed the threshold that distinguished protocol-defined responders from non-responders.

The data management team escalated the finding. The clinical monitor re-reviewed the site's source documents. The source documents, handwritten worksheets maintained at the site, matched the revised EDC values, not the original entries. Whoever had made the revisions had also updated the paper records to match. The original entries, visible only in the EDC audit trail, had no corresponding paper documentation. The audit trail was the only record of what had been entered first.

The sponsor reported the finding to FDA. An FDA investigator arrived at the site within six weeks. The investigation confirmed systematic retrospective data manipulation at a single site affecting primary endpoint data for fourteen subjects. The site was removed from the trial. The affected subjects' data was excluded from the efficacy analysis. The trial timeline shifted by eight months. The total cost of the investigation, data remediation, regulatory response, and timeline delay ran into eight figures. The investigation was possible because the audit trail was complete, intact, and had been reviewed by someone who knew what an anomalous pattern looked like.

Consider what would have happened if the audit trail review had not occurred. The manipulated data would have entered the statistical analysis, influencing an efficacy result that would have been submitted to FDA as a representation of a treatment's actual performance in patients. The paper records matched. The query rates were unremarkable. The site had passed two on-site monitoring visits without the manipulation being detected. Without the audit trail, there was nothing to detect.

> *The audit trail does not merely record what happened to the data. In a clinical trial, it is frequently the only reliable evidence of what actually happened at all*

The Regulatory Mandate

Audit trail requirements for clinical data systems are not a recent invention. The obligation to maintain a secure, tamper-evident record of who did what to a regulated record, and when, has been embedded in the electronic records framework since 21 CFR Part 11 took effect in 1997. What has changed is the breadth of the requirement, the sophistication of regulatory expectations for how audit trails are reviewed, and the consistency with which audit trail failures appear in enforcement outcomes.

21 CFR Part 11 requires that audit trails for electronic records used in lieu of FDA-required paper records be computer-generated, time-stamped, and sequenced. They must capture operator actions, including creation, modification, and deletion. They must be protected from alteration by the individual whose actions they record. They must be retained for a period at least as long as the record itself. These requirements apply to every eClinical system used in clinical investigations subject to FDA jurisdiction.[80]

ICH E6(R3), adopted as the binding international GCP standard on January 6, 2025, addressed audit trails with greater specificity than any of its predecessors. Section 2.12.2 requires that changes to source records be traceable, not obscure the original entry, and be explained where necessary through an audit trail. Section 4.2.4 requires that data corrections be attributed to the person or computerized system making the correction, justified, and supported by source records around the time of original entry. Section 4.2.2 establishes the metadata framework, including audit trails, within which these obligations are operationalized. Taken together, these provisions require that any change to clinical data be documented in a manner that allows identification of the original value, the revised value, the date of revision, and the identity of the individual who made the change, with the rationale for the change captured. E6(R3) does not frame these as technical system specifications. It frames them as sponsor and investigator obligations. The distinction matters because it means a system that technically supports audit trail generation does not satisfy E6(R3) if the organization has not configured it to capture the required information, or has configured it in a way that permits gaps.[81]

Audit Trail Regulatory Sources -- Clinical Trial Context
21 CFR Part 11, Section 11.10(e): Audit trails -- computer-generated, date/time-stamped, secure, operator-action records.
21 CFR Part 11, Section 11.10(k): Operational controls to protect audit trails from alteration.
ICH E6(R3), Sections 2.12.2 and 4.2.4: Changes to source records must be traceable and must not obscure the original entry; data corrections must be attributed to the person or computerized system making the change, justified, and supported by source records. Section 4.2.2 establishes the metadata and audit trail framework within which these obligations are operationalized.
ICH E6(R3), Section 2.12.2: Investigator responsibility to ensure changes to source data are traceable, do not obscure the original entry, and are explained where necessary via an audit trail.
EMA Guideline on Computerised Systems and Electronic Data in Clinical Trials (EMA/INS/GCP/112288/2023), Section 6.2: Audit trail must be enabled for all electronic data creation and modification; field-level capture required; not deactivatable by normal users; proactive and ongoing review expected.
FDA Guidance: Electronic Source Data in Clinical Investigations (September 2013, updated 2019): Source data must be attributable, legible, contemporaneous, original,

Audit Trail Regulatory Sources -- Clinical Trial Context
and accurate; electronic systems used to capture source data must maintain audit trails sufficient to reconstruct the history of data entries and changes.
MHRA GxP Data Integrity Guidance (2018), Section 6.13: Audit trail review as a routine quality activity, not an inspection-triggered event; exception reporting and risk-based review approaches described.
PIC/S PI 041-1 (2021): Audit trails must capture all data changes with rationale; review frequency proportionate to risk.
EU GMP Guide Annex 11 (2011/2024 draft): Always-on requirement; MFA for electronic signature-level access events (draft); audit trail configuration changes subject to change control.
WHO TRS 996 Annex 5 (2016): Audit trail retention commensurate with record retention period; evidence of review maintained.

The European Regulatory Dimension: Section 6.2 and the GCP Inspectors' Framework

The European regulatory framework for audit trails in clinical trials is more operationally specific than its U.S. counterpart, and has become more so since the EMA's 2023 GCP Computerised Systems Guideline (EMA/INS/GCP/112288/2023) entered into effect in September 2023. Before that guideline, EU GCP inspectors applied audit trail requirements through a patchwork of instruments: EU GMP Guide Annex 11, applied by analogy to clinical systems through the GMP/GCP cross-reference structure; ICH E6's implicit data integrity obligations; and GCP Inspectors Working Group questions and answers that addressed specific scenarios without providing a unified framework. From 2010, the EMA's Reflection Paper on expectations for electronic source data and data transcribed to electronic data collection tools in clinical trials (EMA/INS/GCP/454280/2010) provided partial guidance, but it addressed electronic source data capture rather than audit trail requirements specifically, and its interpretation-dependent character meant that inspection findings under it were inconsistent across EU national competent authorities. The 2023 guideline replaced that patchwork with a single operationally detailed instrument. Section 6.2, dedicated entirely to audit trails and audit trail review, establishes requirements that go beyond what 21 CFR Part 11 explicitly prescribes and provides the operational basis for EU GCP inspection findings in ways that the prior reflection paper did not.

What Section 6.2 Requires

Section 6.2.1 of the EMA guideline states that an audit trail should be enabled for the original creation and subsequent modification of all electronic data. This is a broader formulation than Part 11's focus on records used in lieu of paper: the EU standard applies to the creation event, not only to modifications, and applies to all electronic data in the clinical trial context. The guideline specifies that audit trail entries must be protected against change, deletion, and access modification, including modifications to edit rights and visibility rights. The audit trail must be stored within the system itself, not in a separate system or log that could be managed independently.

The field-level versus form-level distinction is explicit in Section 6.2.1: audit trails should capture changes at the data entry field level, not at the CRF page level. This is a significant operational specificity. A system that captures page-level audit trails shows that a page was modified but does not show which field changed, from what value to what value. The EMA's requirement eliminates any ambiguity: field-level capture is the standard. Sponsors whose eClinical systems are configured for page-level or form-level audit trails may be compliant with the technical minimum of Part 11 but are out of step with the EU standard that inspectors are now applying.

The always-on formulation in Section 6.2.1 is precise: it should not be possible for "normal" users to deactivate the audit trail. The guideline adds an important qualification: if it is possible for administrator users to deactivate the audit trail, this should automatically create an entry in a log file. This means that a system in which administrators can disable audit trail generation is not per se non-compliant, provided the disabling action is itself logged and therefore auditable. But a system in which a standard user, or an administrator without automatic logging of the action, can disable the audit trail is non-compliant by design. The design of the access control model is the control, not the procedural restriction on when deactivation is permitted.

Section 6.2.2: Proactive and Ongoing Review

Section 6.2.2 addresses audit trail review with equal specificity. Procedures for risk-based, trial-specific audit trail reviews must be in place, and performance of data review should be generally documented. The guideline states explicitly that data review should be proactive and that ongoing review is expected unless justified otherwise. Manual review and technology-assisted review of larger datasets should both be considered. This is a materially different standard from a review program that is triggered by inspection notification or conducted only at database lock. The EU standard requires ongoing, prospective review as the default, with any departure from that standard requiring documented justification.[82]

The blinding implication in Section 6.2.1 is also operationally significant for the EU context: care should be taken to ensure that information jeopardizing the blinding does not appear in the audit trail accessible to blinded users. This is a system design requirement, not a procedural one. eClinical systems deployed in blinded clinical trials must be configured so that the audit trail accessible to blinded users does not reveal treatment assignment information. For sponsors using cloud-hosted eClinical systems with standard configurations, verifying that blinded audit trail access does not inadvertently reveal unblinded information is a configuration verification step that must be documented in the validation record.

The EU sign-off requirements under Section 6.3 add a dimension that directly interacts with audit trail obligations. The guideline requires investigator endorsement of data at predetermined milestones, with signing of batches of workbooks explicitly identified as not suited to ensure high data quality. This means that the audit trail review program must be aligned with the investigator sign-off milestones: data must be reviewed, and anomalies addressed, before the investigator signs it off. A data review program that operates independently of the sign-off schedule creates a risk that signed-off data contains unresolved audit trail anomalies that were not visible to the investigator at the time of signature.

Requirement	EU (EMA GCP Guideline 2023, Sec. 6.2)	FDA (21 CFR Part 11)	ICH E6(R3)
Audit trail scope	All electronic data creation and modification; field-level, not page-level	Electronic records used in lieu of paper; operator actions	All changes to source data; original value, new value, date, identity, reason
Always-on requirement	Not deactivatable by normal users; admin deactivation must be automatically logged	Protected from alteration by operator; but silent on deactivation logging	Implied by data change documentation obligation; not explicit on deactivation

Requirement	EU (EMA GCP Guideline 2023, Sec. 6.2)	FDA (21 CFR Part 11)	ICH E6(R3)
Field vs. page level	Field-level explicitly required (Section 6.2.1)	Not explicitly specified at field level	Field-level implied by per-change documentation requirement
Review frequency	Proactive and ongoing expected; departures require justification (Section 6.2.2)	Review expected; frequency not explicitly mandated	Ongoing review implied by QMS framework; QTLs must be defined and monitored
Review documentation	Performance of review should generally be documented	Not explicitly required; implied by Part 11 system controls	Monitoring program documentation required; audit trail review included
Technology-assisted review	Manual and technology-assisted review should both be considered	Not specifically addressed	Central statistical monitoring endorsed; automated tools consistent with QMS
Blinding protection	Audit trail must not expose unblinded data to blinded users (design requirement)	Not addressed	Blinding preservation required; audit trail access implicated
Investigator sign-off alignment	Data must be signed off at defined milestones; batch sign-off of workbooks not adequate (Section 6.3)	Not directly addressed	Investigator accountability for source data accuracy

The EU Inspection Approach: How GCP Inspectors Use Audit Trails

EU GCP inspections differ structurally from FDA BIMO inspections in ways that affect how audit trail evidence is evaluated. EMA-coordinated inspections, conducted by national competent authorities, are focused on GCP systems and processes and grade each finding as a critical, major, or minor non-compliance, citing the specific ICH E6 provision violated. This grading system means that an audit trail configuration deficiency that prevents field-level capture is not merely a practice gap; it is a citable non-compliance with a defined severity level. The FDA-MHRA joint paper on data integrity in global clinical trials documented this distinction: FDA inspections take an outcome-focused approach examining data line listings, while EMA inspections assess compliance with GCP systems and processes against E6 requirements.

The practical implication is that EU GCP inspections examine audit trail programs at a structural level before examining specific data anomalies. Inspectors will request the system's audit trail configuration documentation, the procedures governing audit trail review, and records demonstrating that reviews were conducted. A sponsor who can produce complete audit trail data but cannot produce review records, or whose review procedures are not documented and calibrated to risk, has a procedural finding independent of whether the audit trail data itself reveals any concerns. The EU inspection approach is as much a quality systems inspection as a data verification inspection.

The MHRA's GxP Data Integrity Guidance adds its cross-GxP force to the EU framework for UK trials. MHRA's Section 6.13 states that where computerized systems are used to capture, process, report, store, or archive raw data electronically, system design should always provide for the retention of audit trails to show all changes to data. System administrators who amend or switch off the audit trail must leave a record of that action. Routine data review must include a documented audit trail review where risk assessment determines it to be required. An exception reporting process, a validated search tool that identifies predetermined abnormal data or actions, is explicitly identified as an appropriate audit trail review method. The MHRA formulation of exception reporting as a validated tool is more specific than FDA's parallel expectation, and it establishes that the exception reporting system itself requires validation before it can satisfy the review obligation.[83]

EU INSPECTION FINDING CLASSIFICATIONS FOR AUDIT TRAIL DEFICIENCIES

EU GCP inspectors classify audit trail deficiencies using a three-tier finding system: critical, major, and minor. A critical finding indicates a deficiency that directly affects the rights, safety, or wellbeing of subjects or the quality and reliability of data -- it may result in rejection of the trial data for marketing authorization purposes. A major finding indicates a deficiency that could have a significant impact on subject protection or data reliability -- it requires corrective action before the deficiency recurs. A minor finding indicates a deficiency that is unlikely to have a significant impact but should be corrected. Audit trail deactivation by operational users, systematic absence of change reasons, and the absence of documented ongoing review procedures have all been classified as major findings by EU national competent authorities in GCP inspections since the 2023 guideline entered into effect. Audit trail configuration that does not capture field-level changes has been classified as a critical finding where it affected primary endpoint data.

What an Audit Trail Must Capture

The technical minimum for a compliant clinical trial audit trail is defined by the intersection of Part 11's requirements, E6(R3)'s data change documentation standard, and the EMA GCP guideline's field-level specification. Every audit trail entry for a data modification must capture six elements:

1. The identity of the user who made the change
2. The date and time of the change expressed in a controlled and validated time reference
3. The original value before the change
4. The new value after the change
5. The reason for the change
6. The identifier of the data field or record affected

Systems that capture five of these six elements satisfy none of the requirements because the missing element is not optional.

The user identity requirement means that every user must have a unique login credential. Shared accounts are not compliant. A site coordinator who uses the principal investigator's login generates an audit trail entry attributed to the investigator for an action the investigator did not take. FDA's audit trail review methodology specifically looks for patterns suggesting shared credential use: concurrent session events under a single account, access events during periods when the named account holder was demonstrably elsewhere, or data entry volumes that exceed what a single individual could reasonably produce. The EMA guideline Section 5.5 on timestamps adds that user management procedures must ensure that audit trail entries can be reliably attributed to specific individuals throughout the trial lifecycle, including after staff turnover.

The time stamp requirement means that the system clock driving audit trail timestamps must be validated, synchronized to a controlled time reference, and protected from manipulation. The EMA guideline Section 5.5 addresses timestamps specifically: the time and date reference for systems should be validated. For ePRO and eCOA systems, the guideline requires that the timestamp of data entry in the capture tool and the timestamp of data saved to a solid state storage should both be recorded as part of the metadata, and the duration between initial capture in local memory and upload to a central server should be short and traceable. This is a more granular timestamp requirement than Part 11 provides and reflects the specific risks of mobile device-based data capture in decentralized trials.

The change reason requirement deserves particular attention because it is the element most frequently misused. The regulatory purpose of a change reason is to enable a reviewer, at any subsequent time, to understand why the data in the record changed. A change reason that reads "data entry error" without further specification does not serve this purpose. The EMA guideline Section 6.2.1 states that changes to data should only be performed when justified and that justification should be documented. "Correction" is not a documented justification. "Subject disclosed additional medication during follow-up visit; baseline entry corrected per source document review" is.

Audit Trail Element	Regulatory Basis	ALCOA+ Property Protected
User identity (unique, authenticated)	21 CFR Part 11.10(e); E6(R3) 5.5.3; EMA GCP Guideline 5.5 (user management)	Attributable
Date and time (validated, controlled clock)	21 CFR Part 11.10(e); E6(R3) 5.5.3; EMA GCP Guideline 5.5 (timestamp)	Contemporaneous
Original value before change	E6(R3) 5.5.3; Part 11.10(e); EMA GCP Guideline 6.2.1	Original, Accurate
New value after change	E6(R3) 5.5.3; Part 11.10(e)	Accurate, Complete
Reason for change (specific, documented justification)	E6(R3) 5.5.3; MHRA GxP 2018 Section 6.13; EMA GCP Guideline 6.2.1	Attributable, Accurate
Record/field identifier (field-level, not page-level)	Part 11.10(e); PIC/S PI 041-1; EMA GCP Guideline 6.2.1 (explicit field-level requirement)	Attributable, Complete
System and session identifier	Part 11.10(a); Annex 11 draft 2024	Attributable, Consistent
Timestamp of capture vs. upload (ePRO/eCOA)	EMA GCP Guideline Section 6.2.1 (metadata requirement for mobile capture)	Contemporaneous, Traceable

Configuration: Where Compliance Is Made or Broken

Audit trail compliance is not a consequence of purchasing a validated eClinical system. It is a consequence of configuring that system correctly, maintaining the configuration in a controlled state, and verifying that the configuration is operating as intended throughout the trial's lifecycle. These are organizational decisions, not vendor decisions. They require documented design choices, change control, and periodic verification. Under the EMA's Guideline on Computerised Systems and Electronic Data In Clinical Trials Annex 2 (Annex 2) validation framework (addressed in Chapter 7), the audit trail configuration is a trial-specific element that must be validated separately from the platform's generic audit trail capability.

Scope: What the Audit Trail Must Cover

The scope of audit trail capture must be defined during system configuration and documented in the validation package or system configuration specification. Under the EMA's field-level requirement, any configuration that limits audit trail capture to form-level or page-level events is a compliance gap for EU-conducted trials, regardless of whether it satisfies Part 11's less prescriptive language. For sponsors operating multi-regional trials, the EU standard defines the floor: field-level capture for all data domains is the configuration that satisfies both frameworks.

Primary endpoint data fields, eligibility criteria fields, safety data fields, and any field whose value determines protocol-defined outcomes require audit trail coverage as a minimum. The rationale for limiting audit trail scope to a subset of fields must be documented in the risk assessment underlying the system configuration, reviewed by a qualified data governance function, and reflect a considered judgment that the excluded fields are not critical to data integrity. In practice, excluding any field from audit trail coverage introduces risk that is difficult to justify when the cost of capturing the full record is negligible compared to the investigative cost of discovering a manipulation in an excluded field.

Always On: The Non-Negotiable Configuration

Audit trails must be always on. No operational user, regardless of role or permission level, can disable, pause, or restrict audit trail generation during an active period of data management. Under the EMA's Section 6.2.1, if administrator users can deactivate the audit trail, this action must itself be automatically logged. This is an important nuance: the EU standard does not require that it be technically impossible for administrators to deactivate the audit trail, but it requires that any such deactivation leave a traceable record. A system that permits admin deactivation without logging is non-compliant; a system that permits admin deactivation with automatic logging is compliant, but the deactivation event becomes an audit trail entry that will be visible to inspectors.

The always-on requirement has specific implications for system maintenance and upgrade events. Migrations, version updates, and database restructuring activities that require temporary audit trail suspension must be covered by documented procedures, conducted within change control, and recorded such that the period of suspension and its basis are fully documented. Any data entered, modified, or deleted during a period of audit trail interruption must be identified, assessed for risk, and addressed in the validation record for the maintenance activity. A gap in the audit trail timeline that cannot be explained by a documented maintenance event is an inspection finding under any regulatory framework.

The 2024 draft Annex 11 revision's multi-factor authentication requirement connects directly to audit trail integrity. Configuration changes to audit trail scope, behavior, or access controls must require elevated authentication precisely because they affect the integrity of the audit record itself. A system in which the audit trail configuration can be changed with standard user credentials provides insufficient protection against insider manipulation. The authentication requirement is a design control, not a procedural one.[84]

Change Control for Audit Trail Configuration

Any change to the audit trail configuration of a production system used in an active trial must be managed under change control. This means the proposed change must be documented, the data integrity impact assessed before implementation, the change reviewed by a qualified function, implementation tested in a non-production environment, and the change recorded with before-and-after configuration documentation. Under the EMA's Annex 2 A2.10, the change control record must include a risk assessment covering data integrity impact, current functionality impact, and regulatory compliance impact. Changes made outside this process cannot be distinguished, in the regulatory record, from unauthorized configuration modifications made for manipulative purposes.

The change control requirement extends to vendor-initiated changes. Cloud-hosted eClinical platforms may push configuration updates that affect audit trail behavior without the sponsor's explicit awareness. E6(R3)'s clear statement that sponsors cannot transfer regulatory responsibility[85] to CROs and vendors applies with full force: a sponsor whose audit trail configuration was altered by a vendor update, and who did not have a process to detect and assess such changes, owns the compliance gap. Under the EMA's Annex 2, new vendor functionalities must not be used until validated or the vendor's documentation has been assessed, which applies directly to changes that affect audit trail behavior.[86]

SCENARIO: Audit Trail Configuration for Primary Endpoint Field	
COMPLIANT PRACTICE	**NON-COMPLIANT PRACTICE**
eClinical system is configured at study start to capture field-level audit trails for all data domains including primary endpoint assessments. Configuration is documented in the system configuration specification and verified in the OQ test scripts. The configuration satisfies both the EU field-level requirement (EMA GCP Guideline Section 6.2.1) and Part 11 requirements. Change control procedure requires testing and documented sign-off before any modification. System administrator access to configuration settings is restricted and logged separately, satisfying the EU requirement that admin deactivation generate an automatic log entry.	eClinical system is deployed with vendor default configuration capturing audit trails only for certain modules. Primary endpoint assessment fields are in a module not covered by default. No configuration review occurs before first patient enrolled. A post-enrollment discovery that primary endpoint fields lack audit trail coverage is resolved by enabling the configuration mid-trial, leaving a gap in the audit trail for all data entered before the fix. Under EMA GCP Guideline Section 6.2.1, the absence of field-level audit trail coverage for primary endpoint data is a reportable compliance deficiency.
Inspector's View: The mid-trial configuration change and the preceding gap period will be identified immediately by both FDA BIMO and EU GCP inspectors. EU inspectors will cite the deficiency as a specific violation of EMA/INS/GCP/112288/2023 Section 6.2.1 and will grade the finding based on whether the primary endpoint data integrity can be independently verified from other sources. The gap cannot be retroactively populated.	

Audit Trail Review: From Monitoring to Surveillance

An audit trail that is never reviewed is not a compliance program. It is a data warehouse. The EMA GCP Guideline Section 6.2.2 states this directly: data review should be proactive and ongoing review is expected unless justified. The MHRA guidance states that routine data review should include a documented audit trail review where risk assessment determines it to be required. PIC/S PI 041-1 and E6(R3)'s risk management framework both require that review frequency be proportionate to risk and that the review be connected to a quality oversight structure that produces action when anomalies are identified. Under E6(R3) Section 4.2.3, procedures for review of trial-specific data, audit trails, and other relevant metadata must be in place as a planned activity, with the extent and nature adapted to the individual trial and adjusted based on experience during the trial.[87]

The gap between what organizations document in their data management plans regarding audit trail review and what they actually do is one of the most consistent findings in inspections globally. Sponsors that describe audit trail review as a scheduled activity in their Data Management Plan, then demonstrate no contemporaneous records of reviews having occurred, have created a documentation problem on top of a compliance problem. Under the EU inspection framework, the absence of documented review records is itself a citable finding independent of whether the underlying data has integrity problems. The DMP defines the standard the organization has committed to meet; the review records demonstrate whether it was met.

What to Review and When

Audit trail review programs should define, before study start, three things: the scope of review (which fields, data domains, and system events are covered in routine review versus targeted review), the frequency of review (how often routine reviews occur, and what triggers an unscheduled review), and the documentation standard (what constitutes an adequate record of a review, including how anomalies are recorded and resolved). The EMA guideline's requirement that procedures for risk-based, trial-specific audit trail reviews be in place before the trial begins means that these definitions are not optional enhancements to the data management plan. They are prerequisites.

Routine review scope should cover, at minimum, primary endpoint fields, eligibility criteria, and safety data for all subjects whose data has been entered or modified since the last review period. For large multi-site trials, full field-level review of all subjects in every review period may not be operationally feasible; in that case, the DMP should document a risk-based sampling approach. What is not acceptable under any framework is a scope that covers only records flagged by automated validation edits. Validation edits are designed to catch data entry errors, not to detect retrospective manipulation. A data point that passes all validation edits can still be manipulated. Validation edits and audit trail review serve different functions and cannot substitute for each other.

Review frequency should be calibrated to the risk profile of the site and the trial phase. The EMA guideline's reference to ongoing review as the expected default implies that for high-risk data domains and active enrollment periods, review cycles measured in weeks rather than months are the standard. The MHRA's exception reporting approach provides a practical mechanism for maintaining high review frequency efficiently: a validated exception reporting tool that automatically surfaces predetermined anomaly patterns allows reviewers to focus on signals rather than scanning complete audit trail logs, while still satisfying the ongoing review expectation.

Patterns, Not Points

The most important and most frequently absent element of audit trail review is pattern analysis. Individual data changes, reviewed in isolation, are usually explainable. But when the same value has been revised multiple times, each revision following a monitoring visit, each change reason using similar language, and each final value closer to the protocol-defined responder threshold, the pattern changes the analysis entirely. The FDA-MHRA joint paper on data integrity in global clinical trials documented specific inspection cases in which audit trail pattern review revealed systematic data manipulation that individual record review had not detected. Both agencies' inspection methodologies now incorporate aggregate pattern analysis as a standard component.[88]

Pattern recognition requires aggregate visibility. The reviewer must be able to see, for a given field, the complete sequence of changes across all subjects, not merely the current audit trail state of a single record. This requires eClinical audit trail output structured to support query and analysis, and a review process that includes systematic aggregate review, not only record-by-record review. The MHRA's formulation of exception reporting as a validated search tool that identifies and documents predetermined abnormal data or actions is the practical implementation of this requirement.

The most forensically significant patterns in clinical trial audit trail review are:

- Clustered off-hours editing sessions in which multiple fields for multiple subjects are modified in rapid succession
- Change reason uniformity in which the same generic reason is applied across a large proportion of changes at a specific site
- Modifications to primary endpoint fields that occur after monitoring visits, query resolution cycles, or unblinding events
- Changes made under one user's credentials to data attributed to a different user in source documents
- Access events from IP addresses or devices not associated with the documented site location.

None of these patterns is individually conclusive. All of them warrant investigation before they are closed as unremarkable.

Pattern	Potential Significance	Investigative Step and ALCOA+ Implication
Clustered off-hours edits across multiple subjects/fields	Bulk retrospective data modification; potential manipulation	Review source documents for corresponding amendments; verify user authorization at that time. ALCOA+: Contemporaneous, Attributable
Uniform generic change reasons across high proportion of site edits	Change reasons not documenting actual basis for revision; EU GCP Guideline 6.2.1 violation if justification not documented	Request site to provide specific basis for representative sample of changes. ALCOA+: Attributable, Accurate
Primary endpoint modifications post-monitoring visit	Retrospective changes following monitor review; data influenced by monitoring feedback	Correlate change dates with monitoring visit dates and monitor trip report findings. ALCOA+: Contemporaneous, Accurate
Single user account access during documented site closure periods	Shared credentials or unauthorized remote access	Confirm site access logs; verify account holder location; check IP address records. ALCOA+: Attributable
Data entry velocity exceeding plausible single-user rate	Multiple users sharing one account; bulk data fabrication	Review concurrent session logs; check delegation log; confirm subject visit dates. ALCOA+: Attributable, Contemporaneous

Pattern	Potential Significance	Investigative Step and ALCOA+ Implication
Configuration change events not preceded by change control record	Unauthorized system modification; potential audit trail scope alteration -- citable under EMA Annex 2 A2.10	Verify change control documentation; confirm who holds system administrator credentials. ALCOA+: Consistent, Enduring
Field-level audit trail absent for certain data domains	Configuration gap; EU GCP Guideline 6.2.1 non-compliance where primary endpoint data affected	Review system configuration specification; determine when gap was introduced and what data was affected. ALCOA+: Complete, Traceable

The Escalation Pathway

Every audit trail review program requires a defined escalation pathway: the documented process through which an anomaly identified during review is investigated, resolved, and closed. An anomaly that is noted in a reviewer's personal log but never formally documented, investigated, or closed creates a different problem than the one it was intended to address. In regulatory terms, an identified anomaly that was not escalated is not evidence of a functioning quality system. It is evidence of a quality system that identified its own failures and chose not to act.

A functional escalation pathway has four elements. First, a documented trigger definition: which observations require formal escalation as opposed to routine documentation in the review log. Second, an investigation process: who receives the escalation, what documentation must be produced, and within what timeframe. Third, a resolution requirement: every investigated anomaly must be closed with a documented determination of whether it represents a data integrity concern and what action was taken. Fourth, a periodic aggregate review: a structured examination of all anomalies across a review period, considered together, to identify patterns that did not trigger escalation individually but are collectively significant. E6(R3) Section 3.10.1.3 requires that sponsors set pre-specified acceptable ranges, including quality tolerance limits where relevant to critical-to-quality factors, and evaluate deviations beyond those ranges; audit trail anomaly rates, change reason quality metrics, and escalation rates are legitimate parameters within that framework. The EMA GCP Guideline's periodic review provisions explicitly include performance incidents and security incidents among the elements requiring periodic evaluation, connecting the monitoring program output directly to the system's validated state assessment.

eTMF Audit Trails: The Overlooked Record

Clinical trial sponsor and CRO attention to audit trail compliance concentrates overwhelmingly on the eClinical system. But the audit trail obligation extends to all electronic systems used to create, modify, maintain, or transmit regulated records. The electronic Trial Master File is a regulated record system. Its audit trail carries the same requirements as the eClinical System and receives considerably less routine attention.

The eTMF audit trail documents the history of the trial master file: which documents were uploaded, when, by whom; which versions superseded earlier versions; which documents were deleted or marked as not applicable. For EU GCP inspections, which are frequently conducted remotely through eTMF access, the eTMF audit trail is often the first record examined, because it reveals whether the trial master file was compiled contemporaneously with trial conduct or assembled retrospectively in anticipation of inspection. EU CTR 536/2014's 25-year retention requirement for trial master file records makes the eTMF audit trail an obligatory long-term archive element. The requirement to retain eTMF audit trail data for 25 years, in a format readable without the eTMF platform being operational, is an archive design obligation with no U.S. equivalent in its specific duration.[89]

The patterns that matter in eTMF audit trails mirror those in eClinical system audit trails. Bulk upload events not correlated with actual document production periods; document version sequences inconsistent with the version history documented in the corresponding documents; deletions of early versions that would reveal inconsistencies with the version presented at inspection; access patterns suggesting the file was reorganized after inspection notification. These patterns do not necessarily indicate falsification. They may reflect a document management function that has not kept pace with trial operations. The inspection finding is the same either way.

SCENARIO: eTMF Contemporaneity and Audit Trail Evidence	
COMPLIANT PRACTICE	**NON-COMPLIANT PRACTICE**
eTMF system is configured with audit trail capture covering all document uploads, version changes, and access events. Data management plan requires documents to be filed within defined timeframes after execution. eTMF audit trail review is included as a component of the ongoing TMF health check conducted at defined intervals. Upload timestamps are reviewed against corresponding execution dates to identify filing delays. Under EU CTR, the eTMF audit trail is retained for the full 25-year period in a vendor-independent format specified in the system decommissioning plan.	eTMF is maintained primarily as a filing system rather than a contemporaneous record. Monitoring visit reports, protocol amendments, and site correspondence are uploaded in batches, periodically, when staff capacity allows. When an inspection notification is received, a two-week filing effort uploads several hundred documents to bring the TMF to the expected state. The eTMF audit trail shows that 400 documents covering 36 months of trial conduct were uploaded in a 12-day period.
Inspector's View: The 12-day bulk upload pattern is the first thing a remote EU GCP inspection will identify. EU inspectors will classify this as a major finding under EMA/INS/GCP/112288/2023 requirements for contemporaneous TMF maintenance. The sponsor will need to demonstrate that the documents themselves are authentic. The eTMF audit trail, which should be the tool proving authenticity, is instead the primary evidence of the compliance deficiency.	

Common Failure Modes and How They Are Found

The audit trail failure modes that generate inspection findings are not exotic. They recur across inspection cycles, across geographic regions, and across organization types. They are predictable enough that a well-designed audit trail review program should detect most of them before inspection. The reason they persist is that the review programs capable of detecting them are not in place at the organizations that need them.

Disabling or Restricting the Audit Trail

Systems that permit operational users to disable audit trail generation, or that were configured with audit trail capture limited to a subset of data fields without documented rationale, represent the most fundamental failure mode. Under the EMA's Section 6.2.1, any configuration that makes it possible for normal users to deactivate the audit trail is a design non-compliance, not merely a procedural gap. The detection mechanism is straightforward: compare the scope of the audit trail as configured against the regulatory requirement for the data fields in use. Discrepancies are configuration findings. Systems that show periods with no audit trail entries during documented periods of data activity, in the absence of a maintenance record explaining the gap, are showing evidence of audit trail suppression.

Shared Credentials and Inadequate Access Controls

Shared user accounts are one of the most common audit trail compliance failures in clinical trial operations, particularly at investigator sites with small staffs and high coordinator turnover. When one coordinator uses another's login credentials, the audit trail attributes the resulting data entries to the account holder. The attribution is false. A data record attributed to a principal investigator, because the coordinator used the investigator's login, carries an electronic signature commitment that the investigator did not make. Under the EMA guideline's user management framework (Annex 3), each user must have a unique user account that cannot be shared, and the addition and removal of users must be documented and maintained in accessible access logs that are reviewed as part of the audit trail review program.

Detecting shared credential use requires looking at patterns the individual audit trail entry does not reveal: concurrent login sessions under the same account, access events during periods when the account holder was demonstrably in a different location, data entry volumes inconsistent with a single user's capacity during a documented period, and IP address or device records inconsistent with the registered site location. These patterns require cross-referencing the audit trail against other system logs and against the site's operational records.

Post-Hoc Data Modification

Retrospective data modification is the manipulation pattern that audit trails exist to detect. The FDA-MHRA joint paper on data integrity documented two inspection case examples in which audit trail analysis revealed manipulation that had not been detected by on-site monitoring or source data verification. In the first, a data migration had failed to transfer audit trails from the original EDC system, leaving the transferred data without any record of its original entry history. In the second, review of data listings in the clinical study report against audit trail records revealed that subjects appeared to have received opposite treatment assignments from what the audit trail showed, pointing to a systematic problem with the randomization implementation. In both cases, the audit trail was the investigative tool that revealed the problem -- and in the first case, the absence of the audit trail was itself the integrity failure.

The System Clock Problem

Time stamp manipulation is less common than the other failure modes but more damaging when it occurs, because it corrupts the temporal foundation on which all audit trail evidence depends. The EMA guideline's specific requirement that timestamps of data entry and timestamps of data saved to a server both be recorded for ePRO and eCOA systems addresses a particular vulnerability of mobile device-based capture: a device whose local clock has drifted from a controlled time reference will produce timestamps that do not accurately reflect when data was entered. Clock manipulation is detected through cross-referencing eClinical system time stamps against time stamps in other system logs not under the same administrative control: network server logs, eTMF upload timestamps, monitoring system access logs, and external reference sources such as email correspondence with date headers.

Building an Audit Trail Program That Satisfies Regulators

An audit trail program that satisfies regulatory inspection is not primarily a technology achievement. The technology is a prerequisite, not the result. The program consists of three interdependent elements: configuration management, which ensures the audit trail captures the right information throughout the trial's lifecycle; review operations, which ensure the captured information is systematically examined by people with the expertise to recognize what it means; and governance, which connects the review program to the quality management system so that findings produce action.

The Data Management Plan as the Governing Document

The data management plan should contain a dedicated audit trail section documenting, with specificity: the scope of audit trail coverage and its compliance with the EU field-level requirement for any trial subject to EU oversight; the review frequency and sampling methodology calibrated to a documented risk assessment; the change reason requirements imposed on site users with examples of compliant and non-compliant reasons; the escalation pathway for anomalies; the documentation standard for review records; and the procedures for audit trail preservation at system decommissioning, specifying the format and duration of archive retention. For EU-conducted trials, this section must address the EMA GCP guideline's requirement that procedures for risk-based, trial-specific audit trail review be in place before the trial begins.[90]

A DMP audit trail section that consists of a single paragraph affirming that the system has an audit trail and that review will occur is not adequate under any regulatory framework. The regulatory test is not whether the DMP mentions audit trail review. The test is whether, at any point during the trial, a reviewer can determine from the DMP and the review records what was reviewed, when, by whom, what was found, and what was done about it.

Training Site Staff on Change Reason Requirements

Site coordinators who do not understand the regulatory purpose of audit trails will not produce compliant audit trails. Effective audit trail training covers three things: the regulatory basis for the requirement, stated plainly and without bureaucratic abstraction; specific examples of compliant and non-compliant change reasons, drawn from the trial's actual data domains; and the consequence spectrum, from a site query to an inspection finding to a clinical hold, so that the organizational stakes of the choice are visible to the individual making it. For EU-conducted trials, training should explain that EU GCP inspectors cite specific guideline violations and that inadequate change reasons are a documented, gradeable non-compliance, not merely a quality improvement suggestion.

Vendor Qualification and Audit Trail Verification

When a sponsor deploys a cloud-hosted eClinical system or a third-party eTMF platform, the audit trail obligation does not shift to the vendor. The vendor provides the system. The sponsor is responsible for ensuring the system is configured to meet the regulatory standard, that the configuration is maintained in a controlled state, and that the audit trail output can be accessed, exported, and reviewed independently of the vendor's cooperation. Under the EMA's Annex 2, this requires an in-depth examination of the vendor's quality system and specific validation activities, with the examination report available to inspectors. The examination must confirm that the vendor's audit trail implementation satisfies both the field-level capture requirement and the always-on standard, and that the vendor's audit trail data is delivered to the sponsor in a format suitable for independent review.[91]

The service agreement must address at minimum three audit trail-specific provisions: the sponsor's right to audit the system's audit trail configuration and output independently of vendor mediation; the vendor's obligation to notify the sponsor of any changes that affect audit trail behavior before application to the production environment; and the provisions for audit trail data retention and return at the conclusion of the service relationship, including data formats that can be read without the vendor's software. For EU programs, the data return provision must accommodate the 25-year eTMF retention requirement under EU CTR Article 58.[92]

The Audit Trail at Inspection

FDA's BIMO inspection methodology for electronic data systems begins, almost without exception, with the audit trail. EU GCP inspectors, operating under the structured finding classification system described in this chapter, begin with the audit trail configuration documentation and review procedures before examining specific data. The difference in approach reflects the different orientations of the two inspection systems — FDA is outcome-focused; EU inspectors are systems-and-process-focused — but both lead to the same content: what is in the audit trail, how it is reviewed, and what the organization did about what it found.

Organizations that have reviewed their own audit trails systematically, documented what they found, and addressed anomalies before inspection arrive at the inspection room with a decisive advantage: they have already done the analysis the inspector will perform, they know what the inspector will find, and they have documented responses to the questions the findings will generate. Organizations that have not reviewed their audit trails arrive discovering the contents of their own regulatory record alongside the inspector. Under the EU inspection framework, an organization that cannot produce documented audit trail review records will receive a finding on that basis alone, before any data anomalies are even examined.

The inspection question that separates compliant organizations from non-compliant ones is not "Do you have an audit trail?" Every organization with a modern eClinical system has an audit trail. The question is: "What do you do with it?" The answer that satisfies the inspector is specific, documented, and demonstrable. The answer that generates findings is any variation of "Our system maintains the audit trail, and we can access it if needed." The first answer describes a quality activity. The second describes a filing system.

CHAPTER 8 - KEY TAKEAWAYS
The audit trail is the primary forensic record of clinical trial data integrity: it is the mechanism through which the ALCOA+ properties of attributability, contemporaneity, and accuracy can be verified after the fact, and it is frequently the only record that reveals whether data was manipulated.
The EMA GCP Computerised Systems Guideline (EMA/INS/GCP/112288/2023) Section 6.2 establishes the most operationally specific EU audit trail standard to date: field-level capture is explicitly required; it should not be possible for normal users to deactivate the audit trail; if administrators can deactivate it, that action must be automatically logged; and proactive, ongoing review is the expected default.
EU GCP inspections classify audit trail deficiencies using a three-tier finding system (critical, major, minor) citing specific ICH E6 provision violations; audit trail configuration that prevents field-level capture of primary endpoint data has been classified as a critical finding by EU national competent authorities.
The field-level versus page-level capture distinction is a material compliance difference between the EU and U.S. frameworks; FDA's Part 11 does not explicitly require field-level capture while EMA's Section 6.2.1 does; for multi-regional trials, the EU standard sets the floor.
Audit trail configuration must be documented, risk-assessed, and managed under change control; under EMA Annex 2, the audit trail configuration is a trial-specific element requiring separate validation from the platform's generic capability, and configuration changes require formal change control with risk assessment documentation.
Every audit trail entry for a data modification must capture six elements: user identity, validated timestamp, original value, new value, change reason, and field identifier; the EMA guideline adds an eighth element for ePRO and eCOA systems: both the capture timestamp and the server upload timestamp must be recorded.
Change reasons must document specific justification, not merely acknowledge that a change occurred; the EMA guideline Section 6.2.1 states that changes should only be performed when justified and justification must be documented -- "data entry error" is not documented justification.
Audit trail review is a routine quality activity: EMA Section 6.2.2 states that proactive, ongoing review is expected unless justified otherwise; MHRA requires documented audit trail review where risk assessment determines it necessary; both require that review records be maintained.

CHAPTER 8 - KEY TAKEAWAYS
Pattern analysis is the core competency of effective audit trail review: individual data changes are usually explainable in isolation; the patterns that reveal manipulation require aggregate visibility across subjects, sites, and time periods, with cross-referencing against monitoring visit dates, query histories, and access logs.
eTMF audit trails carry the same requirements as EDC audit trails and reveal whether the trial master file was maintained contemporaneously; EU CTR Article 58's 25-year retention requirement makes eTMF audit trail archive design an obligation with material long-term implications.
Vendor qualification for cloud-hosted systems must address audit trail configuration verification, change notification obligations, and post-service data return in accessible formats; under EMA Annex 2, the in-depth vendor examination report must be available to inspectors.
Organizations that have reviewed their own audit trails before inspection, documented findings, and addressed anomalies arrive at the inspection room with the regulatory record already understood; under the EU finding classification system, the absence of documented review records is itself a gradeable non-compliance.

CHAPTER NINE

Electronic Records and Signatures: Getting It Right

> *A system that meets the letter of Part 11 but fails to configure, control, and review its electronic record and signature functions in practice provides no more protection against data integrity failure than a system that ignores Part 11 entirely.*

A mid-sized contract research organization operating investigator sites across three continents had, by any documentation standard, a compliant electronic data capture environment. Every system in its clinical trial portfolio had been validated. The validation packages were current. Access control policies were written, approved, and posted to the quality management system. The standard operating procedures governing electronic signatures, user provisioning, and password management had been reviewed within the past eighteen months. The sponsor audits reviewed those procedures and found them satisfactory. When FDA's Office of Scientific Investigations arrived for a for-cause inspection triggered by anomalous query patterns identified during pre-approval review, the organization's quality team was confident.

The inspection took eight days. What the investigators found was not a failure of documentation. It was a failure of operation. The access control policy required unique user credentials and password complexity meeting NIST standards; the actual eClinical system configurations at four of seven active sites used the platform's default password settings, which permitted single-character passwords and had no session timeout enforced. The electronic signature procedure required investigators to review each case report form page before signing; the audit trail showed a principal investigator who had approved 312 pages in forty-one minutes across a data lock weekend, a rate that permitted approximately eight seconds per page. The user provisioning SOP required accounts for departed staff to be deactivated within twenty-four hours of separation; system access logs showed seventeen accounts belonging to coordinators who had left the organization between four and twenty-two months earlier, several of which had been used to resolve queries after the account-holder's departure date.

None of these findings required the investigators to discover hidden records or decode obfuscated data. They read the configuration settings. They pulled the signature timestamps. They cross-referenced the user account list against the organization's personnel records. The gap between what the policies said and what the systems did was visible to anyone who looked. For the preceding two years, nobody had looked.

The Form 483 issued at the close of the inspection contained eleven observations. Nine of them mapped directly to 21 CFR Part 11 requirements that had been in effect since 1997. The organization had not misunderstood Part 11. It had treated Part 11 as a documentation exercise rather than an operational commitment. That distinction cost it a complete re-inspection, a corrective action program spanning fourteen months, and the suspension of two active trials pending remediation review.

> *The gap between a Part 11-compliant policy and a Part 11-compliant system is not a documentation gap. It is the distance between what an organization wrote it would do and what its systems actually do every day.*

The Regulatory Framework: Part 11, the EMA GCP Guideline, Annex 11, and E6(R3)

21 CFR Part 11 has governed electronic records and electronic signatures in FDA-regulated clinical research since its effective date in August 1997. Nearly three decades later, it remains the foundational U.S. technical standard. Its requirements are neither secret nor complicated: validated systems; audit trails that are computer-generated, time-stamped, and sequenced; access controls limiting system use to authorized individuals; electronic signatures that are unique to one person, non-repudiable, and irrevocably linked to the record they sign; and record retention capabilities that allow production of accurate, complete copies for regulatory review. These requirements apply to every EDC system, every eTMF platform, every electronic patient-reported outcome tool, and every

interactive response technology system used to generate, modify, maintain, or transmit electronic records that serve in lieu of FDA-required paper records.[93]

The European regulatory framework for electronic records and signatures in clinical trials has become substantially more specific with the adoption of the EMA's 2023 GCP Computerised Systems Guideline (EMA/INS/GCP/112288/2023), which entered into effect in September 2023. Section 4.8 of that guideline establishes a four-element framework for electronic signature requirements applicable to all EU-conducted clinical trials:

- Authentication (establishing a high degree of certainty that a record was signed by the claimed signatory),
- Non-repudiation (ensuring the signatory cannot later deny having signed),
- An unbreakable link (ensuring the signed record cannot later be changed without the signature being rendered visibly invalid), and
- A timestamp (recording date, time, and time zone when the signature was applied).

This four-element framework applies to all documents required to be signed under ICH E6, which in the EU context means every investigator endorsement, every sponsor quality oversight sign-off, and every database lock authorization that is executed electronically.

EU GMP Guide Annex 11, whose principles apply to clinical data management systems through the EU GMP/GCP cross-reference structure, governs computerized systems used in EU-regulated activities. The 2011 version established explicit requirements for data backup, disaster recovery, and audit trail configuration that were more operationally specific than Part 11's framework.

Electronic Records and Signatures: Clinical Regulatory Framework
21 CFR Part 11, Sections 11.10(a) and (e): Validation and computer-generated, time-stamped audit trails for electronic records used in lieu of paper records required by FDA regulations.
21 CFR Part 11, Sections 11.50 and 11.100: Electronic signature requirements -- unique to one individual; non-repudiable; cannot be shared, transferred, or falsely denied.
21 CFR Part 11, Section 11.10(d) and (g): Access controls limiting system use to authorized individuals; authority checks confirming permission before use.

Electronic Records and Signatures: Clinical Regulatory Framework
EMA Guideline on Computerised Systems and Electronic Data in Clinical Trials (EMA/INS/GCP/112288/2023), Section 4.8: Electronic signature four-element framework (authentication, non-repudiation, unbreakable link, timestamp); closed vs. open system distinction; eIDAS applicability for EU open systems.
EMA GCP Guideline Section 5.4 and Annex 4: Security and access control; unique user accounts; checks to ensure only authorized individuals have access with appropriate permissions; records of authorization with access levels documented; system records changes to user roles.
EMA GCP Guideline Annex 4, Sections A4.12-A4.13: Authentication method requirements; two-factor authentication for remote access to clinical trial data; risk-based approach to authentication level.
EU GMP Guide Annex 11 (2011): Audit trail configuration changes subject to change control; electronic signatures permanently linked to their respective records; validation required for computerised systems used in regulated activities; supplier assessment required before system use.
ICH E6(R3), Sections 4.3.4 and 4.2.2: Sponsor requirement to validate all computerised systems used in clinical trials throughout the system lifecycle; data traceability requirements including relevant metadata and audit trails.
MHRA GxP Data Integrity Guidance (2018), Sections 6.14 and 6.16: Electronic signatures attributable to individuals; shared logins not acceptable for GxP data; historical access level information must be available.
PIC/S PI 041-1 (2021): Operational requirements for access controls, audit trails, and electronic signatures across GxP computerized systems.
ALCOA+ Properties Protected: Attributable (access controls, e-signatures); Contemporaneous (audit trail timestamps); Original (record immutability after signature); Accurate (system validation).

The European Regulatory Dimension: Section 4.8, Annex 4, and the Closed/Open System Framework

The European Regulatory Dimension: Section 4.8 and the Closed/Open System Framework

The EMA's 2023 GCP Computerised Systems Guideline establishes a closed/open system distinction for electronic signatures that, while structurally parallel to the framework in 21 CFR Part 11 Sections 11.10 and 11.30, carries materially different consequences in the EU context. Under Part 11, open systems require additional procedural and technical controls within the same regulatory framework. Under the EMA guideline, an open system at an EU site may trigger the eIDAS regulation as an entirely separate legal regime, requiring qualified electronic signatures issued by certified trust service providers. That consequence has no U.S. equivalent and has material implications for sponsors designing or qualifying electronic signature workflows for EU-conducted trials.[94]

Closed Systems: The Standard Clinical Trial Case

A closed system, in the EMA guideline's formulation, is one in which the system owner knows the identity of all users and signatories in advance and grants and controls their access rights. This describes the majority of systems used in clinical trials: sponsor-operated or vendor-operated eClinical systems where user accounts are provisioned before use. For closed systems, eIDAS does not apply (eIDAS Article 2.2). Instead, the electronic signature functionality must be proven during system validation to meet the four elements specified in Section 4.8: authentication, non-repudiation, unbreakable link, and timestamp.

This validation obligation is operationally significant. For closed clinical systems, demonstrating compliance with the Section 4.8 framework is a validation deliverable, not a legal compliance determination. The sponsor must test, document, and confirm that the system's signature implementation satisfies each of the four elements before the system is placed in production for an EU-regulated trial. A sponsor who has validated a system against Part 11's signature requirements may need to verify that the unbreakable link requirement is satisfied in the specific sense the EMA guideline requires: that the contents of a signed version of a record cannot later be changed by anyone without the signature being rendered visibly invalid. A system that permits post-signature data modification with only an audit trail entry, without the signature itself being invalidated or flagged, does not satisfy this requirement. This is a more demanding standard than Part 11's permanent linkage requirement and must be specifically tested and documented in the validation record.

Open Systems: eIDAS and EU Site Considerations

An open system is one in which the signatories are not known in advance. In the clinical trial context, this is most likely to arise where investigator or subject signatures are collected through a platform that is not sponsor-provisioned: a generic electronic consent platform, a patient portal accessed through an institution's EHR, or a remote consent tool accessible through a public URL. For EU sites using open systems, electronic signatures must meet the requirements of the eIDAS regulation. Qualified electronic signatures under eIDAS, which require a qualified trust service provider and a qualified signature creation device, are legally equivalent to handwritten signatures across all EU member states and represent the standard applicable to open system signatures in the clinical trial context.

The practical consequence for sponsors is that the classification of a signature platform as open or closed must be made before the platform is deployed in EU trials, and the classification determines which regulatory framework governs the signature implementation. A consent platform that is not sponsor-provisioned and through which any person with an internet connection could theoretically create a user account is an open system under eIDAS, regardless of how tightly it is operationally controlled in practice. Sponsors operating hybrid consent models, in which some subjects use in-clinic eClinical systems (closed) while others sign consent remotely through a patient-facing platform (potentially open), must assess the platform classification for each signature type and ensure the applicable regulatory requirements are met for each.[95]

Authentication and Remote Access: Annex 4 Requirements

Authentication and remote access obligations for EU clinical systems are addressed in Annex 4 of the EMA GCP Computerised Systems Guideline as security requirements distinct from the electronic signature framework. Section A4.12 requires a risk-based approach to authentication method selection. Section A4.13 addresses remote authentication directly, stating that remote access to clinical trial data, for example to cloud-based systems, raises specific challenges, and that two-factor authentication is appropriate or necessary depending on the level of risk. In the cloud-hosted EDC context, every access event by a site coordinator or sponsor data manager is technically a remote access event from outside the system's controlled perimeter. For critical unblinded data and administrator-level access, the risk assessment will almost always support two-factor authentication as necessary. Sponsors whose vendor qualification and access control programs do not specifically address cloud-based remote access authentication have a structural gap under Computerised Systems Guideline Annex 4 that EU GCP inspectors have cited as a standalone finding.[96]

Requirement	FDA (21 CFR Part 11)	EU (EMA GCP Guideline 2023)	ICH E6(R3)
Signature uniqueness	Unique to one individual; cannot be shared or transferred (11.100(a))	Authenticated to high degree of certainty; closed system proven during validation (Section 4.8)	Individual accountability for data entries and changes (implied throughout)
Non-repudiation	Cannot be falsely denied (11.50(a))	System must ensure non-repudiation; signatory cannot later deny (Section 4.8)	Implied by investigator accountability obligations
Record-signature link	Permanently linked to record; cannot be excised or transferred (11.70)	Unbreakable link: signed record cannot be changed without signature being rendered visibly invalid (Section 4.8)	Traceability of signed data required throughout lifecycle
Re-authentication at signature	Required at first signing; at least one component for subsequent signings in same session (11.200(a)(1))	Full re-authentication at every signature; smart card/PIN/previous session auth not acceptable alone (Section 4.8; proven during closed system validation)	Implied by non-repudiation obligation

Requirement	FDA (21 CFR Part 11)	EU (EMA GCP Guideline 2023)	ICH E6(R3)
Signature manifestation	Signature statement required (11.50(a))	Signature manifestation must identify the signer and the meaning of the signature; metadata associated with the signature retained (EMA GCP Guideline Section 4.8; MHRA GxP Guidance Section 6.14)	Not explicitly specified
MFA requirement	Not explicitly required; two-component identification required for first signing	Risk-based authentication required; two-factor authentication appropriate or necessary for remote access to clinical trial data depending on level of risk (EMA GCP Guideline Annex 4, Sections A4.12-A4.13)	Not explicitly required
Open vs. closed system	Open system requires additional controls (11.10 and 11.30)	eIDAS qualification required for open EU systems; closed system validation-proven against Section 4.8 four-element framework	Not explicitly addressed

Requirement	FDA (21 CFR Part 11)	EU (EMA GCP Guideline 2023)	ICH E6(R3)
User account recurrent review	Implied by access control obligations; frequency not specified	Periodic review of user access rights expected; access levels must remain appropriate throughout trial lifecycle (EMA GCP Guideline Section 5.4 and Annex 4)	User management documented (Section 4.3.8)
Inactivity logout	Session timeout expected as operational control	Automatic inactivity logout expected as security control; risk-based implementation (EMA GCP Guideline Annex 4, Section A4.17)	Implied by access control obligations

Access Controls: The First Line of Attribution

Access controls exist for one purpose: to ensure that every action taken in a clinical data system is attributable to an identified, authorized individual. That purpose sounds simple. Its operational execution is where most organizations encounter difficulty.

Part 11 requires that access to electronic records systems be limited to authorized individuals. The EMA's Computerised Systems Guideline Annex 4 (Section 5.4 and Annex 4 of the GCP guideline) frames this as a security and access control obligation that applies across all EU-conducted clinical trials: checks must be used to ensure that only authorized individuals have access to the system and that they are granted appropriate permissions, including the ability to enter or make changes to data. Records of authorization with access levels clearly documented must be maintained. The system must record changes to user roles and thereby access rights. This is a more comprehensive documentation standard than Part 11's framework provides, and it has direct implications for how user provisioning records are structured and maintained.

The access control failures that generate citations cluster around four operational failure modes.

- The first is credential sharing: shared logins that destroy the attribution function for every record created or modified under that credential. The EMA Computerised Systems Guideline's Annex 4 states that for systems generating, amending, or storing GxP data, shared logins or generic user access should not be used; where the computerized system design supports individual user access, this function must be used. The MHRA guidance states the equivalent principle with equal clarity.[97]
- The second failure mode is inadequate provisioning and deprovisioning: accounts created without documented authority grants, and accounts for departed staff remaining active past the separation date.
- The third is generic or role-based accounts, including test accounts, administrative accounts, and sponsor data management accounts associated with a team rather than an individual.
- The fourth is failure to enforce technical controls the policy requires: password settings, session timeout, and other security parameters that exist in the policy document but have not been applied to the actual system configuration.

Multi-factor authentication deserves explicit attention. The EMA GCP Guideline Annex 4 requires a risk-based approach to authentication level for cloud-based clinical data access, with two-factor authentication appropriate or necessary for critical data and administrative access. Section A4.13 addresses remote authentication directly: remote access to clinical trial data, for example to cloud-based systems, raises specific challenges, and the type of access control required must be defined through a risk assessment. For critical unblinded data and administrator-level access, that risk assessment will almost always support two-factor authentication as necessary. Part 11 does not mandate MFA universally, requiring instead two-component identification for the first use of an electronic signature within a session. For new system deployments or upgrades, MFA for signature-level and administrative access events is the design standard that satisfies the current EMA framework and positions the organization for the anticipated direction of FDA's eventual cloud-system guidance.

COMPLIANT: What Good Looks Like	NON-COMPLIANT: What Inspectors Cite
Each system user has a unique login credential documented with name, role, and authorized permissions. EU records include access level changes as system-generated records (EMA GCP Guideline Section 5.4).	Multiple site coordinators share a single EDC login, making individual attribution of data entries and query resolutions impossible. This is a non-compliance under both Part 11 and EMA GCP Guideline Annex 4.
Password policy is configured in the system to enforce the minimum complexity, length, and expiration requirements specified in the SOP. Draft Annex 11 Section 11.5 requires passwords to prevent unauthorized access with length and character complexity requirements.	The password policy in the SOP requires eight-character complex passwords; the system configuration enforces a four-character minimum with no complexity requirement.
Sessions auto-lock after a defined inactivity period; re-authentication is required to resume. Draft Annex 11 Section 11.8 requires automatic inactivity logout that users cannot disable or reconfigure.	No session timeout is configured; logged-in sessions remain active indefinitely at unattended workstations.
User accounts for departing staff are deactivated within the timeframe specified in the deprovisioning procedure, with evidence of timely action retained.	Former coordinator accounts remain active for months following separation; query resolutions are recorded under those credentials after the departure date.
Periodic recurrent review of active user accounts confirms that roles and permissions remain appropriate. Draft Annex 11 Section 11.11 requires	No periodic review of active accounts exists; coordinators who changed roles six months ago still hold permissions appropriate to their former roles.

COMPLIANT: What Good Looks Like	NON-COMPLIANT: What Inspectors Cite
managers to confirm continued access of employees at defined intervals.	
MFA is implemented for signature-level and admin-level access events in cloud-hosted systems; gap documentation exists for platforms not yet supporting MFA. EMA Annex 4 A4.12 requires risk-based authentication; A4.13 addresses remote cloud access.	Generic "Sponsor_DM" team accounts are used for centralized query resolution, making it impossible to identify which individual performed each data management action.

Access Control Configuration: What Inspectors Verify

Inspectors evaluating access control compliance are not reading the access control policy. They are asking the system. FDA BIMO investigators ask consistent, predictable questions: Can you show me a list of all current user accounts? Can you show me who has had administrator-level access to the audit trail configuration? Can you show me accounts that were active during the trial that are no longer active, and confirm when each was deactivated? EU GCP inspectors ask structurally equivalent questions and additionally request evidence of periodic access reviews that the EMA GCP Computerised System Guideline Annex 4 requires: confirmation that access levels remain appropriate for active users throughout the trial lifecycle, and that role changes and permission drift have been identified and addressed on an ongoing basis rather than only at staff departure.

The ability to produce complete, current, and historical access control records is itself a compliance requirement. Systems that cannot generate a comprehensive user access report, cannot show the historical state of access settings at a specific point in time, or cannot confirm that the technical configuration matched the written policy throughout the trial period have failed a basic operational requirement of the electronic records framework. This capability must be verified during system validation and confirmed as part of ongoing system monitoring, not assembled under pressure during an inspection.[98]

Electronic Signatures: The Evidentiary Standard

An electronic signature in a clinical trial record is not a symbol of completion. It is an attestation. Under 21 CFR Part 312 and ICH E6(R3), an investigator's signature on a case report form attests that the data accurately reflects the subject's clinical experience, that protocol procedures were followed, and that the observations documented represent what actually occurred. A sponsor data manager's signature on a database lock record attests that the data has been reviewed, queried, resolved, and confirmed to the standard required for the statistical analysis that follows. These are evidentiary commitments. They carry legal and regulatory weight. They determine, in aggregate, whether the safety and efficacy conclusions drawn from the trial can be trusted.

Part 11 translates those evidentiary commitments into technical requirements. Electronic signatures must be unique to one individual, non-repudiable, and permanently linked to the record they sign. Where post-signature modifications occur, the modification must be documented and the signature's attestation value is limited to the version of the record it signed.[99] The EMA's Section 4.8 framework states the unbreakable link requirement in operationally precise terms: the contents of a signed version of a record cannot later be changed by anyone without the signature being rendered visibly invalid. This is a stricter formulation than Part 11's language in one important respect: the signature must not merely generate an audit trail entry when post-signature modification occurs; it must be visibly rendered invalid. A system that permits post-signature modification with only an audit trail record, without any visual indication that the signed version has been superseded, satisfies Part 11 but does not satisfy the EMA's Section 4.8 standard.

The batch signature problem is the most consistently cited electronic signature failure in inspection outcomes globally. When a principal investigator electronically countersigns case report forms in batches, the audit trail records the time at which each signature was applied. When that timestamp evidence shows that 150 CRF pages were signed in twelve minutes, three distinct regulatory problems arise: the signature is not an attestation of review because no meaningful review occurred; the signature may not be uniquely applied if a coordinator was using the investigator's credentials; and the data underlying those signatures is of uncertain integrity because the investigator who should have been the last line of clinical review was not performing that function. Under the EMA guideline Section 6.3 requirement that investigators sign data at predetermined milestones with the explicit observation that signing batches of workbooks is not suited to ensure high data quality, batch signing is both a BIMO finding and an EMA GCP inspection finding.[100]

Signature Ceremonies and Workflow Design

The design of the electronic signature workflow in an EDC system is not a configuration afterthought. It is a clinical quality decision. Under the draft Annex 11 Section 13.3 requirement for re-authentication at every signature event, systems must enforce credential entry at the point of signature application; relying on the user's existing active session is not sufficient. This requirement directly addresses the batch signing problem: if each signature requires a fresh credential entry, the cognitive friction of signing 300 pages in 30 minutes becomes a material constraint. The workflow design requirement does not prevent batch signing from occurring entirely, but it makes the time-stamp evidence of cursory review even more visible in the audit trail.

Systems can also enforce a minimum time-on-form requirement, preventing signature application before a minimum dwell time has elapsed. Systems can restrict signature authority to the provisioned individual, preventing coordinators from applying investigator signatures under the investigator's credentials even if the coordinator has access to the investigator's login. Systems can require a structured signature statement, surfacing the regulatory attestation language so that the signer is explicitly acknowledging what the signature means. The draft Annex 11 Section 13.5 requires that systems prompt the user for the meaning of the signature where applicable, making the structured statement a design requirement rather than a best practice for EU systems.[101]

Where technical controls cannot enforce the review requirement automatically, procedural controls must. Where procedural controls cannot reliably enforce it, the sponsor's oversight program must verify compliance through audit trail review. The inspection record is unambiguous: when none of these mechanisms is in place, the signature evidence is worthless.

ELECTRONIC INFORMED CONSENT IN EU TRIALS: A SPECIFIC SIGNATURE REGIME

The EMA GCP Guideline Annex 5.3 establishes specific electronic signature requirements for informed consent in EU-conducted clinical trials that go beyond the general Section 4.8 framework. The informed consent form must be signed and personally dated by at least two natural persons: the trial participant or legal representative, and the person who conducted the informed consent discussion. The identity of the persons signing must be ensured. There must be no ambiguity about the time of signature. The system must use timestamps for the signing action that cannot be manipulated by system settings. Any alterations of the signed consent document must invalidate the electronic signature. Where consent is given remotely, the trial participant's identity must be verifiable with documentation available to the investigator, and verification must be done in person when the participant visits the site. These requirements substantially exceed what FDA consent regulations explicitly specify for electronic consent, and sponsors deploying remote or electronic informed consent platforms for EU trials must validate those platforms against the Annex 5.3 requirements, not merely against 21 CFR Part 50.

System Configuration: The Gap Between Policy and Practice

The most preventable category of Part 11 findings is configuration failure: access control settings, audit trail parameters, signature workflow requirements, and session management controls that have been specified in policy documents but have not been applied to the actual system. Configuration failure is not a resource or expertise problem. It is a governance problem. It means that no one with the authority to verify the gap between the policy and the system was asked to look.

The clinical system validation process should include explicit testing of security configuration: verification that the deployed password settings match the policy requirements, that session timeout is enforced, that audit trail capture is enabled across all required data fields, and that access control permissions are provisioned consistently with the authorization matrix. This testing produces a documented baseline. The governance question is whether anyone verifies that the baseline is maintained through the system's operational life.

Software updates, platform migrations, and system reconfiguration events routinely reset security settings to vendor defaults. Vendor defaults are designed for ease of deployment, not regulatory compliance. A password policy configured to meet Part 11 requirements may be silently overwritten when a cloud-hosted eClinical platform releases a version update, if the organization's change control process does not include a post-update configuration verification step. An audit trail that was verified as always-on during validation may be placed in a suspended state by a platform maintenance event that is logged as routine. Under the EMA's Computerised Systems Guideline Annex 2 change control framework, every change must include a risk assessment covering data integrity impact; a change that resets security settings to defaults is a change that affects the validated state of the system and must be assessed accordingly.[102]

Configuration Verification as an Ongoing Obligation

The specific configuration elements requiring periodic verification include: password policy settings; session management settings; audit trail settings; electronic signature workflow settings; and access permission assignments. For EU programs, the verification scope also includes the active user account review required by the EMA GCP Guideline Section 5.4 and EMA's Computerised System Guideline Annex 4 and, for cloud-based systems, the authentication method assessment required by Annex 4 A4.13.

Configuration Element	ALCOA+ Property	Recommended Verification Frequency	EU-Specific Consideration
Password policy (length, complexity, expiration, reuse)	Attributable	Quarterly; after any platform update	EMA GCP Guideline Annex 4 Section A4.15 addresses password policies; EU standard requires documented password policy proportionate to system criticality
Session timeout enforcement	Attributable	Quarterly; after any platform update	EMA GCP Guideline Annex 4 Section A4.17 requires inactivity logout as a security control; risk-based implementation required

Configuration Element	ALCOA+ Property	Recommended Verification Frequency	EU-Specific Consideration
Audit trail enabled and field-level capture active	Attributable, Contemporaneous	Quarterly; after any platform update	EMA GCP Guideline Section 6.2.1 requires field-level capture; form-level insufficient for EU compliance
Audit trail immutability (cannot be modified by users)	Original	At validation; after any platform update	EMA GCP Guideline Section 6.2.1 requires protection against change, deletion, and access modification
Electronic signature re-authentication requirement	Attributable	Quarterly; after any platform update	EMA GCP Guideline Section 4.8 requires full re-authentication proven during closed system validation; session-based auth not acceptable alone

Configuration Element	ALCOA+ Property	Recommended Verification Frequency	EU-Specific Consideration
Signature manifestation completeness	Attributable	At validation; after any platform update	EMA GCP Guideline Section 4.8 and MHRA GxP Guidance Section 6.14 require signature manifestation to identify signer, role, meaning of signature, date and time
Signature-to-record binding (post-signature modification handling)	Attributable, Original	At validation; after any platform update	EMA GCP Guideline Section 4.8 requires signature visibly invalid if record subsequently changed; audit trail entry alone insufficient
Access permission matrix alignment	Attributable	Monthly; within 24 hours of any personnel change	EMA GCP Guideline Annex 4 requires records of authorization with access levels clearly documented; role change records maintained

Configuration Element	ALCOA+ Property	Recommended Verification Frequency	EU-Specific Consideration
Active user account recurrent review	Attributable	Defined interval (e.g., quarterly)	EMA GCP Guideline Section 5.4 and Annex 4 require periodic review to confirm access levels remain appropriate for active users throughout trial lifecycle
MFA configuration for remote/admin access	Attributable	At validation; when cloud access model changes	EMA GCP Guideline Annex 4 Sections A4.12-A4.13 require risk-based authentication; MFA appropriate or necessary for critical data and admin access to cloud-based systems
Administrator access to configuration settings is audit-trailed	Attributable	Quarterly	EMA GCP Guideline Section 5.4 requires records of authorization and system-recorded changes to access rights

Common Gaps That Generate Citations

The enforcement record for Part 11 citations in clinical research is remarkably consistent. The same failure modes appear across sponsor, CRO, and investigator site inspections, across different eClinical system platforms, and across organizations of very different sizes and sophistication. This consistency is informative: the gaps are not the product of obscure regulatory interpretation. They are the product of specific organizational choices that organizations continue to make despite knowing what inspectors find.

Shared Credentials and Delegated Signatures

Shared login credentials and the practice of applying electronic signatures under another person's credentials are the single most universally cited attributability failures in BIMO inspections. They are also among the most consistently cited findings in EU GCP inspections, where the EMA GCP Computerised System Guideline Annex 4 prohibition on shared logins for GxP data systems is cited directly. The regulatory consequences extend well beyond the immediate citation: every record created or modified under shared credentials becomes suspect. The inspector's question shifts from "was this entry correct?" to "can this entry be trusted?" Those are different questions, and the second one has no good answer when attribution has been destroyed.[103]

The investigator delegation log addresses a related but distinct issue. It documents the delegation of specific clinical trial responsibilities from the principal investigator to named sub-investigators and study staff. It does not authorize those staff members to apply the principal investigator's electronic signature. Delegation of responsibilities and delegation of signature authority are not the same thing. Under the EMA GCP Computerised System guideline Section 6.3, only authorized members of the investigator's staff, qualified and documented as such, may perform the sign-off on data. The investigator cannot delegate signature authority to unqualified or undocumented staff, and the authorization must be reflected in the system's user provisioning record, not merely in a paper delegation log.

Audit Trail Gaps and Gaps in Review

Part 11 requires that audit trails be retained for a period at least as long as the records themselves. It does not require that audit trails be reviewed. The EMA GCP Computerised System Guideline Section 6.2.2, however, does: proactive, ongoing review is expected unless justified otherwise. The failure mode documented in inspections is not primarily that audit trails do not exist. It is that audit trails exist but are never reviewed, so that anomalies visible in the audit trail go undetected until an inspector examines them. Under the EU inspection framework, the absence of documented review records is a citable finding before any data anomaly is examined.

Record Retention and Retrievability

The retrievability requirement creates a specific configuration obligation that is frequently overlooked during system selection: the organization must have a plan for producing the complete trial record if the eClinical system vendor's platform becomes unavailable. For EU-conducted trials, the EU Clinical Trial Regulation (CTR) Article 58 twenty-five-year retention requirement for trial master file records makes this obligation more demanding than the U.S. minimum. Vendor contract provisions, data escrow arrangements, and archive export formats must be addressed at system configuration and validated during the validation process. An organization whose entire clinical dataset exists only within a SaaS-hosted eClinical system platform, with no validated archive export capability and no vendor continuity agreement, has a retrievability gap regardless of how well everything else is configured.[104]

Implementation Checklist: Electronic Records and Signatures

The following checklist is organized by functional area and maps each control element to its primary regulatory authority and the ALCOA+ property it protects. EU-specific requirements derived from the EMA GCP Guideline and draft Annex 11 are identified; where the EU requirement exceeds the U.S. standard, the more demanding requirement is listed as the primary control. The checklist represents minimum required controls.

Control Element	Regulatory Authority	ALCOA+ Property	Implementation Note
ACCESS CONTROLS			
Unique user credentials for every system account; no shared logins	21 CFR Part 11.10(d); EMA GCP Guideline Annex 4 (shared logins not acceptable for GxP systems)	Attributable	Verified during user provisioning; confirmed in access control configuration review

Control Element	Regulatory Authority	ALCOA+ Property	Implementation Note
Password complexity, length, expiration, and reuse restrictions configured in system	21 CFR Part 11.10(d); EMA GCP Guideline Annex 4 Section A4.15 (EU: documented password policy required proportionate to system criticality)	Attributable	Configuration screenshot or export retained as validation evidence; EU standard more specific
Session inactivity timeout configured and enforced; user cannot disable it	21 CFR Part 11.10(d); EMA GCP Guideline Annex 4 Section A4.17 (EU: inactivity logout required as security control; risk-based implementation)	Attributable	Tested during validation; reverified after software updates
User provisioning documented with name, role, authorized permissions, effective date, and access level changes	21 CFR Part 11.10(d)(1); EMA GCP Guideline Section 5.4 (EU: system must record changes to user roles and access rights)	Attributable	System-generated access change records required in EU; paper-only record insufficient

Control Element	Regulatory Authority	ALCOA+ Property	Implementation Note
Deprovisioning with defined timeline following separation; documented evidence of timely execution	21 CFR Part 11.10(d); EMA GCP Guideline Annex 4	Attributable	Account deactivation log retained; monthly reconciliation against personnel roster
Recurrent active account review: manager confirmation of continued appropriateness of permissions	EMA GCP Guideline Section 5.4 and Annex 4 (EU: periodic review to confirm access levels remain appropriate for active users); implied by 21 CFR Part 11.10(d)	Attributable	EU requirement for periodic confirmation of all active accounts, not only departing staff
Administrator access restricted; that access itself audit-trailed	21 CFR Part 11.10(d)(2); EMA GCP Guideline Section 5.4	Attributable	Verified in configuration review; administrator action log retained

Control Element	Regulatory Authority	ALCOA+ Property	Implementation Note
MFA for signature-level and admin access events; documented gap assessment where not technically available	EMA GCP Guideline Annex 4 Sections A4.12-A4.13 (EU: risk-based authentication; MFA for remote auth in critical systems); 21 CFR Part 11.200 (two-component identification for first signing)	Attributable	EU framework applies risk-based MFA requirement to cloud clinical data access; document assessment
AUDIT TRAILS			
Audit trail enabled for all required data fields; field-level capture confirmed	21 CFR Part 11.10(e); EMA GCP Guideline Section 6.2.1 (EU: field-level explicitly required)	Attributable, Contemporaneous	EU requires field-level; form-level or page-level insufficient for EU compliance
Audit trail captures original value, new value, date/time stamp, user ID, and specific reason for change	21 CFR Part 11.10(e); ICH E6(R3) Sections 2.12.2 and 4.2.4; EMA GCP Guideline Section 6.2.1	Attributable, Contemporaneous, Original	Generic change reasons are an EMA GCP Guideline Section 6.2.1 non-compliance

Control Element	Regulatory Authority	ALCOA+ Property	Implementation Note
Audit trail cannot be modified or deleted by any user	21 CFR Part 11.10(e) and (k); EMA GCP Guideline Section 6.2.1 (protection against change, deletion, and access modification)	Original	Attempt-to-modify test documented in validation package
Admin deactivation of audit trail generates automatic log entry	EMA GCP Guideline Section 6.2.1 (EU explicit requirement); implied by 21 CFR Part 11.10(e)	Attributable	EU-specific: if admin can deactivate, that action must be automatically logged
Audit trail review procedure: frequency, scope, documentation, escalation pathway	ICH E6(R3) Sections 4.2.2 and 4.2.3; EMA GCP Guideline Section 6.2.2 (EU: proactive ongoing review expected)	Attributable (governance)	EU requires proactive ongoing review by default; departures must be justified
ELECTRONIC SIGNATURES			
Each signature unique to one individual; cannot be shared (closed system validation-proven)	21 CFR Part 11.50, 11.100; EMA GCP Guideline Section 4.8 (proven during validation for closed systems)	Attributable	EU: validation deliverable confirms Section 4.8 compliance; not assumed from platform certification

Control Element	Regulatory Authority	ALCOA+ Property	Implementation Note
Re-authentication required at the point of each signature; session-based auth not acceptable alone	21 CFR Part 11.200(a)(1); EMA GCP Guideline Section 4.8 (EU: full re-auth at every signature proven during closed system validation)	Attributable	EU standard more specific; prevents batch signing under single session auth
Unbreakable link: post-signature modification renders signature visibly invalid	21 CFR Part 11.70 (linked; cannot be excised); EMA GCP Guideline Section 4.8 (EU: must be visibly invalid, not only audit-trailed)	Attributable, Original	EU requires visible invalidation on modification, not merely audit trail entry; verify in validation testing
Signature manifestation includes signer identity, role, meaning of signature, date and time	21 CFR Part 11.50(a) (statement required); EMA GCP Guideline Section 4.8 and MHRA GxP Guidance Section 6.14 (EU: signer, role, meaning, date and time required)	Attributable	EU standard requires more specific manifestation elements than Part 11 currently specifies

Control Element	Regulatory Authority	ALCOA+ Property	Implementation Note
Investigator signature rate monitored; batch signing patterns flagged	ICH E6(R3) Section 4.2.3; EMA GCP Guideline Section 6.3 (EU: batch sign-off of workbooks explicitly inadequate)	Attributable	EU inspection citable finding for batch signing; audit trail review must include signature rate monitoring
EU ELECTRONIC INFORMED CONSENT (EU SITES ONLY)			
eConsent platform signed by at least two persons (participant/legal representative plus consent discussion conductor)	EMA GCP Guideline Annex 5, Section A5.3.2	Attributable	EU-specific requirement; FDA regulations do not specify two-person signature for consent forms
Consent signature timestamps cannot be manipulated by system settings; any document alteration invalidates signature	EMA GCP Guideline Annex 5, Section A5.3.2	Attributable, Original	EU-specific design requirement for eConsent platforms; verify in platform validation

Control Element	Regulatory Authority	ALCOA+ Property	Implementation Note
Open vs. closed system classification determined; eIDAS compliance verified for open EU systems	EMA GCP Guideline Section 4.8; Regulation (EU) No 910/2014 (eIDAS)	Attributable	EU-specific requirement; qualified electronic signature (QES) may be required for open EU systems
SYSTEM CONFIGURATION			
Baseline security configuration documented as part of validation package	21 CFR Part 11.10(a); EMA GCP Guideline validation annex (A2.3)	Attributable (governance)	Configuration export or screenshot retained with validation documentation
Post-update configuration verification triggered by every platform update or migration	ICH E6(R3) Section 4.3.4; EMA GCP Guideline validation annex change control (A2.10)	Attributable	EU change control requires risk assessment including data integrity impact
System clock synchronized to controlled, validated time server	21 CFR Part 11.10(e); PIC/S PI 041-1; EMA GCP Guideline Section 5.5 (timestamp)	Contemporaneous	Time server synchronization verified in validation; drift monitoring in place

RECORD RETENTION AND RETRIEVABILITY			
System can generate accurate, complete copies in human-readable and electronic form	21 CFR Part 11.10(b); EMA GCP Guideline Section 6.2.1 (human-readable audit trail format required)	Enduring, Available	Export function tested in validation; readable output confirmed without native platform access
Archive export capability validated; readable without live production system	21 CFR Part 11.10(b)(c); EMA GCP Guideline Section 6.11	Enduring, Available	Critical for cloud-hosted systems; EU CTR 25-year retention period extends obligation
Retention period requirements addressed in vendor contract; EU CTR 25-year eTMF standard addressed	21 CFR Part 11.10(c); 21 CFR Part 312.62; EU CTR Article 58	Enduring, Available	EU TMF retention of 25 years for authorized products far exceeds US minimum; address in vendor agreement

Hybrid Environments: When Paper and Electronic Coexist

Many clinical trial programs operate hybrid environments in which some records are created and maintained electronically while others remain on paper. Hybrid environments do not reduce the Part 11 requirements applicable to the electronic components. Where electronic records are used in lieu of paper records required by FDA regulations, Part 11 applies to those electronic records fully. The EMA Computerised System Guideline Section 6.1 provides additional specificity for EU-conducted trials: where data is captured first in a direct capture tool such as a trial participant diary or a special questionnaire, a documented procedure must exist to transfer or transcribe information into the medical record where relevant. For transcribed data, the original capture tool record is the source, and its relationship to the eCRF entry must be documented, auditable, and reconcilable.

Organizations designing hybrid environments should ask a foundational question before establishing the source data architecture: which record is the primary source, and why? If the eClinical system is the primary source, paper should not be used as an intermediate capture step, because the intermediate paper record creates an uncontrolled transcription variable. If paper is the primary source, the eClinical system entry is a transcription, and the relationship between the paper source and the eClinical system record must be documented, auditable, and reconcilable. Organizations that answer this question by default, allowing sites to develop their own source data practices, will discover the consequences during data management review or, more expensively, during inspection.

Beyond Technical Compliance: The Operational Discipline

The central problem illustrated in this chapter's opening scenario is not that the organization lacked knowledge of Part 11. Its policies were written by people who understood the regulation. The problem was that the organization treated compliance as a documentation activity: write the policy, file the validation package, and assume the system operates as described. The inspection revealed what that assumption had hidden.

Part 11 and its EU equivalents in practice are not states achieved at validation and maintained through inertia. They are operational disciplines that require systematic attention to the gap between what policies say and what systems do, between what controls are specified and what controls are actually enforced. The organizations that consistently perform well in electronic records and signature inspection findings are not the ones with the most sophisticated policy documents. They are the ones whose quality programs routinely verify that the systems operate as configured, that the configurations match the policies, that the EU-specific requirements for recurrent account review, re-authentication at signature, and field-level audit trail capture are in fact being met in production, and that the oversight activities called for by those policies are actually being performed.

The design checklist in this chapter provides a structural framework for that verification. It is not a substitute for the organizational commitment to actually use it. Configuration verification schedules must be followed, not filed. User access reconciliations must be performed, not planned. Audit trail review activities must be documented, not described. The distance between a compliant program and an inspectable one is measured in execution, not in documentation.[105]

CHAPTER NINE - KEY TAKEAWAYS
21 CFR Part 11 requirements for audit trails, access controls, electronic signatures, and record retention apply to every EDC system, eTMF platform, and electronic patient-reported outcome tool used in lieu of FDA-required paper records; the 2003 guidance narrowed scope but did not reduce the requirements applicable within that scope.
The EMA GCP Computerized System Guideline Section 4.8 establishes a four-element electronic signature framework for EU-conducted trials (authentication, non-repudiation, unbreakable link, timestamp); for closed clinical systems, compliance with this framework is a validation deliverable that must be tested and documented before production deployment.
The EU closed/open system distinction determines which legal framework governs electronic signatures: closed systems (sponsor-provisioned users) must validate against Section 4.8; open systems at EU sites must comply with eIDAS, potentially requiring qualified electronic signatures with certified trust service providers.
Access controls must ensure that every action in a clinical data system is attributable to a uniquely identified, authorized individual; shared credentials, generic accounts, and unrevoked post-separation accounts each independently destroy the attribution function for all records they touch.
Electronic signatures in clinical research are evidentiary attestations, not workflow checkpoints; batch signing patterns, delegated signatures, and post-signature modifications without re-signature each compromise the attestation value; EU GCP Guideline Section 6.3 explicitly states that batch sign-off of workbooks is not adequate.
Electronic informed consent for EU trials is governed by EMA GCP Computerised System Guideline Annex 5.3, which requires signatures by at least two persons, timestamps that cannot be manipulated, and document alteration triggering signature invalidation; these requirements exceed FDA consent regulations.
System configuration must be verified in operation, not only at validation; software updates routinely reset security settings to vendor defaults; EMA GCP Computerised System Guideline Annex 2 change control requires risk assessment for each change covering data integrity impact.
The organizations that perform best in inspection findings are those whose quality programs routinely verify that systems operate as configured and that EU-specific

CHAPTER NINE - KEY TAKEAWAYS
requirements for recurrent account review, re-authentication at signature, and field-level audit trail capture are being met in production.

CHAPTER TEN

Decentralized and Hybrid Trials: New Frontiers for Data Integrity

> *Every data element that informs a regulatory submission must satisfy ALCOA+ requirements regardless of the technology, location, or organizational tier at which it was originally generated; decentralized collection does not create a parallel compliance standard.*

The Phase III trial was, by most operational measures, a success. Patient recruitment met its enrollment target ahead of schedule. Dropout rates were below the protocol assumption. The primary endpoint data arrived at the central database with query rates that any data manager would regard as acceptable. What the sponsor did not know, at the time of database lock, was that the composite endpoint score driving the efficacy analysis was built on a foundation the agency would find impossible to verify.

The trial had used a validated eCOA application to capture daily patient-reported symptom assessments on sponsor-provided tablets. The application had been qualified. The protocol clearly specified eDiary completion as a trial requirement. When the sponsor submitted the marketing application, the clinical dataset included the composite scores exported from the eCOA vendor's platform. What the submission did not include, because the sponsor had not retained it, was the device-level session data: the raw logs recording each patient interaction, the individual item responses underlying each composite score, the timestamps confirming when entries were made, and the metadata showing whether any responses had been modified after initial submission.

The agency requested the underlying session data during review. The eCOA vendor had retained it, but on infrastructure the sponsor could not independently access. The contractual arrangement between sponsor and vendor had not addressed data return obligations or inspection access rights. Retrieval required negotiation, a data format conversion the vendor had not previously performed, and a validation exercise the sponsor had not anticipated. The review clock stopped. The marketing application, for a compound the sponsor had spent a decade developing, sat in a queue while the parties resolved a data custody problem that the trial's data governance framework should have addressed before the first patient was enrolled.

Decentralized and hybrid trials represent the most operationally significant transformation in clinical research methodology in a generation. They expand the patient population that can participate in research, reduce the burden on investigator sites, generate richer longitudinal datasets than periodic site visits allow, and enable trial designs that more closely reflect how patients actually live with their conditions. They also create data integrity challenges that the existing regulatory framework was not built to address and that sponsors, CROs, and eClinical technology vendors are still working out how to manage. This chapter addresses those challenges systematically.

> *The architecture of a decentralized trial distributes data collection across dozens of technologies and thousands of patients; ALCOA+ does not distribute with it.*

What Decentralized and Hybrid Trials Actually Are

The term decentralized clinical trial, often shortened to DCT, encompasses a wide range of trial designs that share a common characteristic: some or all of the clinical activities that traditionally occur at an investigator site occur instead at or near the patient's location. Telehealth visits replace or supplement in-person assessments. Wearable sensors and implantable devices generate continuous physiological data streams. Electronic patient-reported outcome instruments, delivered on smartphones or dedicated devices, capture symptom assessments, functional status measurements, and quality of life data without site staff involvement. Home health nurses conduct procedures that would otherwise require a site visit. Direct-to-patient drug shipment removes the site from the supply chain.

A fully decentralized trial has no traditional investigator site at all: every patient interaction occurs remotely, and the trial infrastructure is distributed across a network of technology platforms, service providers, and patient homes. A hybrid trial combines conventional site activities with decentralized elements, using site visits for procedures that genuinely require them and remote data collection for everything else. Most contemporary DCTs are hybrid: the fully decentralized model works for some therapeutic areas and patient populations, but the investigator site retains essential functions in trials involving complex medical procedures, imaging, or safety monitoring that cannot be replicated remotely.

The regulatory frameworks that govern these trials are the same frameworks that have governed conventional trials for decades. FDA's primary DCT guidance, published in 2023 as a final guidance document, makes this explicit: decentralized elements do not create different data integrity requirements, they create different operational contexts in which the same requirements must be met. ICH E6(R3), finalized in January 2025, applies to all clinical investigations without distinguishing between centralized and decentralized designs. The ALCOA+ properties that define a compliant clinical record apply to a wearable sensor reading with the same force they apply to a CRF entry made by a site coordinator.

The DCT Data Landscape: Source Types and Their ALCOA+ Implications

Data Source Category	ALCOA+ Considerations Specific to DCT Context
Wearable and implantable sensors	Attributability to device and patient ID through device registration; contemporaneity through device clock synchronization; original record is device-level log, not aggregated summary; endurance requires vendor data retention commitment for full regulatory period
Electronic patient-reported outcomes (ePRO/eCOA)	Original record is session-level log, not composite score; completeness requires all individual item responses retained; contemporaneity verifiable through entry timestamps; accuracy requires confirmation that composite algorithm applied matches validated specification
Telemedicine encounters	Attributability requires clinician identity capture; original record is the encounter recording or structured data entry,

Data Source Category	ALCOA+ Considerations Specific to DCT Context
	not a post-encounter summary; completeness requires all clinical observations documented; availability depends on platform retention policies
Electronic health record data	Original record held by the healthcare provider, not the sponsor; traceability from EHR extract to submission dataset must be documented; contemporaneity reflects clinical documentation timing, not study visit timing; accuracy requires reconciliation against protocol definitions
Home health visit data	Attributability requires nurse identity and credentialing documentation; contemporaneity requires contemporaneous capture, not post-visit reconstruction; original record is the structured data entry, not the visit report
Direct-to-patient drug accountability	Original records of shipment, receipt, and return must be attributable to specific patients; audit trail of drug dispensing system constitutes source data for accountability; completeness requires reconciliation of all units dispensed
Central laboratory with remote sample collection	Chain of custody documentation is an ALCOA+ requirement; sample collection timestamp at patient location is source data; original laboratory record is the analyzer output, not the results report transmitted to EDC
Digital biomarkers and AI-generated endpoints	Algorithm version control required; original input data and algorithmic transformation must be retainable for reconstruction; traceability from raw sensor data through processing layers to reported value is an emerging ALCOA+ requirement

The Regulatory Framework for DCT Data Integrity

FDA's 2023 Decentralized Clinical Trial Guidance

FDA's guidance on decentralized clinical trials, finalized in May 2023, is the most operationally detailed regulatory document addressing DCT data integrity from a US regulatory perspective. Its core contribution is not new requirements, but a clear articulation of how existing requirements apply in decentralized contexts. For practitioners who have wondered whether the existing clinical data integrity framework was intended to reach wearable devices, telemedicine encounters, and home-based procedures, the guidance answers that question without ambiguity: it was, and it does.

On electronic source data, the guidance reaffirms the position established in FDA's 2013 electronic source data guidance and reinforced in ICH E6(R3): where data is captured directly by an electronic system designed for that purpose, the electronic record is the source record. For a wearable device capturing continuous heart rate data, the source record is the device-level data stream, not a daily summary report. For an ePRO instrument capturing symptom assessment, the source record is the session log, not the composite score. The guidance states that sponsors must ensure these records are retained in accessible form for the full duration required under 21 CFR Part 312.62, regardless of whether that retention is maintained by the sponsor directly or by a qualified vendor.

The guidance addresses the telemedicine encounter directly. When a licensed healthcare provider conducts a clinical assessment via video, the resulting clinical observations constitute source data. The sponsor must ensure that adequate documentation of those observations exists in a form that permits verification by a monitor or inspector. The guidance does not specify the form that documentation must take, but it is unambiguous that a video recording alone, without structured data capture of the clinical observations, is not adequate. The source document for a telemedicine visit is the documented clinical assessment, and it must satisfy the same attributability, legibility, and contemporaneity requirements as any other source document in the trial.

On investigator oversight in decentralized trials, the guidance preserves the fundamental structure of the investigator's responsibility framework. Even when clinical activities occur at the patient's home, the investigator of record retains responsibility for the conduct of those activities and for the accuracy of the data they generate. The guidance requires that investigators have adequate oversight mechanisms for DCT elements, including procedures to verify that remote data collection is occurring as specified, that patients are using devices correctly, and that data quality issues are identified and addressed in real time. The practical implication is that a sponsor cannot accept remote data passively. Oversight of data quality as it is generated, not at database lock, is required.[106]

ICH E6(R3) and Decentralized Trial Design

ICH E6(R3) addresses decentralized trial elements throughout the guideline rather than in a single dedicated section, which reflects how the guideline conceptualizes the issue: decentralized collection is not a special case requiring special treatment, it is a manifestation of the trial design flexibility that E6(R3) was written to accommodate while preserving the integrity standards that make clinical data trustworthy.

The E6(R3) quality management system framework, described in Annex 1, has particular relevance for DCT programs. The QMS approach requires sponsors to identify the critical data elements and critical processes of a trial prospectively and to implement risk proportionate oversight for each. In a hybrid trial, the remote data collection elements almost always represent higher inherent risk than site-based collection: the investigator's direct oversight is reduced, the technology infrastructure is more complex, the chain from patient observation to database entry involves more intermediary systems, and the opportunity for data quality problems to accumulate undetected before monitoring visits is greater. The E6(R3) QMS framework is not merely compatible with DCT data oversight; it is the appropriate tool for designing that oversight.

E6(R3)'s explicit ALCOA+ mandate, which Chapter 3 addresses in detail, applies to remote data sources with a directness that the original ICH E6 framework, written before the era of consumer wearables and telemedicine-enabled trials, did not contemplate. The contemporaneity requirement means that a patient-reported outcome captured on a smartphone must be captured at the time of the relevant experience, not reconstructed from memory at the end of the day. The attributability requirement means that the system must be capable of identifying which patient completed a given entry and when. The accuracy requirement means that what the patient reports must reach the database unchanged by intermediary processing, or that any transformations applied must themselves be documented and verifiable.[107]

The MHRA Perspective on Decentralized Data

MHRA's framework for decentralized trial data integrity, while not compiled in a single guidance document, represents some of the most practically useful regulatory thinking on the subject. MHRA's inspection experience with DCT programs has informed its guidance development on digital health tools and electronic source data, and MHRA's emphasis on organizational accountability rather than system compliance has particular relevance for DCT data governance.

MHRA's position, consistent with its broader data integrity philosophy, is that the question of whether remote data satisfies ALCOA+ cannot be resolved by vendor attestation or contractual warranty. The sponsor must be able to verify, through its own oversight mechanisms, that the data generated by DCT technologies is attributable, contemporaneous, original, accurate, complete, consistent, enduring, and available. A sponsor that has outsourced DCT data collection to a qualified vendor but has not built oversight mechanisms to verify data quality as it is generated has not satisfied its own obligations under GCP. The vendor qualification provides assurance about the vendor's systems; it does not substitute for the sponsor's ongoing oversight.

The ALCOA+ Properties in Decentralized Context

Attributable: Who Generated This Data and When?

Attributability in a conventional trial is relatively straightforward: a site coordinator's login credentials identify them as the author of an EDC entry, and the system timestamp records when the entry was made. In a decentralized trial, attributability requires considerably more infrastructure. A wearable device generating continuous physiological data must be linked, with certainty, to a specific enrolled subject. The device registration process, the patient consent documentation capturing which device was assigned to which patient, and the chain of custody from device provisioning to patient receipt to data transmission all contribute to the attributability record.

For ePRO instruments, attributability requires that the application can identify the patient completing an assessment. Most modern ePRO platforms accomplish this through patient-specific login credentials, device registration, or biometric authentication. The validation of the authentication mechanism is part of the attributability framework. An ePRO application that can be accessed by multiple household members using shared credentials, or that does not require authentication before each assessment session, does not satisfy attributability, regardless of how well-designed its scoring algorithms are.

Telemedicine encounters present an attributability challenge at both ends of the encounter: the clinician conducting the assessment must be identified, credentialed, and linked to the assessment record, and the patient must be positively identified before the clinical assessment begins. The MHRA guidance on telemedicine in clinical trials requires that identity verification procedures be specified in the protocol or protocol-level procedures and that their execution be documented for each encounter. A telemedicine assessment conducted without a documented patient identity verification step does not satisfy attributability.[108]

Contemporaneous: When Did This Actually Happen?

Contemporaneity is the ALCOA+ property most directly tested by the specific failure modes of decentralized data collection. The regulatory definition is clear: data must be recorded at the time of the activity, not reconstructed from memory, not completed in batches at the end of the week, not pre-filled by site staff on behalf of patients. In practice, ensuring contemporaneous data collection from patients operating independently in their homes, without site staff supervision, requires design choices that go beyond what conventional eCRF design addresses.

Wearable devices that generate continuous passive data streams are, from a contemporaneity standpoint, the strongest DCT data collection mechanism. The device records what it observes at the time it observes it; there is no human decision about when to capture the data, no opportunity for retrospective fabrication at the record level. The contemporaneity risk for passive wearable data lies not in the capture but in the transmission: devices that batch data for periodic upload rather than transmitting continuously may show gaps that represent either genuine data loss or transmission delays. The distinction matters: a gap that represents missing data is a completeness issue, while a gap that represents transmission delay is an availability issue. The audit trail must be capable of distinguishing between them.

For active ePRO instruments requiring patient engagement, contemporaneity depends on patient compliance behavior and on the system's ability to detect and flag non-contemporaneous completion. A diary application that accepts entries backdated to cover missed assessments without capturing a late entry indicator has no contemporaneity protection. Well-designed ePRO systems address this through time-lock windows that prevent entry outside a specified window relative to the scheduled assessment time, clear patient-facing language in the application that explains the purpose of timely completion, and automated flags in the data export identifying assessments completed outside the specified window. These are design requirements, not optional features.[109]

DESIGN REQUIREMENT: ePRO CONTEMPORANEITY CONTROLS

Every ePRO application used to collect efficacy or safety data in a clinical trial must implement time-lock windows that define the acceptable completion window for each assessment type, flag out-of-window completions in both the patient-facing interface and the exported data, prevent retrospective fabrication of missed assessments, and capture the actual completion timestamp in the device-level log independently of any patient-entered date. These controls must be validated as part of the system qualification and their configuration must be specified in the data management plan.

Original: What Is the Source Record in a Multi-Layer System?

The original data question is where decentralized trial data integrity generates the most consequential regulatory complexity. In a system where a wearable device generates raw sensor readings, an on-device algorithm aggregates them into a derived metric, a transmission layer compresses and packages the data for upload, a vendor platform receives and stores the transmission, and an integration layer transfers a processed summary to the sponsor's EDC, there are at least five places that data could be described as the original record. Regulators have a clear answer to which one it actually is.

The original record is the first unaltered capture of the observation. For a continuous heart rate monitor, that is the raw sensor reading before any on-device processing. For an ePRO instrument, it is the individual item response as entered by the patient, not the composite score. For a telemedicine encounter, it is the structured clinical assessment documented during or immediately following the encounter, not a post-encounter summary generated from notes. Every downstream representation of that data, every processed metric, every composite score, every summary report, every EDC entry, is a derived document. The original must be retained and must be accessible for the duration required by the applicable regulations.[110]

The practical implication is that the sponsor's data retention obligation extends to records held by vendors, on infrastructure the sponsor may not directly control. A sponsor that retains composite ePRO scores in its EDC while the vendor deletes the session-level logs after the contract ends has not satisfied its retention obligation. Contractual arrangements with DCT technology vendors must specify data return rights, define what constitutes the original record for each data type, require retention of original records for the full regulatory period, and give the sponsor and regulatory authorities access to those records for inspection. These are not optional contractual provisions. They are the operationalization of the original data principle in a distributed data environment.[111]

Accurate, Complete, and Consistent in Patient-Generated Data

The accuracy requirement creates a verification challenge that is fundamentally different in a decentralized context than in a site-based trial. In a conventional trial, a clinical research coordinator enters data that a site physician has documented in the source record, and a sponsor monitor can conduct source data verification by comparing the EDC entry against the paper or electronic source document. In a DCT, the patient is often both the data generator and the data entry agent, the ePRO application is both the source system and the data capture tool, and the conventional Site Data Verification (SDV) model has no direct analog.

ICH E6(R3) addresses this explicitly. For data captured directly by patients using validated ePRO instruments, source data verification against an independent source document is not the applicable verification model because the ePRO record is the source document. The verification framework must instead focus on the validity of the ePRO instrument itself, the adequacy of patient training on its correct use, the plausibility and consistency of the resulting data patterns, and the audit trail integrity that allows reconstruction of what the patient entered and when. This is a different verification methodology, not an absence of verification.[112]

Completeness in a DCT context requires particular attention to planned versus actual data collection windows. A wearable device that was removed by the patient during a two-week period, generating a gap in the data stream, produces incomplete data for that period. The question of how to handle that gap, whether it represents missing data, whether it can be imputed, and what the regulatory consequence is for the efficacy analysis, must be addressed in the statistical analysis plan and the data management plan before database lock. A sponsor that discovers a systematic completeness problem during the submission review is in a considerably worse position than one that designed its data collection oversight to detect and address such problems in real time.[113]

Vendor Qualification in the DCT Ecosystem

A conventional Phase III trial may use a handful of validated systems: an EDC platform, an IRT system, an eTMF, perhaps a CTMS. A decentralized or hybrid trial of comparable scope may involve a wearable device vendor, an eCOA platform provider, a telemedicine technology provider, a home health service organization, a direct-to-patient logistics provider, a central laboratory with a patient-accessible sample collection network, and a data integration platform aggregating outputs from all of these into the sponsor's clinical database. Each of these vendors generates or handles data that may constitute source data for the trial. Each carries independent obligations under the applicable regulatory frameworks. Each represents a potential failure point in the trial's data integrity infrastructure.

The qualification framework for DCT vendors must be proportionate to the data integrity risk each vendor represents and must be specific to the data types that vendor generates or handles. Qualifying an eCOA platform vendor to use that vendor's platform in a GCP-regulated trial requires, at minimum, evidence that the platform is validated for its intended use, that it generates and retains audit trail data at the level of detail required for GCP compliance, that it implements access controls sufficient to satisfy attributability requirements, that its original session records are retained for the full regulatory retention period and accessible for inspection, and that the data it exports to the clinical database can be reconciled against those original records. A qualification process that reviews only the vendor's SOPs and ISO certification does not provide this evidence.

The wearable device vendor qualification presents additional complexity. A device generating data that will be used as a primary or key secondary endpoint must be qualified not only for its software systems but for the scientific validity of its sensor technology, the clinical validation of its algorithms, and the fitness of its output for regulatory submission. FDA has published guidance on software as a medical device and on digital health technology that establishes the regulatory framework for device qualification; what is often missing in clinical trial vendor qualification programs is the translation of that framework into a GCP-specific qualification process that addresses ALCOA+ properties alongside device performance specifications.[114]

The Vendor Data Return Obligation

Of all the contractual and operational requirements that DCT vendor relationships create, the data return obligation is the one most frequently omitted and most consequentially problematic when it is. The scenario that opened this chapter is not unusual: sponsors discover, at database lock or during submission review, that original records are held by vendors on infrastructure the sponsor cannot access, and that the contractual arrangements governing those relationships did not address data return.

The data return obligation, in its full scope, requires that the sponsor can retrieve the original records held by each DCT vendor in a format that is readable without the vendor's software, for the full regulatory retention period, regardless of whether the commercial relationship between sponsor and vendor remains active. A vendor that retains data on its proprietary platform and provides access only through its own interface has not satisfied the availability requirement. When the vendor's contract expires, when the vendor is acquired, when the vendor discontinues the platform, the sponsor's ability to access those records evaporates. The regulatory retention obligation does not evaporate with it.[115]

Practically sound data return provisions specify: the format in which data will be delivered, with a preference for open standards over proprietary formats; the timeframe within which data will be made available on demand; the scope of data covered, including original session logs, audit trails, and metadata, not only processed outputs; the obligation to return data at contract expiration without additional charge; and the vendor's obligation to maintain retrievability of the data for the sponsor's benefit for the full retention period even after the commercial relationship ends. These provisions require legal review and negotiation. They also require that someone in the sponsor's data management organization understands what records need to be returned, because a provision to return the data is worthless if the requester does not know what to ask for.

Vendor Type	Minimum Data Integrity Qualification Requirements
eCOA / ePRO platform provider	System validation documentation; session-level log retention with audit trail; time-lock window configuration verification; composite algorithm version control; data return obligation for session logs and metadata; audit trail access for inspection
Wearable / implantable device vendor	Device validation for intended clinical use; sensor algorithm version control; raw data stream retention; device clock synchronization documentation; device-to-platform transmission log; fit-for-purpose assessment for regulatory submission

Vendor Type	Minimum Data Integrity Qualification Requirements
Telemedicine platform provider	HIPAA/GDPR-compliant recording or structured data capture; clinician and patient identity verification; encounter documentation retention; audit trail of session activity; data return obligation for encounter records
Home health service organization	Training documentation for nurses/coordinators; protocol-specific procedure verification; contemporaneous data capture capability; attribution records linking staff identity to specific patient contacts; escalation procedures for protocol deviations
Direct-to-patient logistics provider	Chain of custody documentation for each shipment; return and accountability records; temperature/condition monitoring where applicable; attribution of all handling events to identified personnel
Data integration platform	Validated data transformation rules with version control; reconciliation capability between source data and transformed output; audit trail covering all transformation events; original record retention or documented linkage to upstream vendor systems

Electronic Health Record Data as Clinical Trial Source

The use of electronic health record data as a source of clinical trial observations, either to supplement protocol-specified data collection or as a primary data source in trials specifically designed around real-world evidence, presents an ALCOA+ challenge that is qualitatively different from the DCT data challenges described above. In a DCT using wearables or ePRO instruments, the sponsor retains some degree of control over the data collection infrastructure. With EHR data, the sponsor typically has no control at all: the data was generated for clinical care purposes, on systems owned and operated by healthcare providers, according to documentation practices designed for clinical rather than research purposes.

The attributability of EHR data is, in principle, strong: most EHR systems capture the identity of the clinician who made each entry, the timestamp of each entry, and the audit trail of any modifications. In practice, the attributability of specific EHR entries to specific clinical events in the trial timeline requires reconciliation between the EHR's documentation structure and the trial's data collection requirements. A laboratory result documented in the EHR as part of routine clinical care may or may not be contemporaneous with a scheduled trial assessment; it may have been generated by a laboratory not participating in the trial's central laboratory program; it may have been documented by a care team member who is not the trial's principal investigator. Each of these factors affects how the result can be used in the trial's efficacy or safety analysis.

The originality question for EHR data is particularly consequential. The EHR record itself is the original record; what the sponsor receives is an extract of that record, typically in a structured data format such as FHIR or HL7, that represents a subset of the information in the original EHR entry. The extract is a derived document. FDA's position on EHR-derived data in clinical submissions, reflected in its 2019 guidance on electronic health records in clinical investigations, requires that sponsors be able to demonstrate a verifiable path from the extracted data element to its source in the EHR, that the extraction process was validated, and that the mapping between EHR data elements and clinical trial endpoint definitions is documented and consistently applied. These are traceability requirements, and they are demanding ones.

The Real-World Evidence Question

The growing use of real-world evidence in clinical development and regulatory submissions has intensified regulatory attention to the data integrity of non-trial data sources. FDA's framework for evaluating real-world evidence, articulated in a series of guidance documents published since 2019, applies ALCOA+ as the evaluative standard for RWE data fitness: real-world data sources that cannot demonstrate that their records are attributable, contemporaneous, original, accurate, complete, consistent, enduring, and available cannot support regulatory conclusions regardless of their statistical sophistication. The analytical design of an RWE study cannot compensate for source data that does not meet these properties.

For sponsors incorporating RWE elements into decentralized trial designs, such as using claims data to supplement patient-reported outcomes, incorporating EHR laboratory results alongside trial-collected assessments, or using wearable-generated real-world activity data to contextualize clinical endpoint measurements, the ALCOA+ obligations apply to each data stream independently. The weakest data integrity link in the evidence package does not escape scrutiny by virtue of being accompanied by higher-quality data. An integrated analysis built on a mix of ALCOA+-compliant and non-compliant data sources requires a clear and documented rationale for how each data source is used, what its limitations are, and how those limitations affect the conclusions drawn from the integrated dataset.

Common Failure Modes in Decentralized Trial Data Integrity

The inspection and enforcement record for decentralized trial data integrity is, by the standards of more mature regulatory areas, still developing. DCT programs are relatively recent at scale, and the regulatory infrastructure for inspecting them is developing in parallel with the operational infrastructure for running them. That said, the failure modes that have surfaced through FDA BIMO inspections, EMA GCP inspections, and sponsor internal audits of DCT programs are consistent enough to be instructive.

Failure Mode 1: The Composite Score Problem

The most consistently documented data integrity problem in ePRO and eCOA-based trials is the retention of composite scores rather than original session data. The pattern is described at the opening of this chapter. It persists because sponsors and vendors frequently do not distinguish, operationally, between the data they need for the efficacy analysis and the data they are required to retain under GCP. The composite score is what drives the analysis; the session log is what satisfies the original data requirement. Both must be retained. The session log, not the composite score, is the source data.

The error compounds when sponsors conduct source data verification against composite scores rather than session logs, because it means that the SDV process itself cannot detect errors in the compositing algorithm, errors in individual item coding, or patterns in patient response behavior that would be visible in the session log but are obscured in the aggregated score. An SDV process that verifies the composite score in the EDC against the composite score in the vendor's export has verified a derived document against itself. It has verified nothing about the original record.

Failure Mode 2: Device Clock Synchronization Gaps

Contemporaneity in wearable device data depends on the accuracy of the device clock. A device with an unsynchronized clock generates timestamps that may be hours or days offset from actual event time. In a trial where the timing of a physiological measurement relative to a dose or a clinical event is part of the scientific question, clock synchronization failure is not a minor data quality issue. It is a validity problem that can render the relevant data unusable for the intended analysis.

Device clock synchronization must be addressed as a protocol-level design requirement, not as an afterthought. The device qualification process must include verification that clock synchronization occurs at each connection event and that the synchronization is logged in the audit trail. The data management plan must specify how clock synchronization failures are detected, documented, and handled in the analysis. A site-wide clock failure that is not detected until the data lock review, by which point the affected subjects have completed the trial, creates a problem with no clean solution.

Failure Mode 3: Vendor Contract Expiration Without Data Return

DCT vendor contracts frequently expire at or shortly after the clinical database lock, because sponsors structure vendor agreements around the trial's operational timeline rather than the regulatory retention timeline. The minimum retention obligation for records of clinical investigations under 21 CFR Part 312.62 extends two years from the later of the date a marketing application is approved or the date the investigation is discontinued and FDA is notified. Applicable EU requirements under CTR Article 58 impose a 25-year retention period for trial master file records. Sponsors typically apply internal retention policies that exceed the regulatory floor. A vendor contract that terminates at database lock creates a data custody gap that may span the full duration of the applicable retention period.

The industry has not fully internalized this problem, in part because the regulatory consequence typically does not materialize until a post-approval inspection or a litigation demand requires access to original DCT records. By that point, the vendor may be acquired, reorganized, or operating a completely different platform. The data may exist somewhere, in a format no longer supported by available tools, on infrastructure no longer maintained by personnel who understand it. Data return provisions in vendor contracts are not a nice-to-have. They are the mechanism through which sponsors discharge their regulatory retention obligation for data held on vendor infrastructure.

Failure Mode 4: Inadequate Investigator Oversight of Remote Elements

Investigator responsibility does not diminish in a decentralized trial. The investigator of record for a DCT subject is responsible for the conduct of all trial activities for that subject, including activities conducted remotely by patients, home health nurses, or telemedicine clinicians. The practical consequence is that investigators must have oversight mechanisms proportionate to the remote activities they are overseeing, and those mechanisms must be documented and operational.

FDA's 2023 DCT guidance notes that remote principal investigators, investigators who oversee subjects in geographic areas where they are not physically present, must have procedures to verify that protocol-specified activities are being conducted correctly. An investigator whose oversight of remote ePRO completion consists of reviewing summary completion statistics at the weekly data review meeting does not have adequate oversight of a patient who is completing all assessments in a single sitting at the end of each week rather than daily as the protocol requires. The system-level controls that detect and flag non-contemporaneous completion are the investigator's oversight mechanism; without them, the investigator cannot discharge the oversight responsibility the regulations assign.

Non-Compliant DCT Data Governance Patterns	Compliant DCT Data Governance Patterns
• Retaining composite ePRO scores but not session-level logs • Vendor contracts that expire at database lock without data return provisions • Device clock synchronization not included in device qualification scope • SDV conducted against composite scores rather than original session data • Investigator oversight limited to summary statistics without anomaly detection • EHR extract validation not performed or not documented • ePRO time-lock window not configured or not validated as configured • Data return format not specified in vendor contract	• Session-level logs retained as source data; composite scores retained as derived analysis data • Vendor contracts include data return provisions extending for the full regulatory retention period • Device clock synchronization logged in audit trail; synchronization failures trigger data flagging protocol • SDV process references original session logs; composite algorithm version documented and verified • Real-time ePRO compliance monitoring with anomaly flags reviewed by sponsor DM team • EHR extract process validated; mapping to endpoint definitions documented; source records traceable • Time-lock window configuration specified in DMP, verified in system qualification, logged in audit trail • Data return format specified as open standard; return tested before commercial deployment

Designing a DCT Data Governance Framework

A DCT data governance framework is, at its core, the application of the data integrity by design philosophy described in Chapter 5 to a trial architecture that distributes data generation across many technologies, locations, and organizations. The design principles are the same; the implementation complexity is greater. The starting point is the same question that governs all data integrity by design work: what data does this trial generate, where does it come from, how does it move from origination to submission, and what could go wrong at each step?

The DCT Data Flow Map

Every DCT program should produce, before any system is deployed, a data flow map that traces each data type from the point of origination through every intermediary system to its final representation in the clinical database and regulatory submission. The map is not a system architecture diagram, although it should be consistent with one. It is a data provenance document: for each data element, it identifies the original record, the systems through which that record passes, the transformations applied at each step, the retention location for the original record, and the ALCOA+ risks at each transition point.

Data flow mapping for a hybrid trial will typically reveal that the data governance framework has gaps: places where the original record is held by a vendor system with no documented data return obligation, where the transformation between sensor output and composite score is not version-controlled, where the attribution chain breaks because the device is registered to a site rather than a specific patient. These gaps are far easier to address before the trial starts than after the first patient is enrolled. The data flow map is the tool that makes them visible.

The Real-Time Quality Framework

DCT data quality cannot be managed retrospectively. In a conventional trial with periodic monitoring visits, a site that has been generating problematic data for six months can still be visited, the source documents reviewed, and remediation pursued. In a decentralized trial, the patient who completed all ePRO assessments in a single sitting on Sunday afternoon for eight consecutive weeks cannot retrospectively complete them contemporaneously. The data quality problem has already happened; the only question is whether it is detected and documented, or whether it reaches the database unchallenged.

Real-time quality monitoring for DCT programs requires centralized monitoring infrastructure capable of detecting the specific failure patterns associated with remote data collection: ePRO compliance rate by patient with anomaly flags for burst completion; device connectivity gaps by patient with flags for extended loss of data; response pattern anomalies suggesting random or inattentive responding; and timestamp patterns inconsistent with the protocol's data collection schedule. These are not novel monitoring capabilities; they are the natural extension of the centralized monitoring approaches that FDA's 2013 risk-based monitoring guidance endorsed for conventional trials. The key design requirement is that the monitoring system is configured before the trial starts, that its thresholds and escalation criteria are documented in the data management plan, and that the outputs are reviewed and acted upon throughout the trial, not at database lock.

The E6(R3) quality management system framework provides the governance structure for this approach. The QMS requires that quality tolerance limits be defined for critical data elements and critical processes. For a hybrid trial using ePRO as a primary endpoint instrument, the ePRO compliance rate, the rate of out-of-window completions, and the rate of anomalous response patterns are legitimate QTL metrics. Their definition before the trial starts, their monitoring throughout, and the documentation of actions taken when they are exceeded is precisely what the E6(R3) QMS model requires, and it is the data governance infrastructure that makes a DCT program defensible on inspection.

DCT Data Integrity Inspection Readiness Checklist

Area	Inspection-Ready Condition	Common Gap
ePRO original records	Session-level logs retained by vendor under documented retention obligation; accessible for inspection without vendor software dependency	Composite scores in EDC but session logs held only on vendor platform with no data return provision
Wearable device data	Raw sensor data retained with device clock synchronization log; algorithm version documented and version-controlled	Processed metrics in clinical database with no retained raw data or algorithm documentation
Device attribution	Each device registration linked to specific patient ID; chain of custody from provisioning to return documented	Devices assigned to sites, not patients; no individual device-to-patient attribution record

Area	Inspection-Ready Condition	Common Gap
ePRO time-lock configuration	Time-lock window specified in DMP; configuration verified in system qualification; out-of-window completions flagged in data export	Time-lock not configured or configured but not validated; no flag in exported data for out-of-window entries
Investigator oversight documentation	Written procedures for investigator oversight of remote activities; evidence of oversight execution for each subject	No documented oversight procedure; investigator oversight limited to site-level summary reports
Vendor data governance	Qualification documentation addressing ALCOA+ for each vendor system; data return provisions in each vendor contract; data return tested	Vendor qualifications address SOPs and certifications but not ALCOA+ properties; no data return provisions in contracts
EHR data traceability	Extraction validation documented; mapping to endpoint definitions documented; source record identifier retained in clinical database	EHR extracts used without extraction validation or documented mapping; source record identifier not retained
Telemedicine encounter records	Encounter documentation structured to capture clinical observations attributably and contemporaneously; encounter records retained as source data	Encounter records consist of unstructured video without documented clinical assessment; no source document for remote clinical evaluations

Area	Inspection-Ready Condition	Common Gap
Centralized monitoring	Real-time quality monitoring configured with documented QTL thresholds; monitoring outputs reviewed and acted upon with documentation	Quality monitoring performed only at database lock; no defined QTL thresholds; monitoring outputs not documented
Data flow documentation	Data flow map covering all DCT data streams from origination to submission; ALCOA+ risk points identified and addressed	No data flow map; data governance documentation limited to validated system descriptions without end-to-end traceability

What Regulators Are Looking For

FDA's bioresearch monitoring inspection program has adapted its inspection protocols for DCT programs. The adaptation is less about new inspection techniques than about applying existing investigative methods to new environments. An inspector reviewing a hybrid trial program will approach the data integrity question the same way an inspector reviewing a conventional trial would: by tracing a sample of subject data from the clinical database back to the original source record, verifying that the audit trail at each step is complete and consistent, and assessing whether the organizational oversight framework is designed to detect and address data quality problems or to receive and report data passively.

For DCT programs, the backward trace from clinical database to source record is more complex and reveals more potential failure points. The inspector who follows a composite ePRO score from the efficacy analysis through the clinical database to the EDC, then from the EDC to the vendor data export, then from the export to the original session log, and finds that the session log is held on vendor infrastructure that the sponsor cannot access without vendor cooperation, has found a data integrity finding. Not because the data is necessarily wrong, but because it cannot be verified independently. The regulatory framework requires that source data be verifiable; data that can be produced by the vendor but cannot be verified without vendor cooperation does not satisfy that requirement.

EMA and MHRA inspectors bring the same analytical approach to their GCP inspections of DCT-enabled trials, with additional emphasis on organizational accountability. An MHRA inspector reviewing a hybrid trial will ask whether the sponsor's leadership understands its data governance obligations for the remote data collection components and will look for evidence that the sponsor has built its oversight infrastructure based on that understanding, not merely contracted it to vendors. The question is not whether the eCOA vendor has a validated system. The question is whether the sponsor has verified that the vendor's validated system generates ALCOA+-compliant data and that those data are retained and accessible as required.

The emerging area of inspector attention in DCT programs is the digital biomarker and algorithm-generated endpoint. Trials using wearable device data as a primary or key secondary endpoint are arriving at regulatory submission with datasets that inspectors and reviewers are still developing tools to evaluate. The traceability requirement, discussed in the ALCOA+ section of Chapter 3, has particular force here: a reported value derived from a continuous accelerometer data stream through a validated activity algorithm is as much a regulatory claim as a laboratory result, and it must be as fully traceable to its source, through every processing step, as any other efficacy endpoint.

CHAPTER TEN - KEY TAKEAWAYS
ALCOA+ applies to every data element in a decentralized trial without modification; decentralized collection does not create a parallel compliance standard.
The original record for ePRO and eCOA data is the session-level device log, not the composite score; sponsors that retain only composite scores have not satisfied the original data retention requirement.
Vendor qualification for DCT technology providers must address ALCOA+ properties specifically; ISO certification and SOPs are not substitutes for ALCOA+-focused system qualification.
Vendor contracts must include data return provisions that extend for the full regulatory retention period in an open, accessible format; database lock is not the retention deadline.
Device clock synchronization must be treated as a validation requirement and logged in the audit trail; unsynchronized device clocks invalidate the contemporaneity of all sensor data generated during the synchronization gap.
ePRO time-lock window configuration is a GCP compliance requirement, not a design preference; assessments completed outside the specified window must be flagged in the source data.
Real-time centralized monitoring with documented quality tolerance limits is the appropriate oversight model for DCT programs; retrospective database lock review is inadequate.
EHR-derived data used in clinical trial submissions requires a validated extraction process, documented mapping to endpoint definitions, and a verifiable link from each extracted element to its source record.
Investigator responsibility for DCT subject data is not reduced by the decentralized collection model; investigators must have documented, operational oversight mechanisms for remote activities.
The traceability from raw device sensor data through algorithmic transformation to reported endpoint value is the emerging frontier of DCT data integrity; organizations that build traceability into their DCT data governance frameworks now will be prepared for the regulatory expectations that are being formalized

PART THREE: THE HUMAN SYSTEM

Technology alone does not ensure integrity — people do

CHAPTER ELEVEN

The Role of Leadership in Data Integrity

> *When regulators find systematic data integrity failures in a clinical research organization, they do not limit their inquiry to the individuals closest to the data. They follow the accountability chain upward. Senior leadership is both the first line of defense and the last line of responsibility.*

The chief operating officer of a mid-sized CRO learns about a for-cause FDA inspection from the organization's regulatory affairs director on a Wednesday morning. The inspection had been triggered by a pattern of anomalies flagged during FDA's pre-approval review of a marketing application submitted by one of the CRO's sponsor clients. The inspection itself had concluded ten days earlier. The Form 483 had been issued to the site director. The COO is receiving word of it now.

This sequencing is not unusual. It is, in regulatory terms, catastrophic. The ten-day window between inspection conclusion and executive notification is the visible symptom of an organizational design in which leadership accountability for data integrity ends at the quality department. The COO does not know, as of that Wednesday morning, whether this is the first time the organization has received a 483 with data integrity observations or the fourth. She does not know whether the corrective action process that will be initiated in the next twenty-four hours is structurally capable of identifying root causes rather than instances. She does not know how much the sponsor client already knows, how many other studies may be implicated, or whether the agency is satisfied with the Form 483 or is already building the record for a warning letter. What she knows is that something serious happened in her organization and she is finding out about it a week and a half after the fact.

The quality team did not fail. The systems may or may not have failed. What failed was a governance design that treated executive engagement with data integrity as an exception rather than a standing function. The COO is not in this position because she is indifferent to compliance. She is in this position because no one designed an organizational structure that would have ensured she was informed earlier, engaged differently, and positioned to act.

This is a chapter about that organizational design. Not culture in the broad sense addressed in Chapter 11, and not training as discussed in Chapter 12, but the specific executive and governance architecture that determines whether data integrity is a managed organizational function or a documented one. The difference between those two outcomes is, ultimately, a leadership decision.

> *Data integrity governance is not a quality department function that reports to senior leadership. It is a senior leadership function that quality departments support.*

What Regulatory Frameworks Require of Senior Leadership

The conventional framing of regulatory compliance places quality and compliance professionals at the center of data integrity accountability. They write the procedures, conduct the audits, review the audit trails, and manage the corrective actions. Senior leaders set the tone, make resources available, and respond when escalations reach them. This framing is not wrong, but it understates what the primary regulatory frameworks actually require.

ICH E6(R3) is explicit. Its quality management framework places the sponsor organization's governance structure directly in scope, requiring that sponsors establish quality systems with defined accountability for quality objectives at the organizational level, allocate adequate resources to quality functions, and demonstrate that senior leadership engagement with quality outcomes is genuine and documented rather than ceremonial.[116] The framework does not describe a quality department with leadership buy-in. It describes an organizational quality system whose governance reaches the level of the organization that has authority to allocate resources, set priorities, and make decisions that trade operational efficiency against quality assurance.

MHRA's guidance on data integrity is the most direct regulatory statement of senior management accountability in the clinical data governance space. Section 5 of the guidance places the obligation for data integrity culture, resource adequacy, and quality system effectiveness squarely on senior management, not quality functions.[117] MHRA's inspection approach operationalizes this: inspectors evaluate whether management review is substantive or formal, whether resource allocation decisions demonstrate a genuine commitment to supporting compliant practices, and whether the governance documentation reflects actual leadership engagement or a pro forma endorsement of quality outputs. An organization whose executive team signs the annual data governance report but cannot describe its contents when asked by an inspector has failed the MHRA management accountability standard.

PIC/S Guidance PI 041-1 frames management responsibility in operational terms.[118] The expectation is not merely that leaders authorize a quality system. It is that they understand the system's outputs, respond to its signals, and create organizational conditions in which the system can function as designed. Where PI 041-1 is particularly useful is in its connection between self-inspection and management accountability: the guidance requires that self-inspection programs include explicit assessment of whether the organizational environment supports compliant practices, and that the results of those assessments reach management in a form that supports genuine decision-making.

FDA's expectations are communicated through enforcement as much as guidance. The consent decrees and warning letters that followed the Cetero Research and GVK Biosciences investigations did not confine their corrective action requirements to the individuals who performed the falsifications or the systems that permitted them. They required organizational governance remediation: independent oversight boards, executive management review commitments, and governance structures with documented authority to act on data integrity findings across the enterprise.[119] FDA's enforcement record makes clear that it regards systematic data integrity failure as organizational failure, and that its remediation expectations extend to the governance level accordingly.

The Governance Structures That Work

Effective data integrity governance in clinical research organizations is not accomplished by adding data integrity as a standing agenda item in existing committee structures. It requires purpose-built governance that integrates quality and operational information at the level where both are actionable.

The Integrated Quality and Operations Governance Forum

The most persistent structural failure in clinical research governance is the separation of quality information from operational information. Executive teams routinely receive enrollment metrics, timeline dashboards, budget performance summaries, and resource utilization reports through their operational governance. They receive quality metrics separately: deviation counts by study, monitoring visit findings by site, query aging profiles, training completion rates. The two streams of information reach leadership through different channels, at different frequencies, often from different organizational leaders, to different agenda items. The design communicates, implicitly but unmistakably, that quality and operations are parallel functions rather than integrated ones.

In practice, this separation means that the executive who owns the decision to accelerate enrollment into a high-performing site does not have, at the moment of that decision, the site's monitoring finding history, query correction patterns, or data quality trend. The quality information is available. It has been reviewed and documented in a separate committee. It simply has not been presented alongside the operational metric that makes it relevant. The governance structure has organized the information in a way that makes integration harder than separation.

The structural remedy is an integrated governance forum that presents quality and operational data together, not sequentially, for the same studies and the same time periods. When the enrollment performance of a site is reviewed, the site's quality indicators are reviewed in the same session by the same people making the operational decision. When a data lock timeline is discussed, the query resolution pattern, deviation history, and audit trail review status for the study are part of the same discussion. The integration is not achieved by adding a quality section to the operations meeting. It is achieved by designing a governance process that treats quality and operational outcomes as aspects of the same question: is this program being conducted in a way that produces reliable data, on schedule, at acceptable risk?

Management Review: Substantive Versus Formal

Management review is a formal requirement under multiple regulatory frameworks, but the form of the requirement does not guarantee its substance. An organization whose executive leadership reviews a quality management report, signs the management review record, and files the documentation has met the technical requirement. Whether it has met the governance intent of the requirement is a separate question, and one that regulators are increasingly equipped to assess.

Substantive management review requires three elements that formal management review can omit. The first is information in a form that enables decision-making rather than documentation. Executive leaders reviewing aggregate metrics and rate summaries are consuming information that has been processed to the point where the signals that warrant action are often no longer visible. A report that shows ninety-two percent of monitoring visits completed on schedule does not reveal which eight percent were delayed and why, which sites generated repeated findings, or which queries are being closed with generic change reasons that mask systematic data management problems. Substantive management review requires that quality signals reach leaders in forms that make patterns visible, not in forms that make rates reportable.

The second element is organizational authority. A management review that reaches senior leadership but produces no decisions is not governance. Governance requires that the people receiving quality information have the authority and mandate to act on it: to reallocate resources, to modify timelines, to elevate or terminate CRO relationships, to initiate corrective actions at the organizational level rather than the site level. An executive team that reviews quality reports but refers all action items to the quality committee has created a governance structure that looks substantive and functions formally.

The third element is documentation that reflects deliberation rather than endorsement. A management review record that consists of a meeting date, a list of attendees, and a signature block confirms that the meeting happened. A management review record that includes the specific quality signals presented, the analysis of their significance, the decisions made or deferred, and the rationale for those decisions confirms that the meeting was substantive. Regulators assessing governance quality can distinguish between the two in the first five minutes of document review.

The Sponsor Oversight Structure for CRO Data Integrity

The governance principle that requires the most explicit leadership design in clinical research is sponsor oversight of CRO data management. ICH E6(R3) Section 5.2 is unambiguous: the sponsor cannot transfer its regulatory responsibility for data integrity to a CRO regardless of how comprehensively the contractual relationship addresses the subject.[120] The practical implication is that a sponsor whose CRO is found to have manipulated clinical data is not absolved by a well-drafted quality agreement. FDA does not conclude that the sponsor's obligations were discharged because the contract assigned responsibility to the CRO. It assesses whether the sponsor's oversight was adequate to detect or prevent the conduct that occurred.

Adequate oversight, in FDA's enforcement-derived interpretation, is operational rather than contractual. A sponsor that sends periodic audit reports, receives and approves the CRO's quality management procedures, and reviews aggregated study performance metrics has documented oversight. It has not demonstrated that its oversight was capable of identifying the specific failure modes that occurred. The distinction is the difference between oversight as a paper trail and oversight as a functional control.

Functional CRO oversight requires that the sponsor's governance structure includes people with the access, skills, and mandate to evaluate what the CRO's data management practices actually are, not what they are documented to be. This means periodic on-site verification that audit trail review processes are performed as described in the CRO's procedures, not merely that the procedures exist. It means review of query patterns and resolution documentation at the data level, not merely at the metric level. It means escalation pathways that ensure CRO data quality signals reach sponsor leadership with the same priority and through the same channels as CRO performance metrics.

The following table describes the governance elements that distinguish functional oversight from documented oversight in a sponsor-CRO data integrity program.

Governance Element	Documented Oversight	Functional Oversight
Quality Agreement	Comprehensive assignment of data integrity obligations to CRO; annual review cycle	Quality agreement plus periodic verification that stated procedures are operationally active
Audit Program	Scheduled system and process audits per annual plan; findings documented and closed	Risk-triggered audits that examine data-level evidence; escalation pathway for critical findings to sponsor executive leadership

Governance Element	Documented Oversight	Functional Oversight
Performance Metrics	Aggregate quality metrics presented in governance forum on defined frequency	Disaggregated signals — individual site patterns, query resolution anomalies, audit trail exceptions — presented alongside aggregate rates
Issue Escalation	Issue log maintained; critical issues escalated per contractual SLA	Defined pathway from CRO quality event to sponsor executive notification within specified timeframe; sponsor retains authority to direct remediation
Corrective Action Review	CAPA documentation reviewed and approved by sponsor quality function	Root cause analysis reviewed by sponsor leadership; sponsor verifies that CAPA addresses design condition, not only instance
Leadership Engagement	Governance committee receives annual CRO performance summary	CRO data integrity performance is standing agenda item in sponsor clinical governance forum; adverse trends reviewed by sponsor executive leadership

Warning Signs: When Leadership Culture Creates Integrity Risk

Recognizing that leadership conditions create data integrity risk is as important as building governance structures that prevent it. The following patterns are well documented across enforcement cases and inspection findings. None of them requires an executive to order data falsification. All of them produce data integrity failures through organizational conditions rather than individual misconduct.

The Quality-Operations Separation at the Leadership Level

When the executive responsible for clinical operations and the executive responsible for clinical quality report to different organizational parents, resolve tensions through negotiation rather than joint decision-making, and present their respective domains to governance leadership as parallel rather than integrated, the organizational design has created conditions that make integrity failures predictable. The operations leader is accountable for the outcomes that determine the organization's financial performance: enrollment, timelines, budget. The quality leader is accountable for the outcomes that protect the organization's regulatory standing: compliance, documentation, audit findings. These are not the same objectives. When they conflict, the organization resolves the conflict through the relative organizational authority of the two functions, not through a governance structure designed to integrate them. In most clinical research organizations, the operations function has more authority, more visibility, and more direct connection to revenue than the quality function. The integrity risk that follows from this design does not require anyone to make a choice between compliance and performance. It is built into the structure.

Timeline and Enrollment Pressure Without Quality Adjustment

Enrollment pressure is the most reliably documented proximal condition in clinical data integrity failures. A leadership team that communicates enrollment targets without simultaneously communicating the quality conditions that govern those targets is operating a system that will eventually produce the data integrity failures that enrollment pressure without quality constraints reliably generates. The communication does not need to be explicit. It is communicated through the metrics presented in governance forums, through the outcomes that trigger recognition and consequences in performance management systems, and through what questions leaders ask when sites report results.

A sponsor clinical program leader who reviews monthly enrollment updates and asks consistently about pace and milestone achievement is signaling what matters. A sponsor clinical program leader who reviews enrollment updates and asks equally about query resolution profiles, monitoring finding patterns, and data lock readiness is signaling something different. The sites and CROs working for that leader will calibrate their behavior to the signal. The question is whether the calibration is toward documentation adequacy or toward data quality, and that is a question that leadership behavior answers before any policy document is drafted.

Corrective Actions That Address Instances Rather Than Conditions

The corrective action record is one of the most informative diagnostic tools available for assessing leadership quality. An organization whose corrective actions consistently address the specific instance of a finding without addressing the organizational condition that produced it has a quality system that documents problems and a governance system that does not solve them. The pattern is visible in the record: the same type of finding recurs at different sites, different studies, different time periods. Each recurrence generates a corrective action. Each corrective action is closed. The finding continues.

This is not a failure of the quality function. It is a failure of governance. The quality function can identify that contemporaneous documentation failures are recurring across sites. It cannot, without executive authority, change the staffing ratios, enrollment velocity targets, or monitoring program resources that are creating conditions in which contemporaneous documentation is not operationally possible. Root cause analysis that consistently identifies workload and resource constraints as contributing factors, combined with corrective actions that address training and procedure revision, is the signature of a quality system operating without executive engagement. The analysis is correct. The correction is inadequate. The governance level that could make the correction adequate is not engaged.

Compliance Functions Without Organizational Standing

The organizational positioning of the clinical quality function is a governance decision, and its consequences are direct. A quality function that reports to the clinical operations leadership it is charged with evaluating is structurally compromised regardless of the competence and integrity of the individuals in it. A quality function whose leadership does not have direct access to the executive governance forum is structurally positioned to escalate to a level that can escalate further, not to a level that can act. A quality function whose budget is managed by the operational organization it oversees is not designed to exercise independent judgment when independence is operationally inconvenient.

Regulators assess organizational positioning explicitly. MHRA inspectors routinely ask about reporting lines, budget structures, and the documented history of quality function escalations to determine whether the independence of the quality function is organizational or rhetorical. An organization that has written procedures affirming quality independence but has a reporting structure that makes independence functionally impossible has not resolved the underlying governance problem. It has documented a contradiction.

Leadership Risk Indicators: Observable Patterns That Precede Data Integrity Failures

- Quality function reports to the clinical operations leader it is responsible for overseeing, without independent escalation pathway to executive governance
- Enrollment and timeline metrics presented to executive governance more frequently and with greater detail than quality metrics for the same programs
- Corrective action records show recurring finding types across multiple cycles without root cause identification that reaches organizational conditions
- Management review records consist of signature blocks and attendance lists without evidence of deliberation or decision-making
- The ratio of quality findings identified by external auditors or regulators to those identified internally exceeds 1:1 across multiple consecutive audit cycles
- Sponsor executive leadership learns of site-level inspection findings through post-inspection notification rather than through standing escalation protocols
- Quality-related budget reductions are made during periods of enrollment pressure without documented quality risk assessment reviewed at the executive level
- CRO data integrity obligations are governed entirely through quality agreements and audit schedules without operational verification that documented practices are actual practices

Executive Accountability in the Inspection Room

FDA's Bioresearch Monitoring program and its equivalents at EMA national competent authorities, MHRA, and PMDA share a common inspection approach that is relevant to executive leadership: they investigate the organizational conditions that produced the conduct they found, not only the conduct itself. When a for-cause inspection at a clinical site finds audit trail manipulation or data reconstruction, the investigation does not end with the site coordinator who performed the act. It extends to the site management, the sponsor's monitoring program, the CRO's oversight function, and the sponsor's governance structure.

In practice, this means that the executive governance of the sponsor organization is in scope for regulatory assessment even in an inspection that was triggered by conduct at a third-party investigator site. The FDA has issued warning letters that cite sponsors for inadequate oversight of investigator site conduct, for failure to establish monitoring programs capable of identifying the anomalies documented in the inspection, and for quality management systems that could not surface the signals that were present in the data before the agency found them.[121] The warning letters are not directed at the site coordinator. They are directed at the sponsor. The accountability the regulatory framework assigns to sponsors is executive accountability, and inspections assess whether it was exercised.

Executive leaders who understand this dynamic approach data integrity governance differently than those who do not. The question is not whether the organization has policies and procedures that address every regulatory requirement. It is whether the governance structure is designed so that someone with authority could have known about the conditions that led to the finding before the regulator found it. If the answer is no, the governance design is the corrective action item, not the procedure revision.

The Consent Decree as Governance Lesson

The consent decrees that followed the most significant clinical data integrity enforcement actions of the past two decades are instructive precisely because of what they required in addition to operational remediation. The Cetero Research consent decree required, among other things, an independent audit committee with authority to review all clinical data from affected studies, executive management certification of compliance with each corrective action milestone, and a governance restructuring that ensured data integrity oversight reached the board level.[122] These requirements were not incidental. They were FDA's explicit articulation of what governance structures the organization should have had in place before the failures occurred.

The practical implication for organizations that are not in consent decree is straightforward: the governance structures FDA requires as remediation for organizations that have failed are the governance structures it expects to find in organizations that have not. An organization that builds its data integrity governance to the standard that consent decrees impose is building to the standard that inspections assess. This is not an argument for excessive formality or board-level micromanagement of clinical operations. It is an argument for governance architecture that is proportionate to the regulatory accountability that senior leadership actually carries.

Building Leadership Accountability Into Program Design

The operational architecture of leadership accountability in data integrity is not complicated, but it requires decisions that are easier to defer than to make. The following elements define the minimum governance structure for a clinical research organization operating at scale.

Defined Escalation Timelines

Every clinical data integrity program requires a documented escalation pathway that specifies, by finding severity, the timeline within which each organizational level must be notified. A critical data integrity finding, defined as one that affects the reliability of data in a regulatory submission, should reach the sponsor's senior clinical leadership within twenty-four hours of identification, regardless of whether it was identified by an internal monitor, an external auditor, or an FDA inspector. A significant finding that suggests a systemic pattern rather than an isolated occurrence should reach the governance forum within the next scheduled meeting cycle, with an option to convene an ad hoc review if the pattern is severe. A finding that represents an isolated procedural deviation, without evidence of systematic impact, can follow standard corrective action timelines.

The purpose of defined escalation timelines is not primarily to ensure that leadership is informed. It is to ensure that the information is usable when it arrives. A COO who learns of a Form 483 ten days after it was issued has no options. A COO who is notified of an active for-cause inspection on the day it commences can engage the organization's regulatory affairs function, assess the scope of potential findings, begin stakeholder communication planning, and position the organization to respond to the 483 with genuine organizational engagement rather than reactive document assembly.

Data Integrity Metrics in Executive Reporting

Leadership accountability requires information. The metrics that reach executive governance must be designed to support accountability, not to demonstrate compliance. The distinction is between metrics that report rates and metrics that enable decisions.

Rate metrics — percentage of monitoring visits completed, deviation counts, query closure rates — confirm that activities are occurring. They do not reveal what those activities are finding. Decision-enabling metrics for data integrity include: the ratio of internally-identified to externally-identified quality findings for the same period, the recurrence rate of specific finding types across consecutive monitoring cycles at the same sites, the percentage of corrective actions that addressed root cause versus instance, and the escalation rate from the quality function to executive leadership relative to the finding volume that generated it. If the escalation rate is near zero across a high-volume clinical program, it does not mean the program is clean. It may mean the escalation pathway is not being used, which is a governance finding in its own right.

Leadership Behaviors That Signal Priority

The behavioral signals that senior leaders send through their day-to-day engagement with clinical operations are more operationally powerful than any governance document. Chapter 11 addressed the cultural implications of leadership behavior in detail. What requires emphasis here is the governance dimension: the behaviors that send quality signals through formal channels as well as cultural ones.

When senior clinical leaders ask about data quality as a routine element of study status reviews, not as an add-on triggered by a finding, the governance signal is clear. When executive leaders visibly engage with quality metrics in governance forums rather than delegating quality items to the quality representative, the organizational message is different than when they receive the quality report and move to the next agenda item. When a timeline extension for quality remediation is approved at the executive level without requiring the quality function to justify it against enrollment impact, the governance structure has communicated what it values. These are not soft cultural outcomes. They are observable governance behaviors, and they are the ones that regulators assess when they ask whether executive management accountability for data integrity is genuine or performative.

The following reference table maps leadership accountability requirements to the regulatory frameworks that establish them and the governance mechanisms that satisfy them.

Accountability Requirement	Regulatory Basis	Governance Mechanism
Senior management responsibility for data integrity culture	MHRA DI Guidance §5; ICH E6(R3) §5.0; PIC/S PI 041-1 §4	Management review program with documented deliberation; quality function with direct executive access

Accountability Requirement	Regulatory Basis	Governance Mechanism
Adequate resource allocation for quality functions	ICH E6(R3) §5.1; MHRA DI Guidance §5	Executive approval of quality function budgets independent of clinical operations budget pressure; resource adequacy review in management review
Sponsor oversight of CRO data integrity	ICH E6(R3) §5.2; 21 CFR §312.52; FDA oversight guidance (2013)	Operational verification program; CRO quality signals in sponsor governance forum; sponsor authority to direct CRO remediation
Escalation of critical findings to executive level	ICH E6(R3) §5.0; FDA enforcement record; MHRA DI Guidance §5	Defined escalation timelines by finding severity; standing quality agenda in executive governance forum
Self-inspection of data integrity governance conditions	PIC/S PI 041-1 §4; MHRA DI Guidance §5; ICH E6(R3) §5.0	Annual governance audit that assesses whether organizational conditions support compliant practices; results reviewed by executive leadership
Root cause analysis at organizational level	ICH E6(R3) §5.0; FDA CAPA expectations in consent decrees	CAPA review at executive governance level for systemic findings; executive authority to approve corrective actions that require operational change

The Investigator as Local Leader: Principal Investigator Accountability

The governance principles that apply to executive leadership at the sponsor and CRO level apply with equal force, adapted for scope, to the principal investigator at the clinical site. The PI is not merely the most senior clinician at the site. Under 21 CFR Part 312 and ICH E6(R3) Section 4, the PI is the accountable party for the conduct of the investigation at the site, for the integrity of data generated there, and for the supervision of the staff who collect and record that data.[123]

In practice, PI accountability for data integrity at busy investigator sites is frequently nominal. The PI signs protocol amendments, reviews adverse event narratives, and appears at monitoring visits. The day-to-day management of data entry, query resolution, and documentation practices is delegated to the site coordinator or coordinator team. This delegation is operationally necessary and regulatory acceptable, provided the PI has implemented a delegation structure that ensures accountability flows back to them and that they exercise genuine oversight rather than formal coverage.

The FDA bioresearch monitoring inspection framework is explicit that PI oversight is substantive, not formal. Inspectors ask PIs about specific data entries, about the basis for specific clinical decisions documented in the case report forms, and about what the PI knows about the practices of the coordinators working under their supervision. A PI who cannot describe the data management practices at their own site, who does not know the site's query aging profile, and who has not reviewed the audit trail in their eClinical system since validation has failed the substantive oversight standard regardless of their signature on the delegation log.

The organizational implication for sponsors and CROs is that PI oversight assessment is a governance function, not merely a training function. A sponsor whose monitoring program confirms that PIs have been trained on their data integrity obligations but does not verify that they are exercising oversight in practice has a documented training program and an unverified governance structure. Verification requires that monitoring visits include PI-directed conversations about site data management practices, that the site's quality indicators reach the PI in a form that makes their oversight function operational, and that the PI's engagement with data quality is part of the sponsor's site performance assessment.

Leadership in Crisis: When Data Integrity Failures Are Found

The moment when a data integrity failure is identified, whether through internal audit, sponsor monitoring, or regulatory inspection, is a governance test. The organizational response to that moment reveals what the governance structure is actually designed to do.

The first governance decision is the scope assessment. An organization that responds to a single-site, single-study data integrity finding by conducting a risk-based assessment of whether the failure mode could be present in other sites or studies is exercising governance. An organization that responds by closing a corrective action at the affected site is managing an instance. These are not equivalent responses, and regulators distinguish between them. FDA's expectation, derived from enforcement communications and consent decree requirements, is that significant data integrity findings trigger an assessment of whether the underlying conditions are systemic.[124] An organization that waits for the regulator to find the systemic pattern before assessing it has failed the governance standard the regulator will apply.

The second governance decision is the communication strategy. When a data integrity finding has potential implications for regulatory submissions, FDA expects prompt and transparent communication of the issue and its potential scope. Organizations that manage the communication of data integrity findings as primarily a legal or public relations question rather than a regulatory obligation consistently make decisions that compound the original finding into a more significant enforcement outcome. The decision about how and when to communicate a material data integrity finding to the regulator is a governance decision that belongs at the executive and legal level, with clinical quality and regulatory affairs input, and it needs to be made on a timescale that is determined by the regulatory obligation rather than by the organization's readiness to communicate.

The third governance decision is the one that most directly reveals organizational character: whether the response is designed to understand what happened or to demonstrate that it has been addressed. These are not the same. A corrective action plan that closes every observation on the Form 483 within ninety days, without examining whether the observations are symptoms of a broader condition or design failure, may satisfy the immediate regulatory obligation. It will not prevent the next inspection from finding the same pattern under a different set of surface observations. Governance that treats data integrity remediation as a design problem rather than a documentation problem builds organizations that regulators trust. Governance that treats it as a documentation problem builds organizations that generate the next enforcement cycle.

CHAPTER 11 — KEY TAKEAWAYS
ICH E6(R3), MHRA guidance, and PIC/S PI 041-1 assign data integrity accountability explicitly to senior management, not to quality functions; governance structures that confine accountability to the quality layer are non-compliant by design.
Effective governance requires that quality and operational information are presented together in executive forums; separating them into parallel channels is an organizational design decision that consistently produces integrated accountability failures.
Management review is substantive when it presents decision-enabling information, reaches people with authority to act, and produces documented deliberation; it is formal when it produces signatures on reports that have not changed organizational behavior.
Sponsor oversight of CRO data integrity is regulatory non-delegable; FDA's enforcement record treats sponsor governance failure as the primary finding when a CRO is found to have manipulated clinical data under inadequate sponsor oversight.
The warning signs of governance failure — quality-operations separation, timeline pressure without quality adjustment, corrective actions that address instances rather than conditions, quality functions without organizational standing — precede data integrity failures reliably and can be identified before inspection.
Principal investigator accountability under 21 CFR Part 312 and ICH E6(R3) is substantive, not formal; PI oversight assessment is a governance function that requires operational verification, not merely training documentation.
The consent decrees issued following the most significant clinical data integrity enforcement actions define the governance architecture FDA expects to find in organizations that have not yet failed; building to that standard is both the most rigorous and the most efficient compliance strategy.
The organizational response to a data integrity finding is a governance test; the distinction between responding to understand the design condition and responding to close the observation is the distinction regulators use to assess whether governance is functional.

CHAPTER TWELVE

Culture Is the Control: Building a Data Integrity Mindset

> *Regulators assess organizations, not just systems. A technically perfect audit trail in a culturally broken organization is evidence waiting to be used against the sponsor who filed it.*

The inspection had been running for three days when the MHRA investigator asked to speak with the clinical research coordinators without sponsor representatives or site management present. The site head agreed, because the protocol required it, and because declining would have been its own signal.

The coordinator who had managed the most active enrollment period was the third person interviewed. She was experienced, competent, and nervous. She answered the investigator's questions about the eClinical system accurately. She demonstrated that she understood audit trail requirements. She confirmed that she had received training on contemporaneous documentation. Then the investigator asked her a different kind of question: had she ever felt pressure to enter data differently than what she actually observed?

The silence lasted three seconds. In an investigation, three seconds is a long time.

What she described was not a conspiracy. There was no instruction to falsify data, no supervisor directing entries, no awareness that anything crossing a regulatory line was occurring. What she described was a working environment in which enrollment velocity was discussed at every site call and data quality was discussed when there was a problem. Where a sponsor monitor's visit report had flagged her documentation timing as a concern and her site director had asked her to be more careful about it, but the site director had not addressed why it was happening or what would change. Where she had resolved a query by calling the sponsor's clinical data manager and asking what the correct answer should be, because the timeline to lock was forty-eight hours and she was not confident in her own reconstruction. She had not thought of any of this as a data integrity issue. She had thought of it as doing her job under difficult conditions.

> *The most durable data integrity control in any clinical research organization is not a validated system or a written procedure. It is the expectation, shared by everyone from the principal investigator to the most junior coordinator, that accuracy is not negotiable when it conflicts with speed.*

The Regulatory Framework for Culture

It would be convenient if data integrity culture were solely the subject of management consulting literature and organizational psychology journals, because then it could be separated from regulatory obligation. It cannot be. The major regulatory frameworks governing clinical data integrity impose explicit culture requirements, and the enforcement record demonstrates that inspectors treat cultural failure as a primary finding category, not a background condition.

ICH E6(R3), in its Section 3.10 quality management requirements, establishes that sponsors must build a quality culture that supports data integrity throughout the trial lifecycle.[125]

The guidance does not define quality culture as a documentation program. It defines it as an organizational condition: one in which quality objectives are understood and shared, in which concerns are raised and acted upon, and in which the responsibilities for data integrity are clearly assigned rather than collectively assumed. These are cultural requirements, expressed in the language of governance.

MHRA's data integrity guidance is more direct. It states that senior management is responsible for creating an environment in which data integrity is expected, supported, and verifiable, and that organizations must conduct honest self-assessments of whether commercial pressures or organizational incentive structures are creating conditions that make integrity failures structurally likely.

MHRA inspectors do not assess culture through policy review alone. They interview personnel at every organizational level, asking questions designed to surface the gap between the cultural expectations documented in training materials and the cultural expectations actually communicated through management behavior, performance metrics, and escalation response.

PIC/S PI 041-1 establishes equivalent expectations, requiring that management create conditions in which data integrity failures are neither incentivized nor tolerated, and that self-inspection programs include explicit assessment of whether the organizational environment supports compliant conduct.[126]

FDA's approach to culture is expressed less through guidance language and more through inspection practice. FDA investigators conducting bioresearch monitoring inspections assess the organizational conditions that produced the findings they document. A warning letter citing audit trail manipulation at an investigator site is, on its face, a technical finding. The investigative narrative behind it typically describes an organization whose cultural conditions made manipulation the rational response to the pressures the site was under. FDA's remediation expectations in these cases are not limited to fixing the technical controls. They include organizational corrective actions that address the conditions producing the conduct.

Why People Manipulate Data: The Organizational Conditions

The instinct, when data manipulation is discovered, is to explain it as individual misconduct: a dishonest coordinator, a rogue site, a contractor whose practices were inadequate. This explanation is sometimes correct. It is almost never complete. The enforcement record across documented clinical data integrity failures points consistently toward a more structural account: individuals who manipulate data are, in the great majority of cases, operating within organizational conditions that made manipulation predictable.

Understanding those conditions is the prerequisite for changing them.

Pressure Without Support

The most common organizational condition that produces data integrity failures in clinical research is not dishonesty. It is pressure without adequate support for legitimate compliance. Clinical research coordinators managing active enrollment, monitoring visits, query backlogs, and database lock timelines simultaneously are operating under genuine workload constraints. When the path to completing their legitimate work requires practices that are non-compliant, and when the organization's management response to quality concerns is to ask for improvement without providing resources or process changes that make improvement possible, non-compliance becomes structurally inevitable.

The mechanism is well documented. A site coordinator who cannot enter contemporaneous data because she is managing five concurrent consents at the time of the assessments will reconstruct entries later. She will do this not because she is dishonest but because no other path is available to her. If her site management reviews documentation timing and responds with a coaching conversation that confirms the expectation without changing the conditions, the reconstruction will continue. If the sponsor's monitoring program identifies the pattern and responds with a finding that the site is expected to remediate without additional support, the site will improve its response to the next source data verification check without improving its documentation practices. The gap between documented compliance and actual conduct grows. So does the risk.

ICH E6(R3) specifically addresses this dynamic in its quality management requirements, establishing that sponsors must allocate adequate resources for the quality functions that clinical trial conduct requires, and that resource allocation is a sponsor governance responsibility, not a site-level operational issue.[127]

The resource question is inseparable from the cultural one. An organization that communicates high standards and provides inadequate resources to meet them has created a culture of managed non-compliance. It should expect the enforcement record that culture produces.

Metrics That Signal What Actually Matters

Every clinical research organization has formal data integrity values. They are in the quality policy, the training curriculum, the sponsor agreements, and the SOPs. What they communicate to staff is secondary to what the organizational metrics system communicates, because the metrics system tells people what leadership actually measures, which tells them what leadership actually values.

Organizations that track enrollment velocity on a weekly basis and data quality metrics on an exception-only basis are communicating a priority order clearly, regardless of what the quality policy says. Organizations that celebrate enrollment milestones in team meetings and address data quality concerns in individual coaching conversations are telling coordinators and CRAs which performance dimension has organizational visibility and which is a background obligation. Organizations that evaluate CRO performance against delivery timelines and contract terms without equivalent visibility into quality findings are signaling to their CRO partners that the formal data integrity expectations and the evaluated expectations are not the same.

Inspectors read these signals. MHRA investigators, in particular, are trained to look for the gap between formal quality commitments and the actual organizational weight given to quality performance. When that gap is present, it is not a subtle finding. It is visible in the patterns of who attends which meetings, what gets escalated versus managed locally, and whether quality signals receive substantive organizational response or documentation response.

The practical implication is uncomfortable: fixing the metrics system requires senior leadership to be honest about what the current metrics system communicates, and willing to change the performance architecture of the organization, not just the documents that describe it. That is harder than implementing a validated eClinical system. It is also more consequential.

The Normalization of Workarounds

One of the most reliable indicators of cultural integrity risk in a clinical research organization is the presence of normalized workarounds: practices that deviate from the documented procedure and are understood by everyone involved to deviate, but that are treated as standard operating reality rather than non-compliance requiring correction.

Common examples in clinical data management: sites where coordinators are known to complete case report forms at the end of the clinic day rather than contemporaneously, and where monitoring reports note this as a site characteristic rather than a finding. Sponsor data management teams where closing queries on a tight lock timeline is understood to involve accepting resolutions that would not survive rigorous scrutiny, and where this is treated as an operational reality of database lock management. eClinical system configurations where the change reason dropdown is routinely populated with "data entry error" regardless of the actual basis for a change, because the dropdown options do not include an accurate description of what the coordinator is actually doing. None of these practices are individually catastrophic. Collectively, they define an organization whose data is managed for documentation rather than accuracy, and that distinction is precisely what FDA investigators are trained to identify.

The normalization of workarounds is a cultural phenomenon with a specific organizational cause: the failure to close the gap between what the documented procedure requires and what the actual process enables. When that gap exists and persists, people rationalize it as an inevitable feature of clinical trial operations rather than a design failure requiring correction. The first step toward correcting it is refusing the rationalization.

The Reporting Environment

In a clinical research organization with a functional data integrity culture, a coordinator who observes a practice she believes is non-compliant can report it, and something will happen. The report will receive substantive attention. The practice will be investigated. If the concern is valid, it will be corrected. The coordinator who raised it will not face informal consequences for doing so.

This description is an aspiration for many organizations and a reality for few. The reason is not that organizations intend to discourage reporting. It is that the conditions required to support reporting, genuine psychological safety, a responsive investigation process, and protection from the informal social consequences of raising concerns, require deliberate design and sustained leadership attention. They do not emerge from a nonretaliation policy statement, however carefully written.

FDA's guidance on site oversight and monitoring explicitly references the importance of an organizational environment in which monitoring concerns are raised, documented, and acted upon, and characterizes the failure of monitoring programs to surface and escalate quality signals as a governance failure, not merely an operational one.[128]

The reporting environment is both a leading indicator of cultural health and a determinant of whether the organization's quality systems can actually function. A quality system that depends on people raising concerns will not function in an organization where raising concerns carries social risk. The organizations that discover data integrity failures at inspection rather than through their own quality systems are, in many cases, organizations where the reporting environment was not designed to surface them.

The Cultural Signatures Inspectors Recognize

Data integrity culture is not directly observable in a regulatory inspection. What is observable are its artifacts: the patterns of behavior, documentation, and organizational response that culture produces. Experienced FDA investigators and MHRA inspectors have developed well-calibrated pattern recognition for the cultural signatures of organizations under integrity risk, and understanding those signatures is as important for clinical quality professionals as understanding the technical requirements they inspect against.

Cultural Signature	What It Indicates
Monitoring findings are consistently rated as minor across multiple site visits at a site with known enrollment pressure	Monitor may be managing the relationship rather than the risk; findings are being characterized to avoid escalation rather than to reflect actual quality status
Protocol deviations are documented but root cause analysis is consistently attributed to "site training" without process change	Quality system is generating documentation without learning; the same failure mode will recur

Cultural Signature	What It Indicates
Query resolution patterns show large volumes of query closures in the 24-48 hours before a scheduled monitoring visit or database lock	Data is being managed for the review event rather than for accuracy; contemporaneity of the underlying source data is in question
Personnel at multiple organizational levels describe data quality and enrollment velocity as competing priorities	Incentive structure has not aligned these objectives; the gap between them is being managed informally at the individual level
Quality concern escalations are resolved in conversation without documented outcome	Escalation pathway exists procedurally but not functionally; concerns are being closed rather than resolved
CRO partners' data integrity performance is assessed contractually rather than operationally	Sponsor oversight of CRO data quality is document-based rather than evidence-based; the sponsor cannot confirm what the CRO's actual data management practices are
Training records are complete; staff cannot articulate ALCOA+ requirements in the context of their own roles	Training is a documentation exercise; it has not changed understanding or behavior

The clinical hold proceedings arising from CRO data integrity failures documented over the past decade consistently describe organizations where several of these signatures were present simultaneously and were individually rationalized rather than collectively understood as indicators of systemic cultural risk. A single signature is a quality signal. Multiple concurrent signatures are a predictor.

Building a Data Integrity Culture: The Organizational Architecture

Cultural change in clinical research organizations is not accomplished through training campaigns, however well designed, or policy revisions, however comprehensive. It is accomplished through changes to the organizational architecture that shapes behavior: the governance structures, the metrics systems, the escalation pathways, and the leadership behaviors that tell people what the organization actually expects of them. The following elements define the minimum organizational architecture for a data integrity culture.

Leadership Behavior as Primary Signal

The single most powerful determinant of data integrity culture in a clinical research organization is what senior leaders demonstrably do when data quality and operational pressure conflict. Not what they say. Not what the quality policy documents. What they actually do.

An organization whose senior clinical leadership responds to a quality finding that creates timeline risk by asking how the finding can be resolved quickly rather than what produced it is communicating a priority order that every person in that organization will understand and incorporate into their own decision-making. An organization whose leadership responds by asking what design condition made the failure possible, what it will take to correct that condition, and how the timeline will be adjusted to allow for genuine remediation is communicating something categorically different.

Leadership cannot communicate authentic data integrity values through documents. It communicates them through the decisions it makes when data integrity and operational efficiency pull in different directions, which in clinical research they do regularly. The cultural message those decisions send is more durable and more operationally influential than anything a training program can deliver.

MHRA's guidance makes this explicit: it places primary responsibility for data integrity culture on senior management, and its inspection approach assesses whether that responsibility is being exercised through active governance engagement rather than policy ownership.[129]

Governance Structures That Make Culture Visible

Culture is invisible until something makes it visible. In clinical research organizations, the governance structures that most effectively make data integrity culture visible are those that create regular, documented opportunities for leadership to engage with quality signals rather than quality summaries.

The distinction matters. A quality summary reports rates and outcomes: the percentage of monitoring visits with findings, the number of deviations by category, the query aging profile across active studies. These are necessary and useful. They do not tell a governance body what kind of organization it is overseeing. Quality signals do: the specific deviation that is recurring across sites because the protocol design creates a documentation gap that has not been addressed; the CRO partner whose query resolution patterns suggest systematic retrospective data management; the investigator site where audit trail review has repeatedly identified entries made outside plausible clinical windows. These signals require substantive engagement, not dashboard review, and the governance structures that enable that engagement are the ones that produce cultural change rather than merely recording cultural outcomes.

ICH E6(R3)'s quality management requirements establish that clinical quality systems must be capable of generating the quality intelligence that governance review requires, and that the governance review function must have the organizational standing to direct response to that intelligence. Both halves of this requirement are design conditions. Neither emerges automatically from having a quality function.

Sponsor-CRO Relationship Architecture

A significant share of clinical data integrity cultural failures are not internal organizational failures. They are failures of the relationship architecture between sponsors and their CRO partners, in which the formal quality requirements and the actual working relationship pull in incompatible directions.

The most common failure mode is structural: sponsors select CROs through processes that make price and delivery capability primary selection criteria and quality culture indicators secondary or unassessed. They govern CRO relationships through contractual frameworks that create accountability for deliverables and not for the process quality that produces them. They assess CRO performance through milestone completion and financial metrics rather than through direct evaluation of data management practices. And they discover, at inspection, that the contractual quality language they relied on was not operationally implemented.

ICH E6(R3) is explicit on this point: sponsors cannot delegate their regulatory responsibility for data integrity to CROs, and the responsibility for verifying that CRO data management practices meet the required standard rests with the sponsor, not with the CRO's self-assessment.[130]

The practical implication is that sponsor-CRO quality oversight must include operational verification of the CRO's actual data management practices, not merely contractual attestation of their commitment to meeting quality standards. This means audit trail review, query pattern analysis, documentation timing assessment, and direct engagement with CRO data management personnel, not as a compliance exercise but as the substantive oversight that genuine quality assurance requires. The cultural message this sends to the CRO is as important as the oversight itself: it communicates that the sponsor actually evaluates what it contractually requires.

The Speak-Up Architecture

Building a speak-up environment in clinical research is a specific design problem with specific solutions, and it is worth treating it with the same engineering discipline applied to eClinical system configuration. The informal social dynamics that suppress concern-raising in clinical research organizations are consistent across organizations: concerns raised to direct supervisors become organizational noise unless the supervisor has both the authority and the incentive to escalate them; concerns raised through formal quality channels are slow, formal, and socially costly; concerns raised informally are managed conversationally without record or resolution. Each of these is a design gap, not a character gap.

Effective speak-up architectures in clinical research share common design elements. Multiple channels, because some concerns are not safely raised through direct management chains. Defined response timelines, because concerns that disappear into process with no visible outcome teach people that raising concerns is not worth the social cost. Documented outcomes, because the record of what the organization did with the concerns it received is the primary evidence of whether the speak-up culture is functional. And leadership visibility into speak-up activity, because if senior leadership cannot see what quality concerns are being raised and how they are being resolved, it cannot assess whether the reporting environment it has described in policy is the one actually operating.

There is no regulatory requirement that mandates a specific speak-up architecture for clinical research organizations. What the regulatory frameworks require, across FDA,

MHRA, ICH, and PIC/S, is an organizational quality system that can actually surface, escalate, and resolve data integrity signals. A speak-up architecture is the human infrastructure that makes a quality system functional rather than documentary. Organizations that treat it as an HR initiative rather than a quality system element will have policies that describe it and practices that undermine it.

Culture Assessment: Knowing Where You Are

Before an organization can build a data integrity culture, it must honestly assess the one it has. This is harder than it sounds, for a structural reason: the cultural conditions most likely to produce data integrity failures are also the conditions most likely to suppress honest self-assessment. Organizations with compromised reporting environments, normalized workarounds, and misaligned incentive structures will not accurately self-assess through internal surveys administered by quality functions that report to the leadership structures they are assessing.

A genuine culture assessment requires independent access to the people closest to the data and the furthest from the leadership claiming the culture is sound. The clinical research coordinator who reconstructs entries at the end of her clinic day knows exactly what her organization's data integrity culture is. The question is whether the organization has created any pathway through which that knowledge can reach the people with authority to act on it.

Assessment Dimension	Questions to Ask	Evidence to Examine
Leadership behavior	How does senior clinical leadership respond when a quality finding creates delivery risk? Who owns the decision to extend a timeline for quality remediation versus accepting a risk?	Minutes of quality and clinical governance meetings; escalation records showing how quality-delivery conflicts were resolved; corrective action timelines relative to enrollment impact

Assessment Dimension	Questions to Ask	Evidence to Examine
Metrics architecture	What data quality metrics are tracked with the same frequency and visibility as enrollment and delivery metrics? How are they reported to leadership?	Dashboard and reporting templates; meeting agendas; frequency of quality versus operational metric review; whether quality findings appear in the same governance forum as delivery performance
Normalized workarounds	What practices are known to deviate from the documented procedure and are treated as operational reality rather than non-compliance?	Monitoring visit reports over multiple cycles at the same site; audit trail patterns; query aging and resolution timing relative to lock and monitoring windows
Reporting environment	In the past year, how many data integrity concerns were raised through the quality system by coordinators and CRAs rather than identified by monitors or auditors?	Quality event records; ratio of internally-identified versus externally-identified findings; speak-up channel utilization; documented follow-through on reported concerns

Assessment Dimension	Questions to Ask	Evidence to Examine
CRO oversight quality	What direct operational evidence does the sponsor have of the CRO's actual data management practices, beyond contractual attestation?	Audit trail review records for CRO-managed studies; query pattern analysis from CRO data management periods; direct oversight visit records that include data management assessment

The assessment methodology matters as much as the questions. Surveys administered to the full organization will capture the formal culture. Interviews conducted with frontline personnel by individuals they do not report to, using questions that invite honest description rather than program assessment, will capture the actual one. The gap between those two is the organization's cultural integrity risk.

Culture Change Is Not a Training Initiative

The instinct when a cultural problem is identified is to address it through training. This instinct is understandable and nearly always insufficient. Training can communicate expectations. It can build technical knowledge. It cannot change the organizational conditions that make non-compliant behavior rational. A coordinator who understands ALCOA+ completely and is working in an environment that consistently communicates that enrollment velocity matters more than documentation timing will continue to reconstruct entries. She will simply do so with better vocabulary for describing what she should have done differently.

Real culture change requires changes to the things that actually shape behavior: the metrics that determine performance evaluations, the escalation pathways that determine what happens when quality concerns are raised, the resource allocation decisions that determine whether compliant practices are operationally possible, and the leadership behaviors that communicate what the organization actually rewards. These are not training design questions. They are organizational design questions, and they require organizational leadership engagement at a level that treats data integrity culture as a governance priority rather than a quality department project.

ICH E6(R3)'s quality management framework provides the regulatory basis for this engagement. Its requirements for sponsor quality systems explicitly include the organizational governance structures, leadership accountability mechanisms, and resource allocation commitments that constitute a functional quality culture. Organizations implementing these requirements as documentation exercises will have compliant quality management policies and non-compliant quality management practices. The distinction will be visible to a skilled inspector within the first few hours of a bioresearch monitoring investigation.

The organizations that have built genuinely strong data integrity cultures are not the ones that have invested most heavily in training and documentation. They are the ones whose leadership has made the difficult organizational decisions to align the performance management system, the resource allocation model, and the governance structure around the same quality objectives the quality policy describes. That alignment is harder to achieve and harder to sustain than any technical control. It is also the only control that works reliably, across all trial types, all site configurations, and all operational conditions, including the ones no one anticipated when the quality management framework was designed.

The ALCOA+ Culture Connection

Every ALCOA+ property has a cultural prerequisite. The technical controls that protect each property work only in organizational conditions that support them. Examining the cultural prerequisites of each ALCOA+ dimension provides a diagnostic framework for the relationship between culture and integrity that is more operationally useful than abstract discussion of organizational values.

ALCOA+ Property	Cultural Prerequisite
Attributable Data can be traced to the individual who created it	Individual accountability is expected and enforced; shared credentials, practiced for convenience or speed, are treated as the compliance failure they are rather than as operational accommodation

ALCOA+ Property	Cultural Prerequisite
Legible Records are readable throughout the retention period	Documentation quality is treated as a professional standard, not a bureaucratic requirement; entry quality receives the same feedback as entry speed
Contemporaneous Data is recorded at the time of observation	Workload allocation allows contemporaneous entry to be operationally possible; the gap between what the procedure requires and what the workflow enables has been closed by design
Original The first record is preserved	Reconstruction of lost or inadequate records is escalated as a deviation rather than managed as an operational workaround; the original is understood as irreplaceable
Accurate Data reflects what was actually observed	Accuracy is understood as non-negotiable when it conflicts with expected results, enrollment timelines, or database lock schedules; the culture treats a data entry that reflects genuine uncertainty as more compliant than one that resolves it artificially
Complete All required data is present	The completeness requirement is understood to mean genuinely complete, not procedurally complete; the difference between a resolved query and a resolved uncertainty is understood as meaningful
Consistent Data is internally coherent across the record	Inconsistencies are reported as potential findings rather than resolved through interpretation; the instinct to correct apparent inconsistency is treated as a quality signal requiring investigation
Enduring Records are retained for the required period in usable form	Archival requirements are understood as operational commitments, not end-of-study obligations; system changes and storage decisions are evaluated for their archival implications throughout the data lifecycle

ALCOA+ Property	Cultural Prerequisite
Available Records can be produced when required	The ability to produce records under inspection conditions is tested and confirmed, not assumed; the organization's record retrieval capability is a live operational condition, not a contractual commitment

The value of examining culture through the ALCOA+ lens is that it converts abstract cultural objectives into specific, assessable organizational conditions. An organization cannot directly measure whether it has a "data integrity culture." It can measure whether contemporaneous documentation is operationally possible given current workload allocation, whether shared credentials are treated as a compliance finding or an operational accommodation, and whether inconsistencies in the record are reported or resolved. These are auditable conditions, and their presence or absence tells a quality function what kind of culture it is actually managing.

What Good Looks Like: Indicators of a Functional Data Integrity Culture

The cultural risk indicators enumerated earlier describe what organizations should be looking for as warning signs. It is equally useful to identify what a functional data integrity culture looks like in practice, both as an aspirational benchmark and as a set of observable indicators that can be assessed in the organizations a sponsor or CRO is working with.

In a clinical research organization with a functional data integrity culture, quality findings are reported more often internally than they are identified by external monitors or auditors. This is not because the organization has fewer quality failures; it is because the reporting environment works. People who observe documentation concerns raise them through accessible channels that produce documented responses. The ratio of internally-generated to externally-identified findings is one of the most informative single indicators of cultural health available to a clinical quality program.

In a functional culture, protocol deviations are investigated for root cause with the same rigor as safety events, because the organization understands that a data quality deviation is a safety event in process, not in category. Corrective actions address the design condition that produced the deviation, not just the instance of it. The same deviation does not recur at the same site across multiple monitoring cycles unless the root cause was genuinely unaddressable, in which case the design decision to continue at that site is made explicitly and documented.

In a functional culture, conversations about enrollment velocity and conversations about data quality are not treated as separate discussions. A governance forum that receives both sets of metrics is more likely to produce decisions that treat them as genuinely integrated. A governance forum that receives enrollment data from the operations leadership and quality data from the quality leadership, in separate presentations, to separate agenda items, is structurally organizing the information in a way that makes integrating it harder. The governance structure either supports integrated decision-making or it does not, and the decision about how to structure it is a cultural decision made by the senior leadership that designs it.

Finally, in a functional culture, the clinical research coordinators and CRAs who are closest to the data understand that their documentation practices are visible, that the organization takes them seriously, and that raising a quality concern is more likely to result in organizational support than in informal social cost. This is the indicator that is hardest to manufacture through policy design and easiest to destroy through a single leadership response that communicates the opposite.

CHAPTER 12 — KEY TAKEAWAYS
Regulatory frameworks including ICH E6(R3), MHRA guidance, and PIC/S PI 041-1 impose explicit organizational culture requirements, not merely technical control requirements; cultural failure is a primary inspection finding category, not a background condition.
Data manipulation in clinical research is almost always a predictable response to organizational conditions: pressure without adequate support, metrics systems that signal speed over accuracy, normalized workarounds, and reporting environments that suppress concern-raising.
Inspectors assess culture through observable artifacts: documentation timing patterns, escalation records, the ratio of internally versus externally identified findings, and the coherence between formal quality commitments and actual organizational response to quality-delivery conflicts.
Leadership behavior is the primary determinant of data integrity culture; the decisions leaders make when data quality and operational pressure conflict communicate organizational values more durably than any training program or policy document.
Governance structures must create regular, documented engagement with quality signals rather than quality summaries; the ability to surface, escalate, and respond to individual quality indicators is the condition for a functional quality culture.
Sponsor oversight of CRO data management must include operational verification of actual practices rather than contractual attestation; the sponsor's regulatory responsibility for data integrity cannot be delegated regardless of the CRO relationship structure.
Speak-up architectures require deliberate design: multiple reporting channels, defined response timelines, documented outcomes, and leadership visibility into concern-raising activity; they do not emerge from nonretaliation policy statements alone.
Every ALCOA+ property has a cultural prerequisite; examining whether organizational conditions support each property provides a specific, auditable diagnostic framework for cultural integrity risk.
Culture change requires changes to the organizational conditions that shape behavior: the metrics architecture, escalation pathways, resource allocation model, and leadership engagement structure; training initiatives that address knowledge without addressing conditions will not change outcomes.

CHAPTER 12 — KEY TAKEAWAYS
The most reliable indicator of a functional data integrity culture is that quality concerns are raised and identified internally before they are surfaced by external monitors or regulators; this ratio is both an aspirational benchmark and an assessable operational metric.

CHAPTER THIRTEEN
Training That Actually Works

> *ICH E6(R3) requires that all individuals involved in conducting a clinical trial be qualified by education, training, and experience to perform their respective tasks — compliance with this requirement is demonstrated not by training records alone, but by evidence that training has produced the competency it was designed to confer.*

The training coordinator at a mid-sized contract research organization had every reason to be satisfied. Completion rates across the trial portfolio were above ninety-five percent. Annual GCP refresher modules had been assigned, launched, and closed on schedule. Site staff acknowledgment forms were signed. The learning management system showed green across the board. When the sponsor's quality team requested training records ahead of an FDA inspection, the package was ready within the hour.

The inspection did not go well. Investigators asked a clinical research coordinator to walk through the ALCOA+ requirements for electronic source data as they applied to her specific role recording vital signs in the EDC. She described ALCOA as an acronym she had seen in training. She could not explain what contemporaneous meant in practice, could not identify which of her daily documentation tasks the principle governed, and could not articulate what an investigator would look for if they reviewed her entries against source timestamps. She was not uniquely underprepared. The pattern repeated at three of five sites.

The Form 483 observations that followed addressed data integrity at the site level. But the root cause was upstream, in a training program that had been designed to generate documentation rather than competency. The organization had invested substantially in learning management infrastructure, module development, and completion tracking. It had not invested in asking whether any of it changed what coordinators actually did.

This is the central failure mode of GxP training in clinical research: the conflation of documented training with demonstrated competency. The two are not the same. They are not even reliably correlated. An organization that treats training completion as the measure of training effectiveness has substituted an input metric for an outcome metric, and will be surprised, repeatedly, by the gap between its training records and its inspection findings.

> *A training record proves that someone sat through a module. It proves nothing about what they can do when it matters.*

The Regulatory Baseline and Its Limits

ICH E6(R3) states that all individuals involved in conducting a clinical trial must be qualified by education, training, and experience to perform their respective tasks.[131] This requirement is not new. Its predecessor in E6(R2) used nearly identical language. What E6(R3) adds is a quality management framework that makes the operational implications harder to ignore.

The E6(R3) quality management framework requires sponsors to identify the knowledge and skills necessary for each function involved in trial conduct, to verify that individuals performing those functions possess them, and to maintain documentation that supports that verification. Critically, the framework is outcome-oriented: the standard is not whether training was delivered but whether the training delivered what it was intended to. A training program that assigns modules and tracks completion has met the documentation requirement. It has not necessarily met the competency requirement.[132] When an FDA investigator asks whether site staff are qualified to perform their tasks and the only evidence available is a completion certificate, that is an inadequate answer.

21 CFR Part 312.62 establishes investigator recordkeeping requirements that are inextricably linked to training adequacy.[133] Investigators are required to maintain accurate case histories, prepare and maintain adequate and accurate source documents, and ensure that data reported to sponsors accurately reflect source records. These are not clerical obligations. They require clinical research coordinators to understand, at a functional level, what constitutes a source record, when a record must be created, what makes a record

attributable, and what happens to the submission when that record is inaccurate or incomplete. Training programs that do not build this understanding do not satisfy the regulatory purpose of the investigator qualification requirement, regardless of whether the required modules have been completed and acknowledged.

The MHRA's data integrity guidance, applied to the clinical context, is characteristically direct on the same point: the organization is responsible for ensuring that staff understand the importance of data integrity, not merely that they have been informed of the requirements.[134] Understanding and being informed are different cognitive states. Training programs routinely produce the second. They less reliably produce the first.

Where the Checkbox Model Breaks Down

The checkbox compliance model for GxP training persists because it is easy to implement, easy to audit, and produces metrics that look like evidence of compliance. Learning management systems generate completion reports. Completion reports satisfy audit requests. Audit requests close. The underlying question of whether the training changed anything never gets asked because no one has built a mechanism to ask it.

The model breaks down in four predictable places. The first is knowledge transfer under pressure. A coordinator who completed a GCP module eighteen months ago and has since processed several hundred case report forms may or may not retain the ALCOA+ framework when a site is behind on queries and a monitoring visit is scheduled for Thursday. Training that is not reinforced through practice, feedback, and application degrades. The research on adult learning retention is consistent on this point: without active retrieval and application, knowledge acquired in a single exposure fades substantially within weeks.

The second failure point is transfer to novel situations. Clinical trials generate situations that no SOP anticipated. A wearable device produces an unexpected data format. An eClinical system has a configuration error that causes timestamps to display in the wrong time zone. A participant reports a symptom during a home visit that the eCOA instrument does not capture. In each of these situations, a coordinator's response depends on whether they understand the underlying regulatory principle well enough to apply it to a circumstance no training scenario addressed. Checkbox training produces rule followers. Effective training produces practitioners who understand why the rules exist.

The third failure point is the gap between knowledge and behavior. A coordinator can know that ALCOA requires contemporaneous recording and still back-fill entries when the clinic is running behind, because back-filling is faster, no one has explicitly told her that the consequences are serious, and the organizational environment does not signal that documentation timing is monitored or valued. This is not a knowledge failure. It is a behavioral one, and it requires a different intervention.

The fourth failure point is the invisibility of training inadequacy until inspection. Unlike a system configuration failure or a missing source document, inadequate training does not generate an alert. It accumulates silently in the gap between what coordinators know they should do and what they actually do, surfacing only when an investigator asks a coordinator to demonstrate her understanding, or when audit trail patterns reveal documentation practices that competent training would have prevented.

Designing for Competency, Not Completion

Competency-based training design starts from a different question than the checkbox model. Instead of asking what content needs to be covered, it asks what the learner needs to be able to do, and designs backward from that outcome. The distinction sounds straightforward. In practice it requires a significant rethinking of how GxP training programs are structured, delivered, and measured.

A competency-based approach begins with a task analysis for each role involved in clinical trial conduct. For a clinical research coordinator at an investigator site, that analysis identifies every data-generating or data-recording task the coordinator performs, the ALCOA+ properties that each task is designed to protect, the specific failure modes that inadequate performance of each task would produce, and the observable behavioral indicators that distinguish competent from non-competent performance. This analysis is more work than assembling a module from a vendor's GCP content library. It produces a training program that is specifically calibrated to what the coordinator actually does, rather than to a generic GCP curriculum.

The task analysis maps directly to the regulatory framework. ICH E6(R3)'s requirement for role-specific qualification is satisfied not by a single GCP module but by training that addresses the specific tasks, systems, and data integrity risks of the role. A coordinator who processes source documents for a Phase II oncology trial has different training requirements than a coordinator who manages ePRO compliance in a decentralized study.

Treating both with the same module produces the same training record with different levels of actual preparation.

The Adult Learning Framework Applied to GxP Contexts

The research on adult learning provides a practical framework for GxP training design that regulatory training programs routinely underutilize. The core finding is that adults learn most effectively when they can connect new information to existing experience, when they understand why the learning matters for their specific situation, when they practice applying new knowledge before being required to perform independently, and when they receive specific, timely feedback on their performance. GxP training programs that consist of text-heavy modules followed by multiple-choice assessments satisfy almost none of these conditions.

Scenario-based learning addresses the experience connection directly. When training presents a coordinator with a realistic documentation scenario, one that mirrors the specific systems, protocols, and pressures of her actual work, the new regulatory content attaches to something she already knows. The abstraction of ALCOA+ principles becomes concrete when they are applied to a situation the learner recognizes. Scenario-based learning also tests application rather than recall, which is a more accurate measure of what the learner will do in practice.

Spaced repetition addresses the retention problem. A single training event, however well designed, produces time-limited learning. Spacing training content across multiple exposures, with retrieval practice between them, substantially improves long-term retention. For clinical research coordinators, this means replacing the annual GCP refresher with shorter, more frequent reinforcement activities, calibrated to the specific content most likely to degrade and most consequential if it does. The regulatory requirement for ongoing training under E6(R3) provides the framework; spaced practice is the mechanism that makes it effective.

Immediate feedback is the element most consistently absent from GxP training programs. A coordinator who completes a module and receives a score knows whether she answered the questions correctly. She does not know whether her understanding is accurate, which questions she got right for the wrong reasons, or where the gap is between her current knowledge and what she needs to know to perform her role competently. Feedback that addresses these questions requires either instructor-led assessment or well-designed adaptive learning technology. Both require more investment than an off-the-shelf compliance module. Both produce meaningfully different outcomes.

Compliance Training vs. Competency Training: The Structural Difference

Training Element	Checkbox Compliance Model	Competency-Based Model
Needs assessment	Module catalog selected from standard GCP curriculum	Task analysis by role maps required knowledge to specific job functions and data integrity risks
Content design	Declarative content: what the rule is and what it requires	Scenario-based content: how the rule applies to this role's specific tasks, systems, and failure modes
Assessment method	Multiple-choice quiz at module completion; passing score required	Performance-based assessment: learner applies knowledge in a realistic scenario; assessor evaluates decision quality, not just correct answers
Feedback mechanism	Pass/fail score; correct answers revealed after submission	Specific, actionable feedback on the quality of the learner's reasoning and decisions, including explanation of why a correct response was correct
Reinforcement schedule	Annual refresher; curriculum repeats on fixed cycle	Spaced retrieval practice at intervals calibrated to content criticality and retention decay rates; reinforcement triggered by performance signals
Competency verification	Training completion certificate on file	Documented demonstration of competency, including performance assessment results, supervisor verification, or observed performance
Connection to quality system	Training records satisfy audit requests	Training data feeds quality signals: assessment performance by role and site is monitored as a leading indicator of data integrity risk

The ALCOA+ Competency Framework

Every clinical data integrity training program should be organized around ALCOA+ as the evaluative framework, because every regulatory data integrity requirement maps to one or more ALCOA+ properties. A training program built around ALCOA+ is a training program built around the framework FDA, EMA, and ICH will use to evaluate data integrity at inspection. If staff can apply ALCOA+ to their specific tasks, they can answer the inspector's questions. If they cannot, the training record that says they completed a GCP module provides no protection.

Attributability training addresses the specific behaviors required to ensure that every data entry can be traced to the individual who made it. For site staff, this means understanding why shared credentials are never acceptable, even when the system does not prevent them; why proxy entries require specific documentation of who observed the event being recorded; and why an audit trail that shows entries made under a coordinator's credentials when the coordinator was not on site is an inspection finding regardless of the explanation offered afterward. Attributability training should be role-specific and system-specific: a coordinator who works in a particular EDC platform should be trained using scenarios drawn from that platform's actual credential and access control design.

Contemporaneity training is where the gap between knowledge and behavior is most consequential. Coordinators who understand that records must be created at the time of the observation, and who understand the specific regulatory reason, specifically, that after-the-fact records are memory-dependent and outcome-biased, make different decisions under operational pressure than coordinators who know the rule without understanding its basis. The training should address the specific operational scenarios most likely to create contemporaneity pressure: end-of-visit data entry backlogs, eCOA device failure at the time of assessment, discrepancies between paper worksheets and EDC entry windows, and the documentation requirements for observations made during home visits or telehealth sessions. Each scenario should require the learner to make a decision, not just identify the correct rule.

Accuracy and originality training together address the relationship between source data and reported data that is the foundation of submission integrity. Coordinators must understand what a source record is, which records are source for which data fields, what transcription errors look like in the audit trail, and what the difference is between a legitimate data correction documented with a complete change reason and a data manipulation that changes the record without changing the underlying observation. This is not conceptually simple training. It requires that coordinators understand the data flow from their entry through EDC processing to the clinical study report well enough to recognize their role in maintaining the integrity of that flow.

Completeness and consistency training addresses the failure modes that produce incomplete datasets and internally inconsistent records. Coordinators should be trained specifically on the protocol provisions that define what constitutes a complete record for each visit, the documentation requirements for missed assessments and protocol deviations, and the difference between a missing data point that is properly documented and a missing data point that represents an unacknowledged failure of trial conduct. Consistency training should address the cross-system consistency requirement: the eTMF, the EDC, the monitoring visit reports, and the safety database must tell the same story. When they do not, the explanation must be documented, not assumed.

Connecting Training to the Quality System

Training that operates outside the quality system produces training records. Training that is integrated into the quality system produces quality signals. The difference is whether training data informs any quality decision beyond whether the required curriculum has been completed.

A quality-integrated training program treats assessment performance as a leading indicator of data integrity risk. If coordinators at a specific site are scoring below the established threshold on contemporaneity scenarios, that is a signal that the site presents elevated contemporaneity risk. If coordinators in a particular therapeutic area consistently struggle with adverse event documentation scenarios, that is a signal that the protocol's adverse event recording procedures may need clarification, or that the training scenario does not adequately reflect the complexity coordinators encounter in practice. These are actionable signals. A training program that only reports completion rates cannot generate them.

The integration requires that training data be accessible to the quality and monitoring functions, that role-specific competency thresholds be defined prospectively and reviewed systematically, and that training performance by site and role be included in the risk assessment that drives monitoring intensity. This is not a radical departure from existing quality management practice. It is a natural extension of the risk-based monitoring framework that FDA's 2013 guidance established and ICH E6(R3) reinforced.[135] The question is whether training performance is treated as one of the risk signals that monitoring responds to, or whether it is treated as a separate compliance function that runs in parallel with quality without informing it.

ICH E6(R3)'s quality management requirements provide the regulatory basis for this integration. Section 3.10's framework for sponsor quality systems explicitly encompasses the organizational processes that ensure all trial personnel are appropriately qualified and that qualification is verified. An organization that can demonstrate this integration at inspection, that can show how training performance data informed monitoring allocation, how competency gaps identified in training led to protocol-specific remediation, and how the training program was updated when data integrity failures identified patterns of inadequate preparation, has answered the E6(R3) training requirement at a level that a completion certificate cannot approach.

Technology-Enabled Training in Clinical Research

The technology available to support clinical trial training has advanced substantially. Adaptive learning platforms, AI-assisted content generation, simulation environments, and performance analytics tools have created capabilities that the checkbox compliance model was not designed to use. The question for clinical quality organizations is not whether to adopt these capabilities but how to adopt them in ways that improve competency outcomes rather than producing more sophisticated documentation of the same inadequate training.

Adaptive learning platforms adjust content delivery based on learner performance. A coordinator who demonstrates strong understanding of attributability requirements and weaker understanding of audit trail documentation will receive more practice on audit trail content and less repetition of content she has already mastered. This calibration produces more efficient learning and better-targeted reinforcement than a curriculum that delivers the same content to every learner regardless of her starting knowledge. For sponsor and CRO training programs managing staff across dozens of sites and multiple therapeutic areas, adaptive delivery also enables systematic identification of knowledge gaps that are correlated with specific site types, roles, or protocol designs.

AI-assisted content development addresses one of the practical constraints on competency-based training design: the time required to develop high-quality scenario-based content for each protocol, each EDC platform, and each role configuration. A clinical trial with a complex protocol and six active EDC modules requires scenario content that reflects the specific documentation requirements, the specific system configurations, and the specific failure modes of that trial. Developing that content manually for every training update is expensive. AI tools that generate scenario drafts from protocol documents and system specifications, which are then reviewed and validated by clinical quality subject matter experts, substantially reduce that cost while maintaining the specificity that competency-based design requires. The expert review step is not optional: AI-generated content that has not been validated against the actual regulatory standard and the actual operational context will produce scenarios that train to the wrong performance.

Simulation environments allow learners to practice in a replica of the actual system, with realistic scenarios that produce real consequences, without affecting live trial data. A coordinator who practices resolving a discrepancy between a paper source document and an EDC entry in a validated simulation environment, receives feedback on whether her resolution approach was correct and why, and repeats the scenario with variations until her performance is consistently competent, is better prepared to handle the real situation than a coordinator who read about the same scenario in a module. The simulation approach is well established in medical education and in aviation training. Its application to clinical data management training is still emerging but directionally correct.

Performance analytics give training programs visibility into what they actually produce. When assessment data, completion data, and downstream quality data, including monitoring findings, protocol deviation rates, and audit trail anomaly rates by site, are analyzed together, patterns become visible that no individual data source reveals. A site with perfect training completion rates and a high rate of monitoring findings related to source document discrepancies is signaling that its training is producing documentation without competency. A site with lower initial assessment scores that receives targeted reinforcement and subsequently shows improvement in monitoring outcomes is signaling that the reinforcement worked. These signals require data integration that most organizations have not built. Building it is a quality system investment, not a training administration function.

AI-ASSISTED TRAINING TOOLS: DESIGN CONSIDERATIONS FOR CLINICAL QUALITY ORGANIZATIONS

AI tools that generate training content from regulatory documents and protocol specifications can substantially reduce the cost of competency-based course development. They do not reduce the responsibility for the content they produce.

Scenario content generated by AI tools must be reviewed by clinical quality subject matter experts before deployment. The review must verify accuracy against the specific regulatory standard and the specific operational context of the trial.

AI-generated assessments must be validated to confirm they measure the intended competency, not pattern-matching to keywords. Multiple-choice questions that can be answered correctly by a learner who has not understood the underlying principle do not measure competency.

Organizations that use AI tools to generate training content and deploy it without systematic expert review have transferred content development efficiency to a system that does not bear regulatory responsibility for the output. The sponsor retains that responsibility regardless of the tool used to generate the content.

The evidentiary standard at inspection is whether training produced competency. The tool used to develop the training content is not relevant to that evaluation. The output is.

Sponsor Oversight of CRO and Site Training Programs

When sponsors delegate clinical trial activities to contract research organizations, the sponsor's training responsibility does not transfer with the delegation. ICH E6(R3) is explicit: sponsors must ensure that CROs implement and maintain effective training programs, and that the qualification of CRO staff and investigator site personnel meets the same standard as if the sponsor were conducting the activities directly.[136] The contractual representation that a CRO has a compliant training program is not evidence that the program is effective. It is evidence that the CRO made the representation.

Effective sponsor oversight of CRO training programs involves more than requesting training records and curriculum documentation. It requires that sponsors evaluate the design of the CRO's training approach against the competency-based standard: Does the program assess competency or completion? Are assessments role-specific and scenario-based? Is training performance data available to the sponsor for quality oversight purposes? Are competency gaps identified in training fed back into monitoring and quality risk management? These are design questions, and their answers tell a sponsor whether the CRO's training program is producing the qualified staff that E6(R3) requires.

For investigator sites, the sponsor's training obligation extends to ensuring that site staff are trained on the specific protocol, the specific EDC system, the specific eCOA instruments, and the specific source documentation requirements of the trial being conducted.[137] Site initiation training that covers GCP principles in the abstract, without applying them to the specific data collection and documentation tasks the site will perform, does not satisfy the sponsor's obligation to ensure that site staff are qualified for their specific tasks. The subsequent inspection finding that coordinators cannot demonstrate competency on protocol-specific ALCOA+ requirements is a sponsor oversight failure as much as a site training failure.

The qualification of principal investigators carries its own oversight requirement. Investigators are responsible for ensuring the accuracy of case report forms and for supervising the conduct of the trial at their site. Both responsibilities require that investigators understand the data integrity framework that governs the trial, including what their oversight of CRF data is expected to look like in practice, what the audit trail will show about the data management activities at their site, and what their specific responsibility is for the accuracy of the records submitted under their signature. Training programs that treat investigator qualification as a one-time regulatory read-through at site initiation are producing investigators who know the rule. Effective investigator qualification produces investigators who understand their role in maintaining the integrity of the data that will support a regulatory submission.

Training Failure Modes at Inspection

The training-related inspection findings documented in FDA bioresearch monitoring observations follow predictable patterns. Recognizing these patterns allows quality organizations to address them prospectively rather than encountering them during inspection.

Training Failure Mode	Inspection Manifestation
Completion without comprehension: staff completed modules but cannot apply content to role-specific scenarios	Investigator or coordinator cannot explain ALCOA+ requirements as applied to their specific duties; answers to investigator questions reflect surface familiarity without operational understanding
Generic curriculum without role specificity: all staff complete the same GCP modules regardless of function	Site staff training records show identical curricula for investigators, coordinators, and data entry personnel; no evidence of task-specific competency assessment
Assessment that measures recall, not application: multiple-choice quizzes on regulatory text	Staff pass training assessments but cannot demonstrate competency when asked to walk through a documentation decision or explain a change reason they would enter for a specific scenario
No connection to quality system: training data not analyzed as a quality signal	Training completion rates are high; monitoring finding rates are also high; the organization cannot explain the discrepancy because it has never analyzed them together
Sponsor reliance on CRO training representations: contract language treated as verification	CRO training records are available; CRO staff demonstrate the same comprehension gaps as inadequately trained site staff; sponsor cannot produce evidence of CRO training program evaluation
One-time site initiation training without reinforcement	Coordinators hired after site initiation received abbreviated onboarding; their training records show protocol overview acknowledgment, not competency-based qualification; audit trail anomalies at the site correlate with the tenure profile of recent hires
Investigator qualification treated as a signature exercise	Principal investigator signed GCP training acknowledgment; cannot describe the site's audit trail review process, cannot explain the

Training Failure Mode	Inspection Manifestation
	source data verification approach, cannot identify the eTMF location of required investigator documents

Building a Training Program That Produces Competency

The operational requirements for a competency-based clinical data integrity training program are not conceptually complex. They are organizationally demanding, because they require quality functions that typically operate independently to share data, set shared standards, and coordinate on what the training program is actually trying to produce. The following framework addresses the key design decisions.

Define Competency Outcomes Before Designing Content

For each role involved in clinical data generation, processing, or oversight, the training program must define the specific competencies the role requires. These definitions must be specific enough to be assessable: 'understands data integrity requirements' is not a competency outcome. 'Can identify which ALCOA+ properties are relevant to each of the five most common data entry tasks for this role and explain what correct performance looks like for each' is a competency outcome.

The competency definitions should be developed with input from the clinical operations function that designs the workflows, the quality function that identifies the failure modes, and the monitoring function that observes performance at sites. Each function contributes a different perspective on what competent performance looks like and what its absence produces. The resulting competency framework is the specification for the training program and the standard for competency verification.

Design Assessment Before Designing Content

Counterintuitively, the training design process should define how competency will be assessed before designing the content that will be delivered. Assessment design drives content design: if the assessment tests application, the content must build the understanding that application requires. If assessment design is deferred until after content development, the content will be built to the wrong specification and the assessment will measure whatever the content happened to cover.

Effective assessments for clinical data integrity training use realistic scenarios that mirror the learner's actual role, present a decision point that requires application of the relevant principle, and evaluate the quality of the decision and the reasoning behind it. They are not primarily multiple-choice instruments. They require that the learner explain why a particular entry is or is not compliant, what she would do differently, and what regulatory principle governs her decision. This assessment approach is more demanding to develop and score than an automated quiz, but it produces evidence of competency rather than evidence of test-taking.

Build Reinforcement Into the Program Architecture

Effective training programs do not end at module completion. They schedule reinforcement at intervals calibrated to content criticality, build in mechanisms for performance monitoring that can trigger additional reinforcement when quality signals indicate comprehension gaps, and create touchpoints for applying training content to real situations as they arise.

For clinical research coordinators, reinforcement opportunities exist throughout the trial lifecycle. Monitoring visits create natural feedback loops: a monitoring finding related to contemporaneity is an opportunity for targeted reinforcement, not merely a corrective action item. Protocol amendments create natural occasions for protocol-specific training updates. Audit trail review findings create natural occasions for reviewer-level training on what specific patterns mean and what they indicate about documentation practices.

The reinforcement program should be documented well enough to satisfy E6(R3)'s training record requirements. It should also be specific enough to be useful: a training record that shows a coordinator completed a general contemporaneity module after a monitoring finding is less informative than a record that shows she completed a scenario-based module addressing the specific documentation practice that generated the finding and that she passed the associated competency assessment.

Align Metrics to Competency Outcomes

The metrics that drive training program management determine what the program is actually designed to produce. Organizations that track completion rates manage programs designed to produce completion. Organizations that track competency assessment scores, by role, by site, and by training cohort, and that correlate those scores with downstream quality indicators, manage programs designed to produce competency.

The shift from completion metrics to competency metrics requires more from the quality information infrastructure than most organizations have built. Assessment data, training records, monitoring findings, audit trail anomalies, and protocol deviation data must be accessible in ways that allow cross-referencing. This is not a trivial data integration problem. It is also not optional if the objective is a training program that can demonstrate its own effectiveness at inspection. The organization that arrives at inspection with training completion records has documented that training occurred. The organization that can show the relationship between its training program, its assessment data, and its monitoring outcomes has demonstrated that training worked.

CHAPTER 13 — KEY TAKEAWAYS
ICH E6(R3) requires qualification by education, training, and experience for all individuals involved in trial conduct; this requirement is satisfied by demonstrated competency, not by training completion records alone.
The checkbox compliance model for GxP training conflates documented training with demonstrated competency; the two are not the same, and the gap between them is consistently visible at inspection.
Competency-based training design begins with a task analysis for each role, identifies the ALCOA+ properties each task is designed to protect, and designs learning experiences that build the understanding required to apply those properties under realistic operational conditions.
Adults learn most effectively through scenario-based practice connected to their actual work, spaced repetition calibrated to content criticality, and specific feedback on the quality of their reasoning, not just the correctness of their answers.
Training assessments that test application in realistic scenarios produce evidence of competency; assessments that test recall through multiple-choice instruments produce evidence of test completion.
Training data that is integrated into the quality system, analyzed alongside monitoring findings and audit trail data, and treated as a leading indicator of data integrity risk, converts training from a documentation function into a quality function.
Sponsor oversight of CRO and site training programs must extend beyond requesting completion records to evaluating program design, assessing training effectiveness, and verifying that the CRO's training produces qualified staff for sponsor-specific trial requirements.
AI-assisted training tools can reduce the cost of competency-based course development; they do not reduce the sponsor's responsibility for the accuracy and quality of the content deployed, and AI-generated training content requires systematic expert review before use.
The inspection question is not whether training occurred but whether it produced competency; the organization that can demonstrate both, with integrated data linking training performance to quality outcomes, has satisfied the regulatory standard in a way that completion records cannot

PART FOUR: EMERGING CHALLENGES

Staying Ahead Of What Is Already Here

CHAPTER FOURTEEN

AI: Integrity in the Age of Intelligent Systems

> *An AI system that generates a data query, flags a safety signal, or recommends a protocol deviation waiver is making a regulatory decision. The data integrity standards that govern how that decision was reached, what information it was based on, and whether it can be reconstructed and defended are the same standards that have governed human clinical decisions for decades. The system that made the decision is new. The obligation is not.*

A large pharmaceutical sponsor operating a pivotal Phase III oncology program reached the end of its data collection period and initiated database lock procedures. The trial had enrolled patients across forty-one investigator sites in fourteen countries. Across that population, the sponsor had deployed an AI-assisted data review platform that operated in parallel with its standard EDC monitoring program. The platform used a trained anomaly detection model to identify statistical patterns in efficacy data that warranted targeted query generation, prioritizing sites and patients whose data profiles deviated from expected distributions based on the study population as a whole.

The database lock review identified a problem that neither the clinical operations team nor the data management group had anticipated. The anomaly detection model had been retrained at two points during the trial, once after interim analysis and once following a protocol amendment that modified the primary endpoint definition. The retraining events were documented in the system's configuration records. What was not documented was the effect of those retraining events on the queries the model had generated before they occurred. Queries issued under the original model configuration and queries issued under each successive configuration had resolved differently, because the model's sensitivity thresholds had shifted. The sponsor could not produce a reconstruction of which queries had been generated by which model version, or demonstrate that the data cleaning decisions those queries had driven were consistent across the study period.

The pre-approval inspection that followed found no evidence of intentional data manipulation. The investigators found something more troubling for a submission timeline: a dataset whose cleaning history could not be fully reconstructed. The sponsor could not demonstrate that the AI-generated queries that had shaped the final dataset met the traceability requirements that ALCOA+ imposes on any data management decision. The inspection produced a major deficiency finding. The submission was placed on clinical hold pending a full reconstruction of the data cleaning history. Fourteen months and an eight-figure remediation cost later, the submission was refiled.

The sponsor had not used an unvalidated system. It had not bypassed its quality processes. It had done what a technically sophisticated development organization does: it had adopted a capable tool, integrated it into its clinical operations program, and managed it as a technical system rather than as a data integrity obligation. The distinction was catastrophic.

> *AI does not create new data integrity principles. It creates new and more consequential ways to violate the ones that already exist.*

The Core Problem: When the Decision-Maker Cannot Testify

Clinical data integrity has always required that the person who made a data entry or a data management decision be identifiable, that the basis for the decision be documentable, and that the record of the decision be preserved in a form that allows regulatory review. These requirements exist because the regulatory system is, at its foundation, a system of accountability. An FDA inspector reviewing a query resolution record needs to know: who resolved this query, on what date, based on what information, and under whose authorization? The answer to those questions is the chain of custody that makes the data trustworthy.

AI systems interrupt that chain. Not because they produce bad data, but because the question of who decided becomes a question of what decided, and the regulatory framework has not yet fully resolved how to answer it. When an anomaly detection algorithm generates a query, the query does not have an author in the conventional sense. It has a model, trained on a dataset, configured to a set of thresholds, producing an output that a human then acts on. The human action is attributable. The recommendation that produced it is only attributable if the organization has built traceability into its AI infrastructure the way it builds traceability into everything else.

The regulatory expectation is clear in principle, even where it is not yet fully articulated in formal guidance. FDA's May 2023 discussion paper on AI and machine learning in drug development identifies traceability of AI inputs and outputs as a foundational data integrity requirement for AI-supported regulatory submissions. ICH E6(R3)'s governance framework[138] requires that all data management decisions be traceable and that the basis for data changes be documented regardless of the system that initiated them. The 2024 draft Annex 11 revision (still draft as of publication of this book) explicitly requires that AI-assisted data review and cleaning tools be validated, that their outputs be traceable to the underlying data reviewed, and that model changes be subject to change control. The direction of travel across all major regulatory authorities is identical: AI systems used in clinical data management are subject to the same ALCOA+ obligations as the human processes they augment or replace.

The compliance gap is not between what regulators require and what organizations intend. It is between what ALCOA+ requires of an AI system and what most AI system implementations actually provide. Sponsors deploying AI-assisted clinical data tools without a formal traceability architecture are operating with a data integrity gap that inspectors, now trained to look for it, will find.

The Attributability Problem

Attributability, the first ALCOA property, requires that every data entry be identifiable to the person or system that created it. For human entries in a validated EDC system, this is operationally straightforward: the audit trail captures the user account, timestamp, and action. For AI-generated outputs, attributability requires a different kind of documentation architecture.

An AI system that generates a query, flags a potential adverse event, scores a digital biomarker reading, or recommends an analysis exclusion is performing a data management action. That action must be attributable not merely to the system in general, but to the specific version of the model, configured to the specific parameters, operating on the specific input data, at the specific point in time the action occurred. Attributability for an AI output is version-controlled configuration documentation, not just a system name in an audit log.

This creates a practical requirement that most organizations have not built: a version-controlled record of every AI model deployed in a clinical data management role, including the training data used, the configuration parameters in effect, the validation status at each version, and the dates during which each version was operationally active. Without this record, it is impossible to attribute a specific AI-generated query or flag to a specific model version, and the attributability chain for that data management decision is broken.

The Contemporaneity and Traceability Problem

Contemporaneity requires that records be created at the time of the activity they document. For AI systems, this translates to a requirement that the model version, input data, and output be recorded at the time the output is generated, not reconstructed from system logs after the fact. A query generated by an anomaly detection model is a contemporaneous record at the moment of generation. If the model is subsequently retrained, the original query's basis cannot be retrospectively attributed to the updated model; it must have been attributed to the version in effect at generation.

Traceability, the emerging property that extends ALCOA+ in the direction that AI most urgently requires, means that a complete chain of custody can be established from the original data through every transformation, review, and decision to the final dataset used in the regulatory submission. For AI systems, traceability is the requirement that the path from raw clinical data to AI-generated output to human action to data change be fully reconstructable at any point in time after the fact. This is more demanding than most current AI system implementations provide, and it is precisely the requirement that the sponsor in the opening scenario failed to meet.

The Accuracy and Consistency Problem

AI models are not static. They improve, drift, and change. A model trained on early-trial data may behave differently on late-trial data, particularly in studies where the population enrolled shifts from the distribution assumed during training. A model that is retrained during a trial to improve its performance changes its behavior. These are desirable properties in a technology product. They are data integrity problems in a regulated clinical research context unless managed under explicit change control.

Accuracy, in the ALCOA+ sense, means that data and data management decisions reflect the actual state of the clinical investigation. A query generated by a model with degraded accuracy, operating outside its validated range, or producing outputs inconsistent with what a trained human reviewer would have identified, introduces accuracy risk into the dataset that is not recoverable after database lock unless the history of that inaccuracy is documented and correctable. Consistency, the ALCOA+ requirement that a process produces the same result across the same inputs, is structurally challenged by AI systems that are designed to generalize, and whose generalizations can shift between model versions.

Categories of AI Use in Clinical Data Management

AI and machine learning are deployed across the clinical research enterprise in ways that vary enormously in their data integrity risk profile. A system that generates patient scheduling reminders carries a different risk profile than a system that recommends query resolutions or identifies potential adverse events for adjudication. Understanding the categories of AI use, and their respective data integrity implications, is the prerequisite for designing a proportionate compliance framework.

AI AND ML USE CATEGORIES: DATA INTEGRITY RISK PROFILE

AI Application	Data Integrity Risk Level	Primary ALCOA+ Properties at Risk
Anomaly detection / centralized monitoring	High	Attributable, Accurate, Traceable
AI-assisted query generation and resolution	High	Attributable, Contemporaneous, Accurate
NLP for adverse event coding	High	Accurate, Traceable, Consistent
Digital biomarker scoring (wearables, eCOA)	High	Original, Accurate, Attributable
Automated eligibility screening	High	Accurate, Attributable, Traceable

AI Application	Data Integrity Risk Level	Primary ALCOA+ Properties at Risk
Predictive site risk scoring	Medium	Accurate, Consistent
Protocol deviation detection and flagging	High	Accurate, Attributable, Contemporaneous
Automated data cleaning / imputation	Very High	Accurate, Original, Traceable
Patient scheduling and engagement tools	Low	Contemporaneous (limited scope)
Regulatory document summarization (non-decision)	Low	Legible (minimal risk)

High-Risk Category: AI-Assisted Query Generation and Resolution

The single highest-risk deployment of AI in clinical data management is AI-assisted query generation, for the reason illustrated by the opening scenario: it is the point at which AI output directly shapes the final clinical dataset. Every query that an AI system generates, and every query that a human resolves based on an AI recommendation, is a data management decision that must meet all ALCOA+ requirements as if a human data manager had made it independently.

The most common failure mode in this category is not model inaccuracy. It is model version opacity. Organizations that deploy AI-assisted query platforms frequently manage model updates as technical events handled by their technology teams, rather than as change control events handled by their data management quality programs. When a model update changes the queries the system generates, that change has a direct effect on the data that will be in the final dataset. It is functionally equivalent to changing the query resolution procedure in a standard operating procedure. The regulatory framework requires that such changes be controlled, documented, and their impact on existing data assessed.

A sponsor using AI-assisted query generation must be able to answer the following questions for any query in its clinical database: Which model version generated this query?

What was the validation status of that model version at the time of generation? What input data did the model evaluate to generate this query? Was the model operating within its validated performance range on that input? Was this query reviewed and approved by a qualified human reviewer before issuance? What human decision was made in response to this query, and what is the audit trail for that decision? If any of these questions cannot be answered for a query in the database, the data management history for that query does not meet the traceability standard that regulators now apply to AI-assisted clinical data management.

High-Risk Category: Automated Data Cleaning and Imputation

AI-assisted data cleaning, including automated outlier identification, missing data flagging, and machine learning-based imputation, represents the highest-risk category of AI deployment in clinical data management. The Original property, which requires that primary source data be retained and that any changes to it be documented with the original value preserved, is directly implicated in any automated cleaning or imputation process.

An AI system that identifies an apparent data entry error and automatically corrects it, or that fills a missing data point through statistical modeling, has created a derived data record rather than an original one. This is permissible under regulatory frameworks that allow data cleaning, but it requires the same documentation disciplines as manual data cleaning: the original value must be preserved, the basis for the change must be documented, and the system that made the change must be attributable and traceable. An automated correction that overwrites the original value without preserving it in the audit trail is an original-record violation regardless of whether the correction was accurate.[139]

Imputation deserves specific treatment because it introduces a category of record that has no equivalent in manual data management: a data point that was never entered by anyone, generated by statistical modeling from other data. Imputed values used in primary analyses must be identified as imputed, the imputation method must be documented, the model used must be validated, and the sensitivity of the analysis to the imputation must be assessable. A dataset that contains imputed values that are not distinguished from original-source values in the audit trail does not meet the ALCOA+ original standard, regardless of the statistical validity of the imputation method.

Emerging Category: Generative AI in Clinical Documentation

The deployment of large language models for clinical research documentation introduces data integrity risks that are categorically different from those associated with analytical AI systems. A generative AI system used to draft adverse event narratives, summarize protocol deviation explanations, or assist with case report form completion is generating text that may enter the regulatory record. The legibility, accuracy, and attributability requirements that govern any clinical record apply to AI-generated text that enters that record with the same force they apply to text entered by a human clinical research coordinator.

The specific risk is not that generative AI produces inaccurate text, though this remains a genuine technical concern. The specific data integrity risk is that the provenance of AI-generated text may be obscured in the clinical record. A narrative that reads as if authored by the investigator but was drafted by a generative AI system and accepted without substantive modification raises an attributability question: who is the author of this record? FDA's source data guidance requires that the investigator attest[140] to the accuracy of source documents. A narrative the investigator did not write but did sign raises the question of whether the attestation is meaningful. Organizations deploying generative AI in clinical documentation contexts need an explicit position on this question before they encounter it in an inspection.

The Validation Framework for AI Systems in Clinical Research

Chapter 7 addressed computer system validation in the context of traditional clinical software: EDC systems, eTMF platforms, CTMS, and IRT. The CSV framework developed there applies to AI systems, with modifications driven by the properties that distinguish AI from conventional software. Conventional software, when given the same input, produces the same output. Its behavior can be fully characterized by its code. AI systems, particularly trained models, produce outputs that depend on training data and configuration parameters in ways that make complete behavioral characterization through code review alone insufficient.

Computer Software Assurance principles, developed by FDA as the risk-based successor to traditional validation protocols, are better suited to AI system validation than traditional IQ/OQ/PQ approaches, because they focus on what the software does in operation rather than whether it was built according to specification. For AI systems, this means validating performance against clinical data quality outcomes: does the anomaly detection system identify the patterns it was designed to identify, with acceptable sensitivity and specificity, across the range of data inputs it will encounter in the trials where it is deployed?

Key Elements of an AI Validation Program for Clinical Data Management

A validation program for an AI system used in clinical data management must address five elements that go beyond the standard CSV scope: performance characterization, boundary condition documentation, change control for model updates, ongoing performance monitoring, and explainability.

Performance characterization means establishing, before deployment, the model's expected sensitivity and specificity for its intended clinical application, using a dataset representative of the trials where it will be used. This is distinct from the vendor's general performance claims. A model validated on oncology trial data may perform differently on rare disease data; a model validated on EDC data from one platform may perform differently on data from another. The validation program must characterize performance in the specific context of use.

Boundary condition documentation means explicitly defining the conditions under which the model's validated performance cannot be guaranteed, and establishing a protocol for what happens when the system encounters data outside those conditions. AI systems can fail silently: they produce outputs without warning when they encounter inputs outside their training distribution. A clinical data management system must have explicit procedures for detecting when AI outputs should be treated with heightened human review because the system may be operating outside its validated range.

Change control for model updates is the requirement that generates the most friction between clinical AI teams and data management quality programs, and it is the requirement most commonly out of compliance at inspection. Every retraining event, every threshold adjustment, every change to input data features, every update to the model architecture must be assessed for its impact on clinical data management decisions. If the model change affects which queries are generated, which flags are raised, or which cleaning recommendations are made, it has a direct effect on the clinical dataset. It requires the same impact assessment and documentation that any change to a validated system requires.

Ongoing performance monitoring means treating model performance as a quality metric reviewed on the same cadence as other clinical data quality metrics, not as a one-time validation achievement. Model drift, the phenomenon by which a model's performance degrades as the data it encounters diverges from its training distribution, is a known risk in deployed AI systems. A clinical AI system without a performance monitoring program is a validated system without operational quality oversight, and the distinction between initial validation and ongoing monitoring is one that regulatory frameworks across all major authorities explicitly require.

Explainability is the most practically contentious element of clinical AI validation, because it requires that the basis for individual AI outputs be documentable in terms that a human reviewer can understand and evaluate. Not all AI architectures provide this at the individual-output level. A deep learning model may produce an accurate anomaly flag without any mechanism for explaining why it flagged the specific data point it flagged. For clinical data management decisions, where the basis for every data change must be documented, an AI output whose basis cannot be explained creates an immediate ALCOA+ documentation problem. This does not mean that non-explainable AI systems are prohibited in clinical data management; it means that every output from such a system must receive substantive human review before it drives a data management action, and that the human review, not the AI output alone, is the documentable basis for the decision.

Regulatory Frameworks: Where the Requirements Currently Stand

At the time of publication of this book, no major regulatory authority has yet published a final, comprehensive guidance document specific to AI in clinical data management. What exists is a framework of principles drawn from existing guidance, supplemented by discussion papers, draft guidance, and enforcement signals that make regulatory expectations operationally clear even without final guidance.

FDA

FDA's primary statement on AI in drug development is the May 2023 discussion paper, which addresses the use of AI[141] and machine learning across the drug development lifecycle including clinical trials. The discussion paper is not guidance, but it represents FDA's current thinking on the data integrity obligations that apply to AI-generated outputs used in regulatory submissions. Its most significant data integrity provision is the explicit statement that AI outputs used in regulatory decisions must be traceable: the input data, the model version, and the output must be preserved and producible to FDA on request.

21 CFR Part 11 applies to AI systems used to generate[142], modify, maintain, or transmit electronic records that constitute regulated clinical data. The predicate rule framework means that Part 11[143]'s audit trail, access control, and validation requirements apply to any AI system whose outputs enter an FDA-required record. FDA has not published updated Part 11 guidance addressing AI systems; until it does, the existing Part 11 framework is the applicable technical standard.

FDA's bioresearch monitoring program has begun assessing AI system use in clinical data management during inspections. The current inspection focus is on whether AI systems used in clinical data management are validated, whether model change control is in place, and whether sponsors can produce traceability documentation for AI-generated data management decisions. A sponsor that cannot produce this documentation during a BIMO inspection faces the same consequence as a sponsor whose manual data management documentation is deficient: an inspection finding that may delay or prevent approval.

EMA and the 2024 Draft Annex 11

The 2024 draft revision of Annex 11, circulated for consultation[144], contains the most operationally specific regulatory language currently available on AI in clinical data management. Its provisions are formally directed at computerized systems in GMP-regulated manufacturing, but through the cross-reference structure of EU GCP guidance, they apply to clinical data management systems as well. The draft's treatment of AI and machine learning establishes three requirements that go beyond any previously published EU guidance.

First, AI and machine learning systems used for regulated data management decisions must be validated, with validation documentation addressing not just the system's technical specifications but its performance against clinical quality outcomes. This is a higher standard than traditional validation approaches require for non-AI systems, because it shifts the validation focus from implementation compliance to operational effectiveness.

Second, AI outputs used in regulated data management decisions must be traceable to the model version and input data that produced them. This requirement, when adopted, will make version-controlled AI configuration documentation a regulatory requirement rather than a best practice.

Third, changes to AI models must be subject to change control, including impact assessment of the effect of model changes on regulated data management activities. This provision, if adopted as drafted, would require clinical data management quality programs to assess the impact of model retraining events on the clinical dataset, with documentation of that assessment in the trial master file.

ICH E6(R3)

ICH E6(R3) does not address AI systems explicitly, because AI-specific clinical data management guidance was not within the guideline's scope at the time of finalization. What E6(R3) does is provide a governance framework within which AI data integrity obligations sit. Annex 1, Section 4.3.4 requires sponsors to validate computerized systems used to collect, manage, and report clinical trial data, with Principle 9.3 establishing the overarching fitness-for-purpose expectation. The data traceability requirements in Annex 1, Section 4.2 apply to AI-generated outputs that enter the clinical dataset. The sponsor's quality management system obligations in Annex 1, Section 3.10 apply to the processes that govern AI system deployment, change control, and performance monitoring.

The practical implication is that E6(R3) compliance for a sponsor using AI-assisted data management requires more than it would for a sponsor using only conventional EDC systems. The validation obligation under Annex 1, Section 4.3.4 encompasses AI system validation, including performance characterization. The traceability obligation in Annex 1, Section 4.2 encompasses AI output traceability. The quality management system obligation in Annex 1, Section 3.10 encompasses the AI system change control and performance monitoring program. None of these obligations are new; all of them apply more demandingly to AI systems than to conventional software.

REGULATORY FRAMEWORK SUMMARY: AI IN CLINICAL DATA MANAGEMENT

Authority / Framework	Key AI Data Integrity Obligations
FDA / 21 CFR Part 11	Validation required; audit trail for AI outputs entering regulated records; Part 11 technical requirements apply via predicate rule.
FDA / 2023 AI Discussion Paper	Traceability of AI inputs and outputs; model version documentation; not yet final guidance but represents current agency thinking.

Authority / Framework	Key AI Data Integrity Obligations
EMA / 2024 Draft Annex 11	Performance-based validation; traceable outputs; model change control; formal assessment of impact on regulated data — pending final adoption.
ICH E6(R3) Sections 5.0, 5.5.3, Appendix A	Technology validation; data traceability for all clinical data management decisions; quality management system applies to AI program governance.
PIC/S PI 041-1 (2021)	ALCOA+ evaluative standard applies to AI-generated outputs; inspection equivalence framework means PI 041-1 norms apply globally across PIC/S member authorities[145].
MHRA	Culture-first assessment: inspectors evaluate whether organizations have genuine governance of AI tools, not just documented processes; management accountability extends to AI system oversight[146].
February 2026 EMA/PIC/S Consultation	Proposes unified AI/ML validation and change control requirements across EMA and PIC/S jurisdictions; if adopted, becomes simultaneously applicable in the majority of significant clinical regulatory jurisdictions.

AI Data Integrity Failure Modes: Four Documented Patterns

Enforcement actions and inspection findings involving AI systems in clinical data management are not yet as numerous as those involving conventional eClinical system audit trail or access control failures, because AI adoption in clinical data management is relatively recent. But the failure modes that have emerged in early enforcement and inspection experience are instructive, because they are not random. They follow predictable organizational and technical patterns that a well-designed data integrity program can address prospectively.

Failure Mode 1: Model Version Opacity at Database Lock

The most consistently documented failure mode, illustrated by the opening scenario, is the inability to reconstruct the model version history of an AI system at database lock.

Organizations that treat AI system retraining as a technical event managed by a technology team, rather than as a validated system change event managed by a data management quality program, accumulate model version transitions that are not reflected in the trial master file or the audit trail for the clinical dataset. When database lock documentation requires traceability of all data management decisions, and when some of those decisions were driven by AI outputs generated under model versions whose history is not documented, the traceability chain cannot be completed.

Prevention requires one discipline: every model retraining or configuration change during an active trial must be documented in the trial master file with the effective dates of the change, the validation status of the new version, and an assessment of its impact on queries or flags already in the clinical database. This is not a technically complex requirement. It is an organizational discipline requirement, and its absence is an organizational failure rather than a technical one.

Failure Mode 2: Automated Cleaning Without Human Review Documentation

A related but distinct failure mode involves AI-assisted data cleaning systems that make or recommend data changes with documented human approval of the system's outputs in bulk rather than review of individual changes. A data manager who approves the output of an AI cleaning run by signing off that the run completed successfully has not documented what each individual data change was, why it was made, and what the original values were. When inspectors review the audit trail and find batch-approval signatures without individual-change documentation, the original-value preservation requirement and the attributability requirement for each change are both potentially unmet.

Prevention requires that AI-assisted data cleaning systems produce individual-change audit records in the same format and with the same information as manual data changes: original value, new value, basis for change, authorizing review, and timestamp. Bulk approval of cleaning run outputs is not an acceptable substitute for individual-change documentation, regardless of the efficiency cost of individual review.

Failure Mode 3: AI Flag Dismissal Without Documentation

Anomaly detection systems generate flags that human reviewers evaluate and either act on or dismiss. The dismissal of an AI-generated flag is a data management decision: the reviewer has determined that the flagged anomaly does not require a data change or a query. That determination must be documented. An AI system that generates flags and a human review process that dismisses some fraction of them without a documented rationale for each dismissal has created a gap in the data management history. Inspectors who review AI system output logs and find flags that were never addressed, or addressed only by system clearance rather than documented human review, will treat the gap as a quality finding.

Prevention requires that every AI-generated flag have a documented disposition: actioned with a specific data management decision, or dismissed with a documented rationale. The dismissal documentation need not be elaborate, but it must exist in the audit trail and be producible at inspection.

Failure Mode 4: Generative AI Text Without Provenance Documentation

The deployment of generative AI tools for clinical documentation assistance, including adverse event narrative drafting, query response templates, and protocol deviation explanation support, creates a provenance documentation problem that most organizations have not yet addressed through formal policy. When a clinical research coordinator uses a generative AI tool to draft an adverse event narrative and then signs the narrative as the investigator's attestation, the attributability of the record raises a question that did not exist before generative AI was available: is the content of this record attributable to the investigator, or to an AI system whose outputs the investigator reviewed and accepted?

Prevention requires a defined organizational policy for generative AI use in clinical documentation: which uses are permitted, what level of human review is required before AI-drafted content enters the clinical record, and how the use of AI assistance is disclosed in the record if disclosure is required. Some organizations prohibit generative AI use in clinical documentation entirely; others permit it with substantive human review and attestation requirements. Either approach is defensible. No policy, combined with ad hoc deployment, is not.

Designing for AI Data Integrity: The Operational Framework

The organizational response to AI data integrity risk is the same as the organizational response to any data integrity risk: design the system so that compliance is the path of least resistance, not the exception. For AI systems in clinical data management, this means building five operational capabilities before deployment, not after the first inspection finding.

Capability 1: AI System Inventory with Classification

An organization cannot govern what it has not inventoried. The first operational requirement for AI data integrity is a current inventory of every AI or machine learning system in use in clinical data management contexts, classified by the data integrity risk category described earlier in this chapter. The inventory must identify the system, the vendor, the version or model iteration in production, the clinical data management functions it performs, and the ALCOA+ properties most implicated by its use. The inventory is a living document, updated whenever a new system is deployed or an existing system changes version.

Organizations that discover their AI system inventory at inspection, by attempting to reconstruct it from technology team records, are not governing their AI data integrity risk. Sponsors that do not require their CROs to maintain and disclose AI system inventories are not meeting their ICH E6(R3) oversight obligations for the data management decisions those systems drive.

Capability 2: AI-Specific Validation and Change Control Procedures

Standard CSV procedures, written for deterministic software systems, do not address the performance-based validation and model change control requirements that AI systems require. A clinical data management quality program deploying AI tools needs procedures that explicitly address: performance-based validation, including the metrics that define acceptable performance for the specific clinical application; model change control, including what constitutes a change that requires a new validation assessment; ongoing performance monitoring, including the metrics reviewed, the review cadence, and the escalation pathway when performance falls outside acceptable parameters; and boundary condition management, including the procedure for handling AI outputs generated outside the system's validated operating range.

These procedures do not need to be architecturally separate from the existing CSV and data management quality framework. They are most effectively integrated into it, as an AI-specific addendum to existing validation, change control, and quality monitoring procedures. The critical requirement is that they exist as formal documented procedures, reviewed and approved by the clinical data management quality program, before any AI system is deployed in a clinical data management role.

Capability 3: AI Audit Trail Architecture

The audit trail for an AI system used in clinical data management must capture, at minimum: the model version active at the time of each output, the input data processed to generate the output, the output itself, the timestamp, and the human action taken in response. For query-generating systems, the audit trail must be queryable by model version, so that all queries generated under a specific model version can be identified during database lock review or inspection. For data cleaning systems, the audit trail must include original values for every changed record.

This is an infrastructure requirement that must be specified during system procurement and validated before deployment. An AI system that does not provide model-version-tagged audit output is not fit for deployment in a regulated clinical data management role, regardless of its analytical performance. This should be a vendor qualification question for any AI clinical data management platform: can you provide model-version-tagged audit trail output for every data management decision your system drives? If the answer is no, the system cannot be deployed in a role where its outputs enter the clinical dataset.

Capability 4: Human Review Architecture for AI Outputs

AI systems in clinical data management operate as inputs to human decisions, not as autonomous decision-makers, in the current regulatory framework. The human review layer between AI output and data management action is not merely a quality control step; it is the point at which accountability for the data management decision attaches to a qualified person whose identity, qualifications, and authorization can be documented. The design of the human review architecture determines whether that accountability is real or nominal.

Nominal human review, in which a data manager approves AI outputs without individually evaluating them, does not meet the accountability standard. Substantive human review, in which a qualified reviewer evaluates the AI output against the underlying data and makes an independent judgment to accept or reject it, does. The practical challenge is that substantive review of every AI output in a high-volume clinical data management program is resource-intensive. The organizational response to this challenge is not to reduce review requirements; it is to configure AI systems to prioritize human review resources toward the outputs where AI confidence is lowest, and to design review workflows that make substantive individual review operationally feasible.

Capability 5: CRO and Vendor AI Governance

Sponsors that use vendors (CROs, eClinical technology, etc.) for clinical data management, and vendors that use AI-assisted data management tools, must address AI data integrity in their contractual and oversight frameworks. ICH E6(R3)'s governance requirements do not distinguish between data management decisions made by human vendor staff and data management decisions driven by AI tools that vendor staff use. The sponsor's traceability obligation applies to both. A sponsor that cannot produce AI system version documentation for data management decisions made by its vendor, because it never required the vendor to maintain and share such documentation, is not meeting its oversight obligation.

Vendor qualification for AI-assisted clinical data management platforms requires additional assessment criteria beyond those applicable to conventional eClinical systems. The qualification process should include: documentation of the vendor's AI model governance practices, including change control and performance monitoring procedures; review of the vendor's validation documentation for the specific model version deployed in the sponsor's trials; assessment of the vendor's audit trail architecture for AI outputs; and contractual provisions requiring notification of model changes, provision of version documentation, and cooperation with regulatory inspection processes. These are not onerous requirements, and vendors building AI clinical data management tools for the regulated market should be able to meet them. Vendors who cannot should not be deployed in a regulated clinical data management role.

AI DATA INTEGRITY INSPECTION READINESS: ASSESSMENT CHECKLIST

AI System Inventory and Classification

- □ Current inventory of all AI/ML systems used in clinical data management roles exists and is maintained by the quality program.
- □ Each system is classified by data integrity risk level with identification of the ALCOA+ properties most implicated.
- □ CRO and vendor AI system use is disclosed and included in the inventory.

Validation and Change Control

- □ Each high-risk AI system has a validation record including performance characterization for its specific clinical application.
- □ Boundary conditions are documented; procedure exists for handling AI outputs outside the validated operating range.

- □ Model change control procedure is in place; all retraining events during active trials are documented in the trial master file.
- □ Impact assessments exist for all model changes occurring during active trials, documenting effect on existing queries and flags.

Audit Trail and Traceability

- □ AI system audit trail captures model version, input data, output, and timestamp for each data management action.
- □ Audit trail is queryable by model version; all outputs from each version can be identified for database lock review.
- □ Original values are preserved in the audit trail for all AI-driven data changes.
- □ All AI-generated flags have documented dispositions; dismissed flags have documented rationales.

Human Review and Documentation

- □ Human review procedure is documented; individual review of each AI output is required before data management action, not bulk approval.
- □ Reviewer qualifications and authorizations are documented for each AI output review function.
- □ Generative AI use policy exists and is enforced; policy addresses permitted uses, review requirements, and record provenance.

Vendor and CRO Oversight

- □ Vendor qualification for AI platforms includes review of model governance practices, not just technical validation documentation.
- □ Contracts with AI platform vendors require notification of model changes and provision of version documentation.
- □ CRO oversight program includes verification of AI system governance practices, not reliance on contractual attestation alone.

The Strategic Position: Leading the Regulatory Curve

The current regulatory landscape for AI in clinical data management is one of principles without full procedural specificity, moving rapidly toward the latter. Final guidance from FDA on AI in drug development is expected. The EMA/PIC/S consultation that opened in February 2026[147] will, when it produces a final document, simultaneously apply comprehensive AI data integrity requirements across the majority of the world's significant clinical regulatory jurisdictions. Organizations that treat this trajectory as a future compliance event to be addressed when guidance is finalized are making a strategic error.

The inspection record demonstrates that regulators apply existing ALCOA+ and Part 11 principles to AI systems in the absence of AI-specific guidance, and they apply them with the same consequence as to any other clinical data management finding. An organization that cannot demonstrate traceability for AI-generated data management decisions during a pre-approval BIMO inspection today will receive a deficiency finding today, not after FDA's AI guidance is finalized. The absence of specific guidance is not a compliance safe harbor; it is an invitation to apply general principles, and inspectors are doing so.

Organizations that build the five operational capabilities described in this chapter before their next AI system deployment are not preparing for future requirements. They are meeting current ones, and they are building an infrastructure that will accommodate the more specific requirements that guidance documents will eventually impose without requiring fundamental rebuilding. The organizations that implement AI governance at the same speed they implement AI itself are the ones that will complete their regulatory submissions without the detours that the opening scenario represents.

The core argument of this book, introduced in Chapter 5, is that data integrity failures are almost always design failures. AI introduces new design opportunities and new design risks. The organizations that treat AI data governance as a design problem, building traceability, accountability, and quality oversight into AI systems before deployment rather than after the first finding, will use AI as a clinical data management asset rather than a liability. The organizations that treat AI as a technology acquisition and governance as a later-stage concern will relitigate, at significant cost, the lesson the clinical data management field has learned repeatedly since the first Part 11 inspection: that compliance built into a system performs better than compliance retrofit onto one.

CHAPTER 14 — KEY PRINCIPLES
AI systems used in clinical data management are subject to existing ALCOA+ and 21 CFR Part 11 requirements without modification; no AI-specific final guidance is required for these obligations to apply.
Attributability for an AI output means version-controlled configuration documentation linking the specific model version, parameters, and input data to each output at the time of generation — not a system name in a generic audit log.
Model change control is the most consistently deficient element of AI data integrity programs: every retraining event during an active trial must be documented, assessed for impact on the clinical dataset, and reflected in the trial master file.
AI-assisted data cleaning systems must produce individual-change audit records equivalent to manual data changes; bulk approval of cleaning run outputs does not satisfy the original-value preservation or attributability requirements.
AI-generated flags require documented dispositions; a flag dismissed without documented rationale is a data management decision without documentation, not an absence of a data management action.
The FDA May 2023 AI discussion paper, the EMA 2024 draft Annex 11, and the February 2026 EMA/PIC/S consultation establish a consistent global regulatory trajectory: performance-based validation, traceable outputs, and model change control will be formal requirements in all major jurisdictions.
Sponsor ICH E6(R3) oversight obligations apply to CRO and vendor AI system governance; a sponsor that cannot produce model version documentation for CRO data management decisions is not meeting its traceability obligation.
Organizations that build AI governance infrastructure before deployment avoid the remediation costs that follow a BIMO finding; the inspection record demonstrates that regulators are applying existing principles to AI systems now, without waiting for final guidance.

CHAPTER FIFTEEN

Cloud, SaaS, and Third-Party Systems

> *Regulatory obligations for clinical trial data integrity are not diminished by the location of the infrastructure that holds the data. The obligation follows the record, not the server.*

The database lock notification arrives on a Thursday afternoon. The Phase III trial has completed. Three hundred and twelve subjects across eighteen sites in four countries. Forty-two months of operational effort. The clinical data manager begins the final reconciliation, cross-checking the electronic data capture export against the biostatistics handoff package, and notices a discrepancy in the randomization records. Some subject-level randomization data points do not match what the EDC shows. He contacts the interactive response technology vendor for the original transaction logs.

The IRT vendor's customer success team responds the following Monday. The transaction logs he needs are held in the vendor's proprietary cloud environment. The commercial agreement for the trial expired at database lock, sixty days earlier. Access to the archived data requires a new service agreement and a data recovery fee. The transaction logs are not, the vendor explains, included in the standard data transfer package specified in the original contract. They were not discussed during vendor qualification. The sponsor's data management plan does not address them.

The biostatistics submission timeline is six weeks. The regulatory agency for the lead market requires that the IRT transaction records be available for inspection as source data for the randomization sequence. The sponsor's regulatory affairs team knows this. What they did not know, until this moment, was that the original records were held in infrastructure they had no ongoing right to access, by a vendor whose cooperation they now had to purchase, on a timeline dictated entirely by that vendor's internal workload and a payment process that would take fourteen business days to clear.

This is not a hypothetical scenario constructed to illustrate a compliance principle. It is a pattern that recurs across the clinical research industry with enough regularity that it has generated inspection observations, warning letter language, and a growing body of regulatory guidance addressing precisely this failure mode. The shift to cloud-hosted, SaaS-delivered clinical systems has produced genuine operational efficiencies. It has also produced a class of data integrity risk that did not exist when clinical records lived on servers in the sponsor's own facility, and that the industry has been slow to address with the same rigor it applies to other compliance obligations.

> *Outsourcing the infrastructure is a procurement decision. Outsourcing the regulatory obligation is not an option.*

The Infrastructure Shift and Its Regulatory Consequences

The architecture of clinical data management has changed fundamentally over the past two decades. Electronic data capture systems that sponsors once installed, validated, and hosted on internal servers are now almost universally delivered as software-as-a-service platforms, hosted in vendor-operated cloud infrastructure and accessed through a web browser. The same model applies to electronic trial master file platforms, interactive response technology systems, electronic clinical outcome assessments, safety reporting databases, and the integration layers that connect all of these into a coherent clinical data ecosystem. The clinical trial sponsor's physical custody of its own data has, in operational terms, become largely theoretical.

The regulatory framework has not made a parallel shift. The obligations established by 21 CFR Part 11, ICH E6(R3), the EU Clinical Trials Regulation, and PIC/S PI 041-1 were written for[148] a context in which the regulated organization was expected to control the systems holding its data. Those instruments have been interpreted and applied to cloud-hosted environments, but the foundational principle has not changed: the sponsor's responsibility for the integrity, completeness, accuracy, and retrievability of its clinical trial data is not a function of where that data lives. It is a function of the sponsor's regulatory obligations[149]. Those obligations do not travel with the data when the data moves to a vendor's cloud.

The practical consequence of this mismatch is a class of compliance risk that sits at the intersection of contract law, system architecture, and regulatory expectation. Organizations that manage this risk well do so by treating vendor relationships for cloud-hosted GxP systems as compliance engagements, not procurement transactions. Organizations that manage it poorly tend to discover the gap at the worst possible time: at database lock, during inspection preparation, or when a vendor relationship ends unexpectedly.

THE REGULATORY FRAMEWORK FOR THIRD-PARTY AND CLOUD SYSTEMS

Regulatory Instrument	Obligation for Third-Party and Cloud-Hosted Systems
21 CFR Part 11 Section 11.10(k)	Persons who use open systems must employ procedures and controls designed to ensure the authenticity, integrity, and confidentiality of electronic records. The obligation applies regardless of where in the open system those records are held or processed.
ICH E6(R3) Section 3.6 (Agreements)	Sponsors may delegate trial-related duties and functions but cannot transfer regulatory responsibility to contract research organizations or other third parties. Verification obligations remain with the sponsor regardless of contractual arrangements.
ICH E6(R3) Section 4.5 (Validation of Computerised Systems)	All technology used in clinical data management must be validated for its intended use. The validation obligation applies to sponsor-deployed systems and to vendor-operated systems used on the sponsor's behalf.
FDA Electronic Source Data Guidance (2013)	Sponsors are responsible for ensuring that electronic source data meets ALCOA requirements regardless of where it is generated, held, or processed. Third-party custody does not satisfy sponsor obligations.

Regulatory Instrument	Obligation for Third-Party and Cloud-Hosted Systems
PIC/S PI 041-1 (2021)	Supplier qualification for computerized systems includes assessment of the supplier's quality management system, change control procedures, and data integrity controls, not only product documentation.
MHRA Data Integrity Guidance (2018)	Outsourcing data management does not diminish the regulated organization's responsibility for data integrity compliance. Third-party controls must be verified through audit and qualification, not accepted on contractual assurance alone.

The Shared Responsibility Model: What It Means and What It Does Not

Cloud vendors have popularized the concept of shared responsibility as a framework for allocating security and compliance obligations between the vendor and the customer. In its cloud infrastructure variant, the model is straightforward: the vendor is responsible for the security of the infrastructure layer, the physical data centers, the network, and the hypervisor. The customer is responsible for what is deployed on that infrastructure, including data, applications, access controls, and configuration decisions. Neither party is responsible for the other's layer, and the boundary between the two layers is defined by the service agreement.

In a clinical trial context, this model requires substantial refinement before it provides meaningful compliance guidance. The division of responsibility in a GxP SaaS deployment does not follow the cloud security model cleanly, because the regulatory obligations applicable to clinical data do not recognize the infrastructure-application boundary as a compliance boundary. A sponsor whose eClinical vendor has achieved SOC 2 certification for its infrastructure, and whose data center operations meet ISO 27001 standards, has verified the security posture of an environment it does not control. It has not verified that the specific configuration of the eClinical system captures the audit trail data required by ICH E6(R3), that the access control settings satisfy Part 11 attributability requirements, or that the archive export functionality will produce a vendor-independent record set meeting the retrievability standard.

The compliance boundary in a clinical SaaS deployment runs through the system, not between the system and the infrastructure. The vendor's layer encompasses software development practices, release management, system security architecture, and the baseline functionality of the application as shipped. The sponsor's layer encompasses trial-specific configuration, user provisioning and management, operational workflows, query management, audit trail review, and the oversight activities required by E6(R3). In many deployments, the vendor also performs configuration services on the sponsor's behalf, which expands the vendor's functional scope without transferring the sponsor's compliance accountability.

Understanding where the compliance boundary runs is prerequisite to designing a vendor qualification program that addresses the right questions. A vendor qualification that assesses only the vendor's infrastructure and software development practices will miss every compliance risk generated by the sponsor's own configuration decisions. A qualification that assesses only the sponsor's configuration layer will miss every risk arising from vendor software behavior, update practices, and data handling architecture. Comprehensive qualification addresses both, because compliance failures at either layer create sponsor liability.

SCENARIO: Data Availability Upon Vendor Contract Expiration

COMPLIANT PRACTICE	**NON-COMPLIANT PRACTICE**
At system selection, the sponsor negotiates a data return provision requiring the vendor to deliver a complete archive in open-standard formats within thirty days of contract expiration. The provision is validated during system qualification, and a test data return at end-of-study closeout confirms the export is complete and readable without vendor software. Once the commercial relationship ends, the archive resides in the sponsor's long-term storage, accessible for the full retention period without further vendor cooperation.	The sponsor selects the vendor based on functionality and pricing, leaving data return to a standard clause promising "reasonable cooperation upon request"—with no format, timeline, or scope specifications. When the relationship ends, the audit trail data proves readable only through the vendor's now-unlicensed interface, and retrieval requires a new commercial engagement on the vendor's terms.

Vendor Qualification for Cloud-Hosted Clinical Systems

Vendor qualification in the SaaS era is a different activity from vendor qualification when clinical software was licensed for on-premises deployment. On-premises software could be installed in the sponsor's validated environment, subjected to the sponsor's installation qualification and operational qualification testing, and administered by the sponsor's internal IT team. The sponsor had direct access to the system, the database, the audit trail storage, and the configuration settings. Qualification was primarily a matter of confirming that the software performed as specified and that the deployment environment met required standards.

In a SaaS deployment, the sponsor never touches the underlying environment. Installation qualification in the traditional sense is not performed because there is no installation on the sponsor's infrastructure. The sponsor tests its configuration of the vendor's platform, which is a distinct and narrower scope. Verifying that the sponsor's specific configuration meets GxP requirements requires access to the system, defined test scripts, and the ability to execute those scripts in a controlled environment that the vendor controls. It requires vendor cooperation.

The qualification program for a cloud-hosted GxP system must therefore address two distinct scopes: the vendor's quality system and platform management practices, and the sponsor's trial-specific configuration. The first scope is addressed through vendor audit, review of the vendor's validation documentation and quality management procedures, and assessment of the vendor's change control and release management practices. The second scope is addressed through configuration qualification activities executed by the sponsor or by the CRO managing data on the sponsor's behalf.

Vendor Audit as a Qualification Requirement

Sponsors frequently ask whether a vendor's existing audit documentation, ISO certifications[150], SOC reports, and published qualification documentation packages satisfy the sponsor's qualification obligation. The answer is that they satisfy part of it. Reviewing a vendor's documentation confirms what the vendor has represented about its own practices. It does not independently verify those practices. The distinction matters because the regulatory standard requires verification, not merely representation.

ICH E6(R3) Section 3.6 is explicit on this point[151]: sponsors cannot transfer regulatory responsibility to third parties, and contractual assurance from a vendor does not satisfy the obligation to oversee what that vendor does. The practical implication is that sponsors relying exclusively on vendor-supplied qualification packages, without conducting or sponsoring an independent audit of the vendor's quality system, have accepted a representation without verification. Whether that represents an acceptable risk depends on the criticality of the system and the quality of the vendor's documentation, but it does not represent compliance with the oversight expectation.

A proportionate vendor audit program for cloud-hosted clinical systems assesses, at minimum: the vendor's change control practices for software updates that affect GxP functions; the vendor's procedures for notifying customers of changes affecting validated system behavior; the vendor's audit trail architecture and how the system ensures that audit trail data cannot be modified or deleted by operational users or administrators; the data retention and archiving architecture, including the formats in which data can be exported and the vendor's obligations upon contract expiration; the vendor's incident management and business continuity procedures, specifically as they affect data availability; and the vendor's subcontractor and hosting arrangements, including any infrastructure provided by third parties with whom the sponsor has no direct relationship.

Configuration Qualification

A vendor platform that is properly qualified at the infrastructure and software layer can nonetheless fail to satisfy GxP requirements if it is configured incorrectly. The configuration scope is the sponsor's responsibility, and it encompasses decisions that directly determine whether the system captures the data required for compliance. Audit trail configuration is the most consequential configuration decision in a eClinical system. A system deployed with default audit trail settings that do not capture field-level changes for all data domains has a configuration gap regardless of how well the underlying platform is built. The gap is the sponsor's, not the vendor's.

Configuration qualification must verify, at a minimum, that audit trails are enabled for all GxP-relevant data domains and cannot be disabled by operational users; that access controls are configured to enforce unique user identification and prevent shared credentials; that electronic signature implementation meets Part 11 requirements for the specific signature events in the protocol; that the system is configured to capture and retain the change reason information required by E6(R3) for all data modifications[152]; and that the archive export functionality is configured and tested to produce a complete and retrievable record set in a vendor-independent format.

Configuration qualification is not a one-time activity. Every change to system configuration in a production environment requires a documented change control process that assesses the impact on GxP-critical functions. Vendors who provide configuration services must operate under a qualified change control procedure, and the sponsor must have a process for reviewing and approving configuration changes before they take effect in production. A vendor who updates a production configuration without sponsor review and approval has altered GxP-critical system parameters without authorization, regardless of whether the vendor's internal change control process was followed.

Data Sovereignty and Jurisdictional Complexity

Clinical trials conducted across multiple regulatory jurisdictions place data subject records in regulatory environments that may have conflicting requirements for where data may be stored, how it may be transferred across borders, and who may access it. The intersection of GCP data integrity requirements with data sovereignty law creates a compliance dimension that was largely theoretical when clinical data lived on servers in the sponsor's home jurisdiction. In a cloud-hosted model, data sovereignty is an operational reality that must be addressed at system selection, not after deployment.

The European Union's General Data Protection Regulation imposes requirements[153] on the transfer of personal data outside the European Economic Area that directly affect where clinical trial data involving EU subjects may be stored and processed. A cloud-hosted EDC system whose primary data center is located outside the EEA may require data transfer mechanisms, including standard contractual clauses, binding corporate rules, or adequacy decisions, before it can legally receive and store data from EU-subject trials. The validity of those mechanisms has been subject to legal challenge and regulatory evolution, requiring sponsors to maintain current awareness of their legal basis for cross-border data transfers rather than relying on arrangements established at system selection.

The People's Republic of China's Data Security Law and Personal Information Protection Law, effective in 2021 and 2022[154] respectively, impose data localization requirements and cross-border transfer restrictions that affect clinical trials conducted under China National Medical Products Administration oversight. Sponsors conducting trials in China using cloud-hosted platforms must verify that those platforms can operate in a configuration that satisfies Chinese data localization requirements without compromising the global data integrity architecture of the trial. In some cases, separate China-specific data environments are required, creating data reconciliation obligations that must be addressed in the data management plan.

India's Digital Personal Data Protection Act, which entered force in 2023[155], establishes a comparable framework for personal data generated within India. Brazil's Lei Geral de Proteção de Dados similarly governs[156] personal data from Brazilian subjects. Each of these frameworks has jurisdiction-specific provisions that may affect how clinical data from subjects in those countries can be stored, accessed, and transferred. The common thread is that data sovereignty law treats subject data as being subject to the regulatory authority of the jurisdiction in which it was collected, regardless of where the cloud infrastructure storing it is physically located.

The practical compliance obligation for sponsors is to map the jurisdictions in which their trial subjects are enrolled against the data sovereignty requirements of each jurisdiction, and to verify that their cloud-hosted system architecture can satisfy those requirements in a configuration that also meets GCP data integrity standards. These requirements are not always compatible without design work, and the architecture decisions required to reconcile them must be made before first-patient enrollment, not during a regulatory inspection.

DATA SOVEREIGNTY: KEY REGULATORY FRAMEWORKS AFFECTING CLOUD ARCHITECTURE

Jurisdiction / Framework	Cross-Border Transfer and Localization Obligations
EU GDPR (Regulation 2016/679)	Personal data of EU subjects may not be transferred outside the EEA without an adequate transfer mechanism. Cloud-hosted systems processing EU subject data must document their legal basis for cross-border transfer and maintain that documentation throughout the trial.
China DSL / PIPL (2021, 2022)	Data generated within China is subject to localization requirements and may require government security assessments before cross-border transfer. Trials conducted under NMPA oversight using cloud platforms should address Chinese data localization requirements at system selection.
India DPDPA (2023)	Personal data of Indian subjects is subject to restrictions on cross-border transfer. Sponsors conducting trials in India using cloud-hosted systems

Jurisdiction / Framework	Cross-Border Transfer and Localization Obligations
	must assess compliance with DPDPA transfer provisions applicable to the data types collected.
Brazil LGPD (Law 13,709/2018)	Personal data of Brazilian subjects may be transferred cross-border only under specified legal bases. Sponsors conducting trials in Brazil should verify that cloud data transfer arrangements satisfy LGPD requirements.
21 CFR Part 312	U.S. regulatory requirements for clinical data integrity do not impose domestic hosting requirements but require that all trial records be available for FDA inspection on request. Cloud-hosted records in foreign jurisdictions must be accessible to FDA without jurisdictional impediment.

Retrievability: The Most Consistently Under Addressed Requirement

Retrievability is one of the eight ALCOA+ properties. In practical terms, it means that data must be accessible for review and inspection throughout the regulatory retention period, without degradation, without format obsolescence, and without dependence on systems or organizations whose availability cannot be guaranteed for the full retention period. For paper records, retrievability was largely a function of physical storage conditions. For electronic records in cloud-hosted systems, it is primarily a function of contractual architecture and technical design decisions made at system selection.

The retrievability challenge in SaaS clinical systems has three components. The first is format dependency: records held in proprietary formats that require the vendor's software to read are not retrievable in any practical sense if the vendor's software becomes unavailable. The second is access dependency: records held in the vendor's cloud environment are accessible only as long as the commercial relationship authorizing that access remains active. The third is completeness scope: organizations that transfer only the final data values from a system, without transferring the original records, the audit trail, the electronic signatures, and the session logs, have not retrieved the data in a regulatory sense; they have retrieved a subset of it.

The ICH E6(R3) retention standard requires that trial records[157] be retained in a form that allows reconstruction and verification of the trial for the minimum retention period specified by applicable regulatory requirements, as addressed in Annex C of the Step 4 final. Retention periods vary by jurisdiction: the EU Clinical Trials Regulation requires 25 years for products that received marketing authorization; U.S. requirements under 21 CFR Part 312 are shorter but extend beyond the vendor relationships that typically support active trials. The practical implication is that data created in a cloud-hosted system today must remain retrievable on a timeline that extends well beyond any foreseeable commercial relationship with the vendor that currently holds it. Organizations that have not designed their data return and archiving architecture with this timeline in mind have a retrievability gap, even if they have never experienced a vendor relationship ending unexpectedly.

Data Escrow and Archive Architecture

Data escrow arrangements for clinical systems function on the same principle as software source code escrow: a copy of the material held by the third party is deposited with an independent custodian, accessible to the beneficiary under defined triggering conditions. For clinical data, the escrowed material is the trial record in a vendor-independent format, and the triggering conditions include vendor insolvency, platform discontinuation, contract expiration, and sponsor request for data return.

Effective data escrow for clinical systems requires that the deposited material be complete in the regulatory sense, not merely the data values but the full record set including audit trail, electronic signatures, metadata, and any session logs or transaction records that constitute original data for specific system types. The format in which the deposit is made must be readable without the vendor's software; XML exports, SAS datasets, or other open-standard formats are appropriate; proprietary database exports that require the vendor's application to interpret are not. The escrow deposit must be verified at establishment and updated at defined intervals, because an escrow deposit that reflects the system state at study start but not at study completion has diminishing value as the trial progresses.

Organizations that cannot obtain escrow arrangements from their SaaS vendors should assess whether vendor-independent archive export functionality represents an adequate substitute. An archive export that can be executed on demand, that produces a complete and verified record set in an open format, and that has been tested and validated as part of system qualification, may satisfy the retrievability requirement if executed at appropriate intervals and stored in infrastructure under the sponsor's control. The critical question is whether the sponsor can produce the complete trial record from its own resources, without vendor cooperation, at any point during the retention period. If the answer is yes, retrievability is adequately addressed. If the answer requires a qualifying clause about vendor availability or cooperation, it is not.

SCENARIO: Audit Trail Retrievability at End of Retention Period

COMPLIANT PRACTICE	NON-COMPLIANT PRACTICE
At system selection, the sponsor specifies that all audit trail data must be exportable in an open XML format without vendor software dependency. This specification is validated as part of the system qualification. At database lock, a complete archive export is executed, verified against the production system record count, and stored in the sponsor's long-term archive in a format confirmed readable by open-source XML tools. At the twenty-year mark of the retention period, the original vendor has been acquired twice. The sponsor produces the complete trial record from its own archive without contacting any vendor.	The sponsor's system qualification documents confirm that the eClinical vendor can provide data exports on request. No format specification is included. The export mechanism has not been tested as part of qualification. At year eighteen of the retention period, the sponsor receives a regulatory inquiry requiring production of the original audit trail. The export format from the original system is a proprietary binary file. The vendor's current product no longer supports that format. The data is technically present but practically inaccessible.

Vendor Change Control and the Validated State

In an on-premises deployment, the sponsor controls when software updates are applied, what changes are included, and what testing is required before the updated system is returned to production use. In a SaaS deployment, the vendor controls the release schedule[158]. Updates are applied across all customers on a timeline determined by the vendor's development and operations team, with notice periods that vary widely and with customer input that ranges from meaningful to nominal. From a validated state perspective, this means that a clinical system operating in production can be functionally altered by the vendor without any action by the sponsor.

The regulatory consequence is direct. If a vendor update modifies the behavior of a GxP-critical function, such as audit trail capture, access control enforcement, electronic signature mechanics, or data export formatting, the system's validated state has changed.

A sponsor who was not informed of the change, did not assess its impact, did not perform impact testing, and did not update the validation documentation has a retrospective compliance gap for every data management action that occurred in the updated system before the gap was identified.

The vendor change notification obligation must be addressed in the service agreement, not left to the vendor's discretion. Minimum required provisions include: advance notice of scheduled updates that affect GxP-critical functions, with a defined notice period sufficient to allow sponsor impact assessment; a classification of changes by their potential impact on validated system behavior, distinguishing security patches from functional changes; a specification of which change categories require sponsor review before production deployment; and a process for emergency or unplanned changes that preserves the sponsor's ability to assess and document impact on a retrospective but controlled basis.

The practical enforcement of these provisions requires internal sponsor infrastructure: a process owner responsible for tracking vendor change notifications, assessing their impact against the validated system specification, and escalating changes that require validation activity. An organization that has negotiated appropriate contractual provisions but has no internal process for acting on vendor notifications will discover the gap during an inspection, when the investigator asks how the organization maintains the validated state of its cloud-hosted systems and the answer involves a substantial portion of the system's change history that was never assessed.

Subprocessors and Fourth-Party Risk

A sponsor that qualifies its eClinical vendor has performed due diligence on the organization with which it has a direct commercial relationship. That organization, in turn, typically relies on subprocessors for infrastructure hosting, data backup, security monitoring, and other technical services. The subprocessors are not in a direct relationship with the sponsor, and their practices are not assessed by the standard vendor qualification process. They are nonetheless part of the data processing chain for the sponsor's clinical trial records.

The regulatory exposure from unqualified subprocessors is primarily realized when a subprocessor's behavior creates a data integrity or availability event that the sponsor cannot explain to regulatory satisfaction. If the vendor's backup provider experiences a data loss event, if the hosting provider applies a configuration change that affects audit trail behavior, or if a security subprocessor's access monitoring creates an access pattern that looks irregular in the audit trail, the sponsor will be asked to account for these events. Without knowledge of the subprocessor arrangements and their contractual obligations, the sponsor cannot provide that accounting.

The appropriate response is not to qualify every fourth party that touches the data infrastructure. It is to require, in the vendor service agreement, that the vendor disclose its material subprocessors, notify the sponsor of subprocessor changes, and represent that its subprocessors operate under contractual obligations consistent with the data integrity and availability requirements imposed on the vendor. The sponsor should review these representations, assess the risk profile of the disclosed subprocessors, and document that review as part of the vendor qualification record.

Multi-System Environments and Integration Integrity

Few clinical trials operate from a single system. A contemporary Phase III trial might use an EDC system for CRF data, an eTMF platform for essential document management, an IRT system for randomization and supply management, a safety database for adverse event management, a central laboratory data integration platform, a wearable device data aggregator for digital endpoint collection, and a CTMS for site and operational management. Each of these systems may be delivered by a different vendor on a different cloud infrastructure. Data passes among them through interfaces that may themselves be managed by additional third parties.

Each interface in this architecture is a data integrity risk point. Data that is transferred between systems must arrive at the destination with the values it had at the source. Transformations that occur during transfer must be documented, controlled, and reversible in the audit record. Errors that occur during transfer must be detectable and subject to defined remediation procedures. The completeness of the transferred dataset must be verifiable against the source. These requirements apply to every system-to-system interface in the architecture, regardless of whether the systems are provided by the same vendor or by different vendors, and regardless of whether the interface was designed and built by the sponsor or procured as part of a vendor service.

Interface validation is the technical mechanism for ensuring that these requirements are satisfied. A validated interface has defined specifications for what data is transferred, in what format, at what frequency, and with what error handling logic. It has a test protocol that verifies the interface behavior against those specifications. It has a monitoring mechanism that detects and alerts on transfer failures or discrepancies. And it has a change control process that ensures that changes to either connected system are assessed for their impact on interface behavior before production deployment.

The interface validation obligation belongs to the sponsor, even when the interface was built by a vendor. A vendor who provides an integration service between its own platform and another vendor's platform has built an interface to specifications it defined. The sponsor is responsible for verifying that those specifications satisfy the data integrity requirements of the trial, and that the implemented interface performs according to those specifications. Vendor interface documentation confirms what the vendor has built. Sponsor qualification confirms that it is adequate.

The Integration Validation Gap at Database Lock

Integration gaps most commonly surface at database lock or during submission review, because that is when the complete data record is assembled and reconciled for the first time. The laboratory data that arrived in the EDC through an automated interface looks correct in the EDC. The central laboratory's original data output, reviewed directly, contains values that do not match. The discrepancy is traced to a transformation rule applied during the interface transfer that was documented in the vendor's integration specification but was not reflected in the sponsor's data management plan and was not assessed during the sponsor's qualification of the interface.

The clinical consequence of this class of gap depends on which values are affected and how significant the discrepancy is. The regulatory consequence is independent of the clinical consequence: a data set that does not accurately represent the source records, for any reason, has an accuracy problem. An accuracy problem that was not detected before database lock is a more serious accuracy problem than one identified and resolved during the trial. An accuracy problem discovered during regulatory review is the most serious variant of all.

Preventing integration accuracy failures requires that data reconciliation between source system outputs and EDC representations be a routine operational activity, not a database lock task. Risk-based monitoring programs that focus exclusively on site-level data quality, without including systematic cross-system reconciliation as a monitoring activity, are not addressing the full scope of accuracy risk in a multi-system clinical trial architecture. The data management plan should specify, for each system interface, the reconciliation methodology, the frequency, the acceptable discrepancy thresholds, and the escalation path for discrepancies that exceed those thresholds.

Inspection Readiness in the Cloud Era

An FDA investigator conducting a for-cause inspection of a clinical trial site will ask for the original records. In the pre-cloud era, producing original records meant retrieving files from a local server or a paper archive. In a cloud-hosted environment, producing original records means accessing vendor systems, exporting data in a format the investigator can review, and demonstrating that the exported records are complete and unaltered representations of the original. Each of these steps requires capabilities that must be in place before the inspection begins.

The inspection readiness question for cloud-hosted systems is not whether the data exists. In most cases it does. The question is whether it is accessible on the timeline the inspection demands, in a form that allows the investigator to review it effectively, and with documentation sufficient to establish that what is being presented is the original record and not a post-hoc reconstruction. An organization that cannot answer all three parts of that question affirmatively is not inspection-ready, regardless of the quality of the underlying data.

Practical inspection readiness for cloud-hosted systems requires, at minimum: a tested and validated process for producing data exports from each GxP-critical system, including full audit trail exports, in a format reviewable without vendor software; a documented chain of custody for those exports confirming that they are unaltered representations of the system records; a current and accurate inventory of all cloud-hosted systems holding trial records, including their vendor relationships, data return provisions, and retention architecture; and a point of contact for each vendor capable of responding to data access requests on an expedited basis if real-time system access is requested during inspection.

The vendor relationship management dimension of inspection readiness is frequently overlooked. A vendor whose commercial relationship with the sponsor has ended may not respond to an inspection-related data access request on the same timeline as an active customer. A vendor whose standard data access process requires a formal request through a customer success queue, with a five-business-day response time, is not operationally compatible with an inspection timeline that may require data production within hours. Service agreements for GxP-critical systems should include provisions for expedited data access in support of regulatory inspections, with defined response times and a named contact with authority to fulfill the request.

INSPECTION READINESS CHECKLIST: CLOUD AND THIRD-PARTY SYSTEMS For each cloud-hosted GxP system holding clinical trial records, confirm:

1. A validated archive export process exists for this system and has been tested within the past twelve months.
2. The archive export produces a complete record set including audit trail, electronic signatures, and source metadata.
3. The export format is readable without the vendor's software (open standard: XML, SAS, CSV, or equivalent).
4. A chain of custody document exists for each export confirming it is an unaltered representation of the system record.
5. The vendor service agreement includes provisions for expedited data access during regulatory inspections.
6. The data return provision specifies format, scope, and timeline for full data return at contract expiration.
7. Subprocessor disclosure and notification obligations are addressed in the vendor agreement.
8. A vendor change notification process is operational; all notifications are assessed and documented.
9. Interface validation exists for each system-to-system data transfer, with current reconciliation records.
10. Data sovereignty requirements for all enrolled subject jurisdictions have been assessed and documented.

Documented Failure Modes: Cloud and Third-Party Systems

The following failure modes represent patterns observed across FDA warning letters, inspection observation reports, and regulatory guidance documents addressing data integrity in outsourced and cloud-hosted clinical systems. Each illustrates a specific gap between the regulatory expectation and common operational practice.

Failure Mode 1: Vendor Platform Discontinuation Without Data Return

A mid-size CRO operating as data management vendor for a Phase II oncology trial used a cloud-hosted eTMF platform provided by a specialized vendor. The eTMF vendor was acquired by a larger competitor eighteen months after trial closeout. The acquirer discontinued the legacy platform within twelve months of acquisition, providing notice to current subscribers but not to former subscribers whose commercial agreements had lapsed at study closeout. When the sponsor required access to the eTMF records for a regulatory query response three years after closeout, the platform was no longer accessible. The data existed in the acquirer's archive environment, but retrieval required a commercial engagement at consulting rates. The sponsor had no contractual leverage. The records were eventually retrieved at significant cost and timeline impact. The root cause was the absence of a validated data return process executed at study closeout.

Failure Mode 2: Audit Trail Configuration Altered by Vendor Update

A sponsor using a SaaS-hosted EDC platform for a Phase III cardiovascular outcomes trial received a vendor notification, classified by the vendor as a routine security update, indicating that changes were being applied to user session management. The sponsor's internal process for reviewing vendor change notifications had lapsed during a period of organizational restructuring. The notification was received but not assessed. The update altered the session timeout behavior in a way that affected how concurrent access by multiple users was logged in the audit trail. A subsequent FDA inspection found that audit trail entries for a specific time window did not accurately represent the sequence of user access events. The sponsor could not demonstrate that it had assessed the update before production deployment. The observation cited both the audit trail anomaly and the failure to maintain a controlled validated state.

Failure Mode 3: Incomplete Interface Validation for Central Laboratory Data

A sponsor conducting a Phase II metabolic disease trial implemented an automated interface between the central laboratory's data management system and the sponsor's EDC platform. The interface was provided as a standard integration by the laboratory vendor. The sponsor's qualification of the interface reviewed the vendor's integration documentation but did not include sponsor-side testing of the data transfer against actual laboratory output files. A transformation rule in the interface converted laboratory reference ranges from the laboratory's internal coding system to the EDC's coding framework. The conversion was not perfectly bidirectional for a subset of analyte codes. The discrepancy was not identified until database lock review, at which point approximately four percent of laboratory values in the EDC did not match the laboratory's original results. Investigation, remediation, and re-review of the affected records added eleven weeks to the database lock timeline.

Failure Mode 4: Data Sovereignty Non-Compliance Identified at Submission

A sponsor conducting a global Phase III immunology trial enrolled subjects in twelve countries, including China, India, and Brazil, using a U.S.-based cloud EDC platform. The platform's data center was located in the United States. Informed consent forms signed by Chinese subjects transferred personal health data to U.S. infrastructure without a valid cross-border data transfer mechanism under China's Personal Information Protection Law, which had entered force after the trial's EDC selection. The compliance gap was identified during final submission preparation, when the regulatory team conducted a data privacy assessment in preparation for the NMPA submission. Remediation required retroactive consent supplementation for Chinese subjects, modification of the EDC data transfer architecture for the ongoing open-label extension study, and a legal analysis of the original data transfers' regulatory status. The NMPA submission was delayed by nine months.

Designing for Infrastructure Independence

The practical synthesis of this chapter's analysis is a design principle rather than a compliance checklist: clinical trial data systems should be designed such that the sponsor's ability to satisfy its regulatory obligations does not depend on any vendor relationship remaining active. This is a higher standard than what most organizations currently apply, and achieving it requires deliberate decisions at system selection, contract negotiation, validation planning, and operational management. It is also the standard that the regulatory framework, read honestly, requires.

Infrastructure independence does not mean avoiding cloud-hosted systems. It means designing the relationship with those systems such that the regulatory record they contain can be produced, verified, and defended independent of the vendor's ongoing cooperation. It means specifying data return obligations before signing a service agreement, not after the vendor has the data. It means testing archive export processes as part of system qualification, not discovering their limitations at database lock. It means treating vendor change management as a validated state obligation, not a notification-and-forget process. And it means addressing data sovereignty requirements at system selection, when architectural decisions can still accommodate them, rather than at submission preparation, when they cannot.

The sponsors and eClinical system vendors that manage this risk most effectively treat their cloud vendors the same way they treat their contract research organizations: as qualified partners in a regulated activity, whose contributions are valuable and whose obligations are defined, verified, and monitored. The regulatory accountability for what those partners produce sits with the sponsor. The design work required to exercise that accountability in a cloud-hosted environment is not conceptually different from the design work required for any other outsourced clinical function[159]. It is more technically specific, and it requires earlier attention to details that most organizations have historically deferred. The cost of deferring them, as the failure modes documented in this chapter illustrate, is reliably higher than the cost of addressing them[160].

CHAPTER 15 — KEY TAKEAWAYS
The regulatory obligation for clinical data integrity follows the record, not the server; sponsors cannot transfer compliance accountability by placing data in vendor-operated cloud infrastructure.
The shared responsibility model allocates security obligations by infrastructure layer but does not divide regulatory accountability; both the vendor's platform layer and the sponsor's configuration layer carry compliance requirements that must be independently addressed.
Vendor qualification for cloud-hosted GxP systems must assess both the vendor's quality system and the sponsor's trial-specific configuration; documentation provided by the vendor satisfies neither obligation in isolation.
The retrievability requirement demands that clinical records be accessible for the full regulatory retention period without dependence on any vendor relationship remaining active; data escrow arrangements and validated archive export processes are the primary mechanisms for satisfying this requirement.
Data sovereignty law in EU, Chinese, Indian, and Brazilian jurisdictions imposes cross-border data transfer restrictions that must be assessed at system selection and addressed in the cloud architecture before first-patient enrollment.
Vendor change management for SaaS clinical systems requires contractual notification provisions and internal sponsor processes for assessing changes to GxP-critical system functions before they affect the validated state.
System-to-system interfaces in multi-vendor clinical architectures are independent data integrity risk points requiring validation, reconciliation, and change control equivalent to that applied to individual systems.
Inspection readiness in a cloud environment requires tested data export processes, chain of custody documentation, and vendor service agreement provisions for expedited data access during regulatory inquiries.
The design principle that most reliably addresses cloud-related data integrity risk is infrastructure independence: structuring the sponsor's relationship with cloud systems such that regulatory obligations can be satisfied without ongoing vendor cooperation.

CHAPTER SIXTEEN

Preparing for the Inspection You Do Not Know Is Coming

> *Regulators do not announce which organizations they will inspect, or when. The organizations that are ready when investigators arrive are the ones that built their readiness before the inspection was scheduled, not after.*

The letter arrived on a Tuesday. It was addressed to the vice president of clinical operations and identified as a notification from the FDA Office of Scientific Investigations of a forthcoming bioresearch monitoring inspection of the sponsor's clinical operations program. The scheduled dates were three weeks out. The targeted trial was the company's lead Phase III oncology asset, the one that had just completed enrollment after four years of effort and was eight months from its planned NDA filing.

The clinical quality team assembled the same afternoon. What they discovered in the next seventy-two hours would have been comforting if discovered months earlier and was instead alarming: audit trail review records for the trial existed for only eleven of the forty-three sites; the validation documentation for the EDC system had not been updated following a platform upgrade applied by the vendor fourteen months prior; training records for approximately twenty percent of active site coordinators contained only system onboarding documentation, with no protocol-specific competency assessments; and the process for verifying that CRO-operated systems met the sponsor's data integrity standards had never been tested against the actual configuration in production. The trial itself may have been conducted acceptably. The documentation required to demonstrate that to an investigator was not in the shape the team had assumed.

Three weeks is enough time to prepare a conference room and organize a document room. It is not enough time to rebuild a quality program. The organizations that exit inspections with clean records, or with manageable observations that they can defend and remediate credibly, do so because they conducted the inspection before the investigator did. They found their gaps first. They decided which ones to remediate and which ones to explain. They built the records that an inspection requires not in the weeks before the visit but in the months and years of operation that preceded it.

This chapter describes how to do that. It covers how regulators select inspection targets, what FDA and EU GCP investigators actually examine and how they think about what they find, and how to conduct an internal data integrity assessment that surfaces the same problems the investigator would find, on a timeline that allows an organization to address them on its own terms rather than an enforcement timeline.

> *An inspection is a test you cannot study for once it begins. The only preparation that matters is the program you built before it was scheduled.*

How Regulators Select Inspection Targets

FDA: The BIMO Selection Framework

FDA's Bioresearch Monitoring program conducts inspections of clinical investigator sites, sponsors, CROs, and institutional review boards. The program operates across three inspection types, each with a different trigger and a different operational posture.

Pre-approval inspections are the most common type for sponsors and sites contributing to marketing applications. When a new drug application, biologic license application, or abbreviated new drug application is received, CDER's review divisions identify the clinical trials that provide pivotal efficacy and safety support. The Office of Scientific Investigations then conducts a risk-based site selection process, using FDA's Clinical Investigator Site Selection Tool[161], to prioritize which sites contributing to those trials warrant inspection. Selection criteria include the site's contribution to the overall subject population, whether the site has been previously inspected, geographic location, therapeutic area, and statistical signals in the submitted data. The last factor is the one most organizations underestimate: FDA's submission review process includes data reliability assessment, and sites or datasets that generate anomalous statistical patterns during that review are prioritized for inspection regardless of their other characteristics.

For-cause inspections are triggered by specific signals: a whistleblower complaint, a sponsor's own data integrity report submitted to FDA, anomalies identified during pre-approval data review that warrant investigation before review proceeds, or reports from other regulatory authorities about conduct at a site or organization. For-cause inspections are not pre-announced on the same timeline as pre-approval inspections. They may arrive with very short notice and with a specific investigative focus that the organization will not know until the investigator presents credentials.

Surveillance inspections operate independently of specific submissions and target sites and sponsor organizations based on risk signals that do not rise to the level of a for-cause trigger. A site that has not been inspected in several years, a CRO that operates across multiple sponsor programs without a history of inspection, or an organization in a therapeutic area that has recently generated enforcement activity in the sector may appear in the surveillance inspection queue. Surveillance inspections are the least predictable category and the one for which ongoing inspection readiness rather than submission-driven preparation is the only effective strategy.

FDA INSPECTION SELECTION SIGNALS: WHAT ELEVATES RISK

Selection Signal	Mechanism and Implication
Statistical anomalies in submitted data	FDA's data reliability assessment during submission review examines site-level correction rates, endpoint movement patterns, and data completeness profiles. Sites whose data exhibits patterns inconsistent with normal clinical trial conduct are elevated in inspection priority regardless of other selection factors.
High subject contribution to pivotal endpoints	Sites enrolling disproportionate numbers of subjects, particularly in the pivotal endpoint analysis population, receive elevated attention because their data carries commensurately higher weight in the agency's approval decision.

Selection Signal	Mechanism and Implication
Geographic location outside FDA's primary inspection reach	Sites in regions with limited regulatory infrastructure, historical enforcement patterns, or where the agency has documented data integrity concerns in prior inspection cycles are subject to elevated selection probability.
Prior inspection history with findings	A site or organization with unresolved prior observations, or one that has received corrective action commitments not yet verified by re-inspection, is a persistent inspection priority.
Novel or high-risk therapeutic modalities	Gene therapies, cell therapies, and orphan indications with small patient populations generate heightened scrutiny because data anomalies have outsized influence on approval decisions and post-approval safety monitoring.
CRO or vendor concentration risk	Sponsors relying on a small number of CROs or data management vendors may attract inspection attention if those vendors have generated data integrity findings for other sponsors, on the theory that governance failures at the vendor level affect all their clients.

EU GCP Inspections: The National Competent Authority Framework

EU GCP inspections are conducted by national competent authorities, not by EMA directly, for most routine and marketing application purposes. The French ANSM, the German BfArM and Paul-Ehrlich-Institut, the Danish DKMA, and equivalent bodies in each EU member state conduct GCP inspections within their national jurisdictions and, through coordination arrangements under EMA's GCP inspection program, at international sites supporting applications for centrally authorized products.

Marketing application inspections for centrally authorized products are requested by EMA's Committee for Human Medicinal Products, which identifies the trials and sites requiring inspection as part of its assessment of the dossier. The practical experience of sponsors is that EMA-requested inspections are assigned to the national competent authority of the country in which the largest number of relevant sites are located, or to the authority with the most relevant inspection expertise, and that the inspection timeline is driven by the CHMP assessment timeline. An NCA inspection request in connection with a CHMP assessment typically provides eight to twelve weeks of advance notice to the inspected entity.

The EU inspection framework grades findings as critical, major, or minor. A critical finding indicates a deficiency that directly affects subject rights, safety, or wellbeing, or that materially compromises the reliability of the data. A critical finding can result in rejection of the trial data for marketing authorization purposes, regardless of whether the application is otherwise approvable. Major findings require documented corrective action and may delay the assessment clock. Minor findings are documented and addressed in a corrective action plan but do not typically affect the assessment timeline. This grading structure means that every inspection finding in an EU context carries an explicit and documented severity classification that the CHMP and its members will see. A single critical finding at a pivotal trial site can change the trajectory of an application.

MHRA: Systems-Based and Risk-Triggered

MHRA's inspection program is predominantly systems-based rather than study-specific[162], meaning that an MHRA inspection typically evaluates the organization's clinical quality systems across a selection of trials as examples, rather than auditing a single trial end-to-end. This approach means that an MHRA inspection can encompass data integrity issues from trials not identified in advance, if those trials are selected as examples during the inspection itself. Organizations preparing for an MHRA inspection by reviewing only the trials they expect to be examined are systematically under-prepared for this reason.

MHRA's triggered inspection capability is broader than FDA's for-cause mechanism in one important respect: MHRA can and does conduct triggered inspections based on signals from sources other than formal complaints, including public reporting, post-authorization safety signals, and intelligence from other regulatory authorities under information-sharing arrangements. Organizations subject to enforcement action by another major authority should anticipate MHRA triggered inspection activity regardless of whether they have received formal notification.

What Investigators Actually Examine

The FDA BIMO Investigator's Approach

FDA BIMO investigators conduct outcome-focused assessments. Their starting point is the submitted data, and their examination works backward: from the values in the clinical study report to the values in the EDC, from the EDC to the audit trail, from the audit trail to the source documents, and from the source documents to the physical and procedural evidence that the records are genuine. The investigator is not primarily looking for policy non-compliance; they are looking for evidence that the data provided to FDA is reliable.

At a clinical investigator site, an FDA investigator will typically request the following on arrival or within the first day: the protocol and all amendments; the informed consent forms and enrollment log; the electronic data capture system access for the site's trial data; the audit trail export for the study period; the site's training records for all staff involved in the trial; the monitoring visit logs; and the source documentation for a selection of subjects. The subject selection will not be random. It will be based on data features identified during FDA's pre-inspection review of the submitted data: subjects whose data moved in ways that benefited trial outcomes, subjects at data points near protocol-defined thresholds, or subjects with unusually clean data in trials where some data variability would be expected.

At a sponsor inspection, the FDA investigator focuses on oversight: does the sponsor have a functioning quality system that would detect data integrity problems at its sites and CROs, and is there evidence that this system operated throughout the trial? The documents requested typically include the sponsor's monitoring plans and visit reports, the sponsor's data management procedures, audit trail review records, training oversight documentation for investigator sites, and any quality event records, CAPAs, or protocol deviations from the trial period. A sponsor who can produce clean quality event records is not demonstrating that nothing went wrong; they are demonstrating that they were not looking. Investigators are aware of this inference, and they test it.

The investigator's analytical method is pattern analysis, not individual record review[163]. An individual query resolved with a formulaic reason is not finding. A pattern of three hundred queries resolved with the same formulaic reason, sixty percent of which resulted in corrections moving subjects toward the efficacy threshold, is a finding. The difference is scale. An organization whose internal quality monitoring applies individual-record review without pattern analysis is operating with a detection method that will miss the findings most likely to produce a warning letter.

The EU GCP Inspector's Approach

EU GCP inspectors conduct systems-based assessments and document findings against specific ICH E6(R3) provisions. The inspection opening meeting will establish the scope and will typically include a presentation by the organization of its clinical quality system. An organization that cannot clearly articulate its quality management system in the opening meeting, including the structure of its data governance program, the integration of its audit trail review with its monitoring program, and the escalation pathway from site-level findings to sponsor-level oversight, has created a negative first impression that the subsequent document review will need to overcome.

Document requests in an EU GCP inspection are organized around the GCP inspection guideline, which covers the study master file, personnel and training, monitoring, data management, computerized systems, and safety reporting. The data management review will focus on whether the organization has documented procedures for all data management activities, whether those procedures were followed, and whether the audit trail review program provides genuine quality oversight rather than formal compliance documentation. An EU inspector who finds that audit trail review records exist but are identical in structure and conclusion[164] across every review cycle will treat those records as evidence of form over substance, which is itself a quality system finding under E6(R3)'s requirement for genuine oversight.

The EU inspection grading system creates a specific risk that FDA inspections do not present in the same way: a single critical finding can be sufficient to generate a recommendation against marketing authorization, or to require re-inspection before assessment proceeds. EU inspectors are trained to apply the critical/major/minor classification consistently, and an organization that has received a finding it believes should be classified as major rather than critical has limited ability to influence that classification during the inspection. The time to avoid critical findings is before the inspection.

What Investigators Consistently Find

The data integrity inspection record across FDA, EU GCP, and MHRA programs over the past decade reveals consistent finding patterns[165]. Understanding these patterns is the foundation of an effective internal assessment program because it establishes which organizational behaviors generate findings most reliably.

CONSISTENT INSPECTION FINDING PATTERNS: DATA INTEGRITY

Finding Category	Specific Manifestation	Primary Regulatory Citation
Audit trail gaps and manipulation	Audit trail not enabled for all data domains; field-level changes not captured; evidence of backdating or manual timestamp alteration; users sharing credentials producing attributability failures.	ALCOA Attributable, Contemporaneous; 21 CFR 11.10(e); ICH E6(R3) Section 5.5.3; EU GCP Guideline Section 6.2.
Policy-practice gap in access control	User provisioning procedures require deactivation within defined timelines; access logs show accounts remaining active after staff departure; shared credentials in active use despite unique-ID requirements.	ALCOA Attributable; 21 CFR 11.10(d); ICH E6(R3) Section 5.5.4.
Uninformative change reasons	Data corrections documented with formulaic or generic change reason text that provides no auditable basis for the correction; pattern of identical change reasons across hundreds of edits.	ALCOA Accurate, Traceable; ICH E6(R3) Section 4.9.3; PIC/S PI 041-1 Section 5.2.
Query pattern anomalies	Correction rates elevated at sites contributing primary endpoint subjects; endpoint values moving toward significance thresholds	ALCOA Accurate; ICH E6(R3) Section 5.18; FDA Risk-Based Monitoring Guidance (2013).

Finding Category	Specific Manifestation	Primary Regulatory Citation
	following monitor visits; query clusters timed to precede monitoring visits.	
Validation documentation not current	System validation packages not updated following vendor software changes; configuration changes implemented without sponsor impact assessment; validated state not maintained across trial lifecycle.	ALCOA Accurate; 21 CFR 11.10(a); ICH E6(R3) Section 5.5.3; EU Annex 11 Clause 10.
Sponsor oversight gaps for CROs	Sponsor has delegated data management to CRO without documented verification that CRO systems and practices meet the sponsor's standards; CRO audit trail review records not available to sponsor for oversight purposes.	ICH E6(R3) Section 5.2; FDA Electronic Source Data Guidance; MHRA GxP Data Integrity Guidance Section 6.
Training records document completion, not competency	Training records show completion of curriculum but contain no evidence of assessed understanding; site coordinators cannot demonstrate working knowledge of protocol-specific data recording requirements.	ICH E6(R3) Section 4.1.3; GCP requirement for qualified personnel; PIC/S PI 041-1 Section 6.

The Internal Data Integrity Assessment

An internal data integrity assessment is an organization's inspection of itself: conducted with the same analytical framework that an external investigator would apply, designed to surface the same findings before they become regulatory observations, and documented in a way that establishes the organization's awareness and response to its own quality gaps. Done well, it is the most cost-effective quality investment a clinical organization can make. Done poorly, it generates documentation of known problems without generating remediation, which is worse than not having done it.

The distinction between a genuine internal assessment and a compliance exercise is the analytical method applied. A compliance exercise asks: do we have the required procedures, and are they current? A genuine assessment asks: if an investigator applied the analytical methods described in the previous section to our trial records, what would they find? These are different questions, and they require different approaches.

Phase 1: Scoping and Risk Stratification

The scope of an internal assessment cannot be everything simultaneously. A useful assessment prioritizes the systems, trials, and organizational behaviors that present the highest inspection risk, and applies proportionate scrutiny to each. Risk stratification for an internal assessment should consider three dimensions: the regulatory stakes of the asset, the maturity of the quality program supporting it, and the known or suspected weakness patterns in the organization's data management operations.

Assets approaching submission carry the highest regulatory stakes. A program filing an NDA or MAA in the next eighteen months should receive the most thorough data integrity review, because any findings identified during the regulatory submission review will arrive on the applicant's timeline, not the organization's preferred remediation timeline. Assets in active enrollment carry operational stakes: gaps identified here can be remediated while the trial is still running, which is categorically more manageable than gaps identified at database lock or during submission preparation.

Program maturity signals where to look harder. A new CRO relationship that has not been fully integrated into the sponsor's oversight framework is a gap waiting to be confirmed. A recently implemented EDC system whose vendor has released software updates during the trial period may have a validated state issue that nobody has formally assessed. A trial enrolled largely at sites in a region with limited prior monitoring history may have source document verification gaps that centralized monitoring has not reached. These are not certainties; they are risk signals that direct assessment resources toward the most productive areas of examination.

Phase 2: Audit Trail Pattern Analysis

Audit trail pattern analysis is the core analytical technique of any data integrity assessment that aspires to find what an inspector would find. Individual record review is insufficient: it takes too long, and it tests the wrong thing. Pattern analysis examines the distributional properties of audit trail data to identify systemic behaviors that would not be visible in individual record review.

The primary patterns to examine are correction rate distributions, change reason analysis, temporal clustering, and timestamp plausibility. Correction rate distributions compare the rate at which CRF data is modified across sites, data domains, and time periods. Sites with correction rates substantially higher or lower than the trial mean warrant examination of the underlying corrections. Endpoint data domains with higher correction rates than administrative data domains may indicate coaching or selective correction pressure. Correction rates that spike following monitoring visits are a classic signal requiring investigation.

Change reason analysis reviews the substantive content of the change reason text across all corrections. A large proportion of corrections carrying generic reasons, such as "data entry error" without identification of the source of the correct value, identifies a documentation gap that applies to every correction in that category. The relevant question is not whether the individual correction was accurate; it is whether the documentation supports verification of that accuracy on regulatory review. Corrections that cannot be independently verified from the change reason documentation alone are a systematic ALCOA accuracy gap.

Temporal clustering analysis examines the distribution of data entries and corrections across time. EDC entries created exclusively during business hours are clinically plausible. Entries clustered in the hours immediately before monitoring visit dates may indicate last-minute data remediation. Corrections applied across hundreds of records within a very short time window may indicate bulk re-entry or system-driven modification rather than individual clinical review. None of these patterns is automatically a finding. Each is a signal that requires explanation, and the ability to provide that explanation from contemporaneous records, rather than retrospective reconstruction, is the difference between a managed gap and an inspection observation.

Timestamp plausibility analysis examines whether the timestamps on EDC records are consistent with the clinical activity they purport to document. Entries timestamped at times when the clinic was closed, at intervals too rapid for the documented activity to have been performed, or with system clock artifacts that suggest time synchronization issues each represent an ALCOA contemporaneous concern. The FDA-MHRA joint paper on data integrity in global clinical trials documented that both agencies use timestamp plausibility as a primary inspection analysis technique. Organizations that do not apply this analysis internally are not conducting the assessment that regulators will.

Phase 3: Systems and Configuration Verification

The audit trail analysis identifies behavioral patterns in the data. Systems and configuration verification examines whether the technical environment supporting data collection meets the operational requirements that the audit trail was supposed to capture. The two analyses together define the full scope of what an inspector would examine at a system level.

Audit trail configuration verification confirms that the EDC system is configured to capture field-level changes for all data domains, that the audit trail function cannot be disabled by operational users, and that the system's current configuration matches the validated configuration documented at system qualification. A system whose audit trail captures changes at the form level rather than the field level[166] may produce complete audit trail data in volume terms while missing the individual field history that regulatory standards require. This is a configuration gap that looks like compliance until an inspector checks the configuration settings.

Access control verification cross-references the user account list against the personnel records for all sites and all organizations with system access. Accounts belonging to staff who have left the organization or whose roles have changed should have been deactivated or modified contemporaneously. Accounts that remain active after the departure date[167] of their owner, or that carry access rights inconsistent with the current role of their holder, are access control findings waiting to be discovered. This verification takes less than a day to perform on most EDC systems and consistently surfaces gaps that would otherwise appear in a Form 483.

Validation status verification confirms that the current production configuration of every GxP-critical system matches the validated configuration, that all vendor software updates have been assessed for their impact on the validated state, and that the validation documentation has been updated to reflect the current system state. The specific question for cloud-hosted SaaS systems, addressed in Chapter 15, is whether vendor updates have been received, assessed, and documented. Organizations that have been operating cloud-hosted EDC systems through one or more software release cycles without formal impact assessment have a systematic validation gap that an inspector will identify through the vendor change notification record, which they will request.

Phase 4: CRO and Vendor Oversight Verification

ICH E6(R3) Section 5.2 is explicit that sponsors cannot transfer regulatory responsibility to CROs or other vendors. The practical test of whether a sponsor has met its oversight obligation is whether the sponsor can produce evidence that it verified CRO and vendor performance against the required standard, rather than merely contracted for it. An internal assessment that limits its scope to the sponsor's own systems and records, without examining the CRO-operated systems that generated the trial data, has examined perhaps half the relevant compliance picture.

CRO oversight verification examines the record of sponsor oversight activities for each CRO involved in the trial: monitoring of CRO performance against the delegated activities, access to CRO audit trail review records, documented assessment of CRO training program effectiveness, and evidence that the sponsor reviewed and acted on CRO quality event reports. The specific question is not whether the CRO has a quality system; it is whether the sponsor verified that it was functioning. Contractual representations from the CRO that its quality system meets the required standard are not evidence of verification. An audit report, performance review meeting minutes, or documented CRO system access review are.

For vendor systems, the oversight verification assesses whether each GxP-critical vendor system has been qualified, whether the qualification documentation is current, whether vendor change notifications have been received and assessed, and whether the sponsor has current knowledge of the system's configuration and validated state. Vendors who have implemented software changes during the trial period without documented sponsor assessment have altered systems in ways that may not reflect the validated baseline. The sponsor's responsibility to know about those changes and document their impact sits with the sponsor, not the vendor.

Phase 5: The Assessment Report and Remediation Decision

The internal assessment produces findings. Some of those findings warrant immediate remediation. Others represent known gaps that can be addressed on a defined timeline before the trial reaches database lock or submission. A small number may represent gaps that cannot be fully remediated for closed trials, and whose regulatory risk must be assessed and documented rather than eliminated.

The assessment report should characterize each finding in terms that map to the regulatory framework: which ALCOA+ property is implicated, which regulatory provision is at risk, what the potential inspection consequence is, and what remediation is available within the trial's operational timeline. A finding characterized in these terms gives quality leadership and trial management a basis for resource allocation and remediation prioritization that a finding described in operational terms alone does not provide.

Remediation decisions for findings identified during an active trial should be made and implemented before database lock wherever operationally possible. A finding remediated before database lock is a quality improvement. A finding remediated after an inspection observation is a corrective action. The regulatory and reputational implications of these two categories differ substantially, and the choice between them is available only when internal assessment precedes inspection.

Organizations that discover significant findings during internal assessment and choose not to remediate them before the next inspection are making an explicit risk decision. That decision is defensible, provided it is documented as such and the reasoning is sound. An organization that finds a systematic audit trail review gap, assesses it as not likely to be a primary inspection focus given the trial's data characteristics, and documents that reasoning in a risk acceptance record has made a governed decision. An organization that finds the same gap and does nothing because addressing it is inconvenient has made an ungoverned one, and the distinction will be apparent if the gap appears in an inspection observation.

THE STRUCTURED SELF-AUDIT FRAMEWORK: EXECUTION GUIDE

PHASE 1: SCOPE AND RISK STRATIFICATION

- □ Identify all active and recently completed trials by regulatory submission status, enrollment status, and time since last inspection.
- □ Stratify trials by inspection risk: NDA/MAA filing within 18 months (high), active enrollment at sites with no prior monitoring (medium), closed trials with no prior inspection (lower).
- □ Identify specific organizational risk signals: new CRO relationships, recent EDC platform changes, sites in regions with documented enforcement activity.

PHASE 2: AUDIT TRAIL PATTERN ANALYSIS

- □ Export complete EDC audit trail for each high-priority trial; verify export includes all data domains, all user actions, all field-level changes.
- □ Calculate correction rate by site, by data domain (primary endpoint vs. secondary vs. safety), and by time period. Flag outliers exceeding 1.5x the study mean for targeted review.
- □ Analyze change reason text: calculate proportion of corrections carrying generic or formulaic reasons; review specific reason language against the substantive documentation standard.

- ☐ Examine temporal distribution of entries and corrections: identify clusters relative to monitoring visit dates, protocol-defined milestones, and non-business hours.
- ☐ Apply timestamp plausibility analysis: verify entries are consistent with documented clinic hours; identify impossible entry speeds for complex multi-field records.

PHASE 3: SYSTEMS AND CONFIGURATION VERIFICATION

- ☐ Verify audit trail configuration: field-level capture enabled for all data domains; deactivation protection in place; current configuration matches validated specification.
- ☐ Cross-reference user account list against current and departed personnel records for all organizations with system access; document and remediate inactive accounts with residual access.
- ☐ Audit validation documentation currency: confirm all vendor software updates have been assessed for validated state impact; confirm impact assessments are documented and completed.

PHASE 4: CRO AND VENDOR OVERSIGHT VERIFICATION

- ☐ Confirm sponsor has documented verification of CRO quality system adequacy, not merely contractual representations: audit records, performance review documentation, CRO ATR access records.
- ☐ Verify all GxP-critical vendor systems have current qualification documentation and that vendor change notification records are complete and assessed.

PHASE 5: FINDINGS, REMEDIATION DECISIONS, AND DOCUMENTATION

- ☐ Characterize each finding by ALCOA+ property implicated, regulatory provision at risk, and potential inspection consequence.
- ☐ Assign each finding to one of three remediation categories: immediate pre-database lock action, scheduled pre-submission remediation, or documented risk acceptance with supporting rationale.
- ☐ Issue a formal assessment report that serves as the quality record of the assessment activity and provides the evidentiary basis for remediation decisions.

When the Investigator Arrives

An inspection that is well-prepared for is still an inspection. The organization's conduct during the inspection, from the moment of credential presentation through the close-out meeting, affects how the investigator interprets the records they review and, ultimately, how findings are classified and documented.

The First Twenty-Four Hours

The opening meeting sets the tone. Organizations whose quality leadership can articulate the clinical quality system clearly, accurately, and without consulting documentation in real time demonstrate operational familiarity with their own program. Investigators note this. Organizations that deflect opening questions to written policy or that present a program whose description does not match the records subsequently produced generate the working hypothesis that the program is documented rather than operational. That hypothesis is difficult to overcome in the subsequent days of document review.

Document production should be accurate, complete, and timely. A request for training records should produce training records, not a statement that training records will be located and provided tomorrow. Requests that cannot be fulfilled immediately should be acknowledged with an explanation and a realistic timeline. Providing inaccurate or incomplete records in response to an investigator's request, even inadvertently, creates credibility problems that extend to every subsequent document production. Investigators who have received one inaccurate document set apply heightened scrutiny to everything that follows.

The organization's subject matter experts for each inspection area should be identified in advance and available during the inspection. An investigator asking detailed questions about EDC configuration should be able to speak with the person who manages the system, not a quality staff member who is reading from the validation documentation. The ability to answer technical questions accurately from first-hand knowledge rather than document review demonstrates that the organization's quality records reflect its actual operational practice, which is precisely the determination the investigator is making.

Managing the Document Room

Most site and sponsor inspections involve a document room or equivalent space where the organization assembles records for investigator review. The organization should be able to produce, from that room, any record from any inspection-relevant system for any period of the trial. Organizations that are uncertain about what records exist, where they are held, or how to export them from the systems that contain them will demonstrate that uncertainty to the investigator through the production timeline. Slow production of records creates the impression of a disorganized quality system. Very slow production of specific records creates the impression that those records are being edited before production, which is an assumption investigator will investigate.

The document room should be staffed by personnel who understand the records well enough to answer factual questions about their origin and content. Records should be organized to allow rapid location and production by trial, by site, by system, and by time period. If the organization uses an eTMF, the eTMF should be accessible in real time, and the organization should have confirmed in advance that the eTMF contains the complete document set required by its records retention procedures. An eTMF that is missing documents the organization's own procedures require to be there is a finding before the investigator has asked any question about data integrity.

Responding to Observations

The Form 483 issued at inspection close is a list of observations, not a list of violations. An observation describes a condition the investigator found objectionable. The organization has the right and the obligation to respond to each observation in writing within fifteen business days. That response is where the organization can provide context, explain extenuating circumstances, and commit to corrective actions.

The most effective responses to Form 483 observations share three characteristics: they accept the finding rather than arguing it, they provide the context that explains the root cause, and they commit to specific and verifiable corrective actions with realistic timelines. Responses that dispute the finding without providing substantive counter-evidence, or that commit to corrective actions whose timelines are so long they cannot plausibly be genuine, generate follow-up from FDA and may contribute to escalation from Form 483 to warning letter. The fifteen-day response window is a compliance deadline, not a target. Organizations that can respond in five to seven days with a substantive, credible corrective action plan demonstrate organizational competence at the moment it is most visible to the agency.

BREAKING DEVELOPMENT: REMOTE INSPECTION CAPABILITIES

The pandemic-era expansion of FDA's remote inspection toolkit, including remote records review, remote interactive sessions, and hybrid inspection formats, has been formally integrated into FDA's inspection program as a permanent capability rather than a temporary accommodation. The practical consequence for inspection readiness is that organizations should maintain their systems and records in a state that supports remote production and review at any time, not only when an on-site inspection is imminent. EMA and MHRA have developed comparable remote assessment capabilities. The February 2026 EMA/PIC/S consultation proposes harmonized standards[168] for remote and hybrid inspection formats across PIC/S member authorities. Organizations that cannot produce complete, accurate records sets for remote review on short notice are not inspection-ready in the current regulatory environment.

Building Continuous Inspection Readiness

The organizations that sustain clean inspection records over time do not do so by preparing intensively before each inspection. They sustain clean records by operating programs whose ongoing activities produce inspection-ready documentation as a natural byproduct. The internal assessment described in this chapter is a useful tool for organizations building toward this standard, and a safety net for organizations that have not yet reached it. The goal is a program in which the internal assessment finds nothing that an inspector would find, not because the assessment is not thorough, but because the program has already addressed everything it would surface.

Continuous inspection readiness requires four organizational commitments: regular application of the audit trail pattern analysis described above, as an ongoing quality monitoring activity rather than a pre-inspection exercise; validation documentation maintenance as a routine quality process, not a one-time achievement; CRO and vendor oversight that produces documented evidence of verified performance, not just contracted performance; and a quality event management process that identifies data integrity signals, investigates them to root cause, and remediates them before they accumulate into systemic findings.

The regulatory record suggests that the most important single predictor of inspection outcome is whether the organization's quality system detects and remediates its own data integrity gaps before an investigator does. Organizations with functioning quality systems that surface and close findings internally do not typically generate warning letters. Organizations whose quality systems document compliance without detecting operational gaps are the ones the inspection record describes. The design principle that closes this chapter is the same one that opened this book: data integrity failures are almost always design failures, and the most consequential design decision a clinical quality organization makes is whether to build a quality system that finds problems or one that files documentation of having looked.

CHAPTER 16 — KEY PRINCIPLES
Inspection selection by FDA and global regulators is not random; statistical anomalies in submitted data, high subject contribution to pivotal endpoints, and unverified CRO oversight are among the factors that elevate inspection probability.
FDA BIMO investigators conduct outcome-focused pattern analysis, working backward from submitted data values to source records; the finding that matters is not an individual query but a pattern of hundreds that reveals a systematic quality failure.
EU GCP inspectors apply a three-tier finding classification; a single critical finding can be sufficient to recommend against marketing authorization or delay the assessment clock for the entire dossier.
The most consistently documented inspection finding categories are audit trail gaps, policy-practice gaps in access control, uninformative change reasons, query pattern anomalies, and expired or unmaintained validation documentation.
An effective internal data integrity assessment applies the same analytical methods an investigator would use: audit trail pattern analysis, temporal clustering review, timestamp plausibility verification, and access control cross-referencing.
Remediation of findings identified during internal assessment and before database lock is categorically more manageable than remediation following an inspection observation; organizations that conduct genuine self-assessment preserve this choice.
Organizations preparing for an EU GCP inspection should assume that any trial may be selected as an example during a systems-based inspection, not only the trials they expect to be examined.
Continuous inspection readiness is a program design outcome, not a preparation activity; organizations whose quality monitoring regularly applies pattern analysis and validation maintenance as routine activities sustain inspection-ready records without inspection-specific preparation.

CONCLUSION

Integrity as Architecture

> *Data integrity failures are design failures. That statement opened this book. Sixteen chapters later, the enforcement record, the regulatory framework, the inspection patterns, and the organizational evidence all point to the same conclusion.*

Data integrity failures are design failures. That statement opened this book. Sixteen chapters later, the enforcement record, the regulatory framework, the inspection patterns, and the organizational evidence all point to the same conclusion.

Chapter 1 opened with a CRO receiving a warning letter that would cost it $38 million, three major sponsor contracts, and a consent decree requiring four years of independent oversight before it could onboard a new client. That was not a story about fraud. It was a story about accommodation, accumulated across years by a quality system that generated compliance documentation without detecting operational reality. Coordinators under enrollment pressure. Query patterns that moved data toward significance thresholds. Audit trails disabled during key periods. A monitoring program that reviewed metrics rather than records. None of it was deliberate at the organizational level. All of it was the predictable output of a system designed to produce clean packages rather than accurate data.

That CRO's story is not exceptional. It is representative. The enforcement record that Chapter 1 documented, and that subsequent chapters analyzed in granular technical and regulatory detail, describes organizations that were not ignorant of the requirements. They were documented into compliance. Their systems were validated. Their audit trails were enabled. Their access control policies were written and approved. What their systems were not designed to do was make compliant behavior easier than the non-compliant alternative under real operational pressure. The compliance infrastructure existed. The design that would have made it effective did not.

Compliance is a property of documentation. Integrity is a property of systems. The enforcement record confirms they can diverge dramatically, and that they do, repeatedly, in organizations that believe otherwise.

What Design Means

The concept of data integrity by design is simple to state and genuinely difficult to execute. It requires asking, before a system is deployed or a process is written or a training program is built, not whether the output will be documentably compliant, but whether the design makes integrity the path of least resistance. Whether a coordinator under schedule pressure will record data accurately because the system makes accurate recording easier than inaccurate recording, not because a policy says she must. Whether a query will be resolved with a substantive change reason because the workflow requires one, not because a procedure describes one. Whether an audit trail review will surface a signal that warrants investigation because the review is designed to find signals, not because the review form has a checkbox for "reviewed."

Chapter 2 introduced the seven design principles that distinguish programs that produce integrity from programs that document it: making the compliant path easier than the alternative, designing for the failure mode rather than the standard case, building verification into the design rather than the audit, and aligning incentives with the behavior the design requires. Chapters 6 through 16 applied those principles across every domain of clinical data management, from the data lifecycle through computer system validation, audit trails, electronic records, decentralized trials, training, leadership, culture, AI systems, cloud infrastructure, and inspection preparation. The regulatory framework changes; the technology changes; the design principles do not.

Across all of those domains, the finding is consistent. The organizations that exit inspections cleanly, that complete submissions without data integrity deficiencies, and that sustain those outcomes across multiple development cycles and multiple regulatory authorities share one characteristic: they built their quality systems to find problems, not to file documentation of having looked. They applied pattern analysis to their own audit trails before inspectors did. They tested their data return processes before they needed them at database lock. They verified that their CROs' systems matched their CROs' representations before signing the task order. They treated the gap between policy and operational reality as a design failure to be corrected, not a compliance risk to be managed.

What the Regulatory Landscape Requires Now

The regulatory environment for clinical data integrity has never been more demanding, and the trajectory has not reversed. ICH E6(R3)'s explicit adoption of ALCOA+ as binding GCP makes every property an enumerated legal obligation rather than an interpretive expectation. FDA's expanded remote inspection toolkit allows data anomaly detection at a scale and speed that was impossible under traditional on-site monitoring. The February 2026 EMA/PIC/S joint consultation, when it produces its final document, will simultaneously impose comprehensive data integrity requirements across the majority of the world's significant clinical regulatory jurisdictions, covering AI-assisted data management, cloud-hosted systems, and the full spectrum of data governance obligations that earlier guidance left to interpretation.

AI systems used in clinical data management are subject to existing ALCOA+ and Part 11 requirements now, without specific guidance and without waiting for that guidance to be finalized. Cloud-hosted systems create retrievability obligations that extend fifteen years beyond the commercial relationships that support them, and sponsors who have not designed for infrastructure independence have a compliance gap that is not visible until a vendor is acquired, a platform is discontinued, or an inspection arrives. The internal data integrity assessment described in Chapter 16 is the mechanism by which organizations discover these gaps on their own timeline. The enforcement record is the mechanism by which organizations that do not conduct that assessment discover them on the regulator's timeline.

None of this is punitive for its own sake. The regulatory framework governing clinical data integrity exists because the evidentiary basis for drug approval decisions depends on the reliability of clinical trial data. When that data is manipulated, patients receive approvals for treatments whose benefit-risk profiles were misrepresented. When it is merely unreliable, through poor design rather than deliberate fraud, patients receive approvals for treatments whose actual efficacy and safety was never adequately established. The regulatory obligation is, at its core, a patient safety obligation. The organizations that understand data integrity in those terms, rather than as a compliance burden imposed by an adversarial agency, build different programs and sustain different outcomes.

What Technology Cannot Do

Chapters 11 through 13 addressed the parts of the data integrity problem that technology does not solve: culture, training, and leadership. They are the most difficult chapters in the book because the problems they address resist the engineered solutions that the rest of the book proposes. A data integrity culture cannot be configured like an EDC system or validated like a software platform. It is built through the accumulation of leadership decisions, training investments, and organizational responses to the signals that a quality system generates, made consistently over time by people who treat data integrity as a value rather than a requirement.

Chapter 11 documented that organizations whose quality cultures are genuine, where honesty about data problems is encouraged and rewarded rather than suppressed, surface and close findings internally before inspectors find them. Chapter 12 documented that training programs that assess competency rather than completion produce coordinators who understand why accurate data recording matters, not just that it is required. Chapter 13 documented that leadership engagement with data integrity as an operational reality, not merely a quality department concern, is the single most reliable predictor of whether a quality system finds problems or files documentation of having looked.

These are not soft conclusions. They are supported by the enforcement record and by the organizational evidence that the clinical research quality community has generated across two decades of examining why data integrity programs succeed or fail. The technical infrastructure described in Chapters 6 through 10 and 14 through 16 is necessary but not sufficient. It requires a human system that operates it with the understanding that the audit trail is not a compliance artifact: it is the evidence that the data it documents can be trusted.

The warning letter arrives at the end of a long chain of design decisions, each made by someone who was trying to get the work done. The question data integrity by design asks is whether those decisions made accurate recording easier or harder than the alternative.

From Design to Program

The framework this book provides answers the question of what integrity-by-design requires: validated systems, governed data lifecycles, audit trails that are reviewed rather than filed, training programs that assess competency, and leadership structures that connect quality signals to organizational authority. These are design specifications. Applying them produces compliant data as a natural consequence rather than a compliance aspiration.

But a design specification is not the same as a working program. The quality director who finishes this book with a clear understanding of what an ALCOA+-compliant data governance architecture looks like still faces the operational question that understanding alone cannot answer: where does the program actually start, how should progress be measured, and what does the organization need to look different in practice before the next inspection, the next CRO qualification cycle, or the next executive governance review? Those questions require a different kind of answer than the one this book provides. They require a methodology for gap assessment, a framework for resource allocation and prioritization, metrics that tell leadership whether the program is working before an investigator confirms that it is not, and an orientation toward the regulatory developments arriving in the next several years that will expand the obligations this book has mapped.

That is the work of the companion volume, *Data Integrity in Practice: Building, Measuring, and Sustaining Your Program.* The design principles established here are its foundation. The implementation architecture is its subject. For organizations that have read this book and recognized the distance between where their programs are and where this framework requires them to be, that distance is not a compliance gap to be documented. It is a design problem to be solved. The tools for solving it are what the next volume provides.

The Frame

This book closes where it opened: with the recognition that data integrity failures are design failures, and that the organizations that understand this will build different programs than the ones that treat compliance as documentation. The distinction matters for every stakeholder in the clinical research enterprise. For sponsors, it determines whether a marketing application is approvable on its first submission or requires a second. For CROs, it determines whether a data integrity finding ends client relationships or validates them. For clinical investigators, it determines whether the data collected from the patients who trusted them to conduct research with integrity will be used to approve a therapy that works, or will generate a corrective action program that serves no one. For patients, it is the whole point.

The chapters in this book provide the technical, regulatory, and organizational framework for building data management programs that reliably produce integrity rather than document the aspiration for it. The application of that framework is an organizational choice, made by the people who design systems, write procedures, build training programs, and set the quality culture that determines how people behave under pressure. This book is for those people. The design work is theirs.

THE FRAME: FIVE QUESTIONS TO TAKE BACK TO YOUR ORGANIZATION

1. Does our quality system find problems, or does it file documentation of having looked? The difference is the analytical method applied to quality signals, and it determines what investigators will find when they look at the same records.

2. Are our systems and processes designed so that compliant behavior is easier than the non-compliant alternative under realistic operational pressure, or only under ideal conditions that do not persist throughout a trial lifecycle?

3. Does the leadership of this organization treat data integrity as an operational reality that requires their engagement and accountability, or as a quality department concern to which they provide visible endorsement without genuine participation?

4. Have we conducted the inspection of our own data that Chapter 16 describes, applying the same analytical methods regulators use, and made remediation decisions before the next inspection rather than in response to it?

5. When our quality system identifies a data integrity signal, does that signal reach someone with the authority and mandate to address the design condition that produced it, or does it close in the queue where it was generated?

The organizations that can answer these questions well are not necessarily the ones with the largest quality budgets or the most sophisticated technology platforms. They are the ones whose quality programs are built on the recognition that integrity is an architectural property of systems, not a consequence of documentation, and whose leaders act on that recognition every time they make a design decision. That is the argument this book makes. The enforcement record confirms it. The choice of what to do with it belongs to the reader.

Index

Sources & Notes

[1] United States, Food and Drug Administration. "BIMO Inspection Metrics." Clinical Trials and Human Subject Protection, FDA, www.fda.gov/science-research/clinical-trials-and-human-subject-protection/bimo-inspection-metrics.

[2] DiMasi, Joseph A., Henry G. Grabowski, and Ronald W. Hansen. "Innovation in the Pharmaceutical Industry: New Estimates of R&D Costs." Journal of Health Economics, vol. 47, May 2016, pp. 20–33, doi:10.1016/j.jhealeco.2016.01.012.

[3] The financial ranges in the Direct Financial Penalties table are illustrative estimates derived from a composite of publicly reported enforcement outcomes. Sources include DOJ consent decree public filings (www.justice.gov/civil/consumer-protection-branch); SEC Form 8-K and 10-K disclosures by publicly traded CROs and pharmaceutical sponsors following FDA enforcement actions; and Tufts CSDD capitalized cost estimates for full development programs. These figures are not FDA-published data and should be interpreted as order-of-magnitude guidance. Composite estimate methodology: ranges derived from review of ten or more publicly reported enforcement actions from 2010 to 2024 in which remediation costs were disclosed through litigation, SEC filings, or press releases.

[4] United States, Food and Drug Administration. Untitled Letter to Cetero Research, Houston, Texas. Center for Drug Evaluation and Research / Office of Regulatory Affairs, 26 July 2011, www.fda.gov/media/83889/download. See also: Form FDA 483: Cetero Research, Houston, Texas. Inspectional Observations, 3–7 May 2010, www.fda.gov/media/81659/download. FDA's enforcement actions covered multiple Cetero facilities; the aggregate sponsor notification covering approximately 1,900 studies encompasses both the Houston and Fargo, North Dakota facilities. See also: United States, Food and Drug Administration. Warning Letter to Cetero Research, Inc. CDER Bioresearch Monitoring Program, 15 August 2011, www.fda.gov/inspections-compliance-enforcement-and-criminal-investigations/warning-letters/cetero-research-inc-08152011.

[5] United States, Food and Drug Administration. "Notification to Pharmaceutical Companies: Clinical and Bioanalytical Studies Conducted by Semler Research Are Unacceptable." FDA Drug Safety and Availability, www.fda.gov/drugs/drug-safety-and-availability/notification-pharmaceutical-companies-clinical-and-bioanalytical-studies-conducted-semler-research. See also: Form FDA 483: Semler Research Center Private

Limited, Bangalore, India. Inspectional Observations, 29 September–9 October 2015, www.fda.gov/media/97413/download.

[6] European Medicines Agency. "GVK Biosciences: European Medicines Agency Recommends Suspending Medicines over Flawed Studies." EMA Press Release, 22 January 2015, www.ema.europa.eu/en/news/gvk-biosciences-european-medicines-agency-recommends-suspending-medicines-over-flawed-studies. The GVK review was initiated under Article 31 of Directive 2001/83/EC; reference number EMA/591005/2014.

[7] International Council on Harmonisation. "Guideline for Good Clinical Practice E6(R3)." Final version, adopted at Step 4, 6 January 2025; typographical corrections issued 24 October 2025 addressing Sections 1.2.5 and 3.16.4. ICH, database.ich.org/sites/default/files/ICH_E6(R3)_Guideline_Step4_2025_1024.pdf. Citations throughout this book refer to the Step 4 final version as corrected.

[8] Khin, Ni A., Gail Francis, Jean Mulinde, et al. "Data Integrity in Global Clinical Trials: Discussions From Joint US Food and Drug Administration and UK Medicines and Healthcare Products Regulatory Agency Good Clinical Practice Workshop." Clinical Pharmacology & Therapeutics, 2020, doi:10.1002/cpt.1794. The paper documents the joint October 2018 FDA-MHRA GCP workshop findings, including both agencies' position that data integrity concerns affecting audit trail reliability and data management practices directly affect the acceptability of data submitted in support of marketing applications. This paper constitutes primary regulatory authority on both agencies' convergent clinical data integrity enforcement frameworks.

[9] International Council for Harmonisation. ICH E6(R3): Guideline for Good Clinical Practice, adopted at Step 4, 6 January 2025; typographical correction 24 October 2025. The quality management and quality-by-design requirements referenced in this chapter derive from the GCP Principles (Part II, Principle 6) and Section 3.10 (Quality Management) of the guideline body, and from Section 5.0 (Sponsor Quality Management).
database.ich.org/sites/default/files/ICH_E6(R3)_Guideline_Step4_2025_1024.pdf.

[10] International Council for Harmonisation. ICH E6(R3): Guideline for Good Clinical Practice, adopted at Step 4, 6 January 2025, Section 5.1 (Sponsor Responsibilities in the Context of Quality Management) and Section 5.2 (Contracting and Delegation). The principle that sponsors cannot transfer their regulatory responsibility to CROs is a foundational element of the sponsor obligations framework throughout Section 5.
database.ich.org/sites/default/files/ICH_E6(R3)_Guideline_Step4_2025_1024.pdf.

[11] United Kingdom, Medicines and Healthcare products Regulatory Agency. 'GMP Data Integrity Definitions and Guidance for Industry.' MHRA Guidance Document, March 2018, Section 5 (Senior Management Responsibilities). While formally a GMP document, MHRA's GCP inspection guidance applies equivalent management accountability expectations to clinical data governance programs. www.gov.uk/government/publications/guidance-on-gmp-data-integrity.

[12] International Council for Harmonisation. ICH E6(R3): Guideline for Good Clinical Practice, adopted at Step 4, 6 January 2025. The four foundational changes discussed in Chapter 2 of this book derive from Sections 4.9 (ALCOA+ as mandatory standard), 5.0 (organisational data governance), 5.5 (data integrity obligations for all trial systems), and 5.2 (Contracting and Delegation; traceability requirement) respectively. database.ich.org/sites/default/files/ICH_E6(R3)_Guideline_Step4_2025_1024.pdf.

[13] United States, Food and Drug Administration. 'Data Integrity and Compliance With Drug CGMP: Questions and Answers — Guidance for Industry.' FDA Guidance for Industry, December 2018. The principles governing management accountability, design-level controls, and the inadequacy of validation alone as a data integrity strategy in this guidance are applied throughout this chapter in the clinical research context. www.fda.gov/regulatory-information/search-fda-guidance-documents/data-integrity-and-compliance-drug-cgmp-questions-and-answers-guidance-industry.

[14] Pharmaceutical Inspection Co-operation Scheme. 'Guidance on Data Integrity, PI 041-1.' PIC/S Guidance Document, revised July 2021. The framework for distinguishing documented compliance from operational integrity, and the organizational conditions required to sustain each, draws on PIC/S PI 041-1's treatment of data governance, management review, and self-inspection requirements. www.picscheme.org/en/publications.

[15] United States, Department of Health, Education, and Welfare. Final Report of the Tuskegee Syphilis Study Ad Hoc Advisory Panel. Washington, D.C.: DHEW, 1973. The panel's report documented the full scope of the study's ethical violations and directly informed the legislative response that produced the National Research Act (1974) and the establishment of the National Commission for the Protection of Human Subjects of Biomedical and Behavioral Research, whose deliberations produced the Belmont Report (1979). For the Belmont Report, see: https://www.hhs.gov/ohrp/regulations-and-policy/belmont-report/read-the-belmont-report/index.html. For the Tuskegee report, see: Centers for Disease Control and Prevention historical archive, https://www.cdc.gov/tuskegee/index.html.

[16] Beecher HK. "Ethics and Clinical Research." New England Journal of Medicine. 1966;274(24):1354–1360. https://doi.org/10.1056/NEJM196606162742405.

[17] World Medical Association. Declaration of Helsinki — Ethical Principles for Medical Research Involving Human Subjects. Adopted 1964; most recently amended 2013. www.wma.net.

[18] Schneider K. Faking it: The Case against Industrial Bio-Test Laboratories. The Amicus Journal. 1983;Spring. https://www.centerforfoodsafety.org/files/schneider-1983_42309.pdf.

[19] Rosner D, Markowitz G. "Ashamed" to Put His Name to It: Monsanto, Industrial Bio-Test Laboratories, and the Use of Fraudulent Science, 1969–1985. Am J Public Health. 2023;113(6):661–666. https://doi.org/10.2105/AJPH.2023.307247.

[20] United States Senate, Ninety-Fourth Congress. Preclinical and Clinical Testing by the Pharmaceutical Industry, 1976. Joint Hearings, Part II. January 20 and 22, 1976. https://babel.hathitrust.org/cgi/pt?id=umn.31951002815155h&seq=9.

[21] 43 Fed. Reg. 247 (Dec. 22, 1978) (codified at 21 CFR Part 58 — Good Laboratory Practice for Nonclinical Laboratory Studies). Effective June 20, 1979. https://tile.loc.gov/storage-services/service/ll/fedreg/fr043/fr043247/fr043247.pdf.

[22] United States, Food and Drug Administration. 21 CFR Part 312 — Investigational New Drug Application. Code of Federal Regulations, Title 21, Part 312. www.ecfr.gov.

[23] International Council for Harmonisation. ICH E6: Guideline for Good Clinical Practice. Original Step 4 adoption: 1 May 1996. ICH E6(R2) integrated addendum adopted at Step 4: 9 November 2016. www.ich.org. Citations in this chapter to the 1996 ICH E6 framework refer to the original Step 4 guideline; citations to E6(R2) refer to the November 2016 integrated addendum. Both are superseded by ICH E6(R3), adopted at Step 4 on 6 January 2025, which is the operative GCP standard for all new clinical trial activity.

[24] United States, Food and Drug Administration. 21 CFR Part 11 — Electronic Records; Electronic Signatures. Code of Federal Regulations, Title 21, Part 11. Effective August 20, 1997. www.ecfr.gov.

[25] United States, Food and Drug Administration. Part 11, Electronic Records; Electronic Signatures — Scope and Application. FDA Guidance for Industry, August 2003. www.fda.gov/regulatory-information/search-fda-guidance-documents/part-11-electronic-records-electronic-signatures-scope-and-application.

[26] United States, Food and Drug Administration. Electronic Systems, Electronic Records, and Electronic Signatures in Clinical Investigations: Questions and Answers. FDA Guidance for Industry, Revision 1. www.fda.gov/regulatory-information/search-fda-guidance-documents/electronic-systems-electronic-records-and-electronic-signatures-clinical-investigations-questions.

[27] United States, Food and Drug Administration. Oversight of Clinical Investigations — A Risk-Based Approach to Monitoring. FDA Guidance for Industry, August 2013. www.fda.gov/media/71012/download.

[28] United States, Food and Drug Administration. Electronic Source Data in Clinical Investigations. FDA Guidance for Industry, September 2013 (updated 2019). www.fda.gov/regulatory-information/search-fda-guidance-documents/electronic-source-data-clinical-investigations.

[29] Khin, Ni A., Gail Francis, Jean Mulinde, et al. "Data Integrity in Global Clinical Trials: Discussions From Joint US Food and Drug Administration and UK Medicines and Healthcare Products Regulatory Agency Good Clinical Practice Workshop." Clinical Pharmacology & Therapeutics, 2020, doi:10.1002/cpt.1794. Authored by named FDA and MHRA officials; constitutes primary regulatory authority on the convergent data integrity enforcement positions of both agencies. The paper documents the joint October 2018 FDA-MHRA GCP workshop, including both agencies' position that audit trail failures and data management deficiencies directly affect marketing application acceptability.

[30] International Council for Harmonisation. ICH E6(R3): Guideline for Good Clinical Practice, adopted at Step 4, 6 January 2025; typographical correction issued 24 October 2025.
database.ich.org/sites/default/files/ICH_E6(R3)_Guideline_Step4_2025_1024.pdf.

[31] European Medicines Agency, Good Clinical Practice Inspectors Working Group. Guideline on Computerised Systems and Electronic Data in Clinical Trials. EMA/INS/GCP/112288/2023. Final version adopted by the GCP IWG 7 March 2023; published 9 March 2023; came into effect six months after publication (effective September 2023). This guideline formally replaces the 2010 EMA Reflection Paper on electronic source data and establishes ALCOA++ including Traceable as the EU clinical data integrity standard. https://www.ema.europa.eu/en/documents/scientific-guideline/guideline-computerised-systems-electronic-data-clinical-trials_en.pdf.

[32] European Medicines Agency, Data Analytics and Methods Task Force. Data Quality Framework for EU Medicines Regulation. EMA/326985/2023. Adopted by CHMP, 30 October 2023. Establishes a common EU framework for data quality governance across all data types used in regulatory decision-making, including clinical trial data and real-world evidence. https://www.ema.europa.eu/en/documents/other/data-quality-framework-eu-medicines-regulation_en.pdf.

[33] European Commission. Regulation (EU) No 536/2014 of the European Parliament and of the Council on Clinical Trials on Medicinal Products for Human Use. Official Journal of the European Union, April 16, 2014.

[34] European Commission. Regulation (EU) No 536/2014 on Clinical Trials on Medicinal Products for Human Use. Official Journal of the European Union, April 16, 2014.

[35] United States, Food and Drug Administration. Electronic Source Data in Clinical Investigations. FDA Guidance for Industry, September 2013 (updated 2019). www.fda.gov/regulatory-information/search-fda-guidance-documents/electronic-source-data-clinical-investigations.

[36] Khin, Ni A., Gail Francis, Jean Mulinde, et al. "Data Integrity in Global Clinical Trials: Discussions From Joint US Food and Drug Administration and UK Medicines and Healthcare Products Regulatory Agency Good Clinical Practice Workshop." Clinical Pharmacology & Therapeutics, 2020, doi:10.1002/cpt.1794. Authored by named FDA (CDER/OSI and OSIS) and MHRA (Inspection, Enforcement and Standards Division) officials. Constitutes primary regulatory authority on the convergent clinical data integrity enforcement positions of both agencies. The paper documents both agencies' common position that audit trail failures and data management deficiencies directly affect marketing application acceptability.

[37] International Council for Harmonisation. ICH E6(R3): Guideline for Good Clinical Practice, adopted at Step 4, 6 January 2025; typographical correction 24 October 2025. database.ich.org/sites/default/files/ICH_E6(R3)_Guideline_Step4_2025_1024.pdf.

[38] European Medicines Agency, GCP Inspectors Working Group. Guideline on Computerised Systems and Electronic Data in Clinical Trials. EMA/INS/GCP/112288/2023. Final version adopted 7 March 2023; came into effect six months after publication. This document formally replaces the 2010 EMA Reflection Paper on electronic source data. Section 4.5 explicitly adopts ALCOA++ as the EU clinical data integrity standard, including Traceable as the tenth discrete property. https://www.ema.europa.eu/en/documents/scientific-guideline/guideline-computerised-systems-electronic-data-clinical-trials_en.pdf.

[39] European Medicines Agency, Data Analytics and Methods Task Force. Data Quality Framework for EU Medicines Regulation. EMA/326985/2023. Adopted by CHMP, 30 October 2023. Establishes a common EU framework for data quality governance across all data types used in regulatory decision-making, encompassing clinical trial data, real-world data, and electronic health record data. https://www.ema.europa.eu/en/documents/other/data-quality-framework-eu-medicines-regulation_en.pdf.

[40] European Commission. Regulation (EU) No 536/2014 on Clinical Trials on Medicinal Products for Human Use. Official Journal of the European Union, April 16, 2014.

[41] United Kingdom, Medicines and Healthcare products Regulatory Agency. 'GMP Data Integrity Definitions and Guidance for Industry.' MHRA Guidance Document, March 2018, Section 5 (Designing systems and processes to assure data integrity; creating the 'right environment'). The requirement that senior management create an environment in which data integrity is expected, supported, and verifiable, and the obligation to conduct honest self-assessments of whether organizational conditions are creating structural integrity risk, are addressed in Section 5. www.gov.uk/government/publications/guidance-on-gmp-data-integrity.

[42] United Kingdom, Medicines and Healthcare products Regulatory Agency. GMP Data Integrity Definitions and Guidance for Industry. MHRA Guidance Document, March 2018. www.gov.uk/government/publications/guidance-on-gmp-data-integrity.

[43] Khin, Ni A., Gail Francis, Jean Mulinde, et al. "Data Integrity in Global Clinical Trials: Discussions From Joint US Food and Drug Administration and UK Medicines and Healthcare Products Regulatory Agency Good Clinical Practice Workshop." Clinical Pharmacology & Therapeutics, 2020, doi:10.1002/cpt.1794. Authored by named FDA (CDER/OSI and OSIS) and MHRA (Inspection, Enforcement and Standards Division) officials. Constitutes primary regulatory authority on the convergent clinical data integrity enforcement positions of both agencies. The paper documents both agencies' common position that audit trail failures and data management deficiencies directly affect marketing application acceptability.

[44] Pharmaceutical Inspection Co-operation Scheme. Guidance on Data Integrity, PI 041-1. PIC/S Guidance Document, revised July 2021. www.picscheme.org/en/publications.

[45] World Health Organization. Guidance on Good Data and Record Management Practices. WHO Technical Report Series No. 996, Annex 5, 2016. www.who.int/publications/m/item/trs996-annex5.

[46] Japan, Ministry of Health, Labour and Welfare. Partial Revision of Good Clinical Practice for Drugs (Ministerial Ordinance No. 28 of 1997). Revised 2021. www.pmda.go.jp.

[47] China, National Medical Products Administration. Announcement No. 74: Technical Guidelines for Computerized System Validation in Pharmaceutical Companies. 2020. www.nmpa.gov.cn.

[48] India, Central Drugs Standard Control Organisation. New Drugs and Clinical Trials Rules 2019. Ministry of Health and Family Welfare, Government of India. cdsco.gov.in.

[49] Brazil, ANVISA. RDC 658/2022: Good Practices for Computerized Systems. Agencia Nacional de Vigilancia Sanitaria, 2022. www.gov.br/anvisa.

[50] South Korea, Ministry of Food and Drug Safety. MFDS Data Integrity Guidelines for Drug Products. 2020. www.mfds.go.kr.

[51] United States, Food and Drug Administration. 21 CFR Part 11 — Electronic Records; Electronic Signatures. Code of Federal Regulations, Title 21, Part 11, Sections 11.10 and 11.50. The unique user identification requirements of Section 11.10(d) establish the technical basis for attributability in electronic clinical trial systems. www.ecfr.gov/current/title-21/chapter-I/subchapter-A/part-11.

[52] United States, Food and Drug Administration. Electronic Source Data in Clinical Investigations. FDA Guidance for Industry, September 2013 (updated 2019). The guidance establishes that where data is generated by a computerized system, the electronic record is the primary record and derived outputs do not satisfy the source data retention obligation. www.fda.gov/regulatory-information/search-fda-guidance-documents/electronic-source-data-clinical-investigations.

[53] United States, Food and Drug Administration. 21 CFR Part 50 — Protection of Human Subjects. Sections 50.25 and 50.27 establish the informed consent requirements applicable to clinical investigations, including the requirement that consent be obtained prior to initiation of study procedures. www.ecfr.gov/current/title-21/chapter-I/subchapter-A/part-50.

[54] International Council for Harmonisation. ICH E6(R3): Guideline for Good Clinical Practice, Step 4, adopted 6 January 2025, Section 4.9.1 and Appendix C (Glossary). Section 4.9.1 establishes the nine named ALCOA+ properties as the evaluative standard for source data quality. database.ich.org/sites/default/files/ICH_E6(R3)_Guideline_Step4_2025_1024.pdf. See also: European Medicines Agency, GCP Inspectors Working Group. Guideline on Computerised Systems and Electronic Data in Clinical Trials. EMA/INS/GCP/112288/2023, Section 4.5. This section explicitly lists Traceable as the tenth ALCOA+ property and defines data integrity as compliance with all ten properties. https://www.ema.europa.eu/en/documents/scientific-guideline/guideline-computerised-systems-electronic-data-clinical-trials_en.pdf.

[55] United States, Food and Drug Administration. Using Artificial Intelligence and Machine Learning in the Development of Drug and Biological Products. FDA Discussion Paper, May 2023. The discussion of traceability requirements for AI-generated outputs, including the obligation to retain input data and algorithmic specifications sufficient to reproduce the output, is addressed in the paper's section on data integrity considerations for AI in drug development. www.fda.gov/media/167973/download.

[56] Pharmaceutical Inspection Co-operation Scheme. Guidance on Data Integrity, PI 041-1. PIC/S Guidance Document, revised July 2021. PI 041-1 provides the most operationally detailed treatment of each ALCOA+ property available from any regulatory source, including specific inspection questions and illustrative compliant and non-compliant scenarios for each principle. www.picscheme.org/en/publications.

[57] United Kingdom, Medicines and Healthcare products Regulatory Agency. GMP Data Integrity Definitions and Guidance for Industry. MHRA Guidance Document, March 2018. www.gov.uk/government/publications/guidance-on-gmp-data-integrity.

[58] International Council for Harmonisation. ICH E6(R3): Guideline for Good Clinical Practice, Step 4 adoption, January 2025, Section 4.2 (Data Life Cycle Elements). The section introduces an explicit data lifecycle governance requirement applicable to sponsors and investigators, addressing generation, processing, review, reporting, transfer, storage, archiving, and disposition of clinical trial data. www.ich.org/page/efficacy-guidelines.

[59] European Medicines Agency, Data Analytics and Methods Task Force. Data Quality Framework for EU Medicines Regulation. EMA/326985/2023, adopted by CHMP 30 October 2023. The framework defines five data quality dimensions -- reliability, extensiveness, coherence, timeliness, and relevance -- and characterizes their determinants and metrics across primary and secondary use of clinical data. https://www.ema.europa.eu/en/documents/other/data-quality-framework-eu-medicines-regulation_en.pdf.

[60] European Medicines Agency. Guideline on Computerised Systems and Electronic Data in Clinical Trials. EMA/INS/GCP/112288/2023, Good Clinical Practice Inspectors Working Group, adopted 7 March 2023, effective September 2023. The guideline replaces the 2010 reflection paper on electronic source data and addresses the full system lifecycle including retirement phase obligations, ALCOA++ as the operative standard (Section 4.5), direct capture versus transcription obligations (Section 6.1), cloud solution requirements (Section 6.7), and audit trail review frequency (Section 6.2.2). https://www.ema.europa.eu/en/documents/scientific-guideline/guideline-computerised-systems-and-electronic-data-clinical-trials_en.pdf.

[61] European Medicines Agency and Pharmaceutical Inspection Co-operation Scheme. Joint Public Consultation on Clinical Data Integrity and Pharmacovigilance Data Management, February 2026. The consultation addresses digital trial environments, AI-assisted data management, CRO supply chain data integrity, and ALCOA+ harmonization. Expected to produce a globally adopted standard by 2027-2028. www.ema.europa.eu; www.picscheme.org.

[62] Pharmaceutical Inspection Co-operation Scheme. 'Guidance on Data Integrity, PI 041-1.' PIC/S Guidance Document, revised July 2021, Sections 5 and 8. The traceability requirement for data transformations, and the data governance obligations applicable to each stage of the data lifecycle, are addressed in PIC/S PI 041-1's treatment of data governance and computerized system controls. www.picscheme.org/en/publications. See also: United States, Food and Drug Administration. 'Data Integrity and Compliance With Drug CGMP: Questions and Answers -- Guidance for Industry.' FDA Guidance for Industry, December 2018. www.fda.gov/regulatory-information/search-fda-guidance-documents/data-integrity-and-compliance-drug-cgmp-questions-and-answers-guidance-industry.

[63] United Kingdom, Medicines and Healthcare products Regulatory Agency. 'GMP Data Integrity Definitions and Guidance for Industry.' MHRA Guidance Document, March 2018, Sections 6.6 (Data Lifecycle), 6.8 (Data Transfer/Migration), 6.9 (Data Processing), 6.17 (Data Retention), and 6.17.1 (Archive). The MHRA's GxP-scope lifecycle framework, its requirement that processing traceability be maintained regardless of whether outputs are used in reporting, and its treatment of transfer validation and archive access verification are applied throughout this chapter in the clinical GCP context. www.gov.uk/government/publications/guidance-on-gmp-data-integrity.

[64] Williams, James R., et al. 'Data Integrity in Global Clinical Trials.' Clinical Pharmacology and Therapeutics, vol. 108, no. 4, 2020, pp. 727–737. The FDA-MHRA joint paper documents the inspection approaches of both agencies, the convergence in use of audit trail pattern analysis, and the structural differences between FDA's outcome-focused approach and the EU's systems-based GCP inspection model. It is the primary source for the comparative inspection approach analysis in this chapter. https://doi.org/10.1002/cpt.1927.

[65] Khin, Ni A., et al. 'Data Integrity in Global Clinical Trials: Discussions From Joint US Food and Drug Administration and UK Medicines and Healthcare Products Regulatory Agency Good Clinical Practice Workshop.' Clinical Pharmacology and Therapeutics, 2020. The paper documents the convergence of FDA and MHRA inspection approaches to audit trail pattern analysis, including the common use of statistical anomaly detection for review-stage integrity assessment in global clinical trial inspections. The FDA-MHRA joint workshop described in this paper established the framework for ongoing regulatory cooperation on clinical data integrity described in subsequent chapters of this book.

[66] United States, Food and Drug Administration. 'Oversight of Clinical Investigations -- A Risk-Based Approach to Monitoring.' FDA Guidance for Industry, August 2013. The guidance endorses centralized statistical monitoring as a primary method for identifying data patterns indicative of data integrity problems, and establishes that monitoring programs must be designed to detect these patterns, not merely to verify CRF-to-source agreement. www.fda.gov/regulatory-information/search-fda-guidance-documents/oversight-clinical-investigations-risk-based-approach-monitoring. See also: ICH E6(R3) Section 3.11.4.2 (Centralised Monitoring), which requires that the monitoring strategy be designed to detect data quality problems at both the individual record and aggregate pattern level.

[67] International Council for Harmonisation. ICH E6(R3): Guideline for Good Clinical Practice, Step 4 adoption, January 2025, Section 4.2.6 (Finalisation of Data Sets Prior to Analysis). The requirement for consistency between the statistical analysis plan, the analysis performed, and the results reported in the clinical study report is a foundational reporting-stage integrity obligation under E6(R3). See also: European Union. 'Regulation (EU) No 536/2014,' Articles 37 and 58 (CTIS results reporting obligations and eTMF requirements).

[68] European Union. Regulation (EU) No 536/2014 of the European Parliament and of the Council on Clinical Trials on Medicinal Products for Human Use. Official Journal of the European Union, 27 May 2014. Article 58 establishes the 25-year retention requirement for trial master file records after the end of the clinical trial. Articles 37 and 58 establish the CTIS registration and results disclosure obligations discussed in the reporting-stage and retention-period sections of this chapter. https://eur-lex.europa.eu/legal-content/EN/TXT/?uri=CELEX:32014R0536.

[69] United States, Food and Drug Administration. 21 CFR Part 312.62 -- Investigator Recordkeeping and Record Retention. The retention period provisions require records to be maintained in a form that allows reconstruction of the trial and verification of the data. www.ecfr.gov/current/title-21/chapter-I/subchapter-D/part-312/subpart-D/section-312.62. See also: International Council for Harmonisation. ICH E6(R3), Section 4.2.7 (Retention and Access). The 15-year minimum retention period and format durability requirement for electronic records are stated explicitly in this section.

[70] International Council for Harmonisation. ICH E6(R3): Guideline for Good Clinical Practice, Step 4 adoption, January 2025, Section 4.2.8 (Destruction). The section requires that destruction be documented and authorized after confirmation that retention obligations have been met and that no regulatory or legal hold is in place. www.ich.org/page/efficacy-guidelines.

[71] International Council for Harmonisation. ICH E6(R3): Guideline for Good Clinical Practice, Step 4 adoption, January 2025, Section 3.6 (Agreements). The principle that regulatory accountability for clinical trial data cannot be transferred to CROs, vendors, or other third parties, regardless of contractual arrangements, is stated explicitly in Section 3.6. See also: EMA/INS/GCP/112288/2023, Glossary, note that all references to sponsors and investigators also apply to their service providers, while responsibility for validation and data integrity remains with the responsible party.

[72] United States, Code of Federal Regulations. 21 CFR Part 11 -- Electronic Records; Electronic Signatures. The technical requirements for validation, audit trails, access controls, and electronic signatures applicable to electronic records in FDA-regulated clinical research are codified in Part 11, Sections 11.10(a) through 11.10(k). www.ecfr.gov/current/title-21/chapter-I/subchapter-A/part-11.

[73] United States, Food and Drug Administration. "Data Integrity and Compliance With Drug CGMP: Questions and Answers -- Guidance for Industry." FDA Guidance for Industry, December 2018. The principles governing validated state management, change control as a validation activity, and the inadequacy of completed validation packages as ongoing evidence of system integrity are applied throughout this chapter in the clinical research context. While formally a CGMP document, the data integrity principles are applied by FDA inspectors across GxP contexts including clinical research. www.fda.gov/regulatory-information/search-fda-guidance-documents/data-integrity-and-compliance-drug-cgmp-questions-and-answers-guidance-industry.

[74] United States, Food and Drug Administration. "Computer Software Assurance for Production and Quality System Software." FDA Draft Guidance for Industry, September 2022. The CSA framework, including the shift from requirements-based testing to risk-based assurance, the categorization of software as GxP-critical or non-GxP-critical, and the intended reduction of low-value documentation, is drawn from this draft guidance. www.fda.gov/regulatory-information/search-fda-guidance-documents/computer-software-assurance-production-and-quality-system-software.

[75] European Medicines Agency. Guideline on Computerised Systems and Electronic Data in Clinical Trials. EMA/INS/GCP/112288/2023, Good Clinical Practice Inspectors Working Group, adopted 7 March 2023, effective September 2023. The validation annex of the guideline establishes the EU clinical validation framework including vendor examination requirements (Section A2.1), user requirements (A2.2), trial-specific configuration validation (A2.3), traceability of requirements (A2.4), validation and test plans (A2.5), test execution and reporting (A2.6), release for production (A2.7), periodic review (A2.9), and change control (A2.10). https://www.ema.europa.eu/en/documents/scientific-guideline/guideline-computerised-systems-and-electronic-data-clinical-trials_en.pdf.

[76] Pharmaceutical Inspection Co-operation Scheme. "Guidance on Data Integrity, PI 041-1." PIC/S Guidance Document, revised July 2021. The requirements for supplier qualification of computerized systems, including assessment of the supplier quality management system and change control practices rather than reliance on product documentation alone, are discussed in PI 041-1 Sections 6 and 7. www.picscheme.org/en/publications.

[77] United Kingdom, Medicines and Healthcare products Regulatory Agency. "GxP Data Integrity Definitions and Guidance for Industry." MHRA Guidance Document, March 2018, Sections 6.19 (Validation for intended purpose), 6.20 (IT Suppliers and Service Providers). The principle that validation is a lifecycle activity requiring validated state management and change control throughout the system's operational life is stated explicitly. www.gov.uk/government/publications/guidance-on-gmp-data-integrity.

[78] World Health Organization. "Guidance on Good Data and Record Management Practices." WHO Technical Report Series No. 996, Annex 5, 2016. The requirements for lifecycle validation, validated state management, and system retirement planning are consistent with WHO TRS 996 Annex 5 guidance on computerized system lifecycle management. www.who.int/publications/m/item/trs996-annex5.

[79] United States, Food and Drug Administration. "Oversight of Clinical Investigations -- A Risk-Based Approach to Monitoring." FDA Guidance for Industry, August 2013. The risk-based monitoring framework, including centralized statistical monitoring of data patterns, is the regulatory basis for the automated monitoring approaches discussed in this chapter. www.fda.gov/regulatory-information/search-fda-guidance-documents/oversight-clinical-investigations-risk-based-approach-monitoring.

[80] United States, Food and Drug Administration. 21 CFR Part 11 -- Electronic Records; Electronic Signatures. Code of Federal Regulations, Title 21, Part 11, Sections 11.10(e) and 11.10(k). The audit trail requirements applicable to electronic records used in clinical investigations, including the computer-generated, time-stamped, secure, and operator-action-record requirements referenced throughout this chapter, are stated in these sections. www.ecfr.gov.

[81] International Council for Harmonisation. ICH E6(R3): Guideline for Good Clinical Practice, Step 4 adoption, May 2023, Sections 5.5.3 and 4.9.3. The data change documentation requirements, including the obligation to capture original value, revised value, date of revision, identity of the revising individual, and rationale for the change, derive from these sections. www.ich.org/page/efficacy-guidelines.

[82] European Medicines Agency. Guideline on Computerised Systems and Electronic Data in Clinical Trials. EMA/INS/GCP/112288/2023, Good Clinical Practice Inspectors Working Group, adopted 7 March 2023, effective September 2023. Section 6.2.1 establishes the always-on requirement, field-level capture requirement, protection against change and deletion, automatic logging of admin deactivation, human-readable format requirement, and blinding protection obligation. Section 6.2.2 establishes the proactive ongoing review standard, documentation requirement, and technology-assisted review expectation. Section 5.5 addresses timestamp validation. Section 6.3 addresses investigator sign-off alignment with data review. https://www.ema.europa.eu/en/documents/scientific-guideline/guideline-computerised-systems-and-electronic-data-clinical-trials_en.pdf.

[83] United Kingdom, MHRA. GxP Data Integrity Definitions and Guidance for Industry. March 2018, Section 6.13 (Audit Trail). www.gov.uk/government/publications/guidance-on-gmp-data-integrity.

[84] International Council for Harmonisation. ICH E6(R3): Guideline for Good Clinical Practice, Step 4, May 2023, Annex 1 — Clinical Quality Management System. www.ich.org/page/efficacy-guidelines.

[85] International Council for Harmonisation. ICH E6(R3): Guideline for Good Clinical Practice, Step 4 adoption, May 2023, Section 5.18 (Monitoring), Section 5.2 (Contracting and Delegation), and Appendix A (Technology and Data Management). The monitoring framework, CRO oversight obligations, and data traceability requirements establish the primary GCP standards against which inspection findings are cited in EU GCP and MHRA inspections. www.ich.org/page/efficacy-guidelines.

[86] International Council for Harmonisation. ICH E6(R3): Guideline for Good Clinical Practice, Step 4, May 2023, Annex 1 — Clinical Quality Management System. www.ich.org/page/efficacy-guidelines.

[87] Pharmaceutical Inspection Co-operation Scheme. Guidance on Data Integrity, PI 041-1. Revised July 2021. www.picscheme.org/en/publications.

[88] Khin, Ni A., et al. "Data Integrity in Global Clinical Trials." Clinical Pharmacology and Therapeutics, 2020. Documents EMA/FDA inspection-approach differences and audit trail pattern analysis in detecting data integrity problems.

[89] European Union. Regulation (EU) No 536/2014 on Clinical Trials. OJEU, 27 May 2014. Article 58 establishes the 25-year TMF retention requirement. https://eur-lex.europa.eu/legal-content/EN/TXT/?uri=CELEX:32014R0536.

[90] United States, FDA. Oversight of Clinical Investigations — A Risk-Based Approach to Monitoring. August 2013. www.fda.gov/regulatory-information/search-fda-guidance-documents/oversight-clinical-investigations-risk-based-approach-monitoring.

[91] United States, FDA. Electronic Source Data in Clinical Investigations. September 2013, updated 2019. www.fda.gov/regulatory-information/search-fda-guidance-documents/electronic-source-data-clinical-investigations.

[92] European Union. Regulation (EU) No 536/2014 on Clinical Trials. OJEU, 27 May 2014. Article 58 establishes the 25-year TMF retention requirement for eTMF audit trail data. https://eur-lex.europa.eu/legal-content/EN/TXT/?uri=CELEX:32014R0536.

[93] The gap between a Part 11-compliant policy and a Part 11-compliant system is not a documentation gap. It is the distance between what an organization wrote it would do and what its systems actually do every day.

[94] European Medicines Agency. Guideline on Computerised Systems and Electronic Data in Clinical Trials. EMA/INS/GCP/112288/2023, adopted 7 March 2023. Section 4.8 (electronic signature framework), Section 5.4 and Annex 4 (security/access control), Annex 5.3 (eConsent). https://www.ema.europa.eu/en/documents/scientific-guideline/guideline-computerised-systems-and-electronic-data-clinical-trials_en.pdf.

[95] European Union. Regulation (EU) No 910/2014 (eIDAS). Establishes the qualified electronic signature framework for open systems at EU sites; Article 2.2 excludes closed systems. https://eur-lex.europa.eu/legal-content/EN/TXT/?uri=CELEX:32014R0910.

[96] European Medicines Agency. Guideline on Computerised Systems and Electronic Data in Clinical Trials. EMA/INS/GCP/112288/2023, adopted 7 March 2023. Section 4.8, Section 5.4 and Annex 4. https://www.ema.europa.eu/en/documents/scientific-guideline/guideline-computerised-systems-and-electronic-data-clinical-trials_en.pdf.

[97] United Kingdom, MHRA. GxP Data Integrity Definitions and Guidance for Industry. March 2018, Sections 6.14 and 6.16. www.gov.uk/government/publications/guidance-on-gmp-data-integrity.

[98] Pharmaceutical Inspection Co-operation Scheme. Guidance on Data Integrity, PI 041-1. Revised July 2021. www.picscheme.org/en/publications.

[99] United States, FDA. 21 CFR Part 11, Section 11.70. Signature/record linking: electronic signatures shall be linked to their records so they cannot be excised, copied, or transferred to falsify a record. www.ecfr.gov/current/title-21/chapter-I/subchapter-A/part-11.

[100] United States, FDA. 21 CFR Part 11, Sections 11.50, 11.70, 11.100, 11.200, 11.300. Electronic signature requirements. www.ecfr.gov/current/title-21/chapter-I/subchapter-A/part-11.

[101] European Commission. Annex 11: Computerised Systems. EU GMP Guide Annex 11, revised 2011; draft 2024. Sections 11.5, 11.6, 11.8, 11.9, 11.11, 13.3, 13.5–13.8. https://health.ec.europa.eu/medicinal-products/eudralex/eudralex-volume-4_en.

[102] International Council for Harmonisation. ICH E6(R3), Step 4, May 2023, Section 5.5.3 (Data Management Technology) and Appendix A. www.ich.org/page/efficacy-guidelines.

[103] United States, FDA. 21 CFR Part 11, Section 11.10(d). Access controls to ensure records cannot be altered or modified by unauthorized individuals. www.ecfr.gov/current/title-21/chapter-I/subchapter-A/part-11.

[104] United States, FDA. Electronic Source Data in Clinical Investigations. September 2013, updated 2019. www.fda.gov/regulatory-information/search-fda-guidance-documents/electronic-source-data-clinical-investigations.

[105] United States, FDA. Data Integrity and Compliance With Drug CGMP: Questions and Answers — Guidance for Industry. December 2018. www.fda.gov/regulatory-information/search-fda-guidance-documents/data-integrity-and-compliance-drug-cgmp-questions-and-answers-guidance-industry.

[106] United States, FDA. Decentralized Clinical Trials for Drugs, Biological Products, and Devices. May 2023. www.fda.gov/regulatory-information/search-fda-guidance-documents/decentralized-clinical-trials-drugs-biological-products-and-devices.

[107] International Council for Harmonisation. ICH E6(R3), Step 4, 6 January 2025. Sections 4.9, 3.9–3.17, 4.2, and Annex 1. www.ich.org/page/efficacy-guidelines.

[108] United Kingdom, MHRA. GMP Data Integrity Definitions and Guidance for Industry. March 2018. www.gov.uk/government/publications/guidance-on-gmp-data-integrity.

[109] Pharmaceutical Inspection Co-operation Scheme. Guidance on Data Integrity, PI 041-1. Revised July 2021. www.picscheme.org/en/publications.

[110] United States, FDA. Electronic Source Data in Clinical Investigations. September 2013 (updated 2019). www.fda.gov/regulatory-information/search-fda-guidance-documents/electronic-source-data-clinical-investigations.

[111] Pharmaceutical Inspection Co-operation Scheme. Guidance on Data Integrity, PI 041-1. Revised July 2021. www.picscheme.org/en/publications.

[112] United States, FDA. Use of Electronic Health Record Data in Clinical Investigations. July 2019. www.fda.gov/regulatory-information/search-fda-guidance-documents/use-electronic-health-record-data-clinical-investigations.

[113] United States, FDA. Electronic Source Data in Clinical Investigations. September 2013 (updated 2019). www.fda.gov/regulatory-information/search-fda-guidance-documents/electronic-source-data-clinical-investigations.

[114] United States, Food and Drug Administration. 'Digital Health Technologies for Remote Data Acquisition in Clinical Investigations.' FDA Guidance for Industry, December 2023. Addresses qualification of digital health technologies including wearable devices and sensors used for remote data collection in clinical trials. www.fda.gov/regulatory-information/search-fda-guidance-documents/digital-health-technologies-remote-data-acquisition-clinical-investigations.

[115] United States, Food and Drug Administration. 21 CFR Part 312.62 — Investigator Recordkeeping and Record Retention. Code of Federal Regulations. Establishes the minimum retention period for records of clinical investigations; the retention obligation extends to original records held on vendor infrastructure for DCT programs. www.ecfr.gov.

[116] International Council for Harmonisation. ICH E6(R3): Guideline for Good Clinical Practice, Step 4 adoption, May 2023, Section 5.0 (Quality Management System) and Section 5.1 (Sponsor Responsibilities in the Context of Quality Management). The requirement that sponsors establish organizational governance structures with defined accountability for quality objectives at the executive level, and that resource adequacy for quality functions is a senior leadership responsibility, is established in Section 5.0 and elaborated in Section 5.1. www.ich.org/page/efficacy-guidelines.

[117] United Kingdom, Medicines and Healthcare products Regulatory Agency. 'GMP Data Integrity Definitions and Guidance for Industry.' MHRA Guidance Document, March 2018, Section 5 (Senior Management Responsibilities). MHRA places primary responsibility for data integrity culture, adequate resourcing, and quality system effectiveness on senior management; Section 5 establishes the substantive governance obligations and describes the inspection approach used to assess whether those obligations are being exercised in practice. www.gov.uk/government/publications/guidance-on-gmp-data-integrity.

[118] Pharmaceutical Inspection Co-operation Scheme. 'Guidance on Data Integrity, PI 041-1.' PIC/S Guidance Document, revised July 2021, Section 4 (Management Responsibilities). The requirement that management create organizational conditions that support compliant practices, including through self-inspection programs that assess whether the working environment makes compliance operationally possible, is addressed in Section 4. www.picscheme.org/en/publications.

[119] United States, Department of Justice. 'United States Files Consent Decree Against Cetero Research and Its Former Owner.' DOJ Press Release, March 2013. The governance remediation requirements of the Cetero consent decree, including the independent audit committee, executive management certification requirements, and governance restructuring obligations, are described in the consent decree documents filed with the U.S. District Court for the Middle District of North Carolina. www.justice.gov/opa/pr/united-states-files-consent-decree-against-cetero-research-and-its-former-owner.

[120] International Council for Harmonisation. ICH E6(R3): Guideline for Good Clinical Practice, Step 4 adoption, May 2023, Section 5.2 (Contracting and Delegation). The principle that sponsors retain full regulatory responsibility for data integrity regardless of the extent of CRO delegation, and that sponsors must verify CRO compliance through operational means rather than contractual attestation alone, is established in Section 5.2. www.ich.org/page/efficacy-guidelines.

[121] United States, Food and Drug Administration. Warning letters issued to clinical trial sponsors under 21 CFR Parts 312 and 314 following bioresearch monitoring inspections that identified inadequate sponsor oversight of investigator site data integrity. FDA's enforcement record on sponsor oversight accountability is documented in the agency's warning letter database. www.fda.gov/inspections-compliance-enforcement-and-criminal-investigations/compliance-actions-and-activities/warning-letters.

[122] United States, Food and Drug Administration and Department of Justice. Consent Decree of Permanent Injunction, United States v. Cetero Research, Inc., filed U.S. District Court for the Middle District of North Carolina, March 2013. The governance requirements described in this chapter, including independent audit committee authority, executive certification obligations, and board-level oversight provisions, are drawn from the consent decree filed in this matter.

[123] United States, Food and Drug Administration. 21 CFR Part 312, Subpart D (Responsibilities of Sponsors and Investigators), Sections 312.60 and 312.62. Section 312.60 establishes general investigator responsibilities and the prohibition on delegation of investigator accountability; Section 312.62 establishes case history record

requirements that are the primary basis for PI documentation accountability. www.ecfr.gov/current/title-21/chapter-I/subchapter-D/part-312/subpart-D.

[124] United States, Food and Drug Administration. 'Oversight of Clinical Investigations — A Risk-Based Approach to Monitoring.' FDA Guidance for Industry, August 2013. The guidance's description of systemic monitoring, centralized monitoring functions, and the sponsor's obligation to assess whether quality findings represent isolated events or patterns requiring organizational-level response provides the basis for the characterization of scope assessment as a governance obligation. www.fda.gov/regulatory-information/search-fda-guidance-documents/oversight-clinical-investigations-risk-based-approach-monitoring.

[125] International Council for Harmonisation. ICH E6(R3): Guideline for Good Clinical Practice, Step 4 adoption, January 2025, Section 3.10 (Quality Management). The requirements for an organizational quality culture that supports data integrity throughout the trial lifecycle, including the allocation of adequate resources and the assignment of clear accountability for quality objectives, are established in Section 3.10. www.ich.org/page/efficacy-guidelines.

[126] Pharmaceutical Inspection Co-operation Scheme. 'Guidance on Data Integrity, PI 041-1.' PIC/S Guidance Document, revised July 2021, Section 4 (Management Responsibilities). The requirements for management to create organizational conditions that neither incentivize nor tolerate data integrity failures, and for self-inspection programs to include explicit assessment of whether the working environment supports compliant conduct, are addressed in Section 4. www.picscheme.org/en/publications.

[127] International Council for Harmonisation. ICH E6(R3): Guideline for Good Clinical Practice, Step 4 adoption, January 2025, Section 3.2 (Resources) and Section 3.10 (Quality Management). The requirement that sponsors allocate adequate resources for the quality management functions that clinical trial conduct requires, and that resource adequacy is a sponsor governance responsibility, is addressed in Sections 3.2 and 3.10. www.ich.org/page/efficacy-guidelines.

[128] United States, Food and Drug Administration. 'Oversight of Clinical Investigations — A Risk-Based Approach to Monitoring.' FDA Guidance for Industry, August 2013. The guidance's discussion of quality management systems, monitoring program design, and the organizational conditions required for monitoring findings to be escalated and acted upon provides the basis for the characterization of monitoring escalation failure as a governance failure. www.fda.gov/regulatory-information/search-fda-guidance-documents/oversight-clinical-investigations-risk-based-approach-monitoring.

[129] United Kingdom, Medicines and Healthcare products Regulatory Agency. 'GMP Data Integrity Definitions and Guidance for Industry.' MHRA Guidance Document, March 2018, Section 5. MHRA's inspection approach assesses whether senior management accountability for data integrity culture is exercised through active governance engagement or policy ownership alone; this distinction is addressed explicitly in the guidance's treatment of management review requirements. www.gov.uk/government/publications/guidance-on-gmp-data-integrity.

[130] International Council for Harmonisation. ICH E6(R3): Guideline for Good Clinical Practice, Step 4 adoption, January 2025, Section 3.6 (Agreements). The principle that sponsors cannot transfer their regulatory responsibility for data integrity to contract research organizations, and that the responsibility for verifying that CRO data management practices meet the required standard rests with the sponsor, is established in Sections 3.6.5 and 3.6.7. www.ich.org/page/efficacy-guidelines.

[131] International Council for Harmonisation. ICH E6(R3): Guideline for Good Clinical Practice, Step 4 adoption, May 2023, Section 5.1 (Quality Management) and the investigator qualification provisions in Section 4.1.1. The requirement that all individuals involved in the conduct of a clinical trial be qualified by education, training, and experience to perform their respective tasks, and the quality management system obligation to verify that qualification, derive from these sections. www.ich.org/page/efficacy-guidelines.

[132] Pharmaceutical Inspection Co-operation Scheme. 'Guidance on Data Integrity, PI 041-1.' PIC/S Guidance Document, revised July 2021, Section 6 (Personnel). The PIC/S personnel and training provisions, including the requirement that training effectiveness be verified and that training records demonstrate more than training completion, support the competency-based design principles described in this chapter. www.picscheme.org/en/publications.

[133] United States, Food and Drug Administration. 21 CFR Part 312.62 — Investigator Recordkeeping and Record Retention. The investigator's obligation to maintain accurate case histories, prepare adequate and accurate source documents, and ensure that data reported to sponsors accurately reflect source records, which together define the competency requirements that investigator and coordinator training must address, are stated in this section. www.ecfr.gov/current/title-21/chapter-I/subchapter-D/part-312/subpart-D/section-312.62.

[134] United Kingdom, Medicines and Healthcare products Regulatory Agency. 'GMP Data Integrity Definitions and Guidance for Industry.' MHRA Guidance Document, March 2018. The MHRA's principle that organizations must ensure staff understand the importance of data integrity, not merely that they have been informed of the requirements, is stated in the personnel and training section of this guidance and is applied by MHRA inspectors in clinical data integrity contexts. www.gov.uk/government/publications/guidance-on-gmp-data-integrity.

[135] United States, Food and Drug Administration. 'Oversight of Clinical Investigations — A Risk-Based Approach to Monitoring.' FDA Guidance for Industry, August 2013. The risk-based monitoring framework established in this guidance, including the use of centralized monitoring and risk indicators to calibrate monitoring intensity, provides the operational context within which training performance data should be treated as a risk signal. www.fda.gov/media/116754/download.

[136] International Council for Harmonisation. ICH E6(R3): Guideline for Good Clinical Practice, Step 4 adoption, May 2023, Section 5.2 (Contracting and Delegation). The principle that sponsor responsibilities for trial oversight, including the obligation to ensure that staff are appropriately qualified, cannot be transferred to CROs regardless of contractual arrangements, and that sponsors must verify CRO performance against the required standard, is established in this section. www.ich.org/page/efficacy-guidelines.

[137] United States, Food and Drug Administration. 'Electronic Source Data in Clinical Investigations.' FDA Guidance for Industry, September 2013 (updated 2019). The guidance's requirements for training on electronic source data systems, including the requirement that site staff be trained on the specific EDC platform used in the trial, are directly relevant to the protocol-specific and system-specific training design approach described in this chapter. www.fda.gov/media/85183/download.

[138] International Council for Harmonisation. ICH E6(R3): Guideline for Good Clinical Practice, Step 4 adoption, May 2023, Section 5.5.3 (Data Management Technology) and Appendix A (Technology and Data Management). The validation obligation for all technology used in clinical data management, and the traceability requirements for all data management decisions, apply to AI systems through these provisions without AI-specific enumeration. www.ich.org/page/efficacy-guidelines.

[139] United States, Food and Drug Administration. 'Data Integrity and Compliance With Drug CGMP: Questions and Answers — Guidance for Industry.' FDA Guidance for Industry, December 2018. The guidance's treatment of audit trail requirements, original record preservation, and data management documentation is applied throughout this chapter to AI systems through the established principle that CGMP data integrity standards apply to clinical research contexts via the predicate rule framework and the parallel structure of GCP data integrity obligations. www.fda.gov/regulatory-information/search-fda-guidance-documents/data-integrity-and-compliance-drug-cgmp-questions-and-answers-guidance-industry.

[140] United States, Food and Drug Administration. 'Electronic Source Data in Clinical Investigations.' FDA Guidance for Industry, September 2013 (updated 2019). The source data guidance establishes that electronic records meeting the specified system requirements constitute primary source data; this principle applies to AI-generated outputs that enter the clinical record as primary data, subject to the additional traceability requirements discussed in this chapter. www.fda.gov/media/85183/download.

[141] United States, Food and Drug Administration. 'Using Artificial Intelligence and Machine Learning in the Development of Drug and Biological Products.' FDA Discussion Paper, May 2023. The discussion paper addresses the application of data integrity principles, including traceability, to AI-generated outputs used in regulatory submissions and drug development decisions, including clinical trial data management contexts. www.fda.gov/media/167973/download.

[142] United States, Food and Drug Administration. 21 CFR Part 11 — Electronic Records; Electronic Signatures. Code of Federal Regulations, Title 21, Part 11. The predicate rule framework that applies Part 11 requirements to AI systems whose outputs enter FDA-required regulated records is established through the scope provisions of 21 CFR Part 11, Section 11.1(b). www.ecfr.gov/current/title-21/chapter-I/subchapter-A/part-11.

[143] United States, Food and Drug Administration. 'Guidance for Industry: Part 11, Electronic Records; Electronic Signatures — Scope and Application.' FDA Guidance for Industry, August 2003. The scope clarification guidance, which established the predicate rule approach to Part 11 applicability, is the foundational document for understanding which records and systems are subject to Part 11 requirements. www.fda.gov/regulatory-information/search-fda-guidance-documents/part-11-electronic-records-electronic-signatures-scope-and-application.

[144] European Medicines Agency. 'Annex 11: Computerised Systems — Concept Paper for Revision.' EMA Draft Document for Public Consultation, 2024. The draft revision's provisions on AI and machine learning validation, traceable outputs, and model change

control represent the current trajectory of EU regulatory requirements for computerized systems including those used in clinical data management. www.ema.europa.eu.

[145] Pharmaceutical Inspection Co-operation Scheme. 'Guidance on Data Integrity, PI 041-1.' PIC/S Guidance Document, revised July 2021. ALCOA+ as the universal evaluative standard for data integrity, applied throughout this chapter to AI-generated outputs, is established in PI 041-1's definitional and assessment framework. The guidance's treatment of attributability, traceability, and accuracy as distinct but interrelated properties supports the analysis of AI data integrity obligations in this chapter. www.picscheme.org/en/publications.

[146] United Kingdom, Medicines and Healthcare products Regulatory Agency. 'GMP Data Integrity Definitions and Guidance for Industry.' MHRA Guidance Document, March 2018. MHRA's management accountability requirements, which apply the same organizational governance expectations to AI-assisted data management that they apply to conventional clinical data management, inform the chapter's treatment of organizational responsibility for AI system oversight. www.gov.uk/government/publications/guidance-on-gmp-data-integrity.

[147] European Medicines Agency and Pharmaceutical Inspection Co-operation Scheme. Joint Public Consultation on Clinical Data Integrity and Pharmacovigilance Data Management, February 2026. The consultation covers, among other areas, proposed requirements for AI-assisted clinical data management tools, including validation, explainability, and change control provisions. www.ema.europa.eu; www.picscheme.org.

[148] United States, Food and Drug Administration. 21 CFR Part 11 — Electronic Records; Electronic Signatures. Code of Federal Regulations, Title 21, Part 11. Section 11.10(k) establishes that persons who use open systems must employ procedures and controls designed to ensure the authenticity, integrity, and confidentiality of electronic records. This obligation applies to cloud-hosted and SaaS-delivered systems through which regulated clinical trial data is captured, processed, or stored, regardless of where in those systems the records are held. www.ecfr.gov/current/title-21/chapter-I/subchapter-A/part-11.

[149] United States, Food and Drug Administration. 'Electronic Source Data in Clinical Investigations.' FDA Guidance for Industry, September 2013 (updated 2019). The guidance establishes that sponsors are responsible for ensuring that electronic source data meets ALCOA requirements regardless of where it is generated or stored, providing the primary federal basis for sponsor responsibility for data held in third-party cloud systems. www.fda.gov/media/85183/download.

[150] Pharmaceutical Inspection Co-operation Scheme. 'Guidance on Data Integrity, PI 041-1.' PIC/S Guidance Document, revised July 2021. Sections addressing supplier qualification establish that assessment of supplier quality management systems, change control procedures, and data integrity controls is required — not only review of product documentation. This standard applies to cloud-hosted clinical system vendors. www.picscheme.org/en/publications.

[151] International Council for Harmonisation. ICH E6(R3): Guideline for Good Clinical Practice, Step 4 adoption, May 2023, Section 5.2 (Contracting and Delegation). The non-transferability of sponsor regulatory responsibility to CROs and other third parties, established in Section 5.2, is the foundational principle governing sponsor obligations for data held in vendor-operated cloud systems. www.ich.org/page/efficacy-guidelines.

[152] United States, Food and Drug Administration. 'Data Integrity and Compliance With Drug CGMP: Questions and Answers — Guidance for Industry.' FDA Guidance for Industry, December 2018. FDA's treatment of audit trail integrity, original record preservation, and validated state management in this guidance is applied throughout this chapter to cloud-hosted clinical systems through the established parallel between CGMP data integrity standards and GCP data integrity obligations. www.fda.gov/regulatory-information/search-fda-guidance-documents/data-integrity-and-compliance-drug-cgmp-questions-and-answers-guidance-industry.

[153] European Union. Regulation (EU) 2016/679 of the European Parliament and of the Council (General Data Protection Regulation). Official Journal of the European Union, 2016. Chapter V establishes the requirements for international transfers of personal data from the EEA, including the adequacy decision framework, standard contractual clauses, and binding corporate rules applicable to clinical trial data transferred to cloud infrastructure outside the EEA. https://eur-lex.europa.eu/legal-content/EN/TXT/?uri=CELEX:32016R0679.

[154] People's Republic of China. Personal Information Protection Law (PIPL), effective November 2021; Data Security Law (DSL), effective September 2021. The PIPL establishes requirements for cross-border transfer of personal information of Chinese individuals, including security assessment requirements for transfers of sensitive personal information. The DSL establishes data localization obligations for important data. English-language translations are available through official government publication channels.

[155] India. Digital Personal Data Protection Act, 2023. The DPDPA establishes requirements for processing of digital personal data in India, including restrictions on cross-border data transfers. Sponsors conducting trials in India using cloud-hosted systems should assess DPDPA compliance for trial data generated within India. www.meity.gov.in.

[156] Brazil. Lei Geral de Proteção de Dados Pessoais (LGPD), Law No. 13,709/2018. The LGPD governs the processing and cross-border transfer of personal data generated within Brazil. Clinical trial sponsors collecting personal health data from Brazilian subjects using cloud-hosted systems should verify that transfer arrangements satisfy LGPD requirements. www.planalto.gov.br.

[157] International Council for Harmonisation. ICH E6(R3): Guideline for Good Clinical Practice, Step 4 adoption, May 2023, Section 5.5.3 (Data Management Technology) and Section 5.5.7 (Retention of Essential Documents). Section 5.5.3 establishes the validation obligation for all technology used in clinical data management; Section 5.5.7 specifies the fifteen-year minimum retention period and format durability requirements. Both sections apply to records held in cloud-hosted systems. www.ich.org/page/efficacy-guidelines.

[158] European Commission. 'Annex 11: Computerised Systems.' EU GMP Guide Annex 11, 2011; draft revised version published for consultation, 2024. The 2024 draft revision's treatment of cloud-hosted systems, vendor qualification, change control, and audit trail configuration applies to clinical data management systems through the cross-reference structure of EU GMP and GCP frameworks. https://health.ec.europa.eu/medicinal-products/eudralex/eudralex-volume-4_en.

[159] United Kingdom, Medicines and Healthcare products Regulatory Agency. 'GMP Data Integrity Definitions and Guidance for Industry.' MHRA Guidance Document, March 2018. The guidance's treatment of outsourced data management establishes that outsourcing does not diminish the regulated organization's responsibility and that third-party controls must be verified through audit and qualification. www.gov.uk/government/publications/guidance-on-gmp-data-integrity.

[160] European Medicines Agency and Pharmaceutical Inspection Co-operation Scheme. Joint Public Consultation on Clinical Data Integrity and Pharmacovigilance Data Management, February 2026. The consultation addresses, among other areas, cloud-hosted system governance, third-party data management oversight, and the application of ALCOA+ standards to data held in vendor-operated infrastructure. www.ema.europa.eu; www.picscheme.org.

[161] United States, Food and Drug Administration. 'Bioresearch Monitoring Program.' FDA, Bioresearch Monitoring Operations, www.fda.gov/science-research/clinical-trials-and-human-subject-protection/bimo-inspection-metrics. The BIMO inspection metrics published annually by fiscal year provide aggregate data on inspection volume, findings categories, and enforcement outcomes. Annual metrics are the primary quantitative source for BIMO program activity.

[162] United Kingdom, Medicines and Healthcare products Regulatory Agency. 'GMP Data Integrity Definitions and Guidance for Industry.' MHRA Guidance Document, March 2018. MHRA's culture-first approach, self-inspection requirements, and organizational accountability framework, applied by MHRA inspectors in GCP as well as GMP inspection contexts, inform the chapter's treatment of the MHRA inspection posture. www.gov.uk/government/publications/guidance-on-gmp-data-integrity.

[163] United States, Food and Drug Administration. 'Oversight of Clinical Investigations — A Risk-Based Approach to Monitoring.' FDA Guidance for Industry, August 2013. The risk-based monitoring framework, including the identification of statistical anomalies in site-level data as a primary centralized monitoring target, establishes the conceptual basis for pattern analysis as both a sponsor quality tool and an FDA inspection technique. www.fda.gov/regulatory-information/search-fda-guidance-documents/oversight-clinical-investigations-risk-based-approach-monitoring.

[164] European Medicines Agency. 'Guideline on Computerised Systems and Electronic Data in Clinical Trials.' EMA/INS/GCP/112288/2023, effective September 2023. Section 6.2's field-level audit trail requirement, Section 6.3's investigator sign-off provisions, and the guideline's treatment of validation maintenance and vendor qualification establish the EU-specific citation framework for finding classifications in this chapter. www.ema.europa.eu/en/documents/scientific-guideline/guideline-computerised-systems-electronic-data-clinical-trials_en.pdf.

[165] Pharmaceutical Inspection Co-operation Scheme. 'Guidance on Data Integrity, PI 041-1.' PIC/S Guidance Document, revised July 2021. PI 041-1's operational detail on ALCOA+ assessment, data integrity risk assessment methodology, and inspection criteria provides the framework for the internal assessment phases described in this chapter. The guidance's treatment of contemporaneous records, audit trail review programs, and CRO oversight obligations is directly applied in the self-audit framework. www.picscheme.org/en/publications.

[166] United States, Food and Drug Administration. 'Electronic Source Data in Clinical Investigations.' FDA Guidance for Industry, September 2013 (updated 2019). The guidance's treatment of original records, audit trail requirements, and system controls provides the regulatory basis for several of the finding categories documented in the consistent finding patterns table. www.fda.gov/media/85183/download.

[167] United States, Food and Drug Administration. 21 CFR Part 11 — Electronic Records; Electronic Signatures. Code of Federal Regulations, Title 21, Part 11. Sections 11.10(a), 11.10(d), 11.10(e), and 11.10(k) are cited throughout this chapter as the foundational access control, audit trail, and open system provisions that form the basis of FDA inspection findings in electronic records contexts. www.ecfr.gov/current/title-21/chapter-I/subchapter-A/part-11.

[168] European Medicines Agency and Pharmaceutical Inspection Co-operation Scheme. Joint Public Consultation on Clinical Data Integrity and Pharmacovigilance Data Management, February 2026. The consultation proposes harmonized standards for remote and hybrid inspection formats, among other provisions, and establishes the trajectory toward unified inspection methodologies across EMA and PIC/S jurisdictions. www.ema.europa.eu; www.picscheme.org.

www.ingramcontent.com/pod-product-compliance
Lightning Source LLC
LaVergne TN
LVHW080012210926
848481LV00011B/3004
9798234093974